D0340626

A

BADLY FLAWED

ELECTION

A

BADLY FLAWED

ELECTION

Debating Bush v. Gore, *the Supreme Court,*
and American Democracy

EDITED BY RONALD DWORKIN

THE NEW PRESS
NEW YORK

Published in the United States by The New Press, New York, 2002
Distributed by W. W. Norton & Company, Inc., New York

LIBRARY OF CONGRESS CATALOGING-IN-PUBLICATION DATA

A badly flawed election : debating Bush v. Gore, the Supreme Court, and American
democracy / edited by Ronald Dworkin.
p.   cm.
Includes bibliographical references and index.
ISBN 1-56584-737-7
1. Bush, George W. (George Walker), 1946—Trials, litigation, etc.   2. Gore, Albert,
1948—Trials, litigation, etc.   3. Contested elections—United States.   4. Contested
elections—Florida.   5. Election law—United States.   6. Presidents—United States—
Election—2000.   7. Political questions and judicial power—United States.
8. United States. Supreme Court.   I. Dworkin, R. M.
KF5074.2 .B33 2002
342.73'075—dc21   2002019759

The New Press was established in 1990 as a not-for-profit alternative to the large, commercial publishing houses currently dominating the book publishing industry. The New Press operates in the public interest rather than for private gain, and is committed to publishing, in innovative ways, works of educational, cultural, and community value that are often deemed insufficiently profitable.

The New Press, 450 West 41st Street, 6th floor, New York, NY 10036
www.thenewpress.com

Printed in the United States of America

2   4   6   8   10   9   7   5   3   1

Contents

Introduction
Ronald Dworkin   *1*

1. Early Responses
Ronald Dworkin   *57*

2. Lawless Order and Hot Cases
Cass R. Sunstein   *75*

3. Freeing eroG v. hsuB From its Hall of Mirrors
Laurence H. Tribe   *105*

4. Constitutionalizing Democratic Politics
Richard H. Pildes   *155*

5. *Bush v. Gore* as Pragmatic Adjudication
Richard A. Posner   *187*

6. How to Democratize American Democracy
Arthur Schlesinger, Jr.   *215*

7. And to the *C* students: The Lessons of *Bush v. Gore*
Lani Guinier   *231*

8. Holy Cow! Preliminary Reflections on the 2000 Election
Nelson W. Polsby   *265*

Notes   *285*
About the Contributors   *329*
Index   *331*

A

BADLY FLAWED

ELECTION

Introduction

Ronald Dworkin

The presidential election campaign of 2000 was not itself exciting or unusual, beyond the baffling inability of Albert Gore, the Democratic candidate, to pull away in an easy victory over the Republican, George W. Bush, given the extraordinarily successful economy and general good times of the preceding four years, under an administration in which Gore had served as vice president. But what happened immediately after the election—and for the next several weeks—was indeed extraordinary: It rivaled, in uncertainty, dramatic shifts, and political maneuvering, any other election in America's history. It easily surpassed any of them in litigious complexity and, according to a dominant number of scholars and commentators, in judicial incompetence or skulduggery or both.

The post-election battle ended suddenly, on December 12, 2000, when the Supreme Court, in *Bush v. Gore,* stopped recounts that the Florida supreme court had ordered: the Supreme Court's decision meant that Bush would be president. Past Supreme Court decisions have, of course, been attacked as illegitimate and wicked. In recent decades the justices have been vilified and threatened with impeachment for their decisions about school segregation, abortion, and prayer in public schools, for example. But I know of no other instance in which so many distinguished academic and professional critics have criticized the Court in such angry and intemperate language, or even suggested, as they did in this case, that some justices had decided for personal and self-serving reasons. It is now well over a year since the Court's decision, and it is time, we believe, for a deeper inspection of and debate about the issues that *Bush v. Gore,* and the election as a whole, have made so dramatically inescapable.

In an essay published soon after the decision, which is reprinted in Chapter 1 of this volume, I said that I hoped that the fierce attacks on the Court would prove exaggerated, that further reflection would produce a defense of its verdict—or at least an explanation of the various decisions of those five justices—which would restore the Court's and their dignity. I could not find such a defense or explanation then, but I knew that serious attempts would be made to provide one, and it is part of this book's purpose to present and examine some of those attempts.

My own view is that, so far, they have all failed; I continue to think that the Court's decision is inexplicable except on grounds that concede its illegitimacy. In this introduction I try to explain why. But other contributors, in varying degrees, disagree. Professor Sunstein, in Chapter 2, suggests that the Court's intervention at least had the benefit of securing order out of a disorderly postelection contest that had at least prospects of becoming more disorderly, even though he judges that, on balance, this benefit cannot outweigh the legal defects of the Court's arguments. In Chapter 4, Professor Pildes puts the Court's decision in a larger legal and cultural context: He suggests that the five conservative justices whose votes awarded the presidency to Bush may not have acted in a politically partisan way, or for self-serving reasons, but rather out of a predilection for political stability and order—a prediliction that is also discernable, he suggests, in other Supreme Court decisions he discusses. Professor Tribe, who played an active role in the legal contests as one of Gore's attorneys, agrees. In Chapter 3, he offers no opinion about the conservative justices' motives, but argues that their fear of an undisciplined and possibly chaotic democratic process would be enough, in itself, to explain their decision. Judge Posner, who has already published a book defending the Supreme Court's decision, summarizes and deepens his earlier defense here. He says that the decision can be defended, if at all, only "as a pragmatic solution to a looming national crisis," that is, as a decision calculated to produce the best consequences for the nation as a whole.[1]

The Supreme Court's decision was the climax of the protracted postelection struggle, but not its cause, and in the long run it may be more important to consider whether and how we should change the way we elect our presidents, which in considerable part was the cause. Part of the answer to that question is obvious. Misleading and ineffective voting machines and procedures must be replaced and reformed, not only in Florida, which has already begun that process, but in other states as well. In Chapter 7, Professor Guinier discusses, among other crucial social and systemic problems, the malignant role that the fact and heritage of racial injustice plays in our politics. That role was also evident in Florida in 2000. We must at least consider, moreover, whether we should amend the electoral structure laid down in our Constitution. Gore won the national popular vote by a significant margin, but he nevertheless lost the election because the presidency is decided not by national popular vote, but by an electoral college whose members are elected state by state. That system was created as part of our original, eighteenth-century Constitution, and it now strikes many critics as a bizarre way of choosing a national leader. In Chapter 1, I suggest that the electoral college should be abolished or reformed by constitutional amendment, if possible; if not, that its effects should be modified by legislation state by state, to make the chances less likely that the winner of the national popular vote will lose the election. In Chapters 8 and 6, Professors Polsby and Schlesinger offer a detailed and sophisticated account of the complexities and consequences of any such proposal.

This is a book, then, of diverse and often conflicting opinions about a daunting variety of issues raised by the election and what happened after it. We intend the book not as a joint collaborative study, but as a debate through which we hope to refine—and if possible deepen—understanding of those issues. The rest of this introduction continues my own contribution to that debate. I emphasize not the technical legal questions that have already been canvassed in the legal journals, but the more general moral and philosophical puzzles that underlie those legal questions. I try to make plain when and why I disagree with my colleagues in this volume. Those I argue against no doubt have impressive, and perhaps persuasive, replies, but these must await other publications. The debate about our badly flawed election will not end soon.

WHAT HAPPENED

The story is still too fresh in the minds of readers to need much retelling, and my summary of its main events will be brief. The election was held on November 7, 2000. The television networks, as usual, competed with one another to declare victory for one or the other candidate: They hoped to announce the result in each state, based on their exit polls, soon after its polls closed. They all announced victory for Gore in Florida even before all the polls had closed in that state—part of the state is in the central, not the eastern, time zone—and that prediction seemed to guarantee Gore's overall victory. But within an hour the networks recanted, and announced that Florida was "too close to call." Still later they awarded Florida to Bush, and later still returned to their "too close to call" verdict. As the evening ended, it became apparent that that state's electoral votes would be decisive. Given the uncontested results in the other 49 states, if Gore won Florida, he would easily win the electoral college, but if Bush won Florida he would win the electoral college by a single vote.

When all the Florida counties had finally reported, the still unofficial returns showed Bush ahead by a few hundred votes. But in Florida's Palm Beach County, several voters announced that they had voted for the wrong candidate: They said that they had been misled by the confusing "butterfly" ballot used in that county into voting for a third party candidate—Pat Buchanan—when they had meant to vote for Gore. Statistics seemed to confirm their claim. They suggested that several thousand voters—easily enough to give Gore overall victory in the state—had made that mistake, and therefore that more people in Florida intended to, and thought they had, voted for Gore than for Bush. (The butterfly ballot story is discussed at length in Chapter 1.) A group of Palm Beach voters sued, asking for a new election to be held in the county, but the suit failed at every level, largely, I believe, because it seemed impossible to correct the mistake.

Gore's supporters claimed, however, that other voting mistakes had been made, and that the law did allow those mistakes to be corrected. Several Florida counties used "punch card" ballots that require voters to punch out a cardboard "chad" next to the name of their favored candidate. Several voters who intended to punch out a chad had not punched it cleanly through—

in some cases the chad was partly removed, hanging by one or more corners, in others only perforated, so that light could shine through a hole though the chad was fully attached, and in still others only indented or "dimpled," so that no light could shine through, though the indentation might nevertheless be taken to indicate an intention to push that chad out. The counting machines were likely to have recorded all such ballots as non-votes.

Florida law permits candidates to protest election counts and to ask for manual recounts, in which ballots are examined one by one, by hand, to ascertain voter intent. Gore asked for manual recounts in four Florida counties, and these were begun, using to some extent different criteria in each county. Some accepted dimples as evidence of intent, while others insisted on at least a partially detached chad, for example. The Florida election statute provides that counties must submit their vote counts to the secretary of state (who, as it happens, was Katherine Harris, a Republican who was one of Bush's campaign managers in Florida) by seven days after the election, which was November 14. The manual recounts were not completed by that date, and though one provision of the election statute appeared to give the secretary of state discretion to extend the deadline, Harris refused to do so. Gore appealed her decision, and on November 21, the Florida Supreme Court, overruling Harris, extended the manual count deadline until November 26. (On December 4, the United States Supreme Court, in a unanimous decision, vacated the Florida court's decision to extend the deadline, and remanded the case to that court, asking it to explain the grounds of its decision further.) The recounts were not completed even by the Florida court's extended deadline, however, and on November 26 Harris then officially certified Bush as the winner of Florida's twenty-five electoral votes.

The Florida election statute also provides that after a candidate has been officially certified as the winner of an election, other candidates may contest the result in a lawsuit alleging that sufficient legal votes were miscounted to change the result in the election. Gore filed a contest in the Florida courts, but on December 4 the trial court judge, N. Sanders Sauls, rejected Gore's suit. Gore appealed his decision to the Florida Supreme Court, and on December 8, that court reversed Judge Sauls, and ordered a statewide manual recount of all "undervotes"—ballots that machines had identified as containing no vote. Bush appealed to the United States Supreme Court which, on

December 9, issued a stay of the Florida Supreme Court's order, pending its own decision on the merits, and so the recounts stopped. On December 12, the Supreme Court announced its final opinion in the case. The five most conservative justices—Chief Justice William Rehnquist, and Justices Anthony Kennedy, Sandra Day O'Connor, Antonin Scalia, and Clarence Thomas—voted to end the recounts altogether, which meant that Bush would win the presidency.

THE SUPREME COURT'S ARGUMENTS

The opinions of these five justices, taken together, report two very different grounds for that decision, and it is important not only to distinguish these, but also to distinguish the underlying moral charge that gives each whatever appeal it has. One of these arguments was accepted by all five of these justices, and it was therefore the only ground on which a majority of the Court did agree. They declared that the Florida court's recount order was unconstitutional because it permitted different judges, in different counties, to use different standards to gauge voter intent. It permitted some judges, in one county or polling district, to insist, if they wished, that they would count only partially detached chads as votes, while other judges, in others, counted chads that were not even partially detached, but only dimpled. That, the five justices said, constituted a violation of the "equal protection clause"—the clause in the Fourteenth Amendment that forbids states to deny "equal protection of the laws" to any person. In normal circumstances, if the Supreme Court decided that a state court's order was unconstitutional because it was not specific enough, and left too much leeway to subordinate judges or officials, the Court would return the case to the state court with instructions to issue a new, more specific and less permissive order—a recount order that stipulated, for example, that a ballot that was only dimpled could not count as a vote. But the five justices said that sending the case back to the Florida Supreme Court with such an instruction would be pointless, in this case, because even that court had agreed that the Florida legislature would have wanted to take advantage of the "safe harbor" provision of the federal Electoral Count Act, which provided that state certifications of electors could not be challenged in Congress if filed by December 12.[2] Since the Supreme

Court handed down its decision in the late evening of December 12, there was therefore no point, the five justices said, in returning the case to the Florida court. Instead, they simply declared that no more recounts could take place, and that the vote tally that had been certified by Katherine Harris, which favored Bush by a very narrow margin, must therefore be taken to be final.

So there were two parts to the argument all five conservative justices endorsed. The first part held that the Florida Supreme Court's recount order was unconstitutional because it violated the equal protection clause, and the second that there was no time left for the Florida court to correct its error. Much of the initial fury that the decision provoked was directed at the sheer implausibility and, indeed, hubris of the latter part. December 12 was in no sense a final deadline. Results certified to Congress after that date but before December 18, the date on which the electoral college actually votes, might well have been perfectly valid, though they would not have been immune from a challenge in Congress. True, as the Florida Supreme Court said in its initial ruling, the Florida legislature would have preferred to gain that immunity, all else equal. But it hardly follows—nor did the Florida Supreme Court suggest—that the legislature would have wanted to gain the immunity at any cost, including compromising the fairness and accuracy of its election. If the first part of the five justices' argument had been sound, the appropriate remedy would clearly have been to remand the case to the Florida court to allow that court to do what it could to repair the unconstitutionality. That part of the five justices' argument was crucial to the result they reached, and it was plainly wrong.

I will concentrate, however, on the first and somewhat more controversial part of the argument: the claim that the Florida court's recount order violated the equal protection clause because it was too unspecific and left too much leeway to different officials in different counties or polling districts. Even lawyers who defend the Court's overall decision agree that the legal case for that claim was very weak: There was no precedent for it in any past judicial decision. Nevertheless, some lawyers find the argument appealing as a matter of political principle. They think that using different standards in different parts of the state would be arbitrary and unfair, and therefore violate at least the spirit of the equal protection clause, and also the spirit of another clause in the Fourteenth Amendment, the due process clause, which provides that no state should deny any citizen an important liberty, like his right to vote, without "due process of law." (The five justices did not mention the due process clause, but some lawyers think that clause would have provided a sounder doctrinal basis for their decision than the equal protection clause did.) The point of these two clauses, after all, is to protect citizens from unfair and arbitrary decisions by government. (In fact, two of the Court's more moderate justices, Stephen Breyer and David Souter, joined the five conservatives in suggesting that the Florida court's recount order was fundamentally unfair, though they vigorously dissented from the second part of the conservatives' argument.) In Chapter 4 of this book, Pildes says that the Florida court's recount order "sends a chill down my equal protection bones," and in Chapter 2, Sunstein admits that "[t]he equal protection claim does have considerable appeal, at least as a matter of common sense," because if a dimpled ballot is counted as a vote in one county, but not in another, "some voters can legitimately object that they are being treated unequally for no good reason." I disagree with these judgments, as a matter of political principle as well as of law, and in Section 4 of this introduction I try to explain why.

―――――

Three of the conservative justices—Rehnquist, Scalia, and Thomas—offered a further and very different argument: that whether or not the Florida court's order, considered on its own, violated the Fourteenth Amendment, that court had changed the election rules after the election was over, which was in itself unfair. It was not only unfair, they said, but unconstitutional as well, because Article II of the Constitution assigns power to the various state legislatures to direct the "manner" of presidential elections in their states, and by changing the rules that the Florida legislature had established in that state's election statute, the Florida court had unconstitutionally usurped that legislature's authority. That argument did not convince any justice beyond those three, and so it formed no part of the Court's decision, but many commentators believe it to be a stronger argument than the equal protection argument I just described. Charles Fried, for example, who was President Reagan's solicitor general, and who regarded the equal protection argument as the Court's weakest, thought this Article II argument (as it has come to be called) the strongest argument the Court could have presented.[3] As we shall see, the Article II argument is complex. It has been offered in different forms, and I shall try to distinguish and assess each of these. Once again, however, the argument—whatever its legal force—appeals to a moral principle. Changing the rules in the middle of a game—or, still worse, after the game is over—does seem peculiarly unfair, particularly when, as in this case, the stakes are very high. So I shall consider, in Section 5 of this introduction, whether that is what the Florida Supreme Court did.

By far the most popular justification of the Supreme Court's decision to award the election to Bush, however, is an argument which, however much it actually influenced the five conservative justices, makes no appearance in their arguments, which is hardly surprising because it is not a legal argument at all. Many people say that the Court rightly intervened when it did, in that dramatic way, to prevent a constitutional crisis, that it did the nation a favor even if the legal arguments it could muster were very weak, and that if its reputation suffers, that only shows its nobility in making that sacrifice. In Chapter 5 of this book, Posner presents what I believe to be the most articulate and sophisticated form of that hugely popular opinion. In Section 6 of this introduction I take issue with his claims, and try to show that the popular argument is based on a series of mistakes.

Were the Recounts Unfair?

As I said, most commentators agree that the equal protection argument that the five conservative justices offered as their official justification is very weak in law, and even the five justices themselves were suspicious of it. The Supreme Court's decisions, like any court's decisions, are not just ad hoc reactions to unique cases; they are meant to be drawn from and stand on general principles that the Court must therefore respect in later cases as well. As Scalia himself insisted in a recent case, the Court's "principal function is to establish precedent—that is, to set forth principles of law that every court in America must follow."[4] But in this case the five justices stated that that their equal protection argument was not to be treated as a precedent at all: It was to have no application in future cases. It is uncertain how much force that disavowal will have. No court can decide how far its own rulings will serve as precedents for or influence later decisions. But the odd proviso shows a distinct lack of confidence. No wonder. The equal protection clause has never before been thought to require uniform election machinery or manual recount standards, even among the precincts and counties of a single state. In fact, at least thirty states allow local officials to set recount standards, and that policy has never been thought to raise a constitutional problem before.

The weakness of the equal protection argument in law is a sign, not that the law is out of step with political morality, but that the commentators who think that the recounts were in some way unfair to any Florida citizens are wrong. Fairness does not require that government treat all citizens in exactly the same way in all circumstances. On the contrary. Different cities and towns within any particular state inevitably adopt very different laws—criminal laws and other regulations, for example, as well as voting and recount procedures—and the state does not violate any duty to treat all its citizens with equal concern and respect when it permits that. Fairness requires not that all a state's citizens be treated the same, but that none of them be disadvantaged—vis-à-vis other citizens—by laws that are either irrational, or that discriminate against them on some suspect ground, like their race, or in the exercise or value of some fundamental right, like the right to vote. That moral requirement cannot be violated unless a law or legal structure damages some person or puts him at some disadvantage in some way. Being treated differently is not automatically being treated unequally or unfairly. No Florida citizen could sensibly make the objection that Sunstein puts in his mouth—that he has been treated "unequally"—unless he could show, not just that different rules of thumb for identifying voters' intentions were used in his county from those used in other counties, but that the difference in some way constituted a harm or disadvantage to him.[5]

That moral requirement has been an essential part of equal protection law. As Scalia and the other majority justices said in an equal protection case in 1995, "Appellees point us to no authority for the proposition that an equal-protection challenge may go forward in federal court absent the showing of individualized harm, and we decline appellees' invitation to approve that proposition in this litigation." [6] The five conservative justices cited a variety of earlier decisions in an attempt to justify their equal protection claim in *Bush v. Gore,* but in every one of these the plaintiffs had been harmed. They cited, for example, the famous Supreme Court decisions holding that states deny equal protection to their citizens when they create voting districts with more people in some districts than in others, because those who live in more populous districts suffer a greater dilution of their votes. [7] (These decisions gave rise to the principle now expressed in the familiar slogan *one person, one vote.*) Pildes and two coauthors, in a revised edition of their book *When Elections Go Bad,* discuss other past decisions in which federal courts have struck down state court decisions that allegedly changed state election laws after the election took place. [8] But, as the authors make plain, these were all decisions resting on the fact that some voters had indeed been disadvantaged by the change. In one case, for example, the Alabama Supreme Court ordered election officials (after the election was over, and when it was plain that the electoral race between candidates to be chief justice of that very court hung in the balance) to count absentee ballots in spite of the fact that these did not satisfy formal statutory requirements, and that ballots failing those requirements had uniformly been excluded in the past. The federal Eleventh Circuit Court of Appeals reversed the Alabama Supreme Court, and ordered the absentee ballots excluded. The circuit court emphasized that other voters were indeed harmed by the Alabama court's decision in two ways: Adding illegal votes to the total vote count diluted the votes of those who had voted legally, and allowing absentee votes that had not met the formerly understood requirements was unfair to those who would have voted as absentees had they known that these requirements no longer held. [9]

No harm or comparative disadvantage was imposed on any citizen by the Florida Supreme Court's decision not to adopt any more specific standard for manual recounts than the standard laid down in a pertinent section of the Florida statute: The recount should attempt to identify the voting intention of each voter whose ballot is inspected. [10] Suppose two Florida counties—X and Y—both use punch card ballots, and that the judges who conduct the recount in X adopt a rule of thumb stipulating that if a wholly undetached chad is plainly dimpled, and no other dimple appears on the ballot, an intention has been revealed to vote for the candidate whose chad was dimpled. County

Y's judges adopt the very different rule of thumb that no ballot indicates an intention to vote unless one and only one chad has been detached from at least two of its corners. Suppose the machines in County X and County Y had failed to detect any vote on the ballots of X and Y, citizens of the two counties. Is the fact that the two counties use different rules of thumb in their manual recounts unfair to X vis-à-vis Y? Or Y vis-à-vis X? Each county's rule of thumb runs a risk—in County X that an unintended vote will be counted, and in County Y that an intended vote will not be counted. In each case the character of the risk is the same: a voter's intention may be contradicted. There is no discrimination either way. Of course, one of these rules of thumb may be unwise or even unreasonable. We might well think that County Y's rule is too strict, and that this is unfair to Y. But then it wouldn't be *less* unfair to Y if County X had the same unfortunate rule. It would then be unfair to both X and Y.

But why, then, didn't the Florida Supreme Court lay down more specific standards for the manual recount it ordered? Why didn't it stipulate, for example, that no punch card ballot could count as a vote unless at least two corners of a chad were detached? It might well have thought that it was not its role to do that. The Florida statute, after all, laid down nothing more specific than the voter-intention test, and the court might have thought it more in keeping with the spirit of that instruction to allow individual counters to decide, with the evidence of ballots before them, how best to achieve that task. The Florida court had already been attacked as being political, moreover, and it might well have thought that it would encourage rather than defuse that criticism if it made any one choice for the whole state that might be thought to favor one candidate or the other. It may well have decided that the wisest course, as well as the course most in keeping with the statute, was simply to pass on the statute's instruction to those who would study the ballots at first hand. All this is speculation, of course, but, as I said in my earlier article in Chapter 1, the Florida court's decision to do that could hardly be attacked as arbitrary or irrational, or lacking in any justification.

Some commentators, including Pildes in Chapter 4, have suggested that that court's decision not to draft more specific instructions for recounts across the state might have been unfair to voters for a different reason: It encouraged partisan decisions by recounters in different counties, so that those counties dominated by Republicans would adopt strict rules of thumb and those by Democrats more relaxed rules. But that objection seems wrong for a variety of reasons. The alternative, as I just said, was for the Florida Supreme Court to impose one recount standard for the whole state, which would inevitably have been thought massively to favor one party or the other. It might well be wiser, from this perspective as well as others, to allow the decisions, if they were to be influenced by politics at all, to be influenced at a more local level, so that different political biases could cancel themselves out across the state. In any case, the Florida court did everything reasonable it could to protect against partisan decisions. It assigned a highly reputable state court judge (who, incidentally, had already decided in Bush's favor in an earlier, important, ruling) to supervise the recounts, and that judge enlisted other judges to help in that task. The five conservative justices, stretching for any objection to the recount procedures they could find, objected that independent judges would not be experienced in conducting recounts. But (as the vivid television pictures we all saw confirmed) the local election officials were hardly experienced at that either, and it was not unreasonable to expect that judges could learn as quickly as anyone else could. We should note, finally, that any judge hoping to decide on a recount rule of thumb on partisan grounds would have had difficulty in doing so. According to the National Opinion Research Center, which recounted all the Florida votes for a consortium of newspapers including the *New York Times,* the political assumptions on which both Gore and Bush based their strategies in demanding and opposing recounts were wrong. Bush would have won if the recounts the Florida Supreme Court ordered in response to Gore's requests had been continued; Gore would have won if all the votes had been recounted.

I should mention one more ground of unfairness that the five conservative justices said they found in the Florida Supreme Court recount order. That order stipulated that all "undervotes" in the whole state—ballots that the machines had failed to record as casting any vote—be manually recounted, but not "overvotes"—ballots that the machines had discarded because it detected two or more votes on them for the same office. The five justices declared that that distinction was a further piece of unfairness, an additional violation of the equal protection clause. It might be a sufficient answer, in this context, to reply that no one had asked any court or official to recount overvotes, in spite of ample opportunity, and indeed invitation, for either of the candidates to have done so. But let us set that point aside. Suppose that one Florida voter, A, wholly detached two chads on his ballot, and his ballot was therefore disqualified, while another voter, B, did not wholly detach any chad, and his ballot was also disqualified. The Florida court's order meant that B's ballot would be inspected to determine whether there is sufficient evidence that he made a mistake and actually intended to vote for a particular candidate, but A's ballot would not be inspected for evidence that he too made a mistake, and intended to vote for only one candidate. If that would be unfair to A, however, then it would also be unfair not to reinspect all recorded votes as well—that is, all ballots that the machines did count as votes for a particular candidate—because the voters who cast those ballots might have made a mistake too and there may be evidence of that mistake on the ballot. Remember the butterfly ballot in Palm Beach County? Some voter whose ballot had been counted as a vote for Buchanan might have written on the ballot, "I mean to vote for Gore-Lieberman."

It seems absurd to suppose, however, that if any ballots are manually reinspected, all ballots cast in the election must be. If that were true, then a recount conforming to the five justices' announced formula—counting all undervotes and overvotes but not any actual votes—would be as unfair as the recount they condemned. In fact, it is neither arbitrary nor unfair to restrict manual recounts to a designated category of ballots if there is reason to think either that mistakes are particularly likely in that category, or that evidence of such mistakes are particularly likely to appear on ballots in that category, or both. It would not have been arbitrary, I believe, to limit recounts to undervotes on punch card ballots; it was certainly not arbitrary to limit them to undervotes on all ballots. It is distinctly more likely that a voter would mistakenly fail to punch a chad through or not mark his candidate's box on the ballot strongly enough for a machine to register the vote than that he would mistakenly punch through two chads or make two independent marks, each of which is strong enough to be registered. It is also much more likely that a mistake of the first kind would leave evidence of intention on the ballot, in the shape of a partially detached or even dimpled chad, for example, or a weak mark on a candidate's box, or a strong mark very close to it, than it is that a mistake of the second kind would leave such evidence behind. A was not treated unfairly by the Florida court's order, because it was much more likely that B had made a mistake than A, and that his ballot would allow the mistake to be corrected. Any other conclusion would make every selective recount—anywhere—automatically unfair.

Of course, sometimes different treatment for different people is indeed unfair, just because it is different, and the point of the equal protection clause is indeed to guard against that kind of unfairness. A municipality is not required to supply its residents with an ice-skating rink, for example—there would be no injustice in its deciding not to do so—but if it does build a municipal skating rink, it must allow all residents, of all races, to use it on equal terms. It is, however, a moral as well as a legal mistake to suppose that disparate treatment is always unfair, and sometimes focusing on disparity blinds us to the real injustice. The *New York Times's* now well-known study of "irregularities" in Florida's counting of absentee ballots in the 2000 election provides a different kind of example.[11] The *Times* charged that heavily Republican counties failed to enforce the rules governing such ballots; the rule, for example, that requires that absentee ballots must be mailed on or before election day.[12] Republican operatives persuaded election officials in those counties to wink at such violations, but also persuaded officials in heavily Democratic counties to enforce them strictly. The *Times* suggested that if the rules were to be waived in one county, it should be waived in them all, as if the different treatment county by county was the problem. In fact, the problem was the failure to enforce the rules, and though the behavior of the Republican party leaders was appalling, the problem would not have been cured—but only exacerbated—had the violations been more widespread. Violating the rules is unfair to all Florida voters, because it allows illegal votes to compromise legal ones, and the more violations the worse the compromise.

I agree with Sunstein's judgment, however, in Chapter 2, that the Supreme Court's equal protection holding, for all its flaws, might do some later good. Many electoral arrangements and practices are unfair in exactly the way the equal protection clause condemns: They do disadvantage some groups of citizens in the exercise of the fundamental right to vote. Florida's electoral law, in allowing counties to choose their own voting methods, discriminated against the residents of the counties that chose to use punch card ballots because—as the evidence of the 2000 election now makes plain—that system is much more likely than others to count a ballot the voter intended to mark as a vote for one candidate as a non-vote, and residents of those counties are therefore at greater risk of having their votes ignored. In Chapter 7, Guinier describes many other disadvantages that certain voters, particularly black voters, suffered through Florida's election practices. If the Court's equal protection holding is allowed to become a constitutional precedent, in spite of the conservative justices' attempt to prevent it from doing so, that might strengthen the hand of those challenging such discriminatory electoral practices. If it does, those justices' legal and moral error in citing the equal protection clause as their excuse for making Bush president would have had later benefits, but hardly redeeming ones.

DID THE FLORIDA COURT CHANGE THE RULES?

Article II

As I said, three of the five justices who endorsed the equal protection argument—Rehnquist, Scalia, and Thomas—also offered a further, very different, argument in a separate concurring opinion. Though this argument is complex, it carries, once again, a simple and direct moral charge: The Florida Supreme Court, by overruling Katherine Harris's interpretations of the Florida election statute, and then by ordering fresh manual recounts, changed the rules after the election was over, which is patently unfair. Of course, that is exactly what the critics of the Supreme Court's decision accuse the conservative justices of doing—they changed the Constitution, the critics say, so as to elect the candidate they favored. The three justices' argument can therefore be seen as a preemptive strike.

Their argument is often referred to as the Article II argument for a reason I must now explain. Normally, a state supreme court's interpretation of its own state's law is a matter for that court alone; it is not subject to review in the federal courts, including the Supreme Court. Normally, that is, the Supreme

Court would have no business deciding whether some decision of the Florida court invented a new Florida statute in the guise of interpreting the existing one. The Supreme Court would have to accept the Florida court's interpretation at face value. But, the three justices argued, Article II of the national Constitution makes a state court's interpretation of a state election statute, so far as this applies to a national presidential election, an exception. Section 1 of Article II provides, as part of the structure for electing presidents, that "Each state shall appoint, in such Manner as the Legislature thereof may direct, a Number of Electors, equal to the whole Number of Senators and representatives to which the State may be entitled in the Congress . . ." The three justices argued that since this provision assigns power over each state's conduct of presidential elections to the state legislature rather than to the state courts, the national Supreme Court is entitled—and has the responsibility—to see whether the Florida court usurped the Florida legislature's power by, in effect, changing the election statute after the election was over.

As I said earlier, many lawyers who support the Supreme Court's ultimate decision in *Bush v. Gore,* but who agree that the equal protection argument that all five conservative justices endorsed is too weak to justify that decision, believe that the Article II argument is much stronger, and regret that the five justices did not propose that argument as their official justification instead. They point out that the most vulnerable part of the Court's decision—its refusal to send the case back to the Florida Supreme Court to give that body the opportunity to correct the equal protection violation by amending its recount order—would not have been necessary if it had decided the case on Article II grounds, because the latter argument insists, not that the Florida court committed an error in the way it designed the recount, but that it committed an error—at a much earlier stage—by changing the rules so as to make a recount possible. If the Court had reversed on that ground, it could simply have declared that, under the rules as they stood before the Florida court changed them, Bush had won Florida's electoral votes.

It is not clear why the Constitution's framers, in Article II, assigned the power of choosing the manner of selecting presidential electors to the legislature of each state rather than, as in the case of so many other power-assigning provisions, to the states themselves. After all, nothing in the

Constitution requires that states even *have* legislatures. But the choice never-theless had an important consequence, at least in theory, because it gave the state legislators (rather than, for example, the state governor or the people of the state in a referendum) an extraordinary power. Though this fact is not widely appreciated, the Constitution does not require that states allow their citizens to vote for the national president. Florida need not have held a pres-idential election at all in November of 2000; in virtue of Article II, the Florida legislature (controlled by Republicans sympathetic to Bush) might have de-cided that it was wiser—or at least safer—itself to choose a slate of Bush elec-tors rather than allowing ordinary Florida voters any say in the matter. Of course, if any state legislature actually behaved in that ruthless manner, the national Constitution would soon be amended, by irresistible popular de-mand, to prevent such autocracy in the future. But the Florida legislature's decision not to hold a presidential election in 2000 would nevertheless have been constitutionally valid for that election.

In practice, however, the only effect of the Article II provision is to insure what would have gone without saying anyway: that the laws setting up and regulating the presidential election in each state must be adopted by the leg-islature of that state. Since it is the business of a legislature to make laws, it would be their business (and not the business, for example, of the dean of the state university's law school) to make the election laws even if Article II had left the matter to the "states" rather than to the state legislatures. But a sur-prising number of lawyers and scholars (including, apparently, all nine of the Supreme Court justices) apparently think that the language quoted from Ar-ticle II has a much more important consequence than that. They think that it means not only that the legislature rather than some other person or group is to make the election law, but that it is to make the election law in some partic-ularly free and unencumbered way—free, that is, from the normal back-ground provisions and assumptions to which all its other acts of legislation are subject.

That assumption, as we shall see, is indispensable to the Article II argument that the Florida court changed the rules after the election was over. I believe the assumption to rest on a series of confusions about what legislation is, confusions no doubt engendered—at least in part—by conservative lawyers' deep distrust of the justices of the Florida Supreme Court. They believe that the Florida court acted in a partisan and irresponsible manner throughout the postelection contests. The five conservative Supreme Court justices who decided for Bush are widely reported to have been infuriated by the Florida court, and there is some evidence of that state of mind in the comments some of them made in oral argument in the hearings before them. If Article II actually has the result I just reported—that state legislatures are free from the normal restrictions on their powers to legislate when they adopt rules regulating presidential elections—then the power of state court judges to review and interpret state election statutes is sharply limited. But though that fact may explain the popularity of the Article II argument, it cannot improve it, and the argument is a very bad one indeed.

Legislation is not an act of magic: A statute does not spring, full-formed and pellucid, from the collective mind of a group of officials endowed by nature with special legislative powers. Legislation results when a group of people lucky enough to have won the last election—and not all of whom have any great understanding of what they are doing—perform some conventional act, like saying "aye," when particular words are placed before them. But what legislation they have actually enacted—what difference they have made to the law that governs the rest of us by saying "aye"—depends not just on what words were placed before them, but on a good deal else as well. It depends on background rules and practices many but not all of which are encoded in written and unwritten constitutions.

Two of these background practices are pertinent now, because these normally bring judges, like those of the Florida Supreme Court, into the legislative process. First, in many—and an increasing number of—countries, constitutions limit the powers of any legislature to make law. In the United States, for example, the actions of state legislators do not make law if what they attempt to enact would violate the individual rights described in the national or local state constitution. When a putative statute is challenged by individuals or groups who claim that it would violate their constitutional rights, it falls to state and federal judges to decide whether that challenge is justified. Second, what legislation a legislature has enacted—what it has actually done—depends not only on what words the legislators had on their desks when they voted, but on what those words, in that context, mean: how, that is, they are properly interpreted. Though as we shall see legislators can exploit certain conventions in order to more precisely fix the correct interpretation of the words they enact—they can write committee reports setting out what they intend their statute to do, for example—they cannot, in the nature of the case, anticipate or govern every issue of interpretation that may arise. Once again, in the United States, it falls to judges to interpret vague, ambiguous, abstract or otherwise troublesome phrases and statutes, and their interpretive decisions are crucial in fixing what law we are actually governed by. I do not mean that judges, through their responsibility to decide whether a statute is constitutional, or to decide how it should be interpreted, have the power to undo law that the legislature has already enacted. That suggestion misses the crucial point. What legislation a legislature actually *has* enacted depends on what the right answers are to the questions that, in our legal practice, judges must decide. A statute is an interpretive construction, not just a series of punctuated words.

Article II and State Constitutions

When the Florida Supreme Court unanimously ruled on November 21 that Secretary of State Harris had abused her discretion in refusing to extend the deadline for filing election returns, that court said, in the course of its argument, that election laws "are valid only if they impose no 'unreasonable or unnecessary' restraints on the rights of suffrage" set out in the state constitution, and it referred to the state constitution's declaration that "all political power is inherent in the people." [13] On December 4, the Supreme Court, also unanimously, remanded that decision to the Florida court with a question that many commentators thought innocuous. Did the Florida court mean that though the state legislature had intended the deadline to be firm, as Harris had declared, the court was overruling the legislature by declaring that it had violated the state constitution's "people power" provision? The question was anything but innocuous, however, because the Supreme Court, just in asking the question, embraced a dangerous and extraordinary proposition with no foundation in law or logic: That Article II exempts the state legislatures from the constraints of their own state constitutions in their decisions about how elections are to be run.

In fact, on the best understanding of the Florida court's opinion, it appealed to the state constitution not to strike down any part of the Florida election statute, but only as an aid in construing what the election statute meant. It presumed, as courts very often do, that it is desirable, all else equal, to interpret statutes so as to conform to the established values and principles of the state, and it referred to the state constitution as strong evidence of what those values and principles actually are. (That, indeed, is what the Florida court itself said it had done when it finally answered the Supreme Court's question weeks later.) But the Supreme Court was wrong even to suggest that Article II, just in assigning a particular task to the state legislatures, meant to exempt those bodies from the normal background constraints of state constitutions. What possible point could be served by the national Constitution denying the people of Florida authority to protect their own democratic power in that way? What possible point could the framers have thought they were serving by enacting a provision with that consequence? So understood, the clause both undermines democracy and cripples state sovereignty, and has no redeeming features at all.[14]

Nor is that extraordinary reading of Article II forced on us by its text. On the contrary, it would be much more natural, and make much more sense, to interpret that text in the way I suggested: It places positive legislative power over each state's procedures for presidential elections in the legislature of that state, as distinct from other state organs, but does not exempt legislatures from the normal background constraints of all legislation. Nor is it likely that the Supreme Court would have been tempted by its extraordinary reading of Article II had the issue arisen in any other case. The Florida Constitution, like other state constitutions, gives the state governor a limited power to veto any legislation. Suppose that a state's governor had vetoed an election statute on the ground that, in his view, the statute did not allow enough time for the manual recount of disputed ballots. Is it conceivable that the Supreme Court would have declared his action unconstitutional if a challenge had somehow appeared before it? Or suppose a parallel issue arose about some other constitutional provision. Article V of the national Constitution provides that constitutional amendments are to be approved by the state legislatures (rather than, as the Constitution might have specified, by the states). Article X, Section 1 of Florida's constitution provides that "the legislature shall not take action on any proposed amendment to the constitution of the United States unless a majority of the members thereof have been elected after the proposed amendment has been submitted for ratification." Would the Supreme Court have struck that provision down as an unconstitutional violation of Article II?

"Error in the Vote Tabulation"

The three-justice concurring opinion in the Court's final, December 12, decision sets out a different form of the Article II argument. It argues that the Florida court changed the election rules after the election was over because its interpretation of the election statute was "absurd." It was absurd because it "plainly departed from the legislative scheme," and because it produced a new scheme that "cannot reasonably be thought" to represent the preexisting Florida statutory law. The pertinent clause of that statute provides that "if [a sample] manual recount indicates an error in the vote tabulation which could affect the outcome of the election," the county canvassing board may order a full manual recount to see whether there is evidence of a clear voter intent to vote in a particular way.[15] It is crucial, in determining whether the Florida Supreme Court was legally correct in overruling Katherine Harris, and extending the deadline for counties to file the results of manual recounts, to decide what counts as an "error in the vote tabulation" within the meaning of that provision.

The three justices insist that "tabulation" errors must be sharply distinguished from errors by the voters themselves. A tabulation error occurs, they say, only when a device for counting votes does not function as it is designed to function. If a vote-tabulating machine is designed to count a vote when one and only one chad is fully detached from the ballot, and it does not count a ballot with a hanging chad as a vote for anyone, that is an instance of tabulation success, not tabulation error. Since there was no evidence of any substantial tabulation error understood in that way, in the counties that had undertaken manual recounts before the November 14 deadline, those recounts were pointless, because they could not have identified ballots that could lawfully be counted. They could only identify ballots in which voters had erred by not fully detaching a chad, and these ballots could not legally be counted as votes, no matter how clear an intention they displayed to vote for one candidate—even if, for example, one chad on the ballot was almost fully detached and no other chad was even dimpled. So Harris did not abuse her discretion by refusing to extend the deadline. On the contrary, any other decision would have been senseless.

We might call this reading of the phrase *error in vote tabulation* the "machine-error" reading. Katherine Harris had ruled, early in the post-election story, that the machine-error reading was the correct one. But many other readings of the phrase are possible, and soon after she ruled in favor of that one, Bob Butterworth, the Democratic attorney general of Florida, issued his own ruling rejecting the machine-error reading. One alternative, for example, is the "result-error" reading: According to that reading, a tabulation error occurs whenever a voter intended to vote for a particular candidate, and believed that he had, but was not recorded as voting that way. The result-error reading is, of course, much broader than the machine-error reading. On the latter reading, the butterfly ballot used in Palm Beach County produced no tabulation error, even though thousands of voters who intended to vote for Gore—and thought they had voted for him—were tabulated as voting for Buchanan. There was no tabulation error because the machines were designed to count ballots marked in a certain way as votes for Buchanan, and they did so, apparently impeccably. But on the result-error reading, tabulation errors did occur, though these tabulation errors were not remediable through a manual recount, because no evidence of voter intent appeared on the ballots that could override, ballot by ballot, the technical vote for Buchanan. On the result-error reading, tabulation errors also occurred in punch-card-ballot counties because many voters did not succeed in punching a chad completely out, and some of these errors could be corrected through a manual recount that produced evidence, on the ballot itself, of an intention to vote in a particular way. If a manual recount disclosed that one chad was left hanging by one corner and no other chad was even dimpled, for instance, that would provide very strong evidence that the voter intended to vote for the candidate whose chad was left hanging. So, on the result-error reading, Harris's decision not to extend the deadline to permit such recounts had the inevitable result that many errors that the statute contemplated would be corrected by manual recounts would be left uncorrected instead.

Three distinct questions arise. First, do the Florida courts have the initial responsibility to decide which reading of the phrase *error in vote tabulation*—the machine-error reading or some rival reading, like the result-error reading—provides the best interpretation of the statute? Second, if so, was the Florida Supreme Court wrong to reject the machine-error reading, as it did? Third, if so, was that court's reading of the phrase so obviously "absurd," or did it so "plainly" depart from the actual legislative scheme, that the three justices were entitled to treat it as having invented a new statute rather than trying to interpret the existing one?

The answer to the first of these questions is easy enough. Who else but Florida judges are to decide what the Florida election statute means?[16] The legislature that enacted the pertinent clauses of that statute is long gone, and cannot be called back into session to declare how its language should now be understood. The three-justice concurring opinion stated that Katherine Harris, as Florida's secretary of state, "is authorized by law to issue binding interpretations of the election code," and suggested that the Florida Supreme Court was therefore obliged to follow her decision that the machine-reading was the right one. But the language of the Florida statute that the three justices cited, which states that the secretary of state has the responsibility to "obtain and maintain uniformity in the application, operation, and interpretation of the election law,"[17] and that her office's "advisory opinions" shall be binding "on any person or organization who sought the opinion or with reference to whom the opinion was sought,"[18] hardly justifies the claim that Florida courts have no power to review her interpretations to see if they conform to the law. On the contrary, it would be bizarre to interpret that language to have that effect. It would be irresponsible for legislators to place unreviewable power over the meaning of the election law in the hands of an official who is herself elected and might be a candidate for reelection under the terms of that law, even if she were not so political and partisan a figure as Katherine Harris, and it would therefore be wrong to interpret the statutory language to have that effect unless that is its unavoidable meaning.

We must therefore turn to the second and more complex question. Did the Florida court make a mistake in rejecting Katherine Harris's machine-error reading of the phrase *error in the vote tabulation?* The three-justice concurring Supreme Court opinion declared that the machine-error reading is plainly, just as a matter of the literal meaning of words, the right reading, so that the Florida court's contrary reading was not only wrong but "absurd." It is true that some words can properly be used to mean only one thing in the English language, at least literally, almost no matter in what context they appear, and when these words appear in a statute there is rarely room for competing interpretations. The Constitution provides that no one may become president who is younger than thirty-five years of age, and any judge who said that, on reflection, "thirty-five" means "thirty-four" or means "old enough to exercise important responsibilities," would be incompetent or irresponsible. Is the machine-error reading of the Florida statutes recount provision also so evidently correct, just as a matter of what words must mean, that the result-error reading—or any other competing reading—is plainly wrong?

No. A legislative draftsman might well use the words *error in the vote tabulation* with a different, more expanded sense than the machine-error reading allows. He might, with no violence to linguistic propriety, mean to include official errors in the whole process of recording and counting votes. He might regard an error in the instructions furnished to voters as constituting a "tabulation" error in that broader sense, for example. Suppose that in one Florida county that uses punch-card ballots some official had clearly but erroneously instructed voters that if they found they could not actually dislodge the chad, it would be enough—to make an effective vote—if they marked the chad they wanted to dislodge with an *X*. (We needn't suppose that the mistake was deliberate: The instructions might have been approved by representatives of both parties, as the butterfly ballot was approved in Palm Beach County.) A court might well construe "error in vote tabulation," as it occurs in the context of the Florida statute as a whole, to include rather than exclude this error. It would construe *tabulation* to refer to the entire process the county had established for obtaining and counting votes, not just to its process for counting them alone. It would not be outrageous for a court to take that view, particularly since it would be difficult to assign to the legislature any reason for distinguishing between instruction and machine errors in that way.

That is enough to show that the machine-error reading is not dictated simply by plain and indomitable semantics. True, there is no voter error in the story I just told. The error I imagined was official, and someone might argue that "error in the vote tabulation" should be thought to include official as well as machine error, but not voter error. But no one could suppose that this new distinction follows from the plain, unchallengeable, unalterable meaning of *tabulation*. Anyone defending that new reading, which is intermediate between the machine-error and result-error readings, would have to do so by constructing a more complex interpretive argument. He could not rely on what the word *tabulation* just obviously means, all on its own. He would have to show that his intermediate reading was best, all things considered, for some other reason.

How to Read a Statute

What other reason? If a judge cannot rely just on bare semantics in choosing a reading of the error-in-vote-tabulation clause, on what can he rely? Lawyers often say that the meaning of a statutory phrase depends on the intention with which the legislature that enacted the statute used it. But of course a legislature, as an institution, does not have a mind of its own, and cannot intend anything. True, the individual senators and representatives who make up the legislature do have minds, and someone might think that the intention of the legislature as a whole is simply some sum or compound of the various intentions of those individuals. But any attempt to translate the purposes or thoughts or hopes of a large number of individuals into a collective purpose or thought or hope faces insurmountable difficulties. It is unclear, first, which individual legislators should count in fixing the thoughts of the legislature as a whole. Do we take account of the thoughts of all the legislators? Or only those who voted for the clause to become law? If the latter, do we consider the thoughts of each of these, as it were, equally? Or do we pay more attention to those of some—the floor leaders of the bill, for example, if we can identify them? Second, it is unclear exactly which kind of thoughts we should be looking for. It is extremely unlikely that any of the legislators contemplated the specific problems that arose in the 2000 election. If many of them had, they would have tried to write a different, clearer, statute. So we will find nothing if we rummage through their biographies looking for an answer to the specific question whether, when they said "aye" to the clause, they had only machine error in mind, or result errors, or something else. We will surely not find enough direct information about that to construct an overall legislative answer to the question, no matter which combination of individual answers we decide constitutes the collective answer.

We might hope to cure this latter problem by discovering the more general opinions or ambitions or convictions of the individual legislators, and studying these to decide what they would have done if—contrary to actual fact—they had focused on the question of what kind of error should count as one in voter tabulation. Suppose, for example, we discovered that the great majority of the members of the Florida legislature that enacted the clause favored quick and decisive elections and wanted to avoid, if possible, protracted disputes about who won. We might take that discovery as evidence that they would have preferred the machine-error reading, which is the narrowest reading, of tabulation error. But it would hardly be decisive evidence, because we would also discover that many of those legislators had other opinions and convictions as well: in particular that they also wanted the election results to match what Florida voters intended to do, and thought they had done. If all the legislators cared about was a quick end to elections, after all, they would not have provided any recount apparatus at all: They would have been content with the first reported decision, however inaccurate it might be thought to be, unless, perhaps, it was tainted by fraud. The legislators who enacted the disputed clause were faced, like all legislators everywhere, with the problem of accommodating a wide range of goals in a concrete set of rules and principles, and the question of what balance they meant to strike among these—what balance between finality and accuracy, for example—cannot be answered simply by listing the goals themselves. We need more direct evidence about the relative strength of their different convictions in combination with one another, but the only plausible evidence of that relative strength is the statute that emerged from their deliberations and calculations, and it is exactly the question of what that statute is that we began by trying to answer.

In any case, some of the goals the individual legislators undoubtedly had in mind were not even the *kind* of goals that it would be right to take into account at all in interpreting the statute they created. Many legislators, presumably, wanted not to displease their party leaders or major campaign contributors. Others wanted a voting record that would help them in future elections. Others wanted election rules that would benefit their own party in future elections. It would hardly be unrealistic to think that goals like these would be prominent in any sound causal explanation, of the sort that an empirical political scientist might offer, of why individual legislators voted as they did, and of how they would have voted if invited to make "error in the vote tabulation" clearer. Yet it would strike lawyers as obscene to take these goals into account in deciding what they would have done if issued that invitation.

In truth, in spite of traditional lawyers' rhetoric, statutory interpretation has very little to do with deciding what particular people hoped or thought or intended in the past. Lawyers and judges interpret a statute by asking which way of understanding its ambiguous or abstract or troublesome terms would be most consistent with the best justification that the legislators could have offered for enacting the statute they did at the time they did. Lawyers try to reconstruct, that is, not the actual motives and purposes of past lawmakers, but the motives and purposes that would provide the best public *case* for what they did.[19] That case must respect the semantic facts—it must be a case for using the words the legislators enacted—and it must also respect history: Contemporary judges must not interpret a statute by justifying it in a way that would have struck most of the legislators, or the public to whom they spoke, as irrelevant or wrong in principle. In American legal practice, statutory interpretation is also constrained by a variety of conventions, though these are often imprecise and so need interpretation themselves. One convention holds, for example, that if the legislators attach some canonical statement of their purpose or intention to a statute—in a pertinent committee report, for example, or in a formal statement by the manager of a bill on the floor of the legislature—that statement must be given a prominent place in any interpretation of the statute. These constraints often leave room for more than one interpretation, however, and judges must then rely on their own judgment to make political as well as verbal and historical sense of the statute they are interpreting. So a particular interpretation of a statute is better, all else equal, if the statute so construed better serves the general political ideals to which the community in question is already committed through other laws and practices. It was proper, for that reason, for the Florida Supreme Court to call attention to the provision of the Florida constitution that it cited. The court was arguing for an interpretation of the Florida statute that would enable the result of elections more closely to match what the voters collectively intended, and the fact that this goal had been endorsed in the state's constitution was therefore an appropriate part of its case for that inter-pretation.

Process Error

We may now return, with that background in place, to the crucial interpretive question in *Bush v. Gore.* How should we understand the Florida statute's reference to "error in the vote tabulation?" We must construct an interpreta-tion that provides the best justification, subject to the constraints I de-scribed, for enacting that text. The narrowest, machine-error, reading that the three-justice concurring opinion said was "plainly" correct is, on the contrary, indefensible. As I said, it is not dictated by semantic rules, and there was no committee report stating that this was the reading the legislature in-tended. It must be ruled out, then, for exactly the reason the Florida court of-fered. The balance it strikes between accuracy and finality shows too cheap a regard for an ideal that both the state's constitution and its central political traditions take to be of fundamental importance: that each eligible citizen must be offered a fair opportunity to vote, and that the selection of political officials should match, so far as possible, the will of those they govern. It would have been unreasonable, given the importance of those values, for the legislature to allow manual recounts when the source of suspected error was a defect in the counting machines but not when the source of suspected error was some other defect in the process, like inaccurate instructions to voters, when the latter errors could as easily be detected as the former. Judges should not assume that a legislature has acted unreasonably unless semantic compulsion or the force of some convention dictates that unfortunate result.

Once we reject the machine-error reading, we must choose another one.

We might well be persuaded that the result-error reading I described as an alternative goes too far in the opposite direction. We might think that a state has done enough to respect democratic ideals when it has provided a fair, easily understood, and easily managed process for casting votes. It need not take further steps to correct the errors of those who out of carelessness or mischief flout that process—by spoiling their ballot, for example, and then writing "I ♥ Bush" across it. I do not mean that no case can be made for the result-error reading: It is not unreasonable, given the importance of the democratic ideals, to think that a state should try to correct even gross voter errors when the voter's intention is apparent. But there is a reading of "error in the vote tabulation" that is intermediate between the machine reading and the result reading, which I shall call the "process-error" reading, and since even that intermediate reading would sustain the Florida court's decisions, we need not pursue the case for the broader result-error reading now.

A process error occurs when a vote is not recorded in the way a voter intended to vote and believed he had voted, and the failure can be traced to a defect in the state's process of collecting and counting votes. My earlier story, about inaccurate instructions given to voters, is a clear example of a process error. So, at least arguably, is the butterfly-ballot story in Palm Beach County. County officials provided a ballot so misleading (it was not even in conformity with legal regulations) that even average voter attention and care could not prevent a very high number of votes being recorded otherwise than as the voters intended. It is also reasonable to regard the voting errors in punch-card counties—a failure to punch a chad entirely through, for example—as a process error. The punch card system, as we now know, is dangerously susceptible to mistake. The number of ballots rejected as non-votes was strikingly higher in punch-card counties than in counties that used other voting techniques, and the manual recounters in such counties were able to identify, before the recounts stopped, a relatively high number of ballots that machines had rejected as non-votes but that they were confidently able to assign to candidates. Immediately after the election Florida decided to replace punch card ballots with a more accurate system.[20] The punch card system almost guaranteed a significant number of mistakes, and using that system in a presidential election amounted to process error. The process-error reading is an attractive one and nothing narrower, including the machine-error reading, would be acceptable. The Florida court did not misinterpret the Florida statute.

We have now considered two of the questions I listed at the outset of this discussion. I listed a third question, but we can answer that one very quickly. Suppose I am wrong that the Florida Supreme Court's reading of the crucial phrase was the best reading. Suppose that, on balance, the machine-error reading is better. It would still be a separate question whether, as Rehnquist, Scalia, and Thomas claimed, the Florida court changed the rules after the election was over by inventing an entirely new statute altogether. In one sense, of course, any judicial misinterpretation of a statute, unless it is overruled, changes that statute, because the actual statute is defined by the true or correct interpretation. If two lawyers disagree about the correct interpretation of some statute, they are disagreeing about what the statute, properly understood, really is, and when a court resolves the disagreement one of the lawyers will inevitably think, just for that reason, that the statute the court has applied is not the one that the legislature enacted. But if we declare that judges have usurped the power of other institutions whenever we disagree with how they have interpreted some statute, we are in effect denying them the legitimate power to interpret at all. So the charge that the Florida judges invented a new statute must mean not only that they were wrong, but that they were grievously or demonstrably wrong, that no competent lawyer could have reached the decision they did in good faith. That is indeed what the three justices claimed. But even if the argument I made in favor of the Florida court's interpretation fails to show that the interpretation was the best available, I am confident that it shows that the interpretation was not absurd.

DID THE SUPREME COURT DO US A FAVOR?

By far the most popular defense of the Court's decision in *Bush v. Gore* is that the Court saved the nation from a further, and perhaps protracted, period of legal and political battles, and of continuing uncertainty about who the next president would be. On this view, the five conservative justices knew they could not justify their decision on legal grounds, but they decided, heroically, to pay a price in damage to their reputation as jurists in order to save the nation from those difficulties: They "took a bullet," as it has sometimes been put, for the rest of us. In Chapter 5, Posner with his characteristic incisiveness and vigor, sets out the argument for this view more clearly than anyone else has; for that reason this chapter, together with his earlier book, constitutes an important contribution to the national debate.

He says that at least sometimes judges should take a "pragmatic" approach to their work and make decisions they believe will have the best results overall even if these are not decisions that past legal doctrine would authorize. That pragmatic approach, he believes, would have recommended deciding *Bush v. Gore* in the way the conservatives did, and he compares their decision, seen in that light, to Abraham Lincoln's defiance of the Constitution in suspending habeas corpus during the Civil War and, more ominously to the Supreme Court's decision permitting the internment of Japanese Americans during World War II.[21] He does not, however, think that judicial pragmatism should be reserved for exceptional emergencies like full-scale war. On the contrary, he advocates pragmatism as a general style of adjudication, right for judges in quotidian cases as well as in constitutional emergencies. We should therefore look at his formal statements of what pragmatism is and means. I have taken one of these from his earlier book:

> "Pragmatic" as an adjective for anything to do with the judicial process still causes shudders. It seems to open up vistas of judicial willfulness and subjectivity and to mock the rule of law; it seems to equate law to prudence, and thus to be Machiavellian. All that pragmatic adjudication need mean, however—all that I mean by it—is adjudication guided by a comparison of the consequences of alternative resolutions of the case rather than by an algorithm intended to lead the judges by a logical or otherwise formal process to the One Correct Decision, utilizing only the canonical materials of judicial decision making, such as statutory or constitutional text and previous judicial opinions. The pragmatist does not believe that there is or should be any such algorithm. He regards adjudication, especially constitutional adjudication, as a practical tool of social ordering and believes therefore that the decision that has the better consequences for society is the one to be preferred.[22]

In Chapter 5 of this volume, Posner puts this account in a more complex philosophical context. He distinguishes "everyday" pragmatism, which is the consequentialist, "hard-nosed" cost-benefit approach to legal reasoning described in the paragraph just quoted, from two more philosophical forms of pragmatism: "orthodox" and "recusant." [23] The judge who is a pragmatist in this everyday, consequentialist sense, does not despise precedent and technical legal argument. On the contrary, he is aware, and takes into account, the good consequences that flow from systematic judicial respect for traditional legal argument and doctrine, which include encouraging people to plan their affairs with confidence, and the bad consequences that might flow from a judge's ignoring traditional doctrine on particular occasions, which include defeating such expectations and weakening the general benefit of systematic respect for them. But the pragmatic judge is also aware of the dangers of a slavish deference to orthodox legal reasoning; he knows that in some circumstances he can achieve better consequences—even in the long run—by reaching the decision that will produce some particularly important benefit or avoid some particularly grave danger, even though this decision flies in the face of established doctrine. So pragmatic judges must balance the long-term benefits of respecting doctrine against the long–term benefits, from time to time, of ignoring it. "There is no algorithm for striking this balance. . . . He or she should try to make the decision that is reasonable, all things considered, where 'all things' include the standard legal materials . . . but also the consequences so far as they can be discerned of the decision in the case at hand." [24]

In *Bush v. Gore,* Posner says, the Supreme Court had to strike that balance. Would it produce "the better consequences for society," in the long run, to follow precedent and doctrine, which recommended dismissing Bush's appeal and therefore allowing the Florida recount to continue? Or to endorse an unpersuasive legal argument in order to halt the recount so that Bush would become president-elect at once? It was predictable, he says, that if the five conservative justices voted for the second choice, they would be thought to have made a rank partisan decision, and that the Court's reputation for honesty and impartiality, which is important, would suffer. That counted for the first choice. But the possibility of what he calls a "worst-case scenario" following that decision argued more powerfully for the second choice. The recount might have shown Gore the winner in Florida, and the Florida court might then have ordered the state's electoral votes certified for

Gore. Since the Court's decision was to be handed down on December 12, that recount would not have been completed by the "safe harbor" deadline of that very day, which immunizes a state's certification of electors from congressional challenge; indeed, a responsible recount could not have been completed even by December 18, the date on which electors are required to cast their votes. In the meantime, the Florida legislature, dominated by Republicans, might have chosen its own slate of electors pledged to Bush. Congress would then have had to choose between the two slates, but Congress might be divided: the Republican House siding with the Bush slate, but the equally-divided Senate, still presided over by Vice President Gore, who would have cast the deciding vote, endorsing the Gore slate. If Congress was unable to agree, the slate certified by the Florida governor, who is Bush's brother, would be seated. But what if the Florida Supreme Court had ordered the governor to certify the Gore slate, the governor had refused, and the Florida court had declared him in contempt? Who would decide what the governor's official verdict was? Suppose in the end no Florida votes were counted at all. Gore would then have had a majority of the electoral votes cast, but not a majority of the overall number of votes, and then the presidency would depend on the unsettled issue of whether he would need only the former to win. The Supreme Court might refuse to decide that question, on the ground that it is a political question, in which case the impasse would drag on indefinitely. An acting president would be needed and, under certain assumptions—that no vice president would have been elected, that the President's pro-tem of the Senate, Strom Thurmond, would decline to serve, and that the secretary of state was Madeleine Albright, who was born abroad and is therefore ineligible—that would be Lawrence Summers, the secretary of the treasury (and now the president of Harvard University). How would he have handled the delicate situation that arose when the Chinese seized our surveillance plane forced to land in its territory?

Posner sometimes makes modest, negative, claims for the plausibility of this worst-case scenario. He says that it "is by no means fantastic, or even highly improbable,"[25] and later that it is "not inevitable" but "it could not be thought phantasmal."[26] For the most part, however, he argues as if his scenario was—if not inevitable—at least so probable that a pragmatist judge should assume it to be the consequence of his decision to allow the recount to continue. (He called his book *Breaking the Deadlock,* not *Breaking a Not Phantasmal Deadlock.*) In fact, as Sunstein points out in Chapter 2, assignments of probability are indispensable to any genuine consequentialist analysis. It would be irrational for a pragmatist to compare two alternatives by comparing only the worst possible consequences of each, or only the best, or, indeed, only the most likely. He must compare the various possible consequences of each decision, taking into account their gravity, but discounting each by its probability. Posner's pragmatic argument becomes strikingly less impressive, even in its own terms, when we reformulate it in that spirit.

He begins, as I mentioned, by assuming that the manual recounts ordered by the Florida Supreme Court could not possibly have been completed by the "safe harbor" deadline of December 12, and were extremely unlikely to have been completed even by December 18. But this assumption supposes something that a pragmatic consequentialist cannot assume: That something other than a nice balance of long-term consequences required the Supreme Court to stay the Florida recounts on December 9, and also required it to declare, in its December 12 ruling, that the manual recounts under way were defective because they did not stipulate uniform recount standards. A consistent pragmatist would have had to ask himself, in considering whether to issue a stay on December 9, whether the long-term consequences of a decision not to intervene at all, for which the Court would have had ample doctrinal cover, would be better than those of staying the recount on that date and deciding a few days later that recounts were unconstitutional unless subject to uniform standards. He could not have assumed, in asking himself how much disorder the first choice would produce and the second avoid, that the recounts would for some unrelated reason stop until December 13, begin again only after whatever time it took to debate and choose uniform standards, and allow time for adjudication of arguments about the application of those new standards.[27] So the pertinent consequentialist question was whether, if the Florida Supreme Court's recount had been allowed to proceed in the form that court originally ordered, free from Supreme Court interference of any kind, it would have finished in time for Florida to certify a winner on December 12, or, in any case, by December 18. If so—and there is no reason to doubt it—then the rest of the "worst-case scenario" is irrelevant. This is the fallacy not just in Posner's argument, but in the more informal and widely embraced argument that the Court did us a favor by avoiding a crisis. All these arguments ignore the fact that the Court immeasurably worsened the risks before it avoided them. If the Court took a bullet for the rest of us, it also fired the gun.

Even if we set this crucial objection aside, moreover, and assume that the recount process had to begin again—under new standards yet to be chosen—on December 13, the argument that the Court saved the nation from crisis is still much weaker than Posner or the popular view assumes. A pragmatist would have to assume, even under that assumption, that there was a fifty-fifty chance that a recount whenever finished would show Bush the winner, in which case the controversy would end. Even if it showed Gore the winner, none of the steps that would provoke the deadlock Posner describes was inevitable. The Florida legislature might not have elected an alternate slate—there were genuine political risks even for some of the Florida Republicans in doing so. Even if it did, Congress might not deadlock in choosing between the rival slates. Some Republican congressmen might have thought that the case for preferring electors chosen by the people of Florida to those chosen by political officials was too strong to overcome. Some Democratic senators from states carried by Bush might have yielded to political pressure to vote for the Florida electors pledged to him. One or the other candidates might have stepped aside. The moral case for Bush withdrawing would have been very strong: He had lost the national popular vote and knew that many more Florida voters intended to vote for Gore than for him; if, on top of that, a recount had shown that more Florida voters actually had voted for Gore, public opinion might have swung so decisively against his becoming president in a brokered deal, or a Congressional power play, that he would have thought it best to yield. (Many Europeans were surprised that he did not withdraw after the butterfly-ballot episode made it apparent that he was not morally entitled to win on any reckoning.) Or, as the mini-crisis continued, public opinion might have begun to grow, in a self-fueling way, against Gore, and he may have decided that his political future would be enhanced by yielding at once. Or some deal might have emerged more quickly in Congress than Posner imagines. Or, if it became clear that Florida's votes would not be counted, the Supreme Court could have agreed to decide whether a majority of the electoral votes cast or all the electoral votes was necessary to win the presidency. It could plausibly have argued that this was a straightforward question of interpretation that, in the absence of a political resolution in Congress, it had the responsibility to decide. Or, if all the other steps in the worst-case scenario had indeed materialized, Summers, a very intelligent and able man, might have responded superbly to the Chinese retention of the surveillance plane. Some of these possibilities had distinctly lower probabilities than others, of course, and some very low probabilities indeed. But if we begin by supposing that the probability of a recount showing Gore the victor was only about 50 percent to begin with, and then take into account the compound probabilities of Posner's other speculations, his worst-case is exceedingly improbable. Which is only a fancier way of saying that in politics you never know.

Even Posner's worst-case scenario would not have been a national tragedy. It would not have been as bad (to recall Posner's analogies) as a Southern victory in the Civil War or a Japanese victory in World War II. So far, then, Posner's pragmatic defense seems a failure. But we have not yet reached the most serious problem of all. I said that, as of December 9, the balance of pragmatic considerations plainly tilted against Supreme Court intervention. But that judgment, I must now concede, ignores the single most important pragmatic consideration of all. If a pragmatist Supreme Court justice set himself to evaluate, on December 9, the overall consequences of halting the Florida recount, compared to the consequences of letting it continue, it would be irrational of him to ignore the fact that halting the recount would ensure a Bush presidency for at least four years, while letting the recount continue would mean a substantial—let us say a 50-percent—chance that Gore would be president instead. The question of which of these two politicians finally became president would swamp all other factors in a genuine pragmatic comparison of the two decisions.

In the first few months of his presidency, Bush engineered an enormous tax cut, withdrew from the Kyoto treaty on global warming, radically shifted domestic conservation and energy policy, announced a unilateral termination of the nuclear test ban treaty with Russia, drove ahead the immensely speculative missile shield program at considerable danger to other aspects of national security, and shifted American foreign policy sharply away from the consensus internationalist policy that had been followed by presidents of both parties.[28] If, as seems very likely, he makes one or more appointments to the Supreme Court, his appointees will probably be as conservative as he can push past a Senate now controlled by Democrats; he campaigned, after all, insisting that the best of the contemporary justices are Justices Scalia and Thomas. It is safe to assume that Gore's policies and decisions would have been dramatically different in every case. Critics believe that Bush's decisions will seriously harm the nation. They think that the tax cut will seriously damage the economy, just as they believe that Reagan's sharp tax cuts did, that the missile shield program is scientifically silly and diplomatically stupid, and that his environmental and foreign policies will prove disastrous. Bush's supporters think, to the contrary, that the tax cuts will save the economy, that the missile shield program will protect the nation from what they believe to be the genuine risk of nuclear attack by "rogue" states, and that the radical shifts in environmental and foreign policy will improve America's economic position, diplomatic power, and national security.

None of the costs and benefits of a Supreme Court decision either way in *Bush v. Gore* that Posner describes is on the same scale of importance, particularly when probabilities are factored in, as any one of these issues, let alone all of them. Someone who welcomed a Bush presidency would have thought the Supreme Court's decision a consequentialist triumph: It achieved the desired result without the trouble and risks of continuing the postelection battle. But someone who thought Bush dangerous for the nation would have thought the decision a pragmatic disaster. He would have thought—and this is the crucial point—that a continued postelection battle was a small price to pay for a substantial chance of finally avoiding a Bush presidency. A pragmatist justice would have had to decide for himself which of these two consequentialist judgments was right, and that means deciding whether Bush or Gore was better for the country. Of course, that is just what the severest critics think the five conservative justices actually did: They decided that Bush would be a better president and they acted accordingly. Indeed, almost everyone thinks that if the identical case had come to the Court, with only the difference that the candidates' position was reversed—Gore had been certified the winner, Bush had persuaded the Florida courts to order recounts, and Gore was asking the Supreme Court to halt those recounts—the five justices would have voted not to intervene at all. (Even Posner suspects that, though he suggests that the influence of politics and self-interest on the five justices was only to make them "more sensitive to" arguments, like the Article II argument, that they might otherwise have overlooked.[29]) But almost everyone—including, I assume, Posner—believes this fact to be *regrettable*. It is thought to be a devastating criticism of the five justices, if true, that it made a crucial difference to them which candidate would win if they stopped the recounts. But if Posner is right that the justices had a responsibility to reach a "pragmatic" result in this case, then it would have been irresponsible of them *not* to have allowed that to make a crucial difference.

He acknowledges this difficulty. In Chapter 5, he makes the surprising admission that it poses "perhaps the ultimate challenge to pragmatic adjudication," meaning, apparently, that pragmatism would be an unacceptable theory of adjudication if it recommended that judges should sometimes decide election cases so as to elect the best candidate for the nation.[30] He declares, however, that though a good pragmatist would take everything else into account in his assessment of consequences—would take into account, for example, the risk that some "rogue" nation would be tempted to take advantage of a protracted presidential contest to injure us—he would not take account of which candidate's overall policies would be better for us over four years. He describes that result as fortunate, but his defense of it is unconvincing.[31] He falls back on a strategy known to philosophers as "rule-consequentialism." This strategy supposes that people often produce the best consequences, in the long run, by following a rule carefully constructed so that following that rule in every case, whether or not it produces the best consequences in that case, considered on its own, produces the best consequences over time. He insists that judges should follow a strict rule, for that reason, not to make partisan political judgments.

It is unclear why he thinks that following this rule, instead of taking into account who would be a better president in those rare cases in which a judicial decision will decide a presidential election, would indeed produce the best consequences, even in the long run. Of course it would damage the Court's reputation and therefore its effectiveness if people generally thought that the justices had made a partisan decision. But people do think that any-

way about the decision in *Bush v. Gore*. That was, as Posner himself emphasizes, an important and inevitable cost of the Court's intervening in the election, at least once it was clear that only the conservative justices would decide
for Bush. He does not think, in any case, that a pragmatic judge should
openly admit to pragmatism. He suggests that the *Bush v. Gore* majority
should have decided on pragmatic grounds, but constructed the best cover
story of doctrine they could to hide that fact. But then why shouldn't the actual pragmatic grounds for decision, which are to be hidden from the public
anyway, include the decision's single most important consequence? Posner
says that that would derange the balance of powers in the American government. If he means that it would have bad long-term consequences for that
reason, he must explain why. Why is it not better in the long run to allow a
very occasional minor derangement, hidden as well as possible, when that
will save the nation from a calamitous presidency? Posner's argument seems
driven more by the need, at all costs, to deny that a pragmatist judge would
ever base his decisions on partisan political grounds than by any actual pragmatic case for that denial.

He is right, of course, that judges should follow a rule never to rely on
such partisan judgments. But he is wrong to imagine that the conservative
justices' decision in *Bush v. Gore* could be defended as a decision promoting,
in their view, the best overall consequences if they had followed that rule.
Rule-consequentialism provides an argument for not judging consequences
case by case, but deciding in accordance with fixed rules instead. But Posner
is now proposing something very different: a hybrid process in which judges
decide by assessing consequences, case by case, but adopt a rule that requires them to leave the most important consequences out. That is perverse.
It would make good sense to say that, because judges should not be partisan,
they should decide cases involving presidential elections strictly on principle and doctrine, not on any calculation about which result will be overall
better for the nation.[32] It also makes sense—though unattractive sense—to
say that because judges should aim to produce the best consequences, they
should make partisan political judgments in cases, including cases involving
presidential elections, in which an overall assessment of consequences is impossible without them. It makes no sense at all to say that judges should decide such cases pragmatically, by assessing the costs and benefits of a

decision either way, but taking no account of the likely winner of that struggle, which is a fact of absolutely decisive importance in assessing those costs and benefits. How could anyone sensibly decide the true cost of risking even Posner's worst case without considering how good or bad a Bush presidency—the certain outcome of the most certain way of avoiding that worst case—would be? Posner's settled recommendation is a formula, not for pragmatic decision, but for a parody of pragmatism, like asking a doctor to choose between alternate medicines for a patient by comparing their prices, availability, and ease of administration, without also asking which will cure and which will kill him.

So like the fairness argument that appeals to equal protection and the structural defense that appeals to Article II, the good-consequences defense of the Supreme Court's action collapses on careful examination. But since Posner offers, in Chapter 5, a more general defense of judicial pragmatism, we should also consider his more general arguments. *Pragmatism* is a buzzword among lawyers now: It appears everywhere and in the oddest contexts.[33] But since judges, like everyone else, disagree about the relative value of different possible consequences of their decisions, telling them to decide by weighing consequences is only—as Posner conceded many people think it is—an invitation to lawlessness.

The difference between judicial pragmatism and more orthodox theories of adjudication is easy to grasp in dramatic cases when it is clear that a conventional legal analysis would recommend a decision that almost everyone in the community would accept is bad. Posner's example of Lincoln's decision to defy the Constitution by suspending habeas corpus during the Civil War is that sort of case. There is room for doubt, of course, whether Lincoln's assumption that this was necessary to protect the nation's security was sound as a matter of consequential analysis. But the goal he aimed to serve—that the nation's security be protected—was not controversial within the community for whom he acted. In many—probably most—hard cases, however, it will not help simply to say that judges must think about consequences, because the nerve of the controversy is how those consequences should be assessed. The abortion cases provide a dramatic example that I have used before to make this point. Would it produce the best consequences for society to forbid early abortions? Or to permit them? Citizens, lawyers, and judges who disagree about the morality of abortion also, and just for that reason, disagree about which consequences would be best. One side thinks abortion murder, and that any society that permits murder is degraded. They therefore believe that the consequences of permitting abortion are disastrous. The other side thinks that forbidding abortion dooms thousands of women to a miserable life for no adequate reason, and therefore that the consequences of that decision would be dreadful.

If a judge undertook to decide the constitutionality of prohibiting abortion by asking whether the consequences of permitting or banning abortion were better on the whole, he would have to choose between these dramatically opposed convictions, and he would have no choice but to rank the consequences himself, according to his own lights, relying on his own convictions, so that if he himself believed that abortion was murder or otherwise deeply immoral, he would uphold the constitutionality of laws prohibiting it. He would tell himself that, on his own best judgment, and needing no other authority, he deemed the consequences of prohibiting abortion better for society than the consequences of permitting it. That would be a genuinely pragmatic judgment, though almost all lawyers and citizens (and perhaps even Posner) would think it wrong and even irresponsible. It is therefore no surprise that Posner's kind of pragmatism would issue a similar, and similarly irresponsible, command to the justices who decided *Bush v. Gore:* To decide whether, all things considered, a Bush presidency would be sufficiently better than a Gore one to outweigh the damage the Court incurred by accepting the case and deciding, on such flimsy conventional grounds, for Bush.

I should add—though I hope it goes without saying—that judges need not choose between weighing consequences in that personal way and ignoring consequences completely. No one supposes that judges could or should decide cases "by an algorithm intended to lead [them] by a logical or otherwise formal process to the One Correct Decision, utilizing only the canonical materials of judicial decision making, such as statutory or constitutional text and previous judicial opinions." That account of adjudication is a straw man and, I think, always was. Of course, judges must take the consequences of their decisions into account, but they may only do so as directed by principles embedded in the law as a whole, principles that adjudicate which consequences are relevant and how these should be weighed, rather than by their own political or personal preferences.

DEMOCRACY

One More Defense

Even a year after the Supreme Court's decision in *Bush v. Gore,* and in spite of an ocean of academic prose, the best doctrinal defenses that conservative lawyers have been able to construct—the fairness defense, the structural defense, and the pragmatic defense—all fail, and fail badly. They are not enough, singly or together, to dislodge the conviction of most American lawyers and citizens that the five justices acted cynically—not in defense of established law, as they claimed, or even of conservative principles of jurisprudence or political philosophy to which they were otherwise committed, but with a distinct, partisan, and self-interested political goal in mind. On this view, the conservative justices decided as they did in order to elect the president who was most in sympathy with their own political convictions, and who would be likely, when he appointed future Supreme Court justices, to appoint those who would join with them, to strengthen their control of the Court, rather than with their more liberal rivals.

Is that cynical conclusion now irresistible? Three chapters of this book suggest a less severe explanation, though with different emphases. Guinier, Pildes, and Tribe all suggest that the five conservative justices may have acted not in that crude, self-interested way, but in order to pursue a particular conception of American democracy: a conception that stresses order and stability rather than more fluid and experimental structures and devices. They cite past cases in which the five conservative justices could have had no political or personal interest, but in which they voted consistently, in effect, for order rather than experimentation in the democratic process.[34] In the *Timmons* case, for example, the Supreme Court decided, 6–3, to uphold a state's right to prohibit "fusion" candidates—to prohibit, that is, third parties from nominating, at the head of their own slate of candidates, a major party's candidate for the same office.[35] That practice has given additional strength to third parties, because it allows voters to vote for a gubernatorial candidate, for example, with a chance to win, but nevertheless to do so as a supporter of a third party rather than one of the dominant parties. The five conservative justices, in upholding a state's constitutional power to prohibit the practice, cited a state's right to protect the stability of the two-party system. Pildes and Tribe suggest that the same concern for stability and order, rather than more partisan and discreditable motives, might have moved the conservative justices to ignore the law and make Bush president.

That is an ingenious suggestion, but it faces its own difficulties. In the earlier cases that Pildes and Tribe discuss, the conservative justices did not have to ignore established law, as they did in *Bush v. Gore,* in order to protect the stability of some feature of traditional American democracy, like the two-party system. They rather cited the importance of that feature, as in *Timmons,* to explain why, on perfectly traditional grounds, the Constitution either permitted or prohibited some state action. In *Bush v. Gore,* on the other hand, they could not present their preference as part of any argument. It had to operate, if at all, entirely as a hidden, behind-the-scenes, motive. It would be surprising if such a hidden motive could be so powerful unless order, or the stability of traditional institutions like the two-party system, were very much at stake—unless, that is, the opposite decision would have wrecked some havoc. On the contrary, however, political stability was hardly at stake in *Bush v. Gore* at all. In the first place, the situation it adjudicated promised to be, if not unique, at least extremely rare. In *Timmons,* and in the other cases Pildes and Tribe discuss, there were reasons to suppose that the traditional two-party system would be damaged if states could not protect the system—by prohibiting fusion candidates, for example. But no one could think that any traditional feature of our democratic practice would have been jeopardized if, on December 9, the Supreme Court had refused to intervene in the Florida postelection battle, even if (as was very far from inevitable) that meant that the election would be decided through an unruly political battle in Congress. In Chapter 6, Schlesinger describes unruly postelection battles in the past that did not much affect the reigning structure of the democratic process, either for better or for worse. Indeed, it seems likely that—to the degree it had any effect of that kind at all—the Court's decision in *Bush v. Gore* destabilized rather than stabilized the political process: The Court's declarations that it may review and set aside a state court's own interpretation of its state's election statute, and that the very abstract standards of the equal protection clause apply at least in principle to manual recounts in all state elections, pose a greater threat of future destabilization than simply declining to intervene would have done. Of course, we cannot rule out as inconceivable that the conservative justices were moved by a misplaced enthusiasm for order and stability in the democratic process rather than by more personal motives, but it hardly seems likely that they were.

Reforming Our Democracy

The question of democracy's character figures in this book in other, and ultimately more important, ways as well. The story of the 2000 election is about much more than the Supreme Court's performance. The postelection battle dramatically reminded us that we are governed by a constitution whose basic structure embodies an antique, now everywhere rejected, understanding of democracy. On the whole, that constitution, as amended, has served and will serve us well. But some of its provisions, and particularly its procedures for electing our single most important official—who is tritely but accurately called the most powerful person in the world—have little to recommend them beyond their quaintness.

The Constitution provides that each state select members of an electoral college, and that the members of that college vote for and elect a president. In Chapter 6, Schlesinger explains why the original framers of the Constitution adopted that procedure. They did not think that the citizens of the then nation, who were widely dispersed and would have little information about candidates outside their own communities, could choose presidents as successfully as electors, who would be prominent and better informed citizens, could. But in an age of national newspapers, magazines, radio, the internet and, above all, television, that rationale is embarrassingly obsolete. Electors do not exercise independent judgment, in any case—it is considered a scandal when, as has sometimes happened, an elector votes for a different candidate from the one to whom he or she was pledged—and the virtues of the electoral college, if there are any, must be found in a more contemporary argument. Some contemporary case for the electoral college does seem necessary. Gore won over half a million more of the citizens' votes across the country than Bush did, and yet Bush is president because his fewer votes were distributed among states in such a way as to elect more electors. Electoral votes are distributed among states, moreover, in a way that itself seems unfair. The framers assigned to each state a number of electors equal to its total representation in Congress, and since all states, large and small, have the same number—two—of Senators, the smaller states have more electors, in proportion to their population, than the larger states do.

Suppose it were politically possible to amend the Constitution to change the method of electing a president. Should we amend it to abolish the electoral college altogether, and elect our presidents by direct popular vote, so that the candidate winning the most votes across the nation wins the presidency? Or, as some political scientists have suggested, so that the candidate with the most votes wins if he secures at least some large percentage—say, over 40 percent—of the popular vote? If no candidate secures at least that percentage, a runoff election between the two candidates with the most votes in the first election would follow. As these questions show, it is not clear, if we were to scrap the electoral college, what system of direct election would be the best replacement for it. In their probing essays in Chapters 8 and 6, Polsby and Schlesinger offer, from the different perspectives of political science and history, powerful reasons for thinking that the consequences of abolishing the electoral college altogether would be on balance bad. If so, should we amend the Constitution in a less dramatic way? We might, for example, adopt Schlesinger's suggestion that the winner of the national popular vote receive a sufficiently large number of additional electoral votes so as to make it impossible, in practice, that the popular vote winner would not be elected president. That device, Schlesinger believes, would avoid the principal dangers of abolishing the electoral college outright.

Almost all commentators agree, however, that it is very unlikely that there will be sufficiently sustained popular support to amend the Constitution, at least in the foreseeable future. What could we do short of that? In Chapter 1, I suggest that Congress should bribe states to divide their electoral votes in proportion to the popular vote in the state, so that, for example, Florida, on the basis of the vote certified by its secretary of state, would have assigned 13 of its electoral votes to Bush and 12 to Gore. (Gore would then have been proclaimed the winner immediately, on election night, and all the drama would have been avoided.) That would not require a constitutional amendment, but only legislation state by state. That legislation could avoid the third-party threat Schlesinger and Polsby discuss by providing that no candidate receive any electoral votes in the state unless he secures more than, say, 25 percent of the vote, or even by providing that all the electoral votes be split, in proportion to their votes, by the two candidates with the highest total votes in the state. But should we struggle to avoid increasing the power of third parties? In Chapter 7, Guinier argues for greater, not lesser, strength for third parties, and for proportional representation as the best vehicle for ending the static and unfair distribution of power that, in her view, has marked American democracy from its beginning. Her suggestions are in that way the most radical of all. Is she right?

These are all questions of the first importance. But the debate over them often lacks an important dimension: the dimension of principle. The debate is often conducted on the conservative assumption that institutional features that seem to have worked well in the past, at least on the whole, must not be disturbed, or on the instrumental assumption that whatever arrangement produces the most stability, and other consequences deemed good, is for that reason the most desirable. But if any of the traditional features of our practice, or the methods through which they are now protected, are themselves offensive to democratic principles, then we cannot cite the importance of retaining these features as an argument for anything. In this section of the introduction, I hope to clarify those principles, not in order to select among the various recommendations for reform that others defend or question in this volume, but only to provide some background for considering how far these recommendations are consistent with, or indeed supported by, the best account of democracy itself.

Throughout the postelection contests, the candidates, politicians, journalists, and commentators repeated endlessly the mantras of democracy. "The right to vote is sacred; every vote must count; no one must be left out." What do these slogans really mean? What does democracy really require?

Which changes among those recommended, in this book and elsewhere, would improve the democratic character of our government? Which, whatever their other benefits, would compromise that character? That depends, of course, on what democracy, on the best understanding, really is, and that is the question most often neglected in the debates. I shall distinguish and explore two ideals that, alone or in combination, have seemed to many people to define democracy's core. One of these ideals is collective, because it refers to "the people" as a body. It insists that the officials who govern a people must be selected by those people, that the choice of those officials must reflect the people's will. The second ideal is individual rather than collective, because it refers to the right of each and every citizen, as an individual, to participate in the election of officials as an equal. We must explore both the collective and the individual ideals to reach a satisfactory account of how our own democracy, in the particular matter of electing presidents, could be improved.

The Collective Right to Govern

The slogan that government must represent the people's will, though obviously attractive, is also opaque. Which people? We cannot mean the will of them all, at least in any straightforward sense, because people disagree. It might seem natural to say that we mean a majority of them. Or, rather, a majority of those who take the trouble to vote—if we insisted on a majority of all those eligible to vote, no one would ever be elected, because only about 50 percent of Americans bother to vote these days, even in presidential elections. But is it really fair to let the decision of a majority of those who do vote govern the rest of us? Many citizens, including children and convicted felons, are ineligible to vote. It is much harder for some than others to vote, moreover. Citizens living abroad, for example, or citizens in rural or remote areas of the country, must often do much more work to vote than citizens living down the block from a polling booth.

In any case, a majority of those actually voting means those actually voting on a particular day: the second Tuesday in November. If the election had been held the day before or the day after, a different group of people would have voted, and some who voted one way on the actual election day might well have voted differently. What is so crucial about the opinion of one group of people on one day, when they would have been a different group and had different opinions on any other day? How people vote is very much affected, moreover, by political advertising, which means by money.[36] If one candidate had raised more money than he actually did, and the other less, the will of the majority might well have been different. The vote is also, sometimes critically, altered by sheer natural contingencies. The popular vote in a close election may well turn on the weather in different parts of the country—on whose voters, that is, would find it particularly hard to get to the voting booth that day.

No decent electoral system could eliminate all these influences and contingencies. It would be wrong to force people to vote (though some nations do) or to let young children vote. (Felons, however, once they have endured their punishment, should be allowed to vote.) It would be impossible to make it equally easy for all citizens to vote, or to enforce a right to equal climate for all, or to find a date on which citizens' opinions were guaranteed to be more authentic and stable than they would be on other days. But noticing the host of contingencies does seem to draw the magic from the idea of a simple popular majority. It is not the only competent understanding of what we should take "the will of the people" to mean, or even, perhaps, the best understanding.

We might well find a different, more substantive, understanding more attractive. We should begin with a negative requirement: "The people's will" excludes, both historically and analytically, rule by some independently specifiable minority. It would be undemocratic to give ultimate power only to holders of advanced university degrees, rich people, veterans, or descendants of Richard Plantagenet. Now we must add positive requirements. Democracy is served, we might think, not just when people generally—rather than some favored class or group of them—elect their officials, but when these officials, once elected, take account of the will of all the people rather than of only some of them. A truly democratic government is neither hostile to or unconcerned for any group of citizens. It does not specially represent one or more geographical sections of a large continental country, or one or a few ethnic or racial groups in a multinational society. The individual rights enacted in the Constitution, when they are properly understood and enforced by judges, protect Americans against the worst consequences of a government hostile to or unconcerned for them. But we should nevertheless seek an electoral system that protects the collective goals of democracy at a more fundamental level, by making difficult the election of officials detested or distrusted by some large geographical, racial, or other group. Electing a president by a direct national popular vote may or may not be the best practicable method of securing these various aims. Perhaps the electoral college, for all its antiquity, does better. Or perhaps some more complex system, such as enlarging the electoral college in the way Schlesinger suggests, or choosing the electors of each state through some technique of proportional representation, would do better still. Some entirely different system might score higher yet. My point now is not to recommend any of these possibilities, as I said, but only to suggest that we must respect the collective goals of democracy, on the best understanding of what these are, in judging them.

The Individual Right to Vote

Of course citizens, as individuals, have whatever legal rights to vote are provided under the Constitution and election laws as they stand. In my view, as I argue in Chapter 1, the voters of Palm Beach County were denied those rights by the butterfly ballot, and, as Guinier notes in Chapter 7, the Civil Rights Commission report she discusses lists many other rights violations. But we must now be concerned not with citizens' legal rights under current law, but with their background moral and political rights that might justify or require changes in the current law. Posner is correct in objecting to the argument that Gore "really" won the election because he received more popular votes.[37] That, Posner said, is like arguing that someone who won more games but fewer sets really won the tennis match. There is, however, an important difference. Tennis players have no background rights that might entitle them to win a match if they win more games even though they lose more sets: The only pertinent rights they have are those created by the rules of tennis as they stand. But that is not true in politics. Citizens have background rights, under democratic theory, and it is hardly nonsense to say that, when we understand these rights properly, we see that since more Americans voted for Gore, those who did had a moral, though not a legal, right that he become the president. These moral and political rights are relevant in interpreting election laws. The Florida Supreme Court, as we saw, relied on suppositions about citizens' background rights as part of its argument for interpreting the Florida election code as it did. But we must now consider background rights not for their bearing on the law but independently.

The judgment that Gore morally "won" the election seems, at least at first blush, supported by the proposition that each and every American citizen, wherever he or she lives, has a moral right to equal power in the choice of the president. If every citizen were in fact given equal power, and more citizens voted for Gore than Bush, then Gore should have won. But it is not clear that the claim that each citizen is morally entitled to equal power in the choice of president is true, or even what it means.[38] Suppose we define a citizen's electoral power as the influence he can exert, not only through his own vote but in helping to influence others, on the result. We cannot hope to give each citizen equal power in that sense. Some citizens inevitably will, and some should, have more influence than others over how other people vote, and therefore more influence over the election's result. To be sure, we can struggle to overcome the enormous political influence of rich people and organizations. But we would not want to overcome the special political influence of thoughtful or articulate or charismatic people.

So we must distinguish overall electoral power from what we might call electoral impact: A citizen's electoral impact is measured by the difference it makes, on its own, that he votes for a particular candidate. Under the electoral college, political impact is not equal. I suggested one reason earlier. Since all states, small and large, have two extra electoral votes in virtue of their equal number of Senators, voters in smaller states have, *pro tanto,* greater impact than voters in large states. We must be careful not to exaggerate the practical importance of that disparity. As both Polsby and Schlesinger point out, from one perspective the electoral college enhances the power of citizens in the large states that have many electoral votes. It makes more difference how Californians vote, as a group, that how the citizens of Nevada do, and that explains why politicians pay much more attention to the media markets in large states. But it is nevertheless true that people who live in large states, one by one, have less political impact than those who live in smaller ones. It is also true that the electoral impact of citizens who live in marginal states—those in which support for the two major presidential candidates is closely divided—have more impact. It is likely to make a greater difference, to the final result, how they vote than it would have had they moved to a more one-sided state. Direct election by popular vote would eliminate both these sources of impact inequality.

We must now ask, however, whether citizens really do have a right to equality of impact. Suppose that direct popular election would do better in protecting that right than the electoral college, or any of the other electoral schemes that have been suggested to replace it can do, but only at the cost of the other, more collective, values we identified in the last section. We might fear, for example, that direct election would exacerbate the risk that elections would be dominated by urban voters and that the interests of farmers would then be ignored in the government the election produced. We must therefore ask whether equality of impact really is an individual right so important that we should sacrifice important collective goals to protect it. Political influence is what really counts, as a practical matter, and so long as inequality of influence exists, for good or for bad reasons, each citizen's equal impact seems irrelevant to his actual power. Should we really care, then, about equal impact at all?

Yes, but only for a special reason. Equal impact is a badge of equal citizenship, and some of the reasons that might be offered to justify inequality of impact deny that status. Race and gender are obvious examples: When blacks and women were denied the vote, they were denied, collectively, political power, and the country as a whole suffered in consequence. But they were also insulted, one by one, not because they were denied equal impact but because the basis for the denial was insulting. They were deemed not worthy of participation in government as equals. We have rid ourselves of these savage insults in law but, as the stories told by blacks who were turned away from voting booths in Florida remind us, we are not free of the savagery in practice. The most accurate formulation of the background political rights of citizens in elections, therefore, does not insist on equality of impact, but rather on freedom from unequal impact that flows from the wrong reasons.

Prejudice and stereotype are wrong reasons. But so, I believe, are distinctions that have an historical explanation but no contemporary justification. That is important, because it teaches us that we need a contemporary justification in order to feel content with the electoral college as it stands. If we can find none—if we are not satisfied that the electoral college serves the collective goals I described in the last section at least as well as any of the proposals for reform in this volume—then it is urgent to find some way to reform or improve it through a constitutional amendment, or to ameliorate its most inegalitarian features, if possible, without such an amendment. In defending the electoral college it is not enough to say that the Constitution has served us well for centuries, and shouldn't now be tinkered with. This feature of the Constitution did not serve us well in 2000, and on other occasions in the past. On the contrary, it betrayed us badly.

CONCLUSION

The Supreme Court's decision in *Bush v. Gore* has undoubtedly damaged the reputations of the five conservative justices. They have not become pariahs, however. They are still in demand, for example, as speakers and as ornaments at law school celebrations and events. The damage their decision did to the Supreme Court itself is harder to assess, but may be more lasting. Many scholars and theorists of both right and left have long been contemptuous of the idea that the Court decides according to law not politics. These scholars make the mistake of thinking that if a court's decisions are not mechanical derivations from politically neutral principles (which of course the Supreme Court's decisions cannot be) then they are not judicial decisions at all, but only the exercise of naked political power. Fortunately, that opinion has not been shared by the public at large. The public has apparently understood, better than many of the Court's academic critics, that a legal decision is based not on flat, self-applying rules, but on controversial principles of political morality that judges apply in good faith and consistently, even when they disagree among themselves about what these principles are and how they should be formulated.

The decision in *Bush v. Gore* may prove most damaging because it seems so dramatically to undermine that popular opinion. It remains extremely difficult—even after nearly two years and despite the efforts of ingenious defenders—to read the arguments of the conservative justices as based on political principles they sincerely hold, and that have been on display in their other opinions or in their extrajudicial writings. If their decision cannot be understood in that way, if it can only be described in the reductionist language of naked power, then the cynical view has been confirmed in the most widely reported and perhaps most consequential legal decision in most Americans' lifetimes. The people's general willingness in the past to accept the Court's view of the Constitution—sometimes grudgingly but for the most part unreservedly—are sources of wonder in other parts of the world. Whatever else we may say about *Bush v. Gore,* it has put at risk a vital and perhaps indispensable part of America's domestic political capital.

The conservative justices did not act in a jurisprudential vacuum, however, and it is important to notice a more general trend in our legal culture that no doubt contributed to what they did, at least by making it seem more respectable in their eyes. It has become newly fashionable in the legal community to belittle legal argument and to insist that what counts is only reaching a "sensible" result. On this view, arguments are cheap—a dime a dozen—and a clever lawyer can always find an argument for any result. A wise judge concentrates on finding a sensible result in each case, and only then chooses from among the various arguments that might seem to support that result. This attitude, however sophisticated it seems to those who strike it, is simplistic, wrong, and dangerous. Bad arguments—even bad arguments that can be expected to satisfy those who want to be convinced—are indeed cheap. But good arguments—arguments that satisfy a demanding and probing mind—are not cheap: They are sometimes very difficult to find, and sometimes impossible. Learned Hand once announced to me, with great confidence, the result he would reach in some case. He set himself to writing the opinion. I watched him, from my desk opposite his, scribbling furiously on a yellow pad with his amazing eyebrows earnestly furrowed. He threw the sheets away, and began again. And then all over again. Finally he looked up at me. "It won't write," he said. "We're going the other way."

Some judges do not change their minds when they—or their law clerks—discover that they cannot compose an argument for what they want to decide that satisfies them intellectually. They mutter that arguments are cheap and they let the opinion go. Hand was right and they are wrong. Judges do not gain legitimacy from God or election or the will of the governed or their supposed pragmatic skill or inspired reasonableness. The sole ground of their legitimacy—the *sole* ground—is the discipline of argument: Their institutional commitment to do nothing that they are not prepared to justify through arguments that satisfy, at once, two basic conditions. The first is sincerity. They must themselves believe, after searching self-examination, that these arguments justify what they do, and they must stand ready to do what the arguments justify in later, perhaps very different, cases as well, when their own personal preferences or politics are differently engaged. The second condition is transparency. The arguments they themselves find convincing must be exactly the arguments that they present to the professional and lay public in their opinions, in as much detail as is necessary to allow that public to judge the adequacy and future promise of those arguments for themselves.

Of course I do not mean—is it really necessary to repeat this?—that judges' arguments must be algorithms or uncontroversial or convincing to everyone. Sometimes the right argument, the only argument that can meet the twin tests of sincerity and transparency, will call upon principles of interpretation, jurisprudence, and political morality that many other judges— including other judges in the same case—reject. It will sometimes be unclear—in rare cases even to the judge himself—whether he has kept faith with that commitment. But it now seems clear that the majority in *Bush v. Gore* did not keep that faith. Their most fervent supporters describe motives for their decision, like their distrust of the Florida Supreme Court justices, or their anxiety to end the uncertainty and trauma of the postelection period, that are not only not good arguments, but are not even reasons that they would publicly embrace. So their behavior—even according to their supporters—was shabby, but the lazy legal culture in which they live presented less obstacle to shabbiness than it should have. It is time to reform that culture as well.

1. Early Responses

Ronald Dworkin

The Phantom Poll Booth*

As I write, the extraordinary 2000 presidential election remains undecided, because it remains uncertain which candidate will receive Florida's twenty-five electoral votes. By the time this issue is published, the overseas ballots, the legal battles over manual recounts, or both, may finally have given Gore the presidency, or he may have conceded the presidency to Bush. Or the election may still be undecided, because recounts are continuing in Florida, or have been demanded in other states, or because lawsuits challenging the Florida electoral process, some of which have already been filed, are still pending. In any case, however, the election has raised a great number of new and perplexing legal and political issues, and it is important to confront these, for the future, whether or not the presidency still hinges on how they are decided.

Legitimacy is the issue. When an election is so close, and there are serious grounds for suspicion of inaccuracy in the count, how can officials decide who won in a way that the public should and would see as legitimate? It appears that Gore won the popular vote—according to the most recent reports, he received more votes across the country than Bush did. That fact has in itself no legal significance, of course, but neither does it have much moral significance. Which eligible voters actually voted (in fact, approximately only 52 percent of them did) and for whom depended on a host of arbitrary factors or accidents. If the election had been held a day later or earlier, if the weather had been better in one place or worse in another, or if any number of other decisions or chance facts had been different, the popular vote would also have been different, and perhaps different enough to change who "won" it. There is much to be said against the electoral college system. It gives individual voters in small states consistently more impact in presidential elections than those in large states, for example, but the fact that it permits the winner of the popular vote in a very close election to lose in the electoral college is not one of them.

It *is* of central importance to the issue of legitimacy, however, whether more Florida voters actually intended to vote for Gore than for Bush, so that, if the electoral college process had worked as it should, Gore would have won the state's electoral votes and the presidency. The system did not work because the ballot in Palm Beach County was confusing, and many voters—perhaps more than twenty thousand—who intended to vote for Gore actually voted for Pat Buchanan or voted for two candidates and therefore found their ballots ignored. Nor would the system have worked if Gore finally wins because there was a manual recount only in heavily Democratic counties rather than in the whole state. Katherine Harris, the Florida secretary of state and cochairman of the Bush campaign in Florida, has declared that no manual recounts submitted after November 14 will be counted. It is unclear as I write whether her ruling will be overturned, and, if it is, which counties will be recounted. Even a full manual recount in the entire state would not solve the central problem, moreover: If Gore still lost, the confusion in Palm Beach County would still raise doubts about the legitimacy of Bush's presidency.

Some commentators urge that we simply accept the damaged result, because uncertainty and delay is against the public interest. But we have, in any case, a president and an administration until January, and though it is undoubtedly desirable to know who the new president will be as soon as possible, it would not be catastrophic for the nation and world to wait for a few weeks longer (it has been waiting months already) for the answer. Any harm that might come from a short period of delay and uncertainty must be balanced, moreover, against the harm—likely to be both more serious and much longer lasting—of inaugurating a president while a cloud of suspicion hangs over his election. Even if the public were apprehensive about the delay (many polls suggest that it is not[1]) and willing to accept the risk of an inaccurate result in exchange for a quick settlement, that sentiment would be unlikely to hold when the president makes bitterly controversial decisions (about, for example, the nomination of Supreme Court justices) and people are invited to remember that his election was dubious. Rushing the process to an untrustworthy conclusion seems the riskier course.

It is wrong, in any case, to consider the question of legitimacy solely or even largely as a matter of the public's interest because individual rights (the right of each citizen not to be disenfranchised) are at stake. We would not decide whether some ordinance that limited the free speech of particular citizens was constitutional by asking whether the public wanted them to speak or whether the country would be better off if they did not, and we should not use that test to decide whether the basic rights of the voters of Palm Beach County were compromised. True, voters do not have a right to an electoral system that will guarantee perfect accuracy in a large national election: no such system exists. But they do have a right that whatever system has been established by law be respected, and there is a very strong argument that the now infamous butterfly ballot was not only confusing but inconsistent with Florida law.

The Florida code requires that the names of the two major-party presidential candidates be listed first on the ballot, with minority-party candidates below, and that the space for marking or punching a vote for a particular candidate be uniformly to the right of that candidate's name.

The Palm Beach County ballot listed candidates not in one column as other counties did, but in two columns, placing Bush-Cheney in the highest box in the left column, Gore-Lieberman in the box below, and Buchanan-Foster at the top of the right column slightly below the opposite Bush box and slightly above the opposite Gore box, and it placed voting holes not to the right of each candidate, but between the two columns. There were therefore two holes to the right of Gore's box, and the first of these was actually Buchanan's. An arrow in the Gore-Lieberman box pointed to the third hole, but many voters later said that they assumed that the second hole was Gore's, as it should legally have been. Others said that they thought that there were two holes next to the Gore-Lieberman box because it was necessary to vote for each of those candidates separately, and others that they were uncertain where the arrow pointed and so punched out both of the holes next to the Gore box in order to make sure that they voted for him. All ballots with two holes punched (over 19,000 of them) were thrown out altogether. Statistical models show that both the Buchanan vote and the number of ex-

cluded double-punched ballots was much higher than the demography of
the county or the results in comparable counties would have predicted.[2]

What is the appropriate remedy when it is discovered that a completed election was in some important respect illegal? A new election would be expensive and cause delay, and would be unlikely in any case to produce the same
result as a legal ballot would have produced on election day. In Palm Beach
County, for example, many of those who voted for Ralph Nader on November 7 might well vote for Gore in a rerun. Scholars have suggested a variety of
other solutions: that Florida's Supreme Court order it to send no electors to
the electoral college, for example, or that it divide Florida's electoral votes
thirteen for Bush and twelve for Gore. But it would be unprecedented for a
court to make any such radical change in a state's electoral procedures, and
each of these solutions could be attacked as arbitrary and political. And either would automatically make Gore president.

Many lawyers have therefore argued that there should be no remedy at all:
Some innocent violations of complex elections laws are inevitable in any national election, they say; such mistakes are sufficiently random so as not to
benefit any one party or group or region in the long run, and trying to correct
them would involve awkward procedures that would inevitably make our
electoral process more clumsy and litigious. If a new election were ordered in
Palm Beach County, they warn, then every presidential election for decades
would be followed by lawsuits demanding repeat elections in different counties across the nation.

That argument seems decisive against allowing new elections in marginal
cases, or when nothing important turns on how the county in which the
error is alleged has voted. But it would be wrong to declare, as a flat rule, that
no remedy is ever available for demonstrable and grave illegality in the electoral process, no matter how clear the mistake or how evident that it changed
the final national result, because that would value the right to vote too
cheaply. We do not need so absolute a disclaimer of judicial power to ensure
that future elections are not routinely decided in court, and no court, as far as
I am aware, has suggested it. The Florida Supreme Court recently insisted,

for example, that Florida courts have "authority to void an election" when "reasonable doubt exists as to whether a certified election expressed the will of the voters—even in the absence of fraud or intentional wrongdoing."[3] Courts in Florida and in other jurisdictions have ordered new elections when the mistake was not as serious or the results so grave as in the Palm Beach County case.[4] So we should consider what standard for ordering a new election would recognize the crucial importance of the right to vote but nevertheless rarely encourage politicians to seek such an order. Such a standard might provide, for example, that an election will not be voided for a non-fraudulent mistake unless the following four conditions are clearly demonstrated. First, that the electoral process violated legal requirements; second, that the violation more likely than not created a result significantly different from what those who voted collectively intended; third, that based on available evidence, including evidence about vote totals and challenges in other states, the overall result of the election (in this case, the national election of a president) would have been different had the violation not occurred; and fourth, that a new election could be designed so that the result could be expected to be closer to what the voters originally collectively intended. The burden of proof with respect to each element would be on the party seeking the order. This standard does respect the high importance of the right to vote: It allows a new election when there is a substantial chance that the violation of that right defeated the result that the disenfranchised voters hoped to help realize. But it is not likely to encourage much litigation in the future. It is, after all, forty years since the last occasion when it was even suggested that a legal challenge might change a presidential election.[5]

We do not know whether this standard would permit a new election if applied to the Palm Beach County case: the facts have not yet been examined in any court, and may never be.[6] But it is important that we continue to study and debate, even after the 2000 presidential election is finally over, how our electoral process can be improved in the light of what that election revealed, and focusing on the appropriate conditions for a local rerun should be part of that discussion. Allowing important electoral safeguards to be fashioned, tested, and enforced in court is not, as many have claimed, a corruption of our democracy. On the contrary, it is an affirmation of our democracy's strength; even when elections are breathtakingly close, we settle them on the basis of examined principle and not in the streets.

November 15, 2000

A BADLY FLAWED ELECTION†

The 2000 election has finally ended, but in the worst possible way: Not with a national affirmation of democratic principle, but by the fiat of the five conservative Supreme Court justices—Chief Justice Rehnquist and Justices Kennedy, O'Connor, Scalia, and Thomas—over the fierce objection of the four more liberal justices, Justices Breyer, Ginsburg, Souter, and Stevens. The conservatives stopped the democratic process in its tracks, with thousands of votes yet uncounted, first by ordering an unjustified stay of the statewide recount of the Florida vote that was already in progress, and then declaring—in one of the least persuasive Supreme Court opinions that I have ever read—that there was no time left for the recount to continue. It is far from certain that Gore would have been elected if the recounts had been completed; some statisticians believe that Bush would have picked up more additional votes than Gore. But the Court did not allow that process to continue, and its decision ensured both a Bush victory and a continuing cloud of suspicion over that victory.

Though it took six opinions for all the justices to state their views, the argument of the five conservatives who voted to end the election was quite simple. The Florida Supreme Court had ordered a recount of "undervotes" across the state. Instead of adopting detailed rules about how the counters were to decide whether a ballot that the counting machine had declared to have no vote for president was actually a vote for one candidate (rules that might have specified, for example, that if not a single corner of the "chad" of a punch-card ballot had been detached, the ballot could not count as a vote) the Florida court had directed only that counters count a vote if they found, considering the ballot as a whole, a "clear intention" of the voter to vote. The five conservatives noted that this more abstract standard had been applied differently by counters in different counties, and might be applied differently by different counters within a single county, and they therefore held that the use of the standard denied voters the equal protection of the law that the Constitution's Fourteenth Amendment requires.

The natural remedy, following such a ruling, would be to remand the case to the Florida court to permit it to substitute a more concrete uniform counting standard. Breyer, in his dissenting opinion, suggested that course. "[The] case should be sent back for recounting all undercounted votes," he said, "in accordance with a single uniform standard." But the conservatives declared that since the Florida legislature intended to take advantage of the "safe harbor" provision of federal law, which provides that election results certified by states to Congress by December 12 are immune from congressional reexamination, any further recount the Florida court ordered would have to be completed by that date, which ended two hours after the Supreme Court handed down its judgment. The conservatives had remanded the case to the Florida court, for "proceedings consistent with" their opinion, and then told them that no proceedings could possibly be consistent with their opinion. The election was over, and the conservative candidate had won.

———————

The 5–4 decision would hardly have been surprising, or even disturbing, if the constitutional issues were ones about which conservatives and liberals disagree as a matter of constitutional principle—about the proper balance of authority between the federal and state governments, for example, or the criminal process, or race, or the character and extent of individual rights, such as abortion rights or rights of homosexuals, against state and national authorities. But there were no such constitutional issues in this case: The conservatives' decision to reverse a state supreme court's rulings on matters of state law did not reflect any established conservative position on any general constitutional question. On the contrary, conservatives have been at least as zealous as liberals in protecting the right of such courts to interpret state legislation without second-guessing by federal courts, and on the whole less ready than liberals to appeal to the Fourteenth Amendment to reverse state decisions.

It is therefore difficult to find a respectable explanation of why all and only the conservatives voted to end the election in this way, and the troubling question is being asked among scholars and commentators whether the

Court's decision would have been different if it was Bush, not Gore, who needed the recount to win—whether, that is, the decision reflected not ideological division, which is inevitable, but professional self-interest. The five conservatives have made this Supreme Court the most activist Court in history. They aim to transform constitutional law not, as the Warren Court did, to strengthen civil liberties and individual rights, but rather to expand the power of states against Congress, shrink the rights of accused criminals, and enlarge their own powers of judicial intervention.[7]

For three of them (Rehnquist, Scalia, and Thomas) the agenda presumably includes finally abolishing the abortion rights that were first established in *Roe v. Wade* over a quarter of a century ago, a decision they have never ceased insisting should be overruled. The prospects of future success for the conservatives' radical program crucially depend on the Court appointments that the new president will almost certainly make. Those appointments will determine whether the conservatives' activism will flourish (even adding, perhaps, the two new votes that would be needed to overrule abortion rights so long as O'Connor and Kennedy refuse to take that particular step) or whether it will be checked or reversed. Bush long ago signaled, in naming Scalia his favorite justice, his intention that it flourish.

———————

We should try to resist this unattractive explanation of why the five conservative justices stopped the recount process and declared Bush the winner. It is, after all, inherently implausible that any—let alone all—of them would stain the Court's reputation for such a sordid reason, and respect for the Court requires that we search for a different and more creditable explanation of their action. Unfortunately, however, the legal case they offered for crucial aspects of their decisions was exceptionally weak. Their first major ruling, on Saturday, December 9 (soon after the recounting began), was to halt the recount even before they heard argument in Bush's appeal of the Florida Supreme Court decision ordering those recounts. That ruling was in itself lethal for Gore. Even if the Court had ultimately rejected Bush's appeal, and allowed the recount to resume, it could not possibly have been completed by December 12, the date that the conservatives later declared the final deadline.

Scalia argued that this serious injury to Gore was necessary to prevent irreparable harm to Bush: He said that Bush would be harmed if the recounts continued because if the Court later decided that the recount was illegal, the public's knowledge of the results would cast a "cloud" over "the legitimacy of his election." That bizarre claim not only assumes that Bush would have lost in the recount, but also that the public is not to be trusted. Public knowledge that Gore would have won, if the recounts had continued and been accepted, would produce doubt about a Bush election only if the public disagreed with the Court's judgment that the recount was illegal; and it is constitutionally improper for the Court to keep truthful information from the public just because the information might lead it to conclude that the election was a mistake or that the Court was wrong.[8]

The conservatives' second major decision was that the Florida court's "clear intention of the voter" standard for manual recounts violated the equal protection clause because different counties and counters would interpret that standard differently. Two of the more liberal justices (Breyer and Souter) agreed,[9] but the other liberal justices, Ginsburg and Stevens, rejected the argument, and they had the better case. The equal protection clause forbids voting procedures or arrangements that put particular people or groups at an electoral disadvantage. The Court has struck down poll taxes that discriminated against the poor, for example, and citing a "one-person-one-vote" electoral standard, has prohibited electoral districts of very different size because these give each voter in larger districts less impact on the overall election result than voters in smaller districts have. But a general standard for counting undervotes that may be applied differently in different districts puts no class of voters, in advance, at either an advantage or disadvantage. If a voter's county uses a more permissive test to determine "clear intent," then he risks having his ballot counted when he did not intend to vote. If it uses a strict standard, he risks having his ballot ignored when he did intend to vote. One cannot say in advance that either a permissive or strict test is more accurate, and therefore cannot say that a system that combines both within a single state puts any identifiable group at an automatic disadvantage.[10]

As Gore's counsel, David Boies, pointed out in oral argument, Florida's use of different voting machinery in different counties is much more arguably a violation of equal protection, because some types of machine are well known to be much less accurate than others. Punch-card ballot readers, which are used in counties with a high minority population such as Miami-Dade, ignore more than three times as many ballots as optical ballot readers do, and therefore give voters in those counties systematically less chance of having their votes counted.

The Court's equal protection decision is surprising in another way. The one-person-one-vote principle applies not just to presidential elections but to elections for every federal and state office, major or minor, across the country. I do not know how many states use nothing more concrete than a "clear intent of the voter" standard for manual recounts, but several do, and the Supreme Court has now declared that they have all been acting—no doubt for many decades—unconstitutionally. This ruling alone may require substantial changes in the nation's electoral laws, and the Supreme Court may well regret having made it.

———————

The conservatives' equal protection claim is defensible, however, and as I said, two of the more liberal justices also accepted it. But the conservatives' third major decision, and by far its most important, is not defensible. The most natural remedy for the supposed equal protection violation, as all the dissenters insisted, would be to remand the case to the Florida court so that it could establish uniform recount standards and attempt to complete a recount by December 18, when the electoral college votes. But the conservatives held that since the Constitution gives the Florida state legislature authority over its own election law, and since that legislature would wish to take advantage of the federal "safe harbor" law that guarantees a state certification of presidential electors immunity from congressional challenge if the certification is made by December 12, any recounts beyond that date, even those necessary to insure that all valid votes were counted, would automatically be unconstitutional. But the safe harbor provision is not mandatory; it does not provide that a state loses its electoral votes if these are not submitted by December 12, but only that its votes, if submitted after that date, might conceivably be challenged in Congress, if reason can be found to challenge them. Certainly the Florida legislature would wish to meet the December 12 deadline if it fairly could, and its legislation should be interpreted, as the Florida Supreme Court said that it did interpret it, with that aim in mind.

But it goes far beyond that safe assumption to declare, as the five Supreme Court conservatives did, that the Florida legislature meant to insist that the optional deadline be met at all costs, even if it was necessary to ignore the principles of accuracy and fair treatment that underlie the rest of the election code. That would be a bizarre interpretation of any state's election law. What legislature would wish to be understood as purchasing an immunity it would almost certainly never need at the cost of sacrificing its basic commitments of justice? And there is no evidence that the Florida legislature has ever made that choice.[11] Even if the conservative justices thought this bizarre interpretation plausible, moreover, it would still be wrong for them to impose that interpretation on the Florida Supreme Court, which, according to the most basic principles of constitutional law, has final authority in interpreting its own state's law so long as its interpretation is not absurd. The conservatives should, at most, have asked the Florida court to decide for itself whether Florida law, properly understood, declares that the safe harbor must be gained no matter what unfairness to Florida voters is necessary to gain it.

Even the two dissenters who had agreed with the majority that the Florida court's recount scheme violated the equal protection clause thought it absurd to insist on the December 12 deadline, and all of the dissenters feared the impact on the Court itself of so weak an argument for so politically divisive a decision. Justice Stevens said the decision "can only lend confidence to the most cynical appraisal of the work of judges throughout the land." "We do risk a self-inflicted wound," Breyer added, "a wound that may harm not just the court, but the nation," and he also noted, pointedly, that the time pressure the conservatives cited was "in significant part, a problem of the [Supreme Court's] own making."[12] We must try, as I said, not to compound the injury to the Court with reckless accusations against any of its members. But those of us who have been arguing for many years that the Supreme Court makes America a nation of principle have a special reason for sorrow.

The deeply troubling Supreme Court decision in *Bush v. Gore* makes even plainer the urgency of radically changing how we elect our presidents. Our present system is an eighteenth-century antique. It presupposes a starkly elitist conception of government that was popular then but which no politician would dare endorse today. The Constitution's authors did not trust the people to elect the president directly; they expected the members of the electoral college to be distinguished and independent citizens who would make up their own minds, after collective deliberation, about who the president and vice president should be. It was not as important as it later became how those electors were chosen, because, in principle, the selecting body would have no control over or even confidence in the opinions of the independent electors they chose. There was nevertheless some initial disagreement at the Constitutional Convention about the selection of electors. Some delegates wanted them elected by popular vote, some by Congress, and some by the state legislatures. The Convention finally decided, by way of compromise, not itself to establish any electoral method, but to delegate the choice of methods to the state legislatures. Each state was assigned a number of electors equal to the total number of that state's representatives and senators in Congress (that formula was a concession to smaller states, which had fewer representatives but the same number of senators as much larger states) and the state legislatures were directed to decide how their state's electors would be chosen. A majority in the legislature might select the electors themselves, or provide for a popular vote within the state to select them (which might be by a statewide vote for all the electors, or by districts, or by proportional representation). Or, presumably, it might direct that electors be selected by lot. Once all the electors were selected in whatever ways the various state legislatures chose, they would meet in their states, deliberate, and vote for a president. If no presidential candidate received a majority of their votes, then the House of Representatives would choose a president with each state delegation having one vote, so that the smallest state had as much influence as the largest.

America has long since rejected the intellectual premises of this baroque system. Now we embrace the very different principle that the point of elections (and particularly the election of a national president, the one office we elect all together) is to determine and reflect the people's will. Electors are no longer expected to exercise their own judgment: It is candidates, not electors, whose names are on the ballot and it would be a scandal if the electors chose someone other than the candidate to whom most of them were pledged. A partisan majority in a state legislature still has the constitutional power, under Article II, to cancel presidential elections in its state and choose the state's electors by themselves. But if any legislature tried to exercise that power its action would undoubtedly provoke a constitutional amendment ending that power.

———

We have been lucky not to have been seriously damaged by the electoral college system long before this election made its anachronism intolerable. It is dangerous to retain a constitutional structure when its principled base has been so thoroughly repudiated, because the structure then becomes a legal loose cannon. It generates pointless complexities and obstacles, and it is vulnerable to partisan manipulation and bizarre interpretation that cannot be checked by appealing to the structure's purpose, since it now has none. The legal battles in Florida and in the Supreme Court were dominated by a series of deadlines (the Court elected Bush by insisting on the importance of December 12) that are significant only because the eighteenth-century arrangement decreed a stately series of certifications, meetings, and pronouncements that are now only charades. The Republican strategy in Florida of delaying recounts through any means possible—including not only legal challenges but noisy demonstrations outside counting rooms—was made possible only by those pointless deadlines. It makes no sense to demand that a breathtakingly close election be finally decided by any magic date in December in order that a new president be chosen by January 20. The original decision to leave the manner of presidential elections to state legislatures corrupts elections in a different way. The one-person-one-vote principle would suggest, as I said, that we elect presidents through uniform voting methods, with at least roughly equal accuracy, supervised by a national election commission under principles established by Congress. The eighteenth-century compromise guarantees, to the contrary, that different methods of recording votes, which vary dramatically in their accuracy, will be used not only in different states but in different counties within states. It also guarantees that inevitable uncertainties and ambiguities in election law will have to be faced anew in each close election, because even if Florida's law is clarified now, the next set of contests will arise in an entirely different state with an entirely different structure of law and ambiguity.

The present system means, moreover, that politics will play an inevitably ugly role in close elections. It is surely unacceptable that the Florida state legislature, dominated by Republicans, should have the power themselves to elect a set of electors pledged to the Republican candidate whenever they deem this to be necessary because the result of the election is uncertain. Many of the most consequential decisions in Florida were made by political officials whose future might depend either on who won the presidential election or on whether powerful Florida politicians, including Bush's brother, who is Florida's governor, would approve what they had done. Katherine Harris, the Florida secretary of state whose several erroneous rulings contributed enormously to the delays that prevented a fair recount, had been cochairman of Bush's campaign in Florida, and the *New York Times* reported that the Democratic mayor of Miami had been subject to a great deal of local pressure just before the Miami-Dade canvassing board reversed itself and decided to halt manual recounts.[13] It would be a mistake to assume wrongdoing or improper motives in any such case, but it would certainly be better to vest critical decisions in nonpartisan federal election officials who would be much less likely to attract suspicion.

We now have the best chance ever to junk the anachronistic and dangerous eighteenth-century system. The public should demand that Congress begin a process of constitutional amendment that would eliminate that system, root and branch, and substitute for it the direct election of the president and vice president by a plurality of the national popular vote. The amendment should direct Congress to establish uniform election procedures and machinery across the nation and that body might then design and finance voting computers with screens that clearly display a voter's tentative choices and ask the voter to confirm his votes before they are recorded.[14] (It might be possible to allow people with computers, including absentees, to vote through them at home, although special digital identification and security precautions would have to be developed, and care taken to avoid unfairness to voters with no access to a computer.)

Congress should further require that voting booths be open for the same twenty-four-hour period across the different time zones of the country, so that voting stops simultaneously everywhere, and the television networks do not report results in one time zone while voting continues in another; and it should establish a national elections commission with general supervisory power over national elections. Challenges and disputes would no doubt still arise, but these could be adjudicated by officials of such an agency, who would be appointed to provide nonpartisanship, subject to review by federal judges with life tenure, rather than by state political officials and elected state judges.

The nation would benefit in other ways from the change. It does not matter, under the electoral college system, who won the national popular vote, but that fact is nevertheless widely reported and widely thought significant. A president who has won in the electoral college but lost the popular vote, even by a relatively slim margin, is thought by many people to be less legitimate for that reason. Making the popular vote decisive would end the possibility of such a situation. Would we lose anything by the shift? It is said to be a benefit of the electoral college system that it forces candidates to campaign across the nation rather than only in a few highly populated regions with huge media markets and the largest number of potential votes. But in fact the system does not produce genuinely national campaigns. Candidates wholly ignore states that they are very likely either to win or to lose (few presidential campaign ads appeared in the New York media market in this election, for example) and devote most of their time and money to those relatively few states in which the race appears to be close. If the national popular vote were decisive, they would not campaign just in the major population centers (there are too many votes elsewhere) but wherever they thought they could persuade a substantial number of as yet undecided voters.

It has also been said that the electoral college is necessary to protect regional interest groups that are powerful within certain states, and so important to those states' electoral votes, but not large nationally. But interest groups are now much more dispersed across the nation than they once were. Many states that were formerly dominated by agricultural interests, for example, now have a more mixed economy, and farmers might be better protected by voting rules that made their absolute number important even if they were geographically dispersed. It might appear that the electoral college system reduces the number of postelection challenges and contests in close presidential races because candidates have no incentive, under that system, to seek to correct mistakes in a state that the other candidate won so heavily that he would take its electoral votes anyway. Under a popular vote system, however, a candidate who lost the popular vote by a very small margin might canvas the entire country looking for a series of challenges that could yield only a few votes in each case, but might change the overall result collectively.

But there is no reason to think, in advance, that a change from the electoral college to a popular vote standard would produce more postelection challenges or contests. If a national election is close, then the election in states whose electoral votes are crucial is also likely to be close, and many fewer vote changes are needed to make a difference in the state than in the nation. Gore needed only to add a few hundred votes in Florida through challenges, but even in this exceptionally close popular vote contest, Bush would have had to add more than 300,000 votes to his total to win, and there is no indication of irregularities elsewhere in the nation that affected, even cumulatively, that many votes.

The moment seems propitious, as I have said, for pressing for a constitutional amendment. Politicians in either party would have great difficulty claiming that the system we have has worked well, or supplying any principled rationale for it. But we must recognize that it is extremely difficult, and normally takes many years, to amend the Constitution. Short of a new constitutional convention, an amendment requires a two-thirds vote of both houses of Congress, and then approval by the legislatures of three quarters of the states, and the pressure for an amendment may weaken before that long process has been completed. In any case, no amendment can succeed without the consent of many of the smaller states whose citizens benefit unfairly, in the ways I have described, from the very electoral college system that the amendment would end.

―――――――――

It is therefore important to consider how much of the gain that an amendment would bring could be achieved at once without one, or while one is pending. One gain I described (a twenty-four-hour election day ending simultaneously across the country) could be adopted by Congress now, because the Constitution assigns it authority to fix the time of presidential elections. More could be achieved through a model uniform election code, which Congress might endorse and propose to the states, agreeing to finance elections for national office, including providing accurate electronic voting machinery, for those states that adopted that code. The model code would no doubt be adopted in somewhat different form in different states, but Congress could identify core provisions that guaranteed uniform voting machinery and mechanisms of challenge and review, for instance, that could not be changed without forfeiting the benefits Congress offered. There could be no objection under Article II to a state legislature adopting the model code; a legislature would of course be free to repeal the code later, but it would presumably face great political pressure not to do so.

These are extraordinary measures, and many people will be understandably timid about altering a constitutional structure that has been, as a whole, dramatically successful. But the Constitution's original design for elections, rooted in an elitism that is no longer tolerable, has proved its most unsuccessful feature. We have had to amend it before (in 1913, when the power to choose senators was taken away from the state legislatures that originally had that power, and given to the people) in order to keep faith with our most basic constitutional conviction, which is that the Constitution creates and protects genuine democracy. We have now witnessed new and frightening challenges to that assumption, culminating in a deeply regrettable Supreme Court decision, and we must again change the Constitution in order to sustain our deep respect for it and for the institutions that guard it.

December 14, 2000

2. Lawless Order and Hot Cases

Cass R. Sunstein*

Under the leadership of Chief Justice William Rehnquist, the Supreme Court of the United States has not been respectful of democratic prerogatives. The Court has asserted itself vigorously against the elected branches, striking down more federal statutes per year than any other Court in the last half-century. In recent years, many politicians have been complaining about "liberal judicial activism;" but this is a ludicrous complaint. For more than a decade, judicial activism has come from the right, not the left. When the Court has asserted its own, highly contestable vision of the Constitution against the democratic process, it has usually done so in the name of federalism.[1] But the aggressiveness of the Rehnquist Court can be found elsewhere as well, as the Court has struck down campaign finance legislation, affirmative action programs, and efforts to regulate commercial advertising.

It is also true, however, that the Court has generally been minimalist, in the sense that it has typically attempted to say no more than is necessary to decide the case at hand, without venturing anything large or ambitious.[2] To some extent, the Court's minimalism appears to have been a product of some of the justices' conception of the appropriately limited role of the judiciary in American political life. To some extent, the tendency toward minimalism has been a product of the simple need to assemble a majority vote. If five or more votes are sought, the opinion might well tend in the direction of minimalism, reflecting judgments and commitments that can command agreement from diverse people. Notwithstanding its occasional aggressiveness, the Court has almost always been minimalist. Sometimes its decisions have even been "subminimalist," in the sense that they have said even less than is required to justify the particular outcome.[3]

In the Court's two decisions involving the 2000 presidential election, both minimalism and aggressiveness were on full display. The Court's unanimous decision in *Bush v. Palm Beach Canvassing Board*[4] was firmly in the minimalist camp. Here the Court refused to resolve the most fundamental issues and merely remanded to the Florida Supreme Court for clarification. In this way, the Court limited its own role in the election controversy. The Court's 5-4 decision in *Bush v. Gore*[5] was also minimalist in its own way, for it purported to resolve the case without doing anything for the future. But here the Court effectively ended the presidential election. It did so with rulings, on the merits and (most indefensibly) on the question of remedy, that combined hubris with minimalism. This is a characteristic feature of the Rehnquist Court.

The Court's decision in *Bush v. Gore* did have two fundamental virtues. First, it produced a prompt and decisive conclusion to the chaotic postelection presidential campaign of 2000. Indeed, it probably did so in a way that carried more simplicity and authority than anything that might have been expected from the United States Congress (a point that itself says something about the current state of American government). Certainly the Court avoided a mess. Second, the Court's equal protection holding carries considerable appeal in principle. On its face, that holding has the potential to create the most expansive, and perhaps sensible, protection for voting rights since the Court's one person, one vote decisions of mid-century.[6] In the near future, that promise is unlikely to be realized within the federal courts, policing various inequalities with respect to voting and voting technology. But it is not impossible that the Court's decision, alongside the evident problems in the Florida presidential vote, will eventually help to spur corrective action from Congress and state legislatures.

The Court's decision also had two large vices. First, the Court effectively resolved the presidential election not unanimously, but by a 5-4 vote, with the majority consisting entirely of the Court's most conservative justices. It is simply implausible to believe that the five justices who composed the majority would have voted the same way if the parties had been reversed—if, say, Al Gore was complaining about overreaching by the Florida Supreme Court's insistence on manual recounts. Second, the Court's rationale was not only exceedingly ambitious but also embarrassingly weak. However appealing in the abstract, its equal protection holding had no basis in precedent or in history. It also raises a host of puzzles for the future, which the Court appeared to try to resolve with its minimalist cry of "here, but nowhere else." Far more problematic, as a matter of law, was the majority's subminimalist decision on the issue of remedy. By terminating the manual recount in Florida, the Court resolved what it acknowledged to be a question of Florida law, without giving the Florida courts the chance to offer an interpretation of their own state's law.

In a case of this degree of political salience, the Court should assure the nation, through its actions and its words, that it is speaking for the law, and not for anything resembling partisan or parochial interests. A unanimous or near-unanimous decision can go a long way toward providing that assurance, because agreement between diverse people suggests that the Court is really speaking for the law. So too for an opinion that is based on reasoning that, whether or not unassailable, is so logical and clear as to dispel any doubt about the legitimacy of the outcome. The Court offered no such opinion. From the standpoint of constitutional order, the Court might well have done the nation a service. From the standpoint of legal reasoning, the Court's decision was very bad. In short, the Court's decision produced order without law.

In discussing *Bush v. Gore,* I will be covering a lot of territory in a short space, and it will be useful to say at the outset that I seek to draw two general lessons, both of which transcend the case itself. The first involves the nature of the current Court. There are moderates, but no liberals,[7] on the Supreme Court of the United States. We are in the midst of an extraordinary period of conservative judicial activism, in which some Republican judicial appointees are all too willing to read their own political preferences into the Constitution, without a sufficient sense of their own capacity for error. The second lesson involves the nature of voting rights in the modern era, and more particularly the possibility that *Bush v. Gore* will help point the way toward a situation in which everyone's vote has an equal chance to count, regardless of location, ballot, or technology. In the process of discussing these lessons, I will also venture some tentative remarks about the nature of legal judgment in "hot cases"—remarks intended to cast light on the disturbing fact that reactions to *Bush v. Gore* seem to be split along political lines, not only among judges and ordinary people, but among academic specialists as well.

Preliminaries

Bush v. Gore was actually the fourth intervention by the United States Supreme Court in the litigation over the outcome of the presidential election in Florida. In sequence, the Court's interventions consisted of the surprising grant of certiorari on November 24, 2000;[8] the unanimous, minimalist remand on December 4, 2000;[9] the grant of a stay, and certiorari, on December 9, 2000;[10] and the decisive opinion in *Bush v. Gore* on December 12, 2000.[11] All this happened astonishingly quickly. To provide a perspective on what happened, it is important to keep the sequence in mind.

The Unanimous, Minimalist Remand

On November 13, Florida Secretary of State Katherine Harris announced that the statutory deadline of November 14, 2000 was final, and that she would not exercise her discretion so as to allow extensions.[12] On November 21, the Florida Supreme Court interpreted state law to require the secretary of state to extend the statutory deadline for a manual recount.[13] This was a highly controversial interpretation of Florida law, and it might well have been wrong. At the time, however, any errors seemed to raise issues of state rather than federal law.

In seeking certiorari, Bush raised three federal challenges to the decision of the Florida Supreme Court.[14] First, he argued that by changing state law, the Florida court had violated Article II of the United States Constitution, which provides that states shall appoint electors "in such manner as the legislature," and not any court, may direct.[15] Second, Bush invoked a federal law saying that a state's appointment of electors is "conclusive" if a state provides for the appointment of electors "by laws enacted prior to the day fixed" for the election.[16] According to Bush, the Florida court did not follow, but instead changed, the law "enacted prior" to Election Day, and in his view this change amounted to a violation of federal law.[17] Third, Bush argued that the manual recount would violate the due process and equal protection clauses, because no clear standards had been established to ensure that similarly situated people would be treated similarly.[18]

At the time, almost all observers of all political persuasions thought it exceedingly unlikely that the Court would agree to hear the case. Even if the Florida Supreme Court had in some intelligible sense "changed" state law, it appeared improbable that the United States Supreme Court could be convinced to say so. The line between an interpretation and a change is not clear-cut, and even if the Florida Supreme Court was wrong, it would seem to be stretching to say that the law had been "changed."

There was also a point about the limited role of the Supreme Court in American government. Whatever the merits, the Court seemed unlikely to intervene into a continuing controversy over the presidential vote in Florida. This was not technically a "political question," which would require the Court to stay its hand. Because judicial standards did exist for resolving the case, there were legal questions, not merely political ones. But these did not seem to be the kinds of questions that would warrant Supreme Court involvement, certainly not at this preliminary stage. To the complete and utter astonishment of most observers, the Court agreed to grant certiorari, limited to the first two questions raised by Bush.[19]

Bush asked the United States Supreme Court to hold that because the Florida Supreme Court had violated the federal Constitution and federal law, Florida's secretary of state had the authority to certify the vote as of November 14. For his part, Gore wanted the Court to affirm the Florida Supreme Court on the ground that that court had merely interpreted the law. The United States Supreme Court refused these invitations and took an exceptionally small step, asking the state supreme court to clarify the basis for its decision.[20] Did the state court use the Florida constitution to override the will of the Florida legislature? In the Court's view, that would be a serious problem, because the United States Constitution requires state legislatures, not state constitutions, to determine the manner of appointing electors.[21] The Supreme Court also asked the state court to address the federal law requiring electors to be appointed under state law enacted "prior to" Election Day.[22] In its own opinion, the Florida Supreme Court had said nothing about that law.

This was a form of judicial minimalism in action. The Court's decision was minimalist in the particular sense that the Court decided the case at hand, without going beyond the narrow issue presented. To be sure, the Court's decision was not without consequences or meaning. The Court took seriously a quite controversial idea, to the effect that under the federal Constitution, a state court is not permitted to rely on the state constitution in deciding on the content of state law for choosing electors. By taking this idea seriously, the Court signaled its willingness to play an active role in the controversy, and it might well have adversely affected subsequent proceedings in Florida. By itself, however, the Court's decision settled very little, and the Court did no more than was necessary to resolve the particular dispute before it. With its exceedingly narrow requests for clarification, the Court did not settle the dispute over the meaning of the constitutional and statutory provisions at issue in the case.

Why did the Court proceed in this way? It seems possible that some of the justices refused to settle the merits on principle, thinking that the federal judiciary should insert itself as little as possible into the continuing electoral struggle. But the most likely explanation is that the Court sought unanimity and found, as groups often do, that unanimity is possible only if as little as possible is decided. In the first round, the members of the Court evidently thought that unanimity was important and were able to disguise their internal disagreements through this route. The subsequent decision in *Bush v. Gore,* showing a badly splintered Court, suggested that the minimalist remand reflected a narrow ruling that could attract the support of people with very diverse views about the case.

Here, then, are some general lessons about minimalist decisions. Sometimes such decisions reflect a principled commitment, on the part of the key justices, to say and do no more than is necessary to dispose of the case. But sometimes such decisions reflect not principle, but the practical pressures imposed by the need to produce an opinion that can attract the support of a diverse group of people.

THE ASTONISHING STAY

On December 8, the Florida Supreme Court ruled, by a vote of 4–3, that a manual recount was required by state law, and it thus accepted Gore's contest.[23] This decision threw the presidential election into apparent disarray. With the manual recount beginning, it became quite unclear whether Bush or Gore would emerge as the winner. At this stage, the nation reached a new level of uncertainty, and some observers were frightened at the prospect of a chaotic process, without any obvious way to produce an agreed-upon outcome.

On December 9, the Supreme Court issued a stay of the decision of the Florida Supreme Court.[24] This was the first genuinely extraordinary action taken by the United States Supreme Court. It was not only extraordinary but also a departure from conventional practice, and one that is difficult to defend on conventional legal grounds—not because Bush lacked a substantial probability of success, but because he had shown no irreparable harm.

To be sure, some harm would have come to Bush from the continuation of the manual recount. It seemed entirely possible that the recount would have narrowed the gap between Bush and Gore. Indeed, it seemed possible that the recount would, in a day or two, have put Gore in the lead. This would have been an unquestionable harm to Bush, in the nontrivial sense that it would have raised some questions about the legitimacy of his ensuing presidency, if it had subsequently been determined that the manual recount was unlawful.[25]

But the question remains: How serious and irreparable would this "harm" have been? If the manual recount was soon to be deemed unlawful, would the Bush presidency really have been "irreparably" harmed? This is extremely doubtful. At most, there would have been some embarrassment from the fact that the Florida vote would have been seen to have gone Gore's way if votes that should not (by hypothesis) have been counted were in fact counted. This is hardly the kind of harm that ordinarily justifies a stay from the Supreme Court. At the same time, the stay of the manual recount would seem to have worked an irreparable harm to Gore. For Gore, time was very much of the essence, and if the counting was stopped, the difficulty of completing it in the requisite period would become all the more serious. By itself, the Supreme Court's stay of the manual recount did not hand the election to Bush. But it came very close to doing precisely that.

In these circumstances, can anything be said on behalf of the stay? A plausible argument may be available, at least in retrospect. Suppose that a majority of the Court was entirely convinced that the manual recount was unlawful, perhaps because in the absence of uniform standards, similarly situated voters would not be treated similarly. If the judgment on the merits was altogether clear, why should the voting be allowed to continue, in light of the fact that it would undoubtedly have to be stopped soon in any case, and its continuation in the interim would work some harm to the legitimacy of the next president? The question suggests that if the ultimate judgment on the merits was clear, the stay would not be so hard to defend. If the likelihood of success is overwhelming, the plaintiff should not be required to make the ordinary showing of irreparable harm.[26] The stay is therefore best taken to have demonstrated that the Court was determined to reverse the Florida Supreme Court. The problem, then, was less the stay than the Court's ambitious, poorly reasoned judgment on the merits.

Order and Law

In *Bush v. Gore*,[27] the Supreme Court was asked to reverse the Florida Supreme Court on two grounds. Bush urged, first, that the Florida court had violated Article II and Title Three, Section Five of the United States Code by altering what the Florida legislature had done.[28] Bush urged, second, that because no standards had been established to ensure that the similarly situated would be treated similarly, the Florida recount would violate the equal protection and due process clauses.[29]

Merits: What the Court Said

On the merits, there are two especially striking features to the Court's decision. The first is that only three justices were willing to accept Bush's major submission all along, to the effect that the Florida Supreme Court had produced an unacceptable change in Florida law. I will not discuss that issue in detail here, noting only that in my view, the argument becomes less convincing the more one reflects on it. To be sure, a decision by a state court to disregard state law would raise serious questions under Article II. And I am not at all sure that the Florida Supreme Court correctly interpreted state law. But that court's view was not so implausible as to amount to a change, rather than an interpretation. Let us turn, then, to the second striking feature of the Court's decision: The fact that five members of the Court—purely on the merits, seven—accepted the adventurous and unprecedented secondary argument, involving the equal protection clause.

The equal protection claim does have considerable appeal, at least in the abstract and as a matter of common sense. If a vote is not counted in one area when it would be counted in another, something certainly seems to be amiss. Suppose, for example, that in one country, a vote will not count unless the stylus goes all the way through, whereas in another country, a vote counts merely because it contains a highly visible "dimple." If this is the situation, some voters can legitimately object that they are being treated unequally for no good reason. On what basis are their ballots not being counted, when other, identical ballots are being registered as votes?

Announcing its fundamental motivation, the Court wrote, "The right to vote is protected in more than the initial allocation of the franchise. Equal protection applies as well to the manner of its exercise. Having once granted the right to vote on equal terms, the State may not, by later arbitrary and disparate treatment, value one person's vote over that of another." Recall that the Florida Supreme Court had asked for a manual recount in four disputed counties, but without specifying how it would be decided whether ballots would count. The Court's concern was that no official in Florida had generated standards by which to discipline the relatively open-ended inquiry into "the intent of the voter." In the Court's view, "Florida's basic command . . . to consider the 'intent of the voter' " was "standardless" and constitutionally unacceptable without "specific standards to ensure its equal application. . . . The formulation of uniform rules based on these recurring circumstances is practicable and, we conclude, necessary."[30] Without such rules, similarly situated ballots—and hence similarly situated voters—would be treated differently, and for no evident reason.

The Court offered some details on the resulting equality problem. "A monitor in Miami-Dade County testified at trial that he observed that three members of the county canvassing board applied different standards in defining a legal vote."[31] Standards even appeared to have been changed "during the counting process," with Palm Beach County beginning "the process with a 1990 guideline which precluded counting completely attached chads," then switching "to a rule that considered a vote to be legal if any light could be seen through a chad," then changing "back to the 1990 rule," and then abandoning "any pretense of a per se rule." [32] A serious problem was that "the standards for accepting or rejecting contested ballots might vary not only from county to county but indeed within a single county from one recount team to another." [33] This too was not merely speculation. "Broward County used a more forgiving standard than Palm Beach County, and uncovered almost three times as many new votes, a result markedly disproportionate to the difference in population between the counties." [34]

The Court also found a constitutional violation in the unequal treatment of "overvotes" (meaning ballots that machines rejected because more than one vote had been cast) and "undervotes" (meaning ballots on which machines failed to detect a vote, and which had been ordered to be reexamined). The Court objected that "the citizen whose ballot was not read by a machine because he failed to vote for a candidate in a way readable by a machine may still have his vote counted in a manual recount; on the other hand, the citizen who marks two candidates in a way discernable by the machine will not have the same opportunity to have his vote count, even if a manual examination of the ballot would reveal the requisite indicia of intent. Furthermore, the citizen who marks two candidates only one of which is discernable by the machine, will have his vote counted even though it should have been read as an invalid ballot." [35]

To this, the Court added "further concerns." [36] These included an absence of specification of "who would recount the ballots," leading to a situation in which untrained members of "ad hoc teams" would be involved in the process. [37] And "while others were permitted to observe, they were prohibited from objecting during the recount." [38] Thus the Court concluded that the recount process "is inconsistent with the minimum procedures necessary to protect the fundamental right of each voter in the special instance of a statewide recount under the authority of a single state judicial officer." [39]

The Court was well aware that its equal protection holding could have explosive implications for the future, throwing much of state election law into constitutional doubt. Thus far, no constitutional principle requires that everyone's ballot have an equal chance to be counted. If taken seriously, any such principle could produce a great deal of federal judicial involvement in the running of state elections. With this point in mind, the Court emphasized the limited nature of its ruling: "The question before the Court is not whether local entities, in the exercise of their expertise, may develop different systems for implementing elections. Instead, we are presented with a situation where a state court with the power to assure uniformity has ordered a statewide recount with minimal procedural safeguards."[40]

In this way, the Court ensured that its decision was narrow rather than wide—narrow in the sense that it covered the problem at hand without also covering other, apparently similar problems. The narrow ruling ensures that *Bush v. Gore* is an illustration of the kind of judicial minimalism that characterizes the current Court.[41] And if narrowness is a plausible response to ignorance about the consequences of a wider ruling, then the Court's effort to settle the case, without ruling on much more, is not so hard to understand.

At the same time, the Court's opinion was shallow rather than deep, in the sense that it lacked much in the way of theoretical ambition. The Court simply asserted that a manual recount, without a clear standard for determining the intent of the voter, was constitutionally unacceptable. It said little about what the equality principle should be taken to mean, in the context of voting or elsewhere, and relied instead on what it apparently took to be ordinary intuitions. The Court was therefore able to produce an "incompletely theorized agreement" on its equal protection ruling, attracting support from seven justices; the broad support for that ruling seems attributable, at least in part, to the fact that the Court did not offer a deep or contentious argument on its behalf. If incompletely theorized agreements have their virtues,[42] then the minimalism of the Court's approach is not hard to defend.

Merits: Three Problems

Nonetheless, there are three problems with this reasoning. First, the Court's decision, however appealing, lacked any basis in precedent. For this reason it raises serious questions from the standpoint of the rule of law. Second, the Court's effort to cabin the reach of its decision seemed ad hoc and unprincipled, even political—a common risk with minimalism. And third, the system that the Court let stand seemed at least as problematic, from the standpoint of equal protection, as the system that the Court held invalid.

Precedents and Thought Experiments

Nothing in the Court's previous decisions suggested that constitutional questions would be raised by this kind of inequality. The cases that the Court invoked on behalf of the equal protection holding—mostly involving one person, one vote and the poll tax[43]—were entirely far afield. To be sure, the absence of precedential support is not decisive; perhaps the problem had simply never arisen. But manual recounts are far from uncommon, and no one had ever urged, or even seriously thought, that the Constitution requires that they be administered under clear and specific standards. The fact that no court had ever upheld manual recounts lacking such standards attests, not to the strength of the constitutional objection, but to general agreement that any constitutional attack would have been quite implausible.

To make the problem more vivid, suppose that in 1998, a candidate for statewide office—say, the position of attorney general—lost after a manual recount, and brought a constitutional challenge on equal protection grounds, claiming that county standards for counting votes were unjustifiably variable. Is there any chance that the disappointed candidate would succeed in federal court? In all likelihood the constitutional objection would fail; in most courts, it would not even be taken seriously. The rationale would be predictable, going roughly like this: "No previous decision of any court supports the view that the Constitution requires uniformity in methods for ascertaining the will of the voter. There is no violation here of the principle of one person, one vote. Nor is there any sign of discrimination against poor people or members of any identifiable group. There is no demonstration of fraud or favoritism or self-dealing. In the absence of such evidence, varying local standards, chosen reasonably and in good faith by local officials, do not give rise to a violation of the federal Constitution. In addition, a finding of an equal protection violation would entangle federal courts in what has, for many decades, been seen as a matter for state and local government."

Of course, it is possible to think that this equal protection holding would be wrong. Whether the federal Constitution should be read to cabin local discretion in this way is a difficult question. I will suggest some reasons to think that unjustified disparities of this kind should indeed be remedied, by Congress and state legislatures and in extreme cases by courts. The problem is that in a case of such great public visibility, the Court embraced the principle with no support in precedent, with little consideration of implications, and as a kind of bolt from the blue.[44]

In the domain of thought experiments, we can go much further. Imagine if the parties in *Bush v. Gore* were reversed. Imagine, that is, that Gore had originally seemed the winner in Florida, that Bush had demanded a manual recount, that the Florida Supreme Court accepted Bush's demand, and that Gore had resisted the recount on constitutional grounds. Is there any chance that the justices who composed the majority in *Bush v. Gore* would do the same thing in this hypothesized *Gore v. Bush?* My hunch is that not one of those justices would have shown the slightest interest in Gore's complaint. I also doubt that any of the four dissenters would have been willing to press a constitutional objection on Gore's behalf. The best prediction is that such a case would have been resolved within the state courts. With an absence of precedential support, it is simply fanciful to think that a majority of the justices could have been persuaded to rule in Gore's favor under the stated circumstances. The point suggests that *Bush v. Gore* raises serious problems from the standpoint of the rule of law.

Minimalism's Vices

We have seen that the Court attempted to limit the reach of *Bush v. Gore* and to suggest that the equal protection violation is unlikely to be found in other contexts. Here too the Court's opinion gives the appearance of being inadequately principled—of being designed for a single occasion. This is another respect in which the case raises problems for those who believe in the ideal of judicial impartiality.

More specifically, it is not at all clear how the rationale of *Bush v. Gore* can be cabined in the way that the Court sought to do. What is missing from the opinion is a clear explanation of why the situation in the case is unique or even distinctive, and hence to be treated differently from countless apparently similar situations involving equal protection problems. The effort to cabin the outcome, without a sense of the principle to justify the cabining, gives the opinion an unprincipled cast.

Suppose, for example, that a particular area in a state has an old technology, one that misses an unusually high percentage of intended votes. Suppose that many areas in that state have new technology, capable of detecting a far higher percentage of votes. Suppose that voters in the disadvantaged area urge that the equal protection clause is violated by the absence of uniformity in technology. Suppose they object that their votes are less likely to count than are those of their fellow citizens several miles away. Why doesn't *Bush v. Gore* make that claim quite plausible? Perhaps it can be urged that budgetary considerations, combined with unobjectionable and long-standing rules of local autonomy, make such disparities legitimate. Perhaps the sheer expense of producing equality will help to justify inequality. As the Court seemed to suggest, these considerations appear less relevant in the context of a statewide recount administered by a single judge—the situation in *Bush v. Gore*. But this is a complex matter, and it is easy to imagine cases in which those considerations do not seem weighty. I will return to these questions below.

Arbitrariness and Inequality on All Sides

The system that the recount was designed to correct might well have been as arbitrary as the manual recount that the Court struck down—and hence the Court's decision might well have created an even more severe problem of inequality. Without manual recounts, many inequalities were allowed to persist. This is a fundamental problem with the outcome in *Bush v. Gore*. The decision sensibly objected to unjustified inequalities, but it did not come to terms with the fact that without a manual recount, far more troubling inequalities would be permitted to persist. There are a number of complexities here. Political scientist Henry Brady summarizes the evidence with the suggestion that by "any reckoning, the machine variability in undervotes and overvotes exceeds the volatility due to different standards by factors of ten to twenty. Far more mischief, it seems, can be created by poor methods of recording and tabulating votes than by manual recounts."[45]

More particularly, there were several inequalities in the certified vote in Florida. Under that vote, some machines counted votes that were left uncounted by other machines, simply because of different technology. Where optical scan ballots were used, for example, voters were far more likely to have their votes counted than where punch-card ballots were used. In Florida, fifteen of every one thousand punch-card ballots showed no presidential vote, whereas only three of every optically scanned ballot showed no such vote. In all likelihood, these disparities would have been reduced with a manual recount. If the principle of *Bush v. Gore* is taken seriously, manual recounts might even seem constitutionally compelled. But the Court's decision, forbidding manual recounts, ensured that the relevant inequalities would not be corrected.

There were other problems. In the recount that produced the certified vote, some counties merely checked the arithmetic, whereas others put ballots through a tabulating machine. The result is a significant difference in the effect of the recount. In any case the manual recount was picking up many votes that machines failed to include. As Pamela Karlan has written, the Court "never really confronted the magnitude of the inequalities produced in the first instance by Florida's use of different voting technologies in different parts of the state. The Broward County recount discerned votes on about 20 percent of the undervoted ballots, while the Palm Beach County recount, using a more stringent standard, recovered votes on about 10 percent of the undervoted ballots."[46]

If the constitutional problem consists of the different treatment of the similarly situated, then it seems entirely possible that the manual recount, under the admittedly vague "intent of the voter" standard, would have made things better rather than worse—and that the decision of the United States Supreme Court aggravated the problem of unjustified inequality. Now perhaps the best response is that what particularly concerned the Court was not the fact of inequality, but the combination of inequality and process failure, through a manual recount that seemed to have due-process-type problems. Indeed, the Court did speak in due process terms in several points. But its holding was based on unjustified inequalities, and on that count, the certified vote had formidable problems. This does not mean that there was no problem with the manual recount. But it bears directly on the issue of remedy, to which I will shortly turn.

OVERALL EVALUATION

On the merits, then, the most reasonable conclusion is not that the Court's decision was senseless—it was not—but that it lacked support in precedent or history, that it raised many unaddressed issues with respect to scope, and that it might well have authorized equality problems as serious as those that it prevented. In these ways, the majority's opinion has some of the most severe vices of judicial minimalism. In fact, this was a subminimalist opinion, giving the appearance of having been built for the specific occasion.

REMEDY

Now turn to the Court's decision on the issue of remedy. If the manual recount would be unconstitutional without clear standards, what is the appropriate federal response? Should the manual recount be terminated, or should it be continued with clear standards? At first glance, that would appear to be a question of Florida law. If the Florida legislature would want manual recounts to continue, at the expense of losing the federal safe harbor, then manual recounts should continue. If the Florida legislature would want manual recounts to stop, in order to preserve the safe harbor, then manual recounts should stop.

Why did the Supreme Court nonetheless halt the manual recount? The simple answer is that the Court thought it clear that the Florida Supreme Court would interpret Florida law so as to halt the process. As the Court wrote, "The Supreme Court of Florida has said that the legislature intended the State's electors to 'participate [. . .] fully in the federal electoral process. . . . Because it is evident that any recount seeking to meet the December 12 date will be unconstitutional for the reasons we have discussed, we reverse the judgment of the Supreme Court of Florida ordering a recount to proceed.' "[47] Thus the Court concluded that as a matter of Florida law, a continuation of the manual recount "could not be part of an 'appropriate' order authorized by" Florida law.[48]

This was a blunder, and one that seems hard to explain in conventional legal terms. It is true that the Florida Supreme Court had emphasized the importance, for the Florida legislature, of the safe harbor provision.[49] But the

Florida courts had never been asked to say whether they would interpret Florida law to require a cessation in the counting of votes, if the consequence of the counting would be to extend the choice of electors past December 12. In fact, the Florida court's pervasive emphasis on the need to ensure the inclusion of lawful votes[50] would seem to indicate that if a choice must be made between the safe harbor and the inclusion of votes, the latter might have priority. It is not easy to explain the United States Supreme Court's failure to allow the Florida court to consider this issue of Florida law.

Here, then, is the part of the United States Supreme Court's opinion that is most difficult to defend on conventional legal grounds.

Pragmatism, Hysterical and Otherwise

Might anything unconventional help to defend the Court's conclusion? I have suggested that the Court's decision produced order. In fact, it might well have averted chaos. It is worthwhile to spend some time on this question, because it provides the best explanation, though not justification, of the Court's otherwise inexplicable approach. This, in fact, is what (I speculate) helped to motivate the Court's decision: An effort to prevent a difficult situation from spiraling out of control. To understand the underlying issues, let us briefly imagine what would have happened if the Court had affirmed the Florida Supreme Court, or remanded for continued counting under a constitutionally adequate standard. I will attempt a sober account here, and then come to terms with Judge Richard Posner's highly publicized, and quite hysterical, effort to bring "pragmatism" to bear on *Bush v. Gore*.

In the event of an affirmance, manual counting would of course have continued. In the event of a remand, the Florida Supreme Court would have had to sort out the relationship between the legislature's desire to preserve the safe harbor and its desire to ensure an accurate count. That Court had been divided 4–3 on the question of whether a manual recount should be required at all. It is reasonable to speculate that the three dissenters would continue to object to the manual recount. The question is whether any of the four members of the majority would conclude that the December 12 deadline took precedence over the continuation of the contest. There is certainly a good chance that the Florida Supreme Court would have terminated the election at that point. If so, the controversy would have had an ending that was neater, and more legitimate, than was produced by the United States Supreme Court. But if it failed to do so, things would have gotten extremely messy.

Almost certainly, the Republican-dominated Florida legislature would have promptly sent a slate of electors, thus producing two (identical) slates for Bush—the November 26 certification and the legislatively specified choice. The legislative slate would in turn have been certified by the secretary of state and the governor of Florida. In the meantime, the counting would, by hypothesis, have continued well after the expiration of the December 12 safe harbor date. If Bush had won the manual recount, things would be very simple, and such a victory would have been more probable than not. But suppose Gore had won; what then? Would the secretary of state have voluntarily certified the new count? Would the governor of Florida have signed off on the certification? It is not at all clear that Florida's executive officials would do what the Florida courts wanted them to do. And if the secretary of state and the governor refused, how would the Florida courts have responded? Would they have threatened executive officials with contempt? How would they have responded to the threat?

Suppose that this problem had been solved—and that three certified votes from Florida had come before Congress. At that point, both houses of Congress, acting separately, would have to vote on which certification to accept.[51] Almost certainly the Republican-dominated House of Representatives would have accepted a Bush slate. The Senate, then split 50–50, would be much harder to call; perhaps some Democrats, in conservative states won by Bush, would have agreed to accept the Bush slate from Florida. But perhaps there would have been an even division within the Senate. If so, Vice President Gore would have been in a position to cast the deciding vote. Suppose that he did—and that he voted for the third Florida slate, and thus for himself, so as to ensure that the House and the Senate would come to different conclusions. At that point, the outcome is supposed to turn on the executive's certification. But which was that? Here the law provides no clear answers. At this point, a genuine constitutional crisis might have arisen. It is not clear how it would have been settled. No doubt the nation would have survived, but things would have gotten very messy.

The Court's decision made all of these issues academic. It averted what could have been, at the very least, an intense partisan struggle, lacking a solution that is likely to have been minimally acceptable to all sides. If the Court did the nation a large favor, this is the reason. If the Court produced the simplest resolution to a controversy that risked spiraling out of control, then it might have done something with a range of good consequences.

But it is important to be careful with this point. I mean to offer a partial explanation of the Court's decision, not a justification of what the Court did. It will therefore be useful to distinguish what I am saying here from what Judge Posner has said, both in this volume and elsewhere.[52]

Judge Posner thinks that the Supreme Court was right to decide as it did in *Bush v. Gore,* simply because the consequences of the decision were good, all things considered. Judge Posner realizes, of course, that courts need a constitutional "hook" to strike down state practices. He knows that it is not easy to find a legal foundation for the Court's decision in *Bush v. Gore.* Apparently he thinks that Article II, section 1, clause 2 provides a plausible enough ground for the decision. But it also seems as if he doesn't take the Article II argument entirely seriously, urging that the "only possible rationale is pragmatism," and suggesting that "[a]vowedly pragmatic judges" might have been able to avoid embarrassment in producing the outcome in *Bush v. Gore.*

Judge Posner is right on at least two points. First, pragmatic considerations, of the sort that he describes, probably helped to motivate the Court to stop the recount in Florida. Second, consequences do matter to law, not excluding constitutional law; especially when the legal materials leave gaps and ambiguities, an assessment of the consequences can be extremely important. But I believe that Judge Posner's analysis of *Bush v. Gore* verges on the lawless, even the goofy. The problem is that Judge Posner relies on a highly speculative, tendentious, worst-case scenario to approve of a decision that is exceedingly hard to justify on legal grounds. There are lessons here about the appropriate role of pragmatism, and pragmatists, in constitutional adjudication.

Judge Posner thinks that for a pragmatist, the "single most arresting feature of the" *Bush v. Gore* litigation "is the worst-case scenario that it avoided." In Posner's account, continued counting in Florida could have led, among other things, to "greatly impaired authority, amidst virtually unprecedented partisan bickering and bitterness, and after an interregnum unsettling to the global and the U.S. domestic economy and possibly threatening to world peace." Unsettling the global and domestic economy? Threatening to world peace? Judge Posner is not joking. "How would the crisis over the Chinese seizure of our surveillance plane have been resolved by Acting President Summers? And would other hostile foreign powers or groups have tried to test us during the interregnum?" What would we have done *then*?

Judge Posner is borrowing here from the preferred strategy of radical environmentalists, conspiracy theorists, and doomsayers of all stripes: Mobilize public concern, and arouse the citizenry, through the concrete description of a worst-case scenario, however ludicrously unlikely. But this is a diversion. There is always a worst-case scenario. It's always very bad. As every economist knows, the question is how likely it is.

For the election of 2000, it is unlikely in the extreme that continued counting in Florida would have led to an unsettled global and domestic economy, or created a threat to world peace, or "tests" from "hostile foreign powers or groups." (It is a sad irony that serious tests from hostile groups did indeed occur, many months after the 2000 election and *Bush v. Gore.*) If *Bush v. Gore* had not been decided as it was, the overwhelming likelihood is that things would have been settled long in advance of January 20. A congressional resolution would have been messy and even chaotic, but Lawrence Summers would not have become our president, and world peace would not have been at risk. In thinking about legal reasoning in general, the case for Judge Posner's version of pragmatism in law is surely weakened by the fact that someone as sober as Judge Posner can offer, with a straight face, so zany a projection of the "worst case" consequences.

Let us put the factual debate to one side, and investigate the legal issues. As Judge Posner has it, the analysis of *Bush v. Gore* mostly depends on balancing three factors: the worst-case scenario, the harm to the Court's authority, and the effects of one or another decision on the appointments process. A brief analysis of these three factors is the basis for Judge Posner's approval of *Bush v. Gore.* For Judge Posner, the legal materials come up late, and pretty much as an afterthought. Judge Posner agrees that there is no "obvious handle in the Constitution for stopping the recount." He thinks that the equal protection argument is very weak. He even speculates that three of the justices (Rehnquist, Scalia, and Thomas) might not have agreed with it. But in his view, they might have been right to join an opinion with which they did not agree, simply in order to make the outcome seem simpler and to increase its moral authority. (There are obvious questions here, involving not only the consequences but also the ethics of joining an opinion with which one disagrees; I put those questions to one side.)

In the end Judge Posner likes the Article II ground. He says, correctly, that Article II requires electors to be chosen in accordance with the law as enacted by state legislatures; he appears to think that the Court should have said, with Justice Rehnquist, Scalia, and Thomas, that the Florida Supreme Court changed Florida law as enacted by the Florida legislature. But he doesn't say much about to support this claim, and appears not to take it terribly seriously. Perhaps the reason is that as a legal matter, the argument is exceedingly weak. The Florida Supreme Court might well have misinterpreted its own law, but it is a gross overstatement to say that what the Court did went beyond the bounds of legitimate interpretation. In the end Judge Posner seems not to care about the Article II argument after all, acknowledging that *Bush v. Gore* was "a decision whose only possible rationale is pragmatic." He even goes so far as to urge that "avowedly pragmatic judges just might have been able to decide *Bush v. Gore* in Bush's favor without embarrassment."

With this suggestion, Judge Posner appears to be saying that the least embarrassing opinion in favor of *Bush v. Gore* would have been "avowedly pragmatic." But this is doubtful. What would such judges say? That they were attempting to prevent the presidency of Lawrence Summers? To protect the global and domestic economy? To ensure world peace? Any effort to write in this vein would have been widely perceived as illegitimate, simply because it would have involved an explicit abandonment of the legal materials in favor of a highly speculative effort to weigh consequences, on the part of people with no particular expertise in that enterprise. Whether or not the authors of an avowedly pragmatic opinion would have felt personal "embarrassment," an opinion of this kind would have been received far more skeptically, even than *Bush v. Gore* itself.

In fact, there are good pragmatic reasons for judges to attempt to venture a straightforward interpretation of the legal materials. If judges assess the consequences in an ad hoc way, their own prejudices might well come into play, and in any case they are all too likely to err. How can judges possibly get a handle on the nature and likelihood of the worst-case scenario, or the adverse effects of a pro-Bush ruling on judicial credibility and on future nominations? Judges lack the tools to undertake the relevant inquiries. Most of the time, they do better to treat the legal materials with respect. If those materials clearly point to one outcome, that is the outcome that judges should reach.[53] A good pragmatist should avoid ad hoc assessments of consequences, and should try to generate an approach to interpretation that will, among other things, discipline fallible judges.[54] Ad hoc pragmatism, especially of the hysterical variety, fails that test.

It is much too simple to say that judges should follow the law, even if the heavens would fall.[55] Sometimes there is no law to "follow." And if the heavens really would fall, judges should not follow the law. But the legal materials did not plausibly support the outcome in *Bush v. Gore,* and if the Court had followed the law, the heavens would not have fallen. While the Court might well have done the nation a favor, it does not seem unfair to accuse the Court of lawlessness in *Bush v. Gore*—not of seeking to ensure that George W. Bush became president, but of trying to prevent a situation from becoming uncontrollable and chaotic, in part as a result of what the Court saw as highly questionable decisions by the Florida Supreme Court. In fact, Judge Posner's approval of *Bush v. Gore* seems to me part and parcel of an unattractive and even hubristic part of his approach to law—an occasional willingness to treat the legal materials in an irreverent way, when the consequences seem to him to justify the irreverence.

A LARGE NEW RIGHT?

For the future, the most important question involves the scope of the right recognized in *Bush v. Gore.* Notwithstanding the Court's efforts, that right is not at all easy to limit, at least as a matter of basic principle. On its face, the Court appears to have created the most expansive voting right in many decades.

A Minimalist Reading of a Minimalist Opinion

At its narrowest, the Court has held that in the context of a statewide recount proceeding overseen by a single judge, the standard for counting votes must be uniform and concrete enough to ensure that similarly situated people will be treated similarly. This holding extends well beyond the context of presidential elections; it applies to statewide offices, not just federal offices.

By itself this is a substantial renovation of current law, since over thirty states fail to specify concrete standards for manual recounts. This does not mean that state legislatures must set down clear standards in advance; a decision by state judges should suffice. But the inevitable effect of the opinion will be to increase the pressure for legislative reform at the state and possibly even the national level. Any state legislature would be well-advised to specify the standard by which votes will be counted in the context of a manual recount. All this should count, by itself, as a gain for sense and rationality in the recount process.

Equality in Voting

It is hard to understand why the principle of *Bush v. Gore* does not extend much further than the case itself, at least in the context of voting. Consider the following easily imaginable cases:

1. Poor counties have old machinery that successfully counts 97 percent of votes; wealthy counties have newer machinery that successfully counts 99 percent of votes. Those in poor counties mount a constitutional challenge, claiming that the difference in rejection rates is a violation of the equal protection clause.
2. Same as the immediately preceding case, except the division does not involve poor and rich counties. It is simply the case that some areas use machines that have a near-perfect counting rate, and others do not. The distribution of machines seems quite random.
3. Ballots differ from county to county. Some counties use a version of the controversial butterfly ballot, most do not. It is clear that where the butterfly ballot is used, an unusual number of voters are confused, and do not successfully vote for the candidate of their choice. Does this violate the equal protection clause?

4. It is a national election. Citizens in Alabama use different machinery from that used by citizens in New York. The consequence is that citizens in Alabama are far more likely to have their votes uncounted than citizens in New York. Do they have a valid equal protection claim? What if the statistical disparity is very large?

The Court's suggestion that ordinary voting raises "many complexities" is correct; but how do those complexities justify unequal treatment in the cases just given? A number of litigants have already raised this question, initiating lawsuits to force states and localities to justify inequalities. The best answer would point to two practical points: budgetary considerations and the tradition of local control. In light of these points, it might be difficult for some areas to have the same technology as others. Wealthy counties might prefer to purchase more expensive machinery, whereas poorer communities might devote their limited resources to other problems. Perhaps judicial caution in the cases just given can be justified in this way. But this is not altogether clear. Why shouldn't states take steps to ensure that voters in different countries have an equal chance to have their ballots count? The expense of equality is unlikely to be high. It is not at all clear that disparities in treatment can be justified—especially if those disparities are closely connected to race or wealth.

Even if courts should tread cautiously here, *Bush v. Gore* plainly suggests the legitimacy of both state and national action designed to combat disparities of this kind. It is for this reason that the Court's decision, however narrowly intended, set out a rationale that might well create an extremely important (and appealing) innovation in the law of voting rights. Perhaps legislatures will respond to the invitation if courts refuse to do so.

A General Requirement of Rules?

In fact, the Court's rationale might extend more broadly still. Outside of the context of voting, governments do not impose the most severe imaginable constraints on official discretion. Because discretion exists, the similarly situated are treated differently.[56] Perhaps the most obvious example is the "beyond a reasonable doubt" standard for criminal conviction, a standard that different juries will inevitably interpret in different ways. Is this unacceptable?[57]

In the abstract, the question might seem fanciful; but related constitutional challenges are hardly unfamiliar. In the sixties and seventies, there was an effort to use the due process and equal protection clauses to try to ensure more rule-bound decisions, in such contexts as licensing and admission to public housing.[58] Plaintiffs argued that without clear criteria to discipline the exercise of discretion, there was a risk that the similarly situated would not be treated similarly, and that this risk was constitutionally unacceptable. But outside of the most egregious settings, these efforts failed,[59] apparently on the theory that rule-bound decisions produce arbitrariness of their own, and courts are in a poor position to know whether rules are better than discretionary judgments. Does *Bush v. Gore* require courts to extend the limited precedents here?

Perhaps it could be responded that because the choice between rule-bound and more discretionary judgments is difficult in many cases, judicial deference is generally appropriate—but not when fundamental rights, such as the right to vote, are at risk. If so, *Bush v. Gore* has a limited scope. But does this mean that methods must be in place to ensure against differential treatment of those subject to capital punishment? To life imprisonment? I cannot explore these questions here. But for better or for worse, the rationale in *Bush v. Gore* appears to make it necessary to consider these issues anew.

LAW OR POLITICS?

It is now time to address a broader question, one that is especially troubling for those who believe, as I do, in the possibility and the integrity of legal reasoning. One of the most striking features of the decision in *Bush v. Gore* is the much-remarked fact that the most conservative justices made up the five-person majority, with the least conservative justices constituting the four-person minority. Before and after the Court's final decision, it was easy to detect a similar division within the nation.

People who supported Gore, or who identified themselves as left-of-center, tended to be enraged by the Supreme Court's involvement; people who supported Bush, or who identified themselves as right-of-center, tended to approve of it. A similar division could be found over assessments of the Florida Supreme Court. Observers who supported Bush tended to think that the Florida court had not interpreted Florida law but instead changed it. Observers who supported Gore tended to think that the Florida court had acted well within the legitimate bounds of interpretation. Of course few of these people were experts in Florida law. But the same pattern seems to have held among those who knew nothing about Florida law and those who studied it in some detail.

Much the same division can be found among academic observers. Of course, there are exceptions and qualifications. But in general, there is, even among academic students of law, a clear and sharp difference between Gore supporters and left-of-center people on the one hand and Bush supporters or right-of-center people on the other. The former are generally skeptical of the Court's decision, whereas the latter think, broadly speaking, that it was correct. Judge Richard Posner and Professors Richard Epstein and John Yoo, for example, tend to support the Court, whereas less conservative professors, likely Gore voters, tend to think that the Court was wrong.[60] How can we account for this?

The most natural way would be to acknowledge the enduring truth in the view conventionally associated with the legal realist movement of the thirties: The line between legal judgment and political judgment is far from crisp and simple. At least where the legal materials leave gaps, people will do what they like, on political grounds. In *Bush v. Gore,* perhaps the legal materials left gaps, and thus people did what they liked, on political grounds. I have suggested that the result in *Gore v. Bush* would be quite different from that of the actual case, and that a majority could not have been mustered, in that hypothetical case, for the equal protection ruling of the real-world Court. Even if I am wrong on this, I am sure that at the very least, most people's reactions to *Gore v. Bush* would be very different from their reactions to *Bush v. Gore*— and hence that judgments about this case have a great deal to do with the identity of the parties. This may be less true for legal specialists than for non-lawyers; but it is certainly true for specialists too. At the very least, this fact seems to be an embarrassment for those who believe in the separation between law and politics.

To understand what is going on here, I would like to propose, very briefly and tentatively, what might be called a *neo-realist account of legal judgment,* designed especially for what we might consider "hot cases." The account is meant to be purely descriptive, not normative. The core of the account is that in such cases, people's initial evaluations play a large role in their ultimate judgments, and their initial evaluations are highly emotional. Often the relevant emotion involves indignation or outrage. Take, for example, another high-profile legal dispute: whether President Clinton had committed an impeachable offense. Of course the Congress was split down the middle on that issue, with party identification being a near-perfect determinant of people's votes. It defies belief to think that we would have seen the same pattern of evaluations if President Clinton had been Republican.

In the impeachment case, legal evaluations were greatly affected by an intense, emotional reaction, either in the form of, "it's outrageous that a president of the United States has committed such acts," or instead, "it's outrageous that Kenneth Starr's investigation has gone so far with essentially private misconduct." Now it is important to be careful with the idea of "emotions" here. With respect to law, as elsewhere, emotions are not cognition-free.[61] They are based on and surrounded by thoughts—in the case of impeachment, thoughts about the character and performance of President Clinton. What is crucial is that the intense emotional reaction tends to dominate people's reaction to the topic at hand, dampening their responsiveness to other considerations, even making it hard for people on both sides to ask: What would I think if the person alleged to have committed these acts were someone of a different political party? What would I think if the parties were reversed? The difficulty of asking such questions is a characteristic feature of emotional reactions to certain political and legal events, and it ensures that the relevant judgments will be more or less impervious to further thinking.

There are three aggravating factors here. First: When like-minded people talk with one another, they tend to move toward extremes.[62] If three members of a group tend to think that the Florida Supreme Court was stealing the election from George W. Bush, their discussions will push them toward a more extreme version of what they already thought. The effect is heightened if such people think of themselves as alike along some dimension: Republican, liberals, conservatives, and so forth. At the same time, people engaged in deliberation are not likely to be much moved by people who disagree with them *if* those people can be said to follow in a different social category. Deliberating Republicans are not likely to be moved by deliberating Democrats, or vice-versa, even if the same arguments might have some appeal if labels were unassigned to those who make those arguments. I speculate that in *Bush v. Gore,* and in other cases involving politically charged legal questions, like-minded people, including like-minded judges and specialists, fortified one another's opinions, thus contributing to the neo-realist model that I have outlined.

Second: It is well established that while people care about fairness, their judgments about what is fair are systematically self-serving and hence, biased.[63] When an observer favors one or another side in a sporting event, in politics, or in law, their prejudices much affect their judgments about what is right. Where legal materials are ambiguous, a similar effect should be at work: Judgments about what is fair, and about what is lawful, will partly be a function of what is in people's interests, broadly understood.

Now one of the points of legal reasoning, and even of the ideal of the rule of law, is to quiet the intense emotional reactions that often crowd out other factors. Perhaps we can see the ancient image of justice, equipped with blindfolds, as a signal that certain considerations—above all, the identity of the parties—are not a legitimate basis for judgment. And it seems clear that well-trained lawyers and judges are, as a rule, more impervious to emotions of this kind. But they are not entirely impervious to them, and in politically charged cases, justice is not blind in the least.

Third: People are subject to *confirmation bias,* in the sense that when they hear two contending sides in an argument, they will often be fortified in their preexisting belief, thinking that the debate has only served to confirm what they thought before.[64] For example, people who favor capital punishment are likely, after hearing arguments for and against capital punishment, to be fortified in their belief, because they will see the strength in the arguments on their side, and stress the weaknesses in the opposing position. To the extent that Gore supporters were able to talk to Bush supporters, and vice-versa, the discussion might well have failed to break down disagreements, partly because positions had become congealed when like-minded people spoke, at first, largely with one another. Judges and academics, like ordinary people, are not immune from confirmation bias.

I think that these factors were extremely important in *Bush v. Gore,* and that initial emotional reactions drove people's ultimate judgments about the law, including the judgments of Supreme Court justices and academic commentators. I also believe that these intense reactions produced serious mistakes on the part of the Court and its defenders, in academic circles and elsewhere. Of course, similar mistakes can be found on both sides of intense legal controversies. It is simply the case that the legal materials did not support the outcome in *Bush v. Gore,* especially on the question of remedy, and hence the Court acted in a lawless fashion.

CONCLUSION

If the Supreme Court is asked to intervene in an electoral controversy, especially a presidential election, it should try to avoid even the slightest appearance that the justices are speaking for something other than the law. Unanimity, or near-unanimity, can go a long way toward providing the necessary assurance. Whether or not this is possible, the Court's opinion should be well-reasoned and rooted firmly in the existing legal materials.

In *Bush v. Gore,* the Court did not succeed on these counts. The 5–4 division was unfortunate enough; it was still worse that the five-member majority consisted of the most conservative justices. Regrettably, the Court's opinion had no basis in precedent or history. To be sure, the equal protection argument had a certain appeal in common sense. But even if it were correct, the natural remedy would have been to remand to the Florida Supreme Court, to ask that court to say whether Florida law would favor the manual recount over the safe harbor provision, or vice-versa. This remedy seems especially sensible in light of the fact that the inequalities that the Court condemned might well have been less serious than the inequalities that the recount would have corrected.

Nonetheless, there are two things to be said on behalf of the Court's ruling. First, the Court brought a chaotic situation to an abrupt end. From the standpoint of constitutional order, it is reasonable to speculate that any other conclusion would have been worse. The outcome might have been resolved in Congress, and here political partisanship might have spiraled out of control. Second, the principle behind the equal protection ruling has considerable appeal. In a statewide recount, it is not easy to explain why votes should count in one area when they would not count elsewhere. In fact, the principle has even more appeal if understood broadly, so as to forbid similarly situated voters from being treated differently because their votes are being counted through different technologies. Understood in that broader way, the principle of *Bush v. Gore* should bring a range of questionable practices under fresh constitutional scrutiny.

Bush v. Gore is likely to intensify public concern about unjustifiably aggressive decisions from the Supreme Court, and perhaps that concern will give the Court an incentive to be more cautious about unsupportable intrusions into the democratic arena. The Rehnquist Court has combined, far too much of the time, judicial hubris with minimalism. One of the unintended consequences of the decision might be to eliminate, once and for all, the widespread view that the federal judiciary is a bastion of liberal thinking, and the myth that a form of liberal judicial activism is playing a large role within the federal courts. Actually, there are no liberals on the current Court; the supposed left-wing consists only of moderates. *Bush v. Gore* might well become a symbol of the Court's tendency toward right-wing judicial activism, as it certainly deserves to be.

Equally important, *Bush v. Gore* might come to stand for a principle, in legislatures if not courts, that greatly outruns the Court's subminimalist holding—a principle that calls for an end to the many unjustified disparities in treatment in voting and perhaps beyond. It would be a nice irony if the Court's weak and unprecedented opinion, properly condemned on democratic grounds, led to significant social improvements from the democratic point of view.

3. Freeing eroG v. hsuB From its Hall of Mirrors*

Laurence H. Tribe†

Once Upon a Time:

There was a presidential election so close that its outcome turned on the electoral votes of one state, Florida, where the margin of error probably exceeded the margin of victory. Many votes slipped through the cracks, either because of archaic tabulation systems, confusing ballots, and inadequate voting assistance, or because voters were too careless to read and follow directions. Unwilling to accept the razor-thin victory that the rules in place on Election Day gave his opponent, the unofficially proclaimed loser convinced the state's highest court, all of whose members had been appointed by governors of the loser's political party, to extend the statutory deadline for recounting doubtful ballots. The state court let each county election board make up its own rules as it went along, either recounting ambiguous ballots to "divine" the intent of the voters, or throwing out potentially legal votes in accord with the "letter of the law." The apparent margin of victory grew increasingly narrow. . . .

And this is where our now too-familiar story diverges into the saga that has become *Bush v. Gore*.[1] Depending on where your political loyalties lie, one of these stories may seem more accurate to you than the other:

Version one: the shrinking margin of victory reasonably caused fear that unprincipled partisans would succeed in overturning the people's democratic choice. Compelled by an activist Florida court that had read new terms into the Florida election code while reading old terms out, influenced by an unprecedented demand for speedy adjudication and realizing that whatever it did or failed to do would be widely criticized, the U.S. Supreme Court soberly intervened. And not a minute too soon, for the Court stopped the recount just hours before the people of Florida, by missing the December 12 safe harbor set by Congress, would have lost their right to cast an unchallengeable slate of electoral votes for president, conceivably ending in the "election" of the sore loserman, rewarding him and his band of merry lawyers for changing the rules of the game after his opponent had crossed the finish line. Whatever one might think of the Court's decision, this version concludes that we should all be grateful we avoided a constitutional crisis that might have lasted even beyond the next inauguration day or, worse still, imperiled our democracy.

Version two of the final chapter is quite different. In it, the state court emerges in hindsight as the tribunal that earnestly—if without clear legal support—tried to preserve democracy by counting all the votes cast. And a conservative majority of the Supreme Court, heedless of the critics' cries, concocted a transparent excuse to blow the whistle while its preferred candidate, the conservative, was ahead. According to this ending, the Court's intervention and the presidency it brought about are delegitimated by the Court's brazenly partisan motives.

Showing both these variants to be false lest either be assimilated into the national psyche—whether as conventional wisdom or as just a widely accepted account—is the aim of this essay. Can someone with an obvious ax to grind[2] succeed in such a project? The proof of that pudding will have to be in the eating.

ELECTION 2000: THE GRINCH THAT ALMOST STOLE CHRISTMAS[3]

It's hard not to think the air has been all but sucked out of whatever breathing room once existed for sober reflection about the notorious saga of *Bush v. Gore*. Collections of thoughtful essays have appeared in print[4] and will continue to[5]; spirited defenses of the decision's bottom line (if not its widely criticized reasoning)[6] have been and will continue to be published, and the celebrity authors have predictably had their say.[7] Yet rarely has a case so much studied been so little understood, even by those who have looked at it most closely. It is as if the case comes equipped with its own hall of mirrors, the better to project misleading images of what was at stake, leading critics and defenders alike down false trails of inquiry.

What I find most intriguing about *Bush v. Gore* isn't just how wrong its legal reasoning seems, but what shaped the Court's perceptions and how its performance fit the Rehnquist Court's signature patterns of decision when it plunged so eagerly into the presidential election thicket in the face of such evident obstacles to rendering, and being *seen* to render, a nonpartisan decision driven by legal principle. In trying to understand the Court's likely perceptions, it may help to begin with what led to and surrounded the case, what the public saw, and what every participant in the saga experienced.

The public image of *Bush v. Gore* began to take shape with the first premature announcement of Gore winning Florida's crucial 25 electoral votes on Tuesday evening, November 7. That faded into a morass of "never mind" mea culpas from the media, proclamations of a Bush victory, and embarrassed explanations that the election was technically too close to call by early Wednesday morning. The marketing war began immediately. The Bush campaign's PR machine depicted Gore as a sore loser too selfish to read the handwriting on the wall. An outspent Gore PR team tried to convince people to be patient while Florida's complex election protest provisions made sure that "every vote counted." Emerging reports boosted Gore's case. It seemed that Pat Buchanan had a new group of core supporters: elderly Jewish voters in Palm Beach, many of whom would as soon vote for Buchanan as vote for Adolf Eichmann. When these voters complained that the butterfly ballot had caused them to spoil their votes, and when televised pictures made clear to millions of Americans just how easy such a mistake would have been, many began to believe in the urgency and the justice of hunting for uncounted legal votes.[8]

The images of outraged voters faded quickly as the Bush spinmeisters weaved a web of images and sound bites destined to linger mockingly over the painstaking effort to recount ballots. Packs of reporters from every corner of the nation flooded into counties named Volusia, Seminole, and Palm Beach. Directed by an army of partisan loyalists and looking for a bold and dramatic image to speak where words fell short, the reporters pointed their cameras at the ordinary, and all too fallible, human beings holding ballots up to the lights to "divine" the intent of the voters. Almost overnight, *dimples* and *hanging chads* became household words, evoking close-up glimpses of election fraud to many, while conjuring images emblematic of democracy and the voting rights struggles of the sixties to others.

By this time, the news shows started with the caption: *Looming Constitutional Crisis?* The talking heads predicted a disaster: The election would be tossed into the chaos of Congress unless the deus ex machina of the Supreme Court, described in hushed tones suggesting a latter-day Wizard of Oz, could save us; the fact that our nation's founders envisioned Congress—not the Court—deciding mattered little to the televised ministers of truth. It mattered even less when, shortly before midnight on December 11, the Court ruled the recounting had to end. The man behind the curtain had brought the presidential election of 2000 to a suitably dramatic, if dramatically undemocratic, close.

I first became involved with *Bush v. Gore* when, four days after the election, George W. Bush filed a lawsuit in a federal district court in Florida, seeking an order preventing the continued counting, under state judicial supervision, of disputed ballots. In that federal suit, which seems already to have vanished from memory, Bush claimed that principles of judicial federalism—which would ordinarily counsel abstention from federal intrusion into the ongoing processes of a state's judicial system, requiring a challenger to climb the ladder to the state's highest court and, if he lost there, hope to interest the U.S. Supreme Court in the case—should give way in light of the federal constitutional and statutory principles supposedly at risk were the counting to proceed: equal protection for every ballot, abiding by the rules in place on election day, and resolving all election contests by December 12.[9]

I agreed to argue the case at Vice President Gore's request, believing freedom from this sort of short-circuiting of a state's legal processes to be an important part of our constitutional architecture and the constitutional pluralism I've long embraced[10]—especially given the Constitution's Article II delegation to each state of the responsibility to select a slate of presidential electors,[11] which I saw as an added shield against federal intrusion. We won the federal lawsuit,[12] but Bush prevailed in his request that the Supreme Court invoke its discretionary power of direct review first to question, and ultimately to overturn, the way Florida's highest court was conducting the ballot recount.

In a case that would abound with ironies, Article II—which helped shield Gore from Bush's lower federal court attack—turned out to provide sword enough to lead a unanimous Supreme Court on December 4[13] to ask Florida's highest court to explain how, as required by Article II, its *state legislature* had authorized it to extend the ballot-counting deadline from November 21 to 26.[14] And Article II would later serve as the context permitting three justices of the Court, concurring in the Court's December 11 decision to end the election on equal protection grounds,[15] to conduct an independent analysis of state law concluding that the state court had departed from the legislative scheme.[16] As we shall see, it was the Court itself that acted in conflict with the rules Florida's legislature put in place before the election, invoking equal protection principles as well as a safe harbor statute that its own decision did not protect but violated. It is as though the Bush lawyers persuaded the Court first to imagine the strongest arguments available *against* what they asked it to do—and then to bounce those arguments off a trick mirror aimed at what the Florida Supreme Court had done. To borrow an image the Court once used in another context, Bush's lawyers had to nudge five justices "through an analytical looking glass" to succeed.[17] And they were all too ready to be nudged.

THE RED HERRING OF ARTICLE II

Central to the ways in which observers have been misled has been the role, in resolving the election stalemate, of Article II, section 1, clause 2 of the Constitution, providing that "[e]ach State shall appoint, in such Manner as the Legislature thereof may direct, a Number of Electors," charged with selecting the United States president. Critics of the Supreme Court's intervention have proceeded as though they had to attack the Court for disagreeing with the Florida court's interpretation of Florida law—a step seemingly authorized in some circumstances by Article II's explicit delegation of authority to the Florida *legislature,* not to its *judiciary.* And supporters of the Court's intervention have proceeded as though they had to defend the Court for intruding into the internal structure of Florida's government, finding in Article II the authority to reject a state constitution's allocation of authority between the state legislature and the state judiciary.

Both positions are awkward for those forced into them. For critics, an aversion to federal supremacy over state election processes coexists uneasily with arguments they themselves have made in support of state efforts to impose term limits on a state's federal officers.[18] For defenders, an embrace of federal supremacy over those processes is in tension with their own arguments that a state's control over the federal officials representing its people is too central to state sovereignty to be limited by federal constraints.[19]

Once we bring *Bush v. Gore* into proper focus, however, it should become clear that both the critics and the defenders of the Court's decision have been aiming at phantom targets: The critic's argument that the Supreme Court had no business second-guessing the Florida court on a question of Florida law notwithstanding Article II makes two mistakes. First, the Supreme Court did not in fact reject any reading of Florida law propounded by the Florida court. Only the concurring opinion of Chief Justice Rehnquist was bold enough to declare Florida's court incapable of properly interpreting its own election code. The only piece of text to which five justices assented, the voiceless per curiam opinion, held that the recount ordered by the state court violated the federal equal protection clause. What remedy was proper? There, the per curiam disingenuously translated the Florida court's opinion that the legislature wanted all recounts to be completed by December 12 (so as to take advantage of the promise contained in Congress's safe harbor statute[20]) into a bright-line rule halting the recount at midnight, December 11—at the cost of throwing out countless legal votes. But the Florida court had penned no such bright line,[21] and hindsight gives cause to doubt the Florida court, if asked, would have penned it.[22] At a minimum, the Court had no business guessing about the Florida court's views rather than remanding for the Florida court to decide whether it read the state legislature to have set December 12 as an absolute deadline. Failing to remand was unpardonable—but it was different from rejecting a decision of Florida's highest court on the meaning of Florida law.

But what if the Court had done that? Apart from wasting their ammunition by shooting at a target not really in play here, the critics are beating a dead horse. *Of course* the federal judiciary has a role to play in policing how a state's courts handle the choice of presidential electors. Suppose the Florida court had issued an opinion that said: "Notwithstanding the state legislature's plain preference for a popular vote, it is the view of this court that the people are dunderheads and that this court should, and it hereby does, designate the presidential electors as follows. . . ." Would anyone doubt that the federal judiciary could—and should—intervene?

The point is straightforward: Whenever a provision of the Constitution specifies how a decision otherwise internal to the state's system of governance is to be made, enforcing that provision is a matter for the federal judiciary, subject only to principles committing so-called "political questions" to Congress and/or the president for decision. In the post–*Bush v. Gore* case of *Rogers v. Tennessee*,[23] for example, the Court had to construe the ex post facto clause,[24] which provides: "[n]o State shall . . . pass any . . . ex post facto Law." To the Court, the words *pass* and *Law* were clearly meant as "a limitation upon the powers of the Legislature, and [. . .] not . . . the Judicial Branch of [state] government."[25] This federal judicial interpretation leaves state *legislatures* more constricted than state *courts,* however differently a state might prefer to allocate authority between those two branches. Yet Justices Ginsburg and Souter, both of whom were exercised in *Bush v. Gore* about federal judicial intervention into the allocation of authority between the state legislature and judiciary, joined Justice O'Connor's majority opinion in *Rogers* without reservation. What's more, that opinion arrived at its conclusion only after carefully dissecting previous state supreme court opinions, thus second-guessing the highest state court's interpretation of state law.[26]

Indeed, although Justice Ginsburg's *Bush v. Gore* dissent, joined by Justices Souter and Breyer,[27] doubted the Court's authority to prevent a state from organizing "itself as it sees fit,"[28] even the chief justice's concurrence raised that issue only as a side note. For it did *not* hold Florida had violated Article II by assigning to its judicial rather than its legislative branch the task of deciding how presidential electors would be chosen. Instead, the concurrence held that Florida's highest court, while discharging its responsibility to interpret state legislation in accord with its constitution, had so *misinterpreted* the governing legislation as to require federal correction. As will shortly become clear, that conclusion was indefensible. But that is a substantive matter, not a charge that the concurring opinion poked its three-headed nose into a realm that was none of its business. For it plainly *was* the Court's business, as it always is when a federal constitutional norm speaks directly to a challenged exercise of state power.

Thus those critics of *Bush v. Gore* who accuse the justices of unauthorized federal sallies into exclusively state territory have been tackling a phantom runner—there were no such sallies here—and aiming at the wrong goalposts—such a sally cannot be dismissed as automatically improper.

The defenders of *Bush v. Gore* likewise make unnecessary work for themselves when they assume it depends for its lawfulness upon putting Article II on a collision course with state sovereignty[29]—whose core, as the Court recognized in *Gregory v. Ashcroft,*[30] is the allocation of responsibility among the state's three branches. For, aside from a passing dictum, even the concurring justices did not rely upon an assumed federal judicial power to revise a state's assignment of responsibilities among its branches. Finally, although we will see how the concurring opinion went awry in rejecting the relevant Florida Supreme Court interpretation of the state election code, the institutional function of checking state judicial construction of state election legislation to assure compliance with federal constitutional ground rules is altogether unexceptional.

It is not only unnecessary but also futile for *Bush v. Gore's* defenders to talk as though a state's highest court's interpretations of state law may be discarded whenever a federal constitutional norm makes state legislation decisive. For, even then, the Court may reject only *manifestly unreasonable* state judicial constructions of state statutes; it has no warrant simply to substitute its own preferred construction for the state court's, within an outer perimeter whose definition is a matter of federal law. Thus, shortly after *Bush v. Gore,* in *Rogers v. Tennessee,*[31] Justice Scalia, joined by Justices Thomas and Stevens, treated a merely "reasonable reading of state law by the State's highest court" as binding upon the Court.[32] In any event, the concurring opinion in *Bush v. Gore* purported to defer to the state court and erred not because of how it postured itself vis-à-vis that court but because its own reading of the state's election law was simply untenable.

FLORIDA ELECTION LAW: THE LAW OF STANDARDS

The Chief Justice's concurring opinion argued (and the Court itself hinted) that the Court's intervention was needed to halt a lawless process launched injudiciously by Florida's highest court. Building on the concurrence, Judge

Richard A. Posner paints *Bush v. Gore* as a pragmatic response[33] reasonably calculated to contain the damage threatened by the Florida court's lawless decisions of November 21 (extending the deadline for certification)[34] and December 8 (ordering a statewide manual recount of all undervotes[35]). But Florida's Supreme Court, by resolving textual ambiguities in the Florida election code to permit the tabulation of as many clearly intent-revealing ballots as possible, did not "butcher [. . .] the state's election statute."[36] To the contrary, it remained faithful both to the primacy that Florida law attaches to the right to vote and to the literal text of the Florida code. If you are willing to accept that claim on my say-so, you needn't delve into the following somewhat tedious exercise in technical statutory construction. Those not already convinced that the Florida court adhered fully to the state election code must bear with me awhile.

Round 1: The Extension

The Florida Supreme Court initially demonstrated its unwillingness to be boxed in by self-contradictory bright-line rules during the protest phase of the election 2000 litigation, which arose out of the decisions by four counties to grant the Florida Democratic party's November 9 requests for manual recounts.[37] Soon realizing they might not complete these recounts before the November 14 statutory deadline for submitting certifications of election results,[38] the county canvassing boards inquired of Florida Secretary of State Katherine Harris in what circumstances she would accept late returns. Harris had to resolve a conflict in the Florida election code: Section 102.111 said the secretary "shall ignore" returns filed after the seven-day deadline, while section 102.112 said the secretary "may ignore" the same returns.[39] In accordance with a division of elections advisory opinion,[40] the secretary ruled that her office would reprieve a county only in cases of voter fraud, substantial noncompliance with election procedures, or "an act of God."[41]

On November 21, the Florida Supreme Court rejected that ruling as legally unsound. It reasoned that the state legislature had not chosen to teach tardy canvassing boards a lesson at the cost of excluding tens of thousands of votes and held "the Secretary may reject a Board's amended returns *only* if the returns are submitted so late that their inclusion will preclude a candidate from contesting the certification or preclude Florida's voters from participating fully in the federal electoral process."[42] That holding was a manifestly reasonable way of reconciling the confusing code provisions with the clear preference in Florida law for counting, whenever possible, every lawfully cast ballot.[43] No doubt, those who saw only the images of a frenzied circus outside the Florida Supreme Court, and who heard only the made-for-TV sound bites that the court's alchemy had turned "may" or "shall reject" into "must accept," saw the state court's reading of Florida's legal rules as a fast-and-loose concoction,[44] one that could only aggravate the tensions and the sense of uncertainty taking hold in Florida. But those media-enhanced emotions bore little relation to the legal reality.

Such sentiments were exacerbated by the state court's admittedly inadequate explanation of what it was doing and why—especially in permitting the recounts thwarted by executive officials' (mis)interpretation of the election code to continue until November 26, a date it seemed to have pulled from thin air—until it belatedly provided its rationale in a December 11 opinion,[45] issued just hours before the Supreme Court rendered its final ruling. Responding finally to the Court's December 4 request for clarification,[46] the Florida court explained that, even without any protests or recounts, counties would have had until November 18 to certify their final results; a federal consent decree required that no certification take place until after the tenth day following the election to allow for the tabulation of overseas ballots.[47] The division of elections' November 13 misinterpretation of the state's election code deprived the counties of five days to recount ballots manually—so, on November 21, the Florida court simply gave back those five days by extending the deadline to November 26. Contrary to popular belief, this move did not add "twelve days to a phase that had no real legal significance."[48] Instead, it combined the federal consent decree's November 18 deadline with the ten-day contest filing period allowed by Florida election code section 102.168.[49] Whereas the literal text of the statute would have allowed a contest to be filed until November 28, the Florida Supreme Court permitted an extension only until November 26.

The state court's explanation came too late to placate those who had perceived the November 21 ruling as ad hoc judicial legislation. Vivid images raised eyebrows, and subsequent rulings from that same court would meet with deep distrust by those who saw Florida's highest court as flouting the aphorism that the "rule of law" is "the law of rules."[50]

Round 2: The Statewide Recount Order

The chapter of the Election 2000 saga that would ultimately end as the Supreme Court's final word on *Bush v. Gore* began on November 27, when Vice President Gore filed suit under section 102.168(3)(c), a provision of the Florida election code that permits an election contest whenever the "receipt of a number of illegal votes or rejection of a number of legal votes [is] sufficient to change or place in doubt the result of the election."[51] Florida's highest court determined that Gore had made a threshold showing that enough "legal votes" had been rejected—i.e., not counted—to "place in doubt" the results of the presidential election in Florida as certified on November 26. So it turned to the question of remedy. Inferring from the broad grant of authority in section 102.168(8)[52] a mandate that the court "do everything required by law to ensure that legal votes that have not been counted are included in the final election results,"[53] the court expanded its focus beyond the votes specifically identified by Gore to order a statewide manual recount of all undervotes on which one could discern a "clear indication of the intent of the voter."[54]

What do "Damaged" and "Defective" Ballots Have to do With All This?

The Florida Supreme Court, in formulating its "intent of the voter" standard, relied on §101.5614, the section of the election code that regulates the canvassing of election returns.[55] The provision mandates that "*[a]ll* valid votes shall be tallied by the canvassing board,"[56] that *any* "damaged or defective" paper ballot "shall be counted manually at the counting center,"[57] and that "*[n]o* vote shall be declared invalid or void *if there is a clear indication of the intent of the voter as determined by the canvassing board.*"[58] The section further provides that "[t]he return printed by the automatic tabulating equipment, to which has been added the return of write-in, absentee, and *manually counted votes,* shall constitute the official return of the election."[59]

One recurring criticism of the Florida court's reading of the statutory text, seemingly traceable to the December 8 dissent by Florida Chief Justice Wells,[60] is that section 101.5614(5) is inapplicable when determining a *general* definition of "legal vote" because the section applies *only* when a "ballot card . . . is *damaged or defective* so that it cannot properly be counted by the automatic tabulating equipment."[61] Chief Justice Rehnquist adopted this objection wholesale without any independent analysis of the statutory text.[62] Judge Posner likewise claims "the provision about recording a vote when there is a clear indication of the voter's intent is for cases in which the ballot is damaged or defective, which is different from its being spoiled by the voter, and is indeed a kind of tabulating error."[63]

With all due respect to its distinguished sources, this criticism is wrong to the point of embarrassment. It tortures the statutory text and conflicts squarely with a Florida Supreme Court decision authoritatively interpreting § 101.5614(5) two years before election 2000: In *Beckstrom v. Volusia County Canvassing Board*,[64] the Florida Supreme Court "construe[d] 'defective ballot' to include a ballot which is marked in a manner that cannot be read by a scanner."[65] This definition of "defective ballots," surely, encompasses those that are incompletely punched through. Although referring to *Beckstrom* elsewhere in his opinion,[66] Chief Justice Rehnquist notably ignored the only portion of that opinion addressing the meaning of "defective ballot" in § 101.5614(5). Judge Posner likewise gives *Beckstrom* short shrift, suggesting the court could not really have meant what it said.[67] The reason, clearly, is an unwillingness to concede the possibility that a voter who didn't follow directions nonetheless cast a "legal vote."

They Should've Read the Directions!

On that view, shared by Chief Justice Rehnquist, no "legal votes" could have been missed if all ballots were counted without mechanical error by machine. The logic of that position rests on circularly defining a "legal vote" as a ballot marked such that it can be read properly by a vote-counting machine. As Chief Justice Rehnquist put it, "No reasonable person would call it an 'error in the vote tabulation' or a 'rejection of legal votes' when electric or electromechanical equipment performs precisely in the manner designed."[68] Judge Posner observes that punch card votes are "tabulated by computers that are programmed to reject ballots that are not punched through,"[69] echoing Chief Justice Rehnquist's incredulity that anyone could complain when a machine "fails to count those ballots that are not marked in the manner that [the] voting instructions explicitly and prominently specify."[70] This tough-love view conveniently ignores, first, that the much-lauded voting instructions were not uniform from county to county; second, that the instructions may have violated Florida law by being provided solely in English in areas with large Hispanic populations;[71] and third, that Florida election code did not require county canvassing boards to provide voters with *any instructions whatsoever* on how to cast a ballot unless specifically requested—demonstrating the fallacy of the assumption that the legislature intended to make the right to vote depend on correctly reading a sign.[72] Still, Judge Posner asks how the failure of machines deliberately programmed not to count votes from ballots incompletely punched through could possibly be thought an error in tabulation: "If you put a steel bar into a meat grinder and hamburger meat doesn't come out, do you call this an error by the meat grinder?"[73] Well, yes—if by the "meat grinder" you mean the poor fellow who was busily grinding meat and innocently reached for a steal bar instead. Perhaps more to the point: If you put a circular definition of *legal vote* into a word processor and an argument that begs the question comes out, do you call this an error by the word processor?

The problem, of course, is that voting machines translate marks or punches on a ballot into votes in an imperfect manner and with varying degrees of accuracy. Why should the degree of accuracy achieved by the machines automatically equal the degree of accuracy the Florida legislature intended to require in the election code? After all, it explicitly required automatic machine recounts in very close elections;[74] it allowed for country-based protests with on-demand sample manual recounts and full manual recounts wherever such recounts would be likely to make a difference;[75] and it flatly required, in manually counting ballots, that "[n]o vote shall be declared invalid or void if there is a clear indication of the intent of the voter as determined by the canvassing board."[76] The legislature neither programmed the voting machines nor created a scheme whereby machine results are entitled to anything beyond a presumption of accuracy.

The frequent refrain that no legal votes had gone uncounted because every ballot cast had in fact been "read by voting machines . . . and there-after reread by virtue of Florida's automatic recount system"[77] ignores the fact that ballots are *translated* into votes; they are not *votes* as such. This is not just a matter of logic, but rather, a legislative mandate that counting all the ballots by machine is a necessary but not sufficient condition to recording all legal *votes*. Once a manual recount has been ordered, ballots transform into mere vehicles by which the election code achieves its stated end: namely, the counting of remaining votes.

The Florida Supreme Court's reading of the state election code to mandate counting each ballot that expresses a clear manifestation of voter intent, notwithstanding the voter's failure to follow the rules, was no innovation designed to add votes to Gore's column. Apart from its 1998 *Beckstrom* precedent, the Florida court pointedly refused to reject as illegal large blocks of *Republican* absentee ballots, in which required information had been filled in not by the voters themselves but by Republican party workers, undeniably violating statutory requirements.[78] To secure a Gore victory, rigorously enforcing the election code against all absentee ballots would have been the simplest and most certain strategy. Instead, the state court used the "voter's intent" standard to count most of those ballots as votes for Bush—something the defenders of *Bush v. Gore* have inexplicably forgotten or conveniently forgiven.

Because the Executive Said So!

The state court's critics next claim that their interpretation at least accords with that of the election officials upon whom the state legislature conferred the primary duty of construing and applying Florida's election laws.[79] Thus, the secretary of state's determination that ballots unreadable by vote tabulation machines were automatically illegal should have received great deference.[80] But neither the statutory provision governing election contests, nor any other Florida law, says anything of the sort. To the contrary, the statute stipulates that "[t]he *circuit judge* to whom the contest is presented may fashion such orders *as he or she deems necessary* to ensure that each allegation in the complaint is investigated, examined, or checked, to prevent or correct any alleged wrong, and to provide any relief appropriate under such circumstances."[81] And the statutory language offers no support for the assertion that broodingly omnipresent "principles of administrative law required the contest court . . . to defer to the canvassing boards, as the experts in counting votes, unless their decisions were unreasonable."[82]

Besides, even within that supposedly universal administrative law framework, deference to an executive ruling is inappropriate if it contradicts the plain meaning of the statute's words.[83] Any fair-minded examination of Florida case law reveals that the narrow definition of "legal vote" provided by the division of elections cannot be reconciled with Florida law as it has existed since 1975.

Florida Election Law is Not the Law of Per Se Rules

In the midst of the seventies, when President Bush was frolicking in his "nomadic days,"[84] the Florida Supreme Court was busy developing its approach to interpreting state election statutes. In *Boardman v. Esteva*,[85] the court stated definitively that it would henceforth read the statutes to treat as valid all votes that were cast in "substantial compliance" with state regulations.[86] Thus, in *Boardman,* the court ruled that a group of imperfect absentee ballots should be included in the total despite the existence of a number of examples of voter error[87] and the loss of many outer envelopes containing absentee voters' affidavits.[88] Applying the "substantial compliance" rule in subsequent disputes, Florida courts have refused to invalidate ballots on which voters or officials did not follow the letter of the law,[89] and have agreed to reject votes in large numbers only in cases where the plaintiff has overwhelmingly shown fraud on the part of election officials.[90]

The Florida court's adoption of the "substantial compliance" rule accords with the state's constitutional protection of the right to vote. Article 1, section 1 of the Florida constitution proclaims that "[a]ll political power is inherent in the people." Some have identified the court's reliance on the state constitution as an instance in which it "was going beyond conventional statutory interpretation," since nowhere does the text direct attention to Article I or speak the magic words *right to vote*.[91] Such simplistic treatment of the state constitution's relation to state statutes overlooks the nature of republican government, not to mention decades of persuasive case law. The

Florida court had previously held that "the primary consideration in an election contest is whether the will of the people has been effected;"[92] that "[t]he right to vote, though not inherent, is a *constitutional right in this state*;"[93] and that the "fundamental purpose of the election laws" in Florida is "to facilitate and safeguard the right of each voter to express his or her will in the context of our representative democracy."[94] Reading the relevant statutes in light of this basic right did not *replace* the scheme set up by the Florida legislature, but simply served as a heuristic for determining what that scheme required in light of background constitutional principles.

A Voter's Intent: In the Eye of the Beholder?

The preference of the state court's critics for machine-generated results over manual counts may evince a lack of faith in the trustworthiness of human vote tabulators, but something deeper must underlie their belief that no reasonable legislature would have left so much in the hands of human counters. It may be that this obsession with mechanization derives from the recognition that a ballot is by no means a "neutral" object, being instead the conveyor of a distinctly partisan message. That message, when examined by a human tabulator, may "look" different depending on that tabulator's personal political preferences. Machines may err, but at least such errors, even if abundant, are random. Human "errors," by contrast—whether deliberate or reflecting the vote counter's unconscious desire to see one candidate prevail—are anything but.

Those to whom this problem looms large[95] not only lack faith in the individuals designated by the Florida legislature to count votes manually on a regular basis,[96] but also ignore the many statutory safeguards Florida law provides to control partisan maneuvering in the manual counting process. The state election code requires recount teams to consist of members of both parties[97] and mandates that all recounts be open to public view.[98] That not every recount team in every single county rigidly observed those procedural requirements[99] may justify a few raised eyebrows but, without actual proof of improper conduct, hardly warrants a categorical renunciation of the entire undertaking—particularly given the role of the supervising state magistrate, against whose adequacy no challenge was yet ripe.

More importantly, the anxiety about partisanship at the recount stage *as a justification for halting the recount* implies that the *initial* count is itself above such reproach. Such a claim belies reality. It disregards the well-known political calculations that often go into the choice of what type of ballot to use; how long to keep particular polling places open; which voters to turn away either for want of adequate identification or for suspicion that they have criminal records; whose requests for clarification of ambiguities at the polling place to treat seriously and whose requests to dismiss; and a host of other similar variables all plainly subject to partisan manipulation. Blind faith in the underlying count despite these realities also ignores the manually counted ballots that were included in the November 26 certification and the important role that human counters play in literally every election in the tabulation of absentee ballots. Given the sophisticated and regularly updated polling data available throughout the election process to many who are in a position to take advantage of such knowledge and let it shape how they treat such absentee ballots,[100] why in a close election would we *ever* include those votes? To pose the question is to expose the futility of making demands of perfect neutrality at *any* stage of an election.

There is an even deeper problem with the outcry against manual recounts using a voter's intent standard. Beyond the subjectivity inherent in deciding *which* rigid rules should replace those slippery standards, the outcry itself is, at bottom, an outcry against entrusting political power to fallible human beings who might at any moment abuse it. That outcry assails democracy itself. Consider that in the Florida election of 2000, all candidates had an equal opportunity both to protest how ballots were or were not counted and to request manual recounts; that all candidates and voters could contest the certified results of the election if the protest phase did not fully vindicate their interests; and that all candidates' political parties[101] could send representatives to observe the recounting process to help ensure that the vote tabulators were properly discharging their duties. Given this structure, the existence of partisan motives that color nearly everyone's perceptions cannot be deemed a defect to be cured, whether by the ostensibly impersonal agency of machines or by the purposefully mechanical application of formal rules. For if that is the "cure," then the Constitution's basic scheme for curbing the abuse of power—to let "ambition counteract ambition,"[102] to balance the self-interest that tugs one way with self-interest that tugs the other, all the while seeking in the long run to instill virtues of civic republicanism—must be the disease. If the ever-present possibility of bias, or even of chicanery, on the part of people entrusted with the duty to exercise their best judgment, became so great as to require replacing people with machines and judgment with mechanical rules, then the whole enterprise of popular government—government of, by, and for the people—seems doomed.

Predicated on a very different premise, Florida's election code entrusts people with considerable power and discretion at every step. Relying on the fundamental constitutional choice of competition in the marketplace of ideas, Florida's election code harnesses partisan motives and political self-interest in a model of supervised combat and contest, not a model of lockstep command and control. Thus, Florida's protest system encourages each candidate to file protests in large-population counties that lean heavily toward that candidate's party.[103] Meanwhile, the state election code's unequivocal reliance on the human judgment of canvassing-board officials reveals the legislature's confidence that closely watched election officials will perform their duties ethically even amidst intense partisan wrangling. The Florida court did not arbitrarily decide to reject uniform, mechanically applicable, statewide rules and to rely instead on nothing beyond the legislature's "intent of the voter" standard, as implemented on a county-by-county or even a case-by-case basis, all subject to oversight by a single state judge. To the contrary, its decision arose naturally from the preferences evinced by Florida statutes; first, that county canvassing boards can and should be relied upon to conduct manual recounts with integrity; second, that conducting manual recounts in a judicially supervised, public, and open way would either uncover or deter egregious abuses of process; and third, that this is the best way to ensure that all legal votes get counted.

Despite the legislature's evident acceptance of political struggle as a way to facilitate democratic choice; despite its explicit declaration that election officials are presumed to be tabulating votes accurately in that partisan environment; despite its unequivocal embrace in 1999 of an increasing number of election contests and, thus, of more manual recounts; and despite its overwhelming preference for standards over rules in the election context, Chief Justice Rehnquist, echoed by Judge Posner, advances an utterly inconsistent vision, one that would "depart from the legislative scheme." [104] Had they but viewed their own arguments in an undistorted mirror, they would have seen that those very arguments, and not the state court's rulings, flouted the letter and the spirit of the statutory scheme that the Florida legislature put in place, while the image of a partisan state court run amok—an image that seemingly drove the Court and continues to haunt its defenders—can only have been the product of trick mirrors.

We are left with a puzzle: Why might the three justices who joined in the Supreme Court's concurring opinion—and to a lesser degree the two others who were persuaded to halt the recount instantly even on the premise that it complied with Florida's election statutes—have been so profoundly averse, along with Judge Posner, to the very idea of manual recounts as a matter of course in excruciatingly close elections? Why the sense on their part that, no matter what the Florida statues might say, no rational legislature would ever choose a system in which voters who can't read or don't follow directions might still be counted? Why the feeling that sometimes unruly partisan combat, with its close ties to rough-and-tumble popular democracy, must be cabined, buttoned down, rendered rule-like and predictable rather than being embraced and celebrated? Perhaps the answer is the fear that democracy itself breeds disorder.

The Topsy-Turvy Nature of the Equal Protection Claim

There was a time when an aroused and active citizenry gathering political support for a favored cause or candidate didn't seem terribly alarming to the Supreme Court. In 1986, when I represented a group of Berkeley activists agitating for rent control against landowners who felt threatened by that grassroots effort, the Court, in *Fisher v. City of Berkeley*, [105] ruled 8–1 that federal antitrust law could not be used to preempt such citizen-based action. Barely a decade later, the landscape had changed. In *Timmons v. Twin Cities Area New Party*, [106] I represented a minority political party challenging a state ban on "fusion" candidacies (in which two parties, usually a minor party and one of the two major parties, nominate the same candidate), candidacies that the major parties saw as threatening to their dominance. The Court's 6–3 decision upholding the state's power to assure political stability by preserving the shared hegemony of those two parties decisively awakened me to the drumbeat sounded by a cohesive Court majority. Chief Justice Rehnquist and Justice O'Connor, both of them members of the *Fisher* majority, joined by Justices Scalia, Kennedy, and Thomas, supported quite often by Justice Breyer, and at times by Justice Souter as well, had by the nineties coalesced around an alliance committed to judicial invocation of the Constitution to avoid political ferment and fragmentation,[107] preserve order and hierarchy, and impose, whenever possible, mechanical rules in preference to contextual standards requiring discretion and subjectivity in their application.[108]

The succession of television images that framed *Bush v. Gore* inflamed that commitment. More than simply bring us the story of the case, it necessarily shaped the Court's understanding of the stakes involved and its ultimate holding that the Florida court's December 8 order—and the disorder it unleashed—violated the Fourteenth Amendment's equal protection clause. Recall the televised close-ups that became the enduring legacy of the entire dispute—the close-ups of election officials holding partly perforated ballots up to the light, squinting to see what dents or holes or hanging chads they might detect and quarreling over how to tally those ballots in the presidential race. For those exposed to this dizzying, almost intoxicating, barrage of images accompanied by punchy scrolling text lines, it quickly became axiomatic that ballots identical in appearance might end up being counted differently in different counties or in the same county at different times. In breathlessly conducted litigation with unheard-of deadlines, crowding what would normally be six weeks of briefing and months of judicial reflection into a matter of days, those pictures were worth not thousands, but tens of thousands, of words.

SIX DIMENSIONS OF THE SEEN AND UNSEEN

Invisible History

But there were a number of crucial dimensions the TV screen couldn't show. The first consists of the unique histories lying behind the similar-looking ballots that the election canvassers visually inspected on camera; it further explains why uniform statewide rules would necessarily introduce their own distinct inequalities. In any given county, unusually many of the punch-card voting machines might be outdated or in poor repair; or the chads might have been cleared out less recently than the statewide norm; or more of the voters might be elderly or frail; or voting instructions, which the law required to have been printed in Spanish *and* English, may have been written in English only—as was the case in Osceola County, with a 29 percent Hispanic population.[109] For an election canvasser in such a precinct to use a more inclusive standard than the one applied by a canvasser in another precinct, where an identical-looking ballot could have an entirely different history, might be the best way to respect, not violate, the principle of "one person, one vote." Remembering that the goal is "one *person,* one vote," not "one ballot, one vote," is rendered more difficult by the image of the ballot being held in the air and scrutinized with squinted eyes. The voter who cast that ballot, and the story connecting that person to the machine that failed to register that person's vote, must be constructed in the mind's eye.

Florida's highest court plainly recognized how futile, and almost certainly counterproductive, would have been any effort to mechanize, standardize, and ultimately dehumanize the process of assessing from a ballot's appearance what the voter who cast that ballot probably intended. The Supreme Court faulted Florida's highest court for failing to promulgate a rule worthy of a science fiction novel: the very idea that a machine-like algorithm could workably replace human judgment in deciphering machine-rejected ballots depends on breakthroughs in artificial intelligence and computerized pattern-recognition unknown to the modern world.

Imagine, for instance, rigorously enforcing a rule saying a punch card ballot counts only where the chad has been detached on at least two corners. Suppose that, in one county, the ballots were printed on such thick cardboard that no chads were detached on more than a single corner, and most were merely indented. Or suppose that another county found hundreds of ballots with no detachments but with the name *Bush* or *Gore* clearly circled, obviously violating the instructions but making the voter's intent unmistakably clear. Some would reply that, of course, the uniform standards would make exceptions for such cases. This response abandons the quest for objective criteria articulable in advance. The only way to accommodate cases that merit exceptional treatment is to demote the uniform rules to the status of mere guidelines, all to be applied with a dollop of subjective judgment and a pile of common sense.

Even if the county boards' initial choice of recount standards wouldn't always have been well calibrated to each county's relevant characteristics, the supervising state judge would have been there to compel them to take critical variations into account. That task too might have been performed imperfectly, but no more so than the alternative of a one-size-fits-all standard. And the Court offered no rebuttal to Justice Stevens's dissenting observation that the "single impartial magistrate" ordered by the Florida court to supervise the process statewide could best relieve the concerns raised by "differing substandards for determining voter intent." [110] Straining all the multifaceted background facts through one uniformly metered sieve would yield an unequal stream of results, not a stream that flows evenly in accord with "one person, one vote." The equal protection holding of *Bush v. Gore* thus preserves at best the surface *appearance* of equality, a common feature of the Rehnquist Court's jurisprudence. [111] And the Court's evident assumption that this surface appearance is what it takes "to sustain the confidence that all citizens must have in the outcome of elections," [112] while characteristic, reflects a sorry view indeed of politics and of the American electorate. [113]

Yet some commentators and advocates not only buy into this surface vision of equality, they see it as the *only* constitutional alternative. In his brief for the Florida legislature, [114] for example, Professor Charles Fried suggested that the "intent of the voter" standard is "capacious and unconstraining," and so "vague and devoid of guidance as to invite arbitrary or discriminatory treatment." [115] Professor Fried concluded that "there must be narrow, objective and definite standards governing the exercise of official discretion," [116] and that state election codes must adopt only those procedures capable of mechanical and nondiscretionary application. Although appealing in its elegant simplicity, that argument reifies the ballot—which is, after all, only the *means* of voting—and in so doing appears to lose sight of the *end:* An election is not a test of the electorate's ability to follow directions, but a process whose goal is to determine the aggregate preferences of all voters. Assuming an eligible voter makes an apparently good-faith effort to comply with reasonable voting procedures, the only justifiable basis for excluding a vote is that the voter's intent cannot be determined, or that efforts to determine it would prove impracticable. Any number of voters might, on any given Election Day, leave an infinite variety of indentations, or marks in pencil or ink, with stylus on a punch card, or with other methods not much discussed in the popular press.[117] The resulting indented squares or hanging chads can in many cases clearly reveal the voter's intent in the context of the entire ballot and against the backdrop of the particular polling place. Ballots of which this can be said should not be excluded solely because the voter behind the ballot did not follow each word of the instructions as if it were gospel.

Professor Fried's argument would suggest that, in a jurisdiction whose rules tell voters to "punch all the way through," a ballot with only a dimpled chad and the following note should be rejected: *Vote tabulators, please take notice: I tried and tried to punch this damn thing all the way through in the Bush column for president, but no matter how hard I tried, the stylus just wouldn't poke through. But know this: I meant to, and attempted to, vote for George W. Bush for president.*[118] Failing to count such a vote when one encounters it in a manual recount seems altogether arbitrary. Examples like this show that there is something otherworldly about the whole idea of reducing the vote-tallying process to one from which all discretionary judgments are banished in a futile attempt to prohibit partisan fudging and cheating. Such a project would not only require eliminating all manual counting, including manual processing of overseas and other absentee ballots; it would also seem to require us to tolerate an ocean full of disenfranchisement to prevent a teacup full of fraud. Whatever else may be said of such a venture, it surely cannot be mandated by the Constitution.

A Comedy of Errors

A second dimension flattened into obscurity by the TV screen is the reality that election officials can err in at least two diametrically opposed directions: They can wrongly fail to count a vote that someone intended to cast as such; or they can wrongly attribute a vote to someone who either intended to cast no vote at all or intended to cast a vote for an opposing candidate. Machines can do that too, of course—as they did to the Palm Beach citizens who intended to vote for Gore and who unwittingly became "Buchanan supporters." And, in just the same way, an error during a manual recount can turn a "none of the above" voter into a phantom supporter of one of the leading candidates ("false inclusion"), or can turn a supporter of either of those candidates into an imaginary supporter of the other ("false reversal"), or can turn someone who intended to vote for one of those two into a "no vote" statistic ("false exclusion"). The inevitable and yet unpredictable nature and distribution of these errors makes it impossible to treat differences in recount standards as though they neatly correspond to differing degrees of accuracy in discovering previously uncounted votes.[119] The Court erred when it implied that the use of a more stringent recount standard in Palm Beach County had violated the "one person, one vote" principle by diluting the votes of people in Palm Beach relative to the votes of people in counties with "more forgiving standard[s]."[120] For the Court was wrong to assume that Broward County's recovery of "almost three times as many new votes" as Palm Beach County recovered, "a result markedly disproportionate to the difference in population between the counties," somehow translated into a higher rate of disenfranchisement for Broward County voters.[121] In reality, no such equation is possible.

The Untold Story of the Underlying Count

The third dimension absent alike from the TV images and the Court's opinion was an absolutely crucial comparative analysis. All seven justices who saw or suggested equal protection problems in the recount process simply assumed that they could validly put to one side, and relegate to another day and another lawsuit, the multitude of errors and inequities that were visible on no screen but that made a mockery of the underlying vote count leading to the November 26 certification of Bush as the winner by just 537 votes out of over *six million* cast. Many believe that simple prudence dictated decisive Supreme Court action, blowing the whistle without further ado, however rickety a theoretical justification the Court could cobble together in the time available. But any such theory has to assume the *underlying* vote count is entitled to be treated as at least comparatively reliable despite all the flaws in the process generating it—including ample opportunities on the part of state and local officials to tailor the processing of voters, and the handling of both live and absentee ballots, to the latest reports from East Coast broadcasters of how the election was going, keeping in mind how those officials' adoption of one practice rather than another might shape the outcome—and despite the equally obvious likelihood that adjusting the underlying count with the results of the recount, *whether with its supposed flaws or with the state being given time to correct them,* would at least yield a *more* reliable determination of who won.

To offer a few telling examples: Florida law unambiguously mandated at least one initial recount in all sixty-seven counties because the vote totals in the initial count came within half of one percent of each other.[122] Yet eighteen of Florida's counties *did no such recount.*[123] And there's no doubt that other differences among the counties, many of which were understood to be positively correlated with socioeconomic status and thus with likely ethnic background and political affiliation, rendered the initial count not only less reliable than Florida law required but also less than politically and racially neutral in the distribution of error rates. Thus, for example, far more ballots were rejected in the twenty-four punch-card counties (3.9 percent) than in the twenty-four optical-scan counties with second-chance capability (0.6 percent),[124] in the fifteen optical-scan counties without second-chance capability, the rejection rate was highest of all (5.7 percent).[125] Minority voters were roughly *ten times* as likely not to have their votes correctly counted in this election as were nonminority voters;[126] and that's to say nothing of the obstacles that prevented minority voters from even obtaining a ballot that anyone *could* count. In some of the forty-one optical-scan counties, ballots had been counted as valid in the initial counting process even when voters simply checked or circled a candidate's name;[127] other counties had excluded all ballots that were not machine-readable.[128] Moreover, eleven counties used the infamous butterfly ballot (Palm Beach) or some other confusing form of wraparound ballot that *no* amount of recounting could translate into a vote mirroring the voters' actual intent.[129] Yet only Justice Ginsburg's dissent put the logically crucial *comparative* question: What was there in the Court's opinion or in the dissenting opinions of Justices Souter or Breyer that demonstrated "that the recount adopted by the Florida court, flawed as it may be, would yield a result any less fair or precise than the certification that preceded the recount?"[130] The inescapable answer is: Nothing.

Nor is it enough, in response, to extol the possible virtues of decentralized decision-making with respect to the choice of how much to spend on better voting equipment, as Justices Souter and Breyer may have supposed.[131] *First,* any interest in localism that the Court or those agreeing with its equal protection holding deem cognizable with respect to differences in underlying voting mechanisms, ballot designs, or automatic recount practices should be no less cognizable with respect to differences in how ballots were to be recounted under the December 8 order. There is no mystical difference between the count and the recount for equal protection purposes. If there were, it would be a nice question how to classify the automatic recount mandated by Florida law but actually undertaken in just 49 of Florida's counties in this election. *Second,* the fact that the decision to decentralize decision-making with respect to the underlying vote was the *legislature's* is irrelevant, since we've already seen that the Florida court's recount order derived from the legislation enacted to discharge the state's duty under Article II.

A "ONE-TIME-ONLY" EQUAL PROTECTION OFFER

In any event, the inequities marring the underlying vote count and the election certification embodying it cannot so simply be swept under a rug emblazoned with the motto, *Another problem for another day.* Because a presidential election cannot be rerun after its flaws have been extinguished, *to strike down the recount is to uphold the count itself.* Talk of the "fundamental right of each voter" cannot be permitted to obscure that what is at stake is *the aggregation of votes into a single result.* Yet, as we've seen, the Court obscured just that, obsessing over the arrangement of deck chairs rather than on the plight of the *Titanic* itself. At the end of the day, the Court offered only one justification for not asking whether the state court's recount order would yield an outcome less fair or precise than the certification *preceding* that outcome (or than the certification produced by uniform statewide standards) might yield: An unsatisfying suggestion that "the problem of equal protection in election processes generally presents many complexities" supposedly absent when one focuses on "the minimum procedures necessary to protect the fundamental right of each voter in the special instance of a statewide recount under the authority of a single state judicial officer."[132]

If the Court is successful in limiting its equal protection rationale to "the present circumstances," [133] it will have effectively precluded *Bush v. Gore* from having any significant precedential value. Not only are elections that fall within the margin of error for vote counts extremely rare, but advances in vote-counting technology, spurred in large part by this past election, will hopefully make the chad a thing of the past. Since a similar scenario may never again arise, the legal effect of *Bush v. Gore* could be a virtual nullity, despite the best efforts of voting rights advocates to leverage it into a brave new world of voter equality. [134]

Many see this attempt to limit the case all but to its precise facts as profoundly illegitimate. [135] In so doing, these critics argue, the Court was trying to free itself from the discipline of stare decisis, which forces a court to eat its own words in future cases or else give good reasons why it is spitting them out. Whenever a real court renders a decision, these commentators argue, that decision must have precedential effect. It is no good for a court to employ reasoning that resembles a one-way, nonrefundable railroad ticket, good for *this* day and *this* destination only. [136] These objections to *Bush v. Gore* depict the decision as so unprincipled and result-driven as to be less than true adjudication. Not only was the Court's chosen candidate installed in office, but it wouldn't have to bother with annoying new civil rights lawsuits premised on its equal protection "reasoning." By ushering in a new president and then dispensing with the reasoning by which it reached that result, the Court effectively had its cake and ate it too. "President, yes; precedent, no" is no formula for adjudication.

Yet the question of what precedential value to accord an opinion is nearly always a matter of degree, and the Court is often criticized most sternly for rendering decisions that roam too far beyond the facts at hand, [137] supposedly "legislating from the bench" when announcing broad holdings like those requiring certain warnings during any custodial interrogation [138] or restricting state regulation of abortion procedures more severely before fetal viability than after. [139] In fairness, the Court's critics can't expect to have it both ways.

Nonetheless, a decision limited to a set of circumstances only by a "principle" that is so internally incoherent as to be meaningless or so internally inconsistent as to "imply" anything and therefore nothing[140] may well be indistinguishable from a decision literally limited to its own unique set of facts and hence indistinguishable from a wholly unprincipled adjudication—an exercise of power judicial in name only. Although *Bush v. Gore* might be thought to fit that category, that its purported limits are wholly irrational, rather than simply indefensible, is more than I wish to claim of a line that struck seven justices as at least intuitively plausible—and more than I need to show in order to condemn what the Court did as profoundly wrong.

The Due Process Plight of the Beleaguered Ballot

How could so deeply flawed and problematic an equal protection claim have prevailed? Answering that question exposes a fourth dimension of the problem: Part of the intuitive appeal and rhetorical force of the equal protection claim was the ease with which the elusive concept of "one person, one vote" could be applied to distinct constitutional interests. Proponents conflated two different ways of thinking about equal protection into one slippery amoeba of "equality under law" capable of oozing back and forth between the architectural or *systemic* value of assuring that election systems do not dilute the influence of any *discernable group of voters,* and the quite distinct *individualistic* value of procedural fairness to *each voter* regardless of the comparative weight of votes between various groups or communities.

The Court's December 11 per curiam opinion is perched unsteadily on the cusp between an overview of the electorate as a whole and a focus on the imagined individual voter. Much of the opinion's work is done by borrowing doctrinal imagery from each realm in order to shore up the inadequacy of the argument in the other. Thus, according to the Court, the absence of objective, uniform rules "has led to unequal evaluation of ballots in various respects," in which "standards for accepting or rejecting contested ballots might vary not only from county to county but indeed within a single county from one recount team to another."[141] The Court's verbal sketch is designed to conjure individual *persons* being deprived, one at a time, of something to which they are entitled. Meanwhile, the Court depicts *ballots* as though they *are* persons in their own right, grouped and counted according to criteria that deliberately risk diluting their weight should they happen to be cast in counties adopting more restrictive measures of inclusion. The per curiam opinion departs almost entirely from the "one person, one vote" decisions in the Court's canon, dismissing the concern that *Bush v. Gore* did not involve *grouping* voters, by geography or otherwise,[142] with an insistence that the right to equal protection belongs to individual voters, not to groups.

Excuse me? Has not the Rehnquist Court insisted that *no process at all is constitutionally due* to an individual unless the state's law first confers some positive *entitlement*—such as a job held with tenure—that the state itself has promised the individual will not lose absent some specified cause?[143] The *Bush v. Gore* majority faulted Florida for failing to provide something that the Rehnquist Court has held countless times is not required by due process: The conversion of the individual voter's undoubted *interest* in having her vote counted so long as her ballot clearly indicates her intent, into a full-fledged *entitlement* to trial-like evaluation of her ballot through the application of objective criteria that the state has never supplied and that nothing in the Rehnquist Court's arsenal of due process decisions even begins to suggest. Admittedly, such "objective" criteria formulated by the state's highest court might reduce the room for partisan manipulation. But so might whatever criteria the state court's supervisory magistrate would employ. Besides, partisan considerations could just as easily enter into the state supreme court's selection of (supposedly objective) criteria for various types of ballots—a selection that six justices thought would overcome all constitutional objections.

That selection would face yet another constitutional objection from the five authors of the per curiam opinion if it failed to include those *overvotes*[144] that were left out of the Florida court's December 8 recount order. That opinion faulted the recount because "three counties were not limited to so-called undervotes but extended to all of the ballots,"[145] thus treating overvotes in those counties differently from overvotes elsewhere. Perhaps more importantly, a standard that excluded overvotes generally would harm "overvoters" vis-à-vis all "undervoters" in the state,[146] and of course would do the same with respect to "the citizen who marks two candidates, only one of which is discernable by the machine, [who] will have his vote counted even though it should have been read as an invalid ballot."[147]

These putative overvote violations highlight the Court's own errors throughout its per curiam opinion, which focused on saving a tree while burning down the forest. First, while it may be true that *three* counties' *recounts* included overvotes, it is also true that *thirty-four* counties examined overvotes for mistakes *during the original machine count* and subsequently included, in their initial vote tallies, overvotes that revealed the voter's intent.[148] The Court tried to have it both ways despite this fact, but if the three counties erred by including their overvotes, then surely the thirty-four counties erred as well. And if the Constitution requires the recount to be invalided because of selective inclusion, then the initial count must be invalidated on *exactly the same* grounds. But the majority had already elided a true examination of the underlying differences among county voting machines; it was thus no surprise that it zeroed in on an overvote "problem" that could be detected only in the shadow of the larger equal protection problems the Court itself would go on to create.

In fact, the per curiam did not even notice the reflection of the overvote issue in the mirror of its own narrow holding. The Court saw an equal protection violation because overvotes were treated differently from undervotes. But, taking the Court on its own terms, a recount standard that *uniformly* excludes overvotes should be perfectly constitutional—every overvote is treated the same as every other.[149] Instead, the Court seemed to suggest that overvotes have some positive right to be counted—that, because *some* dimpled chads are considered under positive law, dimpled chads on *overvotes* must receive that same consideration. But this line of argument leads to an absurd conclusion: Voting jurisprudence would no longer be one person, one vote; or even one ballot, one vote; but one *dimple,* one vote. Each mark would have to be given the same treatment on any ballot where it appeared— to avoid denying due process to *that mark.* But it makes no sense to say "a dimple is a dimple is a dimple" when a dimple next to two punched-through holes may not mean nearly as much as a dimple next to two other merely dimpled chads.

Because, in any event, the positive law of Florida expressly precluded counting any overvotes,[150] no Florida voter can complain that overvotes were not counted—at least not without raising a substantive right to have one's vote properly counted whenever one's intent was clear. And that standard, after all—as adopted by the Florida legislature and approved by the Florida Supreme Court—is the very one overturned by the Supreme Court's per curiam decision on what turned out to be the real "election day."

The Catch-22: Changing the Rules Midway Through the Game

Even if one felt comfortable with the majority's equal protection amoeba, a fifth dimension would remain. As the Court could not deny, the Florida Supreme Court's December 8 recount order, in directing all the canvassing boards to apply the statute's general intent standard, carried out the electoral ground rules that the Florida legislature put in place before election day. Whatever might be said for enforcing some sort of bright-line rule for recounting ballots, the text, context, and history of Florida's election code make plain that the Florida legislature opted for an "intent of the voter" standard instead. Recall the insistent rallying cry against the Florida court: Article II plus the safe harbor statute make the rules laid down by each state legislature *prior to the election* the binding guide for choosing presidential electors. But the "fix" proposed by the Court and by Justices Souter and Breyer—in which newly promulgated uniform statewide criteria for counting votes would, time permitting, govern the recount process—would obviously require adopting *new* rules after Election Day. So there is an irreducible, if little-noted, clash between the universally accepted importance of judging an election's results in accord with standards and methods adopted in advance, and the equal protection theory that attracted seven justices.

Ballots as Castaways

After its unjustifiably narrow focus on the constitutional defects in the December 8 court-ordered recount, and despite all its talk about the "minimum procedures" that must be followed in such "special instance[s]" to preserve the "fundamental rights" of individual voters,[151] the Court devised a remedy that sent the *Titanic*'s deck chairs—on whose salvaging the Court had so myopically focused—down with the ship. The sixth dimension eluding both the television cameras and the Court's radar screen was the invisible spectacle of literally thousands of ballots being jettisoned into oblivion when the Court ordered the recount to stop before all legal votes could be counted.

The Court's only justification for *ending* the recount rather than at least allowing the Florida court to *try* fashioning a remedy for the alleged defects in its December 8 order was the state's supposed interest in finality. Not exactly second-guessing the state's highest court on the meaning of state law, the Court in essence pre-guessed it by claiming it had to defer to the state court's "holding" that the Florida legislature wished to ensure Florida could "participat[e] fully in the federal election process," [152] and "therefore" would opt for a December 12 deadline, whatever the cost in uncounted votes. But the "therefore" didn't follow, and the Florida court, never having been asked, had never held December 12 to be a firm legislative deadline.[153]

Chief Justice Rehnquist's concurrence argued that, in conferring power specifically on the *state legislature,* Article II in any event limited the degree to which the Court could properly defer to the state judiciary's reading of the state's election code.[154] But the concurring opinion's "independent" analysis of Florida's election statutes led it to conclude that, given the benefits of resolving all election contests in time to fit within the federal safe harbor, the Florida legislature, in empowering state courts to grant "appropriate" relief, "*must have meant* relief that would have become final by" December 12.[155] That meant the Florida court had violated Article II by ordering a recount on December 8 that could not possibly have been completed by the deadline, leading the chief justice to conclude that the November 26 certification of Bush as the winner by 537 votes[156] had to stand as the final result.[157]

That dog won't hunt. You can read the Florida statutes backwards and forwards without finding the slightest *clue* that the state legislature ever decreed all recounts in a contested presidential election must stop by December 12. For that matter, nowhere does the legislature indicate that recounts must stop at any time before the electors meet to vote on December 18 or before Congress counts the votes on January 6. And nothing hints the Florida legislature had ever considered—much less resolved—what to do when confronted with a trade-off between the safe harbor benefits and those of counting all legal votes. Particularly unreal is the suggestion that the legislature that enacted the 1999 election contest provision involved in *Bush v. Gore* preferred, much less mandated, that the safe harbor's advantages trump the imperative of counting every legal vote. For that legislature's members were, with few exceptions, the same as those of the Florida legislature in 2000— and *that* legislature was notoriously poised on December 11 to name its own electoral slate committed to Bush *after* the December 12 deadline had passed,[158] apparently with the Court's blessing.[159]

It required no genius to ascertain that, all other things being equal, Florida's legislature wanted its electors to be counted in the national tally, but there was no way any court could extract a firm December 12 deadline from the legislature's obvious wish to have the state's 25 electoral votes counted.[160] For one thing, concluding all election contests by that safe harbor date wouldn't in any event guarantee that Congress would honor the promise made by the 1887 Congress in the Safe Harbor Act.[161] And, as Justice Ginsburg's dissent noted without rebuttal, the 1887 statute under which the January 6 count was to be conducted contained later deadlines and alternative ways of getting an electoral slate bulletproofed for the congressional count.[162] All anyone can say with certainty is that if *anything* made Florida ineligible for the safe harbor, it wasn't the Florida court's December 8 recount order, but the *Supreme Court's* December 9 decision to stay that order and halt the recount. That stay guaranteed Florida couldn't possibly produce by December 12 any final resolution *using the rules and procedures in place on November 7.*[163]

Even if the Court were correct that its ending the recount would have allowed Florida's electors, as certified on November 26, to sail right into Congress's safe harbor, the Court's own criteria would have rendered unconstitutional any reading of either state or federal statutes to mandate this purchase of electoral security at the price of ditching into the sea thousands of ballots, many of which clearly expressed a voter's intent but didn't happen to get machine-counted. As Justice Stevens tellingly noted in dissent, the five-member unsigned majority had accepted Florida's definition that "all ballots that reveal the intent of the voter constitute valid votes."[164] Under the *Court's own reasoning,* then, the Fourteenth Amendment would preclude any legislative or judicial determination to put the state's interest in finality above the rights of those voters to have *all* of their ballots counted. As the Supreme Court itself had told the Florida high court: "The press of time does not diminish the constitutional concern."[165] And it would be question-begging to say that the rights of *all* the voters, including those whose ballots would never be counted, would be safeguarded by shielding from challenge the electors certified on November 26—because, of course, the Court's decision destroyed any such shield and, besides, the whole question was whether counting the remaining ballots would have shown that the wrong electors had been certified!

The Court's emphasis on the supposed interest in finality, and its decision allowing that interest to trump all other constitutional concerns, disregarded a central point: although we often think of an election as a single "event," to which we must turn our attention on "Election Day," it in fact involves an ongoing *process*. Even in a "normal" election, that process begins well before the media-hyped "day," when absentee ballots begin to pour in; continues on the West Coast for some three hours after the polls close in the East; and does not end until much later, after all of the absentee ballots have been counted. For not until every legal vote is included do we have the "actual" result. Presidential elections last even longer, for even after the polls close, even after the absentee ballots come in, even after the electors vote, Congress ultimately has the final say. We often think of Congress's counting of the electoral votes as just ceremonial because it usually *is,* in practical terms, a mere formality. Rarely is any election so close that tabulating the absentee ballots might actually put a different candidate in office. Even rarer are presidential elections so close that the slate of electors the House and Senate select to represent a single state could prove pivotal. But election 2000 *was* that close, and the Court's decision to end it before the process had run its course drew an imaginary—but devastating—line between the "count" of November 7 and the "recounts" thereafter, demanding a surface equality of appearance in the latter while actively tolerating a genuine inequality of opportunity in the former.

It is surely not enough to say in defense of *Bush v. Gore* that almost any judicial ruling involves line-drawing and that, although one can disagree over where the cut should be made, the Court's solution—to require equality in the recount process, but not in the underlying count—was as plausible as any other. For the Court decreed an election outcome that transmuted the underlying count into a presidency and, in the process of so doing, *created* divisions—between the count and recount; between December 12 and December 18; between December 18 and January 6—where in fact none existed in the real world. Each was one stage of a continuous process that did not end (and *could not* end in a constitutional sense) until Congress had tabulated the votes of the electors. The Supreme Court, in drawing its imagined count/recount line, not only ignored the partisan influences[166] and inevitable inequalities[167] that shape the process at *every* stage, but also forgot that political reality does not carve up that process into distinct segments. Thus, the "line" along which *Bush v. Gore* would have us divide the electoral world turns out not to be a *line* at all but a mirage. Deciding what belongs on one side of it and what belongs on the other is rather like asking whether a postulated "line" is heavier than a rock is long.[168]

Surreal is the only word for the Court's decision to stop the counting at a point when the pending election contest could no longer be resolved by December 12—a decision that arbitrarily distinguished among ballots all of which reflected legal votes the machines missed but only some of which had the good fortune to be counted before the Court called "time" in the name of a constitutional pronouncement with no basis in the rules or principles in place on Election Day, committing the very sins the justices accused the Florida court of committing. One need only peer past the hall of mirrors to glimpse the irony verging on hypocrisy behind *Bush v. Gore*'s judicial facade.

The Mystery of the Court's "Unsought Responsibility"

Are we expected, then, to overlook these gaping flaws in the Court's argument just because of the insufficiency of the record and the time pressures under which the Court's "unsought responsibility,"[169] as its opinion puts it, forced it to work? *Unsought responsibility?* Please! The Court talks as though, simply because the "contending parties invoke[d] the [judicial] process," it had *no choice* but "to resolve the federal and constitutional issues [it] ha[d] been *forced* to confront."[170] But cases abound in which the Court, extolling the virtues of abstention or avoidance, has let a cup laced with far less poison than this pass from its lips. It is insult enough for the nation to be lectured about "the vital limits on judicial authority," and to be told that "[n]one are more conscious of [those] limits . . . than are the members of this Court,"[171] in a case where the Court has reached out to grant discretionary review—and has then said not a word to explain why *it*, rather than Congress, is the proper decision-maker. But asking the nation to endure that lecture from a Court boasting that "none stand more in admiration" than it does "of the Constitution's design to leave the selection of the president to the people, through their legislatures, and to the political sphere,"[172] pours salt in the wound.

Precisely what *is* the Court's justification—even assuming, counterfactually, that its ruling on the merits had been defensible—for first interrupting, and then bringing to a close, the national conversation that became *Bush v. Gore* before the matter could reach Congress? Florida Chief Justice Wells, dissenting from the 4–3 recount order of December 8, quoted a mathematician's view that the "margin of error in this election is far greater than the margin of victory, no matter who wins."[173] With every recount, the state would emerge with just another conclusion, not necessarily any closer to the truth. Given the futility of identifying an unambiguous winner, the game wasn't worth the candle. Worse, "prolonging [the] judicial process in this counting contest propels this country . . . into an unprecedented and unnecessary constitutional crisis" that "will do substantial damage to our country, our state, and to this Court as an institution."[174] That's not a bad approximation of the most sophisticated of the published defenses of what the Supreme Court *did*, if not of what it *said*, in agreeing to review *Bush v. Gore*, issuing its stay, and then bringing the election to a close on December 12.

The Supreme Court was less forthright than Chief Justice Wells but appears to have had much the same end in view. But exactly what "crisis" it feared remains mysterious. I part from the cynics who are confident that the "crisis" the Court was determined to avert was a Gore presidency. Had the Court cared only about blocking Gore's victory, it would probably have calculated, based on what was known at the time, that it could safely let the December 8 recount continue. If that recount emerged with a victory for Bush, that would have ended the matter. If it instead emerged with what Florida's highest court was prepared to certify as a Gore victory, there was every indication that the Florida legislature stood ready to certify a slate of Bush electors, something the Court's December 12 opinion strongly (and carelessly) suggested the state legislature could properly do at any time.[175] Only the Court would have been in a position to stop the state legislature from construing its constitutional mandate more broadly, and the Court must have known that it could simply have declined to enjoin the state legislature when it certified Bush the winner.

Had the Supreme Court opted for that course—which would in essence have recognized that breaking the virtual tie in Florida was a nonjusticiable "political question" textually committed to Congress under the Twelfth Amendment rather than the sort of legal question properly resolved by a court created under Article III of the Constitution—the odds were great that Bush would still emerge victorious. The 1887 Electoral Count Act contained a labyrinthine procedure by which the Congress that would convene on January 6 was to resolve disputes over election results in contested states and was to break any remaining ties. It's true that even that procedure, untested during the 114 years it had been in place, was shadowed by constitutional doubt over the power of one Congress to bind its successors in such matters.[176] But, even so, the relative power of the Republicans and Democrats in the Congress that would do the counting made it likely that, in the end, Bush would have emerged the winner.

It bears noting here that the technical legal case for treating the matter as a "political question" was particularly powerful. The requisite textual commitment to a political branch could hardly be clearer.[177] And the appearance of impropriety, even conflict of interest, attaching to the spectacle of five justices deciding who will name their own successors was unmistakable. After all, the same Court had identified a similar but less extreme appearance of impropriety and conflict as one reason to treat the impeachment and removal of federal judges as a political question committed to Congress and hence unreviewable by the Courts.[178]

That leaving the matter to Congress looked like a fairly secure way to hand the election to Bush underscores the fact that the Court's dramatic intervention need not have reflected a wish to assure a Bush presidency (and hence to secure the almost incestuous appointment of like-minded successors to the Court), but could well have reflected nothing beyond dismay at the very processes that lay ahead regardless of their result, including a wish to have the presumed Bush succession unmarred by what Justice Scalia described—in an opinion accompanying the December 9 decision of a bare majority of the Court to issue a stay—as "a cloud upon . . . the legitimacy of [Bush's] election." [179]

What cloud?

Presumably, it was the cloud the majority thought implicit in the very knowledge of ever more apparent (but, by the Court's lights, illegal) votes for Gore, perhaps even enough to overturn the razor-thin edge then held by Bush. But that concern seems irreconcilable with the First Amendment, for the Court could set the record straight later by announcing that the recounted "votes" had not been tallied in a lawful manner should that be its ultimate conclusion, and the freedoms of speech and press plainly prevent government from suppressing information lying at the political core of free expression on the theory that the minds of adult citizens would be so polluted by learning of it that no subsequent refutation could undo the "harm."

Had the Court stayed out of the whole controversy, leaving the ultimate resolution to Congress, it would of course have forsaken the ability to clear away the impression (which it thought false) that the "votes" recounted for Gore were actually *legal* votes. Chief Justice Rehnquist would still, in all likelihood, be swearing in George W. Bush as the forty-third president, but only after a messy and unsettling bout of politics, and with a cloud of pro-Gore pseudo-numbers raining on his inaugural parade—and perhaps shadowing his presidency beyond the Court's ability to correct. Avoiding that scenario seems the best account of what the Court was up to. In essence, it made a deliberate decision to short-circuit the elaborate set of political processes that otherwise lay ahead.

A Herculean Pretension [180]

What can have seemed so distressing about those processes? One can only surmise that, to five justices, images of ballots across the state being counted in front of a nationwide TV audience—images that, for many others, conjured thrilling memories of the voting-rights struggles of decades past—must have brought to mind instead dismaying thoughts of chaos, partisan manipulation, and mob rule. And the spectacle of Congress sorting out the mess at the end probably seemed no more reassuring. Anything so visibly threatening to stability, good order, the established hierarchy, and stately decorum qualified as a "crisis" this Court had jurisdiction to halt. Never mind about the partisan maneuvering, less open and visible but no less real, that had led to the radical maldistribution of reliable voting machines and methods among Florida's sixty-seven counties, or about such other less apparent sources of inequality and political favoritism as the subjective and variable standard for deciding which absentee ballots to accept. *Those* machinations evidently seemed to the Court part *of* the stable order to be preserved, not a threat *to* it.

Understanding *Bush v. Gore* in this light requires a candid recognition of the Rehnquist Court's staggering confidence in its own ability to define and prioritize values of constitutional magnitude, and to decide which measures are needed to realize them. Low on that list of values is an energized, politicized electorate engaged in such democratic business as the election of a president. The Court's self-confidence is matched only by its disdain for the meaningful participation of other actors in constitutional debate. Thus, despite the case that many[181] have made for giving Congress substantial latitude in defining constitutional terms for purposes of exercising its power to enforce the Fourteenth Amendment,[182] the Court has been rigidly doctrinaire in dismissing out of hand any such pluralistic approach to constitutional interpretation and enforcement,[183] striking down in rapid succession key provisions of the Religious Freedom Restoration Act,[184] the Patent Reform Act,[185] the Trademark Remedy Clarification Act,[186] the Age Discrimination in Employment Act,[187] and the Americans with Disabilities Act.[188] In so doing, the Court has repeatedly concluded that Congress failed either by going beyond what *it* regarded as the *only correct* understanding of Fourteenth Amendment rights or, having hewed to the Court's understanding, by taking more far-reaching steps than the Court deemed necessary.

One more example should suffice. The joint 1992 opinion of Justices O'Connor, Kennedy, and Souter, reaffirming the core of *Roe v. Wade*[189] in *Planned Parenthood of Pennsylvania v. Casey,*[190] is an opinion that, for the most part, I admire as one of the Court's most eloquent explications of liberty and equality. However, the impatience of the authors with dissent from their wisdom was starkly evident in their announcement that retreating from a decision as basic as *Roe* would betray those who had cast their lot with the

Court, calling into doubt the legitimacy of that august tribunal as the oracle of last resort on fundamental national matters. Unbelievably, the Court insisted that even more was stake: "If the Court's legitimacy should be undermined, then, so would the country be in its very ability to see itself through its constitutional ideals. The Court's concern with legitimacy is not for the sake of the Court, but for the sake of the Nation to which it is responsible." [191] Evidently, far from being the "least dangerous" branch, the Court turns out to be the one truly indispensable branch: without it, sadly, we would have no one to define our "constitutional ideals" for us (especially given that the Court flatly refuses to let any other branch even help out with the task). Such an "unsought responsibility" must be an awfully heavy load to bear, for, as Justice Kennedy put the matter to a reporter in his chambers just before the Court announced its decision in *Casey*, it is hard for a justice in his position to know "if you're Caesar about to cross the Rubicon or Captain Queeg cutting your own tow line." [192]

The Forgotten "Rule of Law": The Political Question Doctrine

Given that set of attitudes, the Court's sense that its destiny was to intervene—to take the hit to its short-term reputation, if need be—need not have been driven by fear that the nation was about to go over some constitutional precipice. For this Court, incentive enough was provided by the spectacle of perhaps another week of state and local officials holding ballots up to the light and squinting to get a better view of dimpled chads or of partial perforations, followed by posturing and horse-trading in Congress—images that doubtless struck the *Bush v. Gore* majority as the very antithesis of the rule of law. To those for whom, in Justice Scalia's phrase, "the rule of law is the law of rules," [193] the fact that the rules laid down in this case—by the Twelfth Amendment, by Congress in 1887, and by the Florida legislature as its words had been reasonably construed by Florida's highest court—would appear to have invited this boisterous political brawl must have seemed an oversight by the framers, deserving of no particular respect.

The political incentives were aligned too powerfully in favor of decisive Supreme Court intervention to bring closure to an election that had already overstayed its welcome as the Christmas season neared—even if that meant distrusting the people and insulting democracy. And for a Court that believes its own press, having absorbed the TV image of a tribunal above the fray that alone can speak with authority about the Constitution, nothing could have seemed more natural.

Creating Constitutional Dialogue

But there is another vision of the Court's proper relation to democracy, a vision in which the order the Court sought by *avoiding* politics is instead the *work* of politics, in which order is *earned* rather than *decreed*. When the Court proclaimed the unconstitutionality of racial segregation in public schools,[194] it entered into a still-ongoing dialogue with the political branches, and particularly with Congress,[195] recognizing that a sweeping declaration of principle was all the nation could handle in a single gulp. And when the Court ordered President Nixon to turn over the tapes sought by the Watergate special prosecutor for use in a pending criminal trial,[196] it was engaged in facilitating, not circumventing, the opportunity of the political branches—the executive, in pursuing a criminal prosecution; Congress, in conducting its impeachment hearings—to carry on their constitutionally defined roles.

In this other vision of the Court's proper role vis-à-vis political action, Congress is less to be feared than challenged; it may or may not rise to the occasion, with ordinary politicians winning for themselves a measure of respect. Who knows but that a kind of bipartisanship appropriate to a virtually tied election and to a challenge of historic proportion mightn't have developed in the House and Senate? What if it did not? Well, the meaning of extraordinary challenges encompasses the risk of failure. And, in a democracy, politics exists to be attempted, not circumvented.

Supreme Distraction: The Court's Alleged Extraconstitutional Motive

Some of the most vocal critics of *Bush v. Gore* accuse the Court of an even baser motive: having acted out of sheer partisan zeal and crude self-interest.

In so doing, they have ignored or denied the simplicity and naiveté emblematic of the caricatures they create. Forgetting Dostoevsky's "general rule" that "people, even the wicked, are much more naive and simple-hearted than we suppose" and that "we ourselves are too," [197] these critics act as if they alone possess the shrewd sophistication required to discover the authentic meaning behind why and how the Court did what it did.

But Where's the Pudding?

Commentators determined to attack the Court for the shamefully partisan motives they believe they can prove impelled the five justices in the majority [198] confront an initial difficulty in the fact that the equal protection theory adopted by those five was shared by Justices Souter and Breyer, whom no one could plausibly suspect of being foolish enough to contribute unwittingly to a partisan conspiracy or corrupt enough to go along knowingly.

Apart from the fact that *Bush v. Gore* cannot be deemed comparable to any issue the Court had ever previously confronted—and the fact that, as we have seen, the Court's equal protection theories and its hubris were sadly characteristic of, rather than inconsistent with, the superficial analysis and arrogant stance that had become this Court's signature—the entire strategy of inferring from the supposed novelty of the Court's ruling, or from its alleged inconsistency with past decisions, a corrupt scheme to install Bush in office seems ill-conceived. For the theory rests on a transparent fallacy: If someone is not very smart or thinks he's not being closely watched, then a departure from his usual routine may be cause for suspicion, perhaps even evidence that he's up to no good. But if an actor is very clever and knows that his every step will be dissected by equally clever observers from the moment he acts until historians cease to care, then as nefarious a scheme as pulling off a virtual coup is likely to be covered up by conducting business as usual, not by making conspicuously novel—even unprecedented—moves.

The body of this essay argues that, surface inconsistencies aside, the justices in the *Bush v. Gore* majority acted very much in accord with their previously manifested deeper proclivities. That demonstration, of course, is consistent with the possibility that the action of those justices was overdetermined, being a product *both* of those self-aggrandizing proclivities *and* of a preference for candidate Bush. No doubt, the justices in the majority shared, at a minimum, that baseline preference. But the *role* that this shared preference played in each justice's mind remains ultimately unknowable—probably even to that justice. So I believe these critics to be wrong on both counts: The justices did *not* depart from their modi operandi and, even if they had, that proof would establish nothing remotely close to improper partisan motivation.

Beyond being unknowable, the "real" motives behind *Bush v. Gore* ought to be of no particular interest, notwithstanding our culture's endless preoccupation with discovering what makes people tick. We are not, after all, talking about setting aside a conviction or a judgment awarding a sum of money on the ground that it was procured by fraud or some other form of corruption that requires the result to be undone. Unlike any such judgment, the decision in *Bush v. Gore* that led Gore to concede the election to Bush on December 13, 2000, and that in turn led first the electoral college and then Congress to make Bush president cannot be undone. For this reason, the only truly relevant legal question is whether good and sufficient reasons can be put forth in defense of that judicial decision—not whether, if it *could* be undone, the motives underlying it were so corrupt that such relief would be warranted *whatever* reasons might be advanced in its support.

There is a fundamental, although rarely articulated, distinction between attacking a government action on the basis that its operative effect on particular identified persons is void and should be set aside or otherwise concretely redressed because the government actor was impermissibly motivated, and attacking an action of any branch of government on the basis that its legal consequences for the world at large are so tainted by impermissible motive that it should be deemed a nullity and that anyone addressed by it should be free to disregard it with impunity.[199]

The first kind of attack is routine; we witness it daily in charges that a government employer terminated an individual on a forbidden ground such as race, religion, national origin, gender, sexual orientation, or political philosophy where that individual's job lacks any of the protections of tenure and could thus have been lawfully terminated for no reason at all. If *Bush v. Gore* were, say, a contest between the two gentlemen whose names appear in the caption of that decision—if one had sued the other to collect on an alleged debt arising out of a bet made on the vote spread in the election, for exam-ple—it would be routine to ask whether the judge who ruled, let us assume, for Bush had done so because a Bush partisan had corruptly offered to pay her, or because she had been cochair of the Bush campaign and felt indebted to Bush for appointing her to the federal bench. Proof of such charges might be hard to come by, but no one could say that they were immaterial. And no one could doubt what sort of remedy would be appropriate were such charges established. The tainted ruling would be set aside and the proceed-ing would be conducted afresh.

But *Bush v. Gore* manifestly is not that kind of case. It is a case about the lawfulness of a process put in motion by a state's highest court for concluding that state's part in a national presidential election in which that state's elec-toral votes turned out to be decisive. Attacking the Court's holding that the process was unlawful, or its decision to end the process without allowing the state to correct its mistake, is fair enough. But it becomes an attack of a differ-ent stripe altogether when it is made to turn on *why* the justices ultimately voted as they did—and, in that sense, why the judicial branch of the United States government declared the election at an end. When government does something that alters the legal landscape itself, whether by promulgating a general rule of behavior for the future[200] or by ruling that a legislatively set deadline for counting ballots in a presidential election has arrived, the fact that such an action indisputably has significant effects on *all* of us doesn't suddenly give any *one* of us a basis to overturn that rule or that deadline. We cannot claim a right to behave as though the rule had not been promulgated or the deadline had not yet passed by showing that the motives underlying the rule or ruling were improperly partisan or otherwise shameful.

This is not to say that, as a moral or political matter, when passing judg-ment on those who chose to cast their lot with the *Bush v. Gore* majority, such speculations as to motive are immaterial. For those broader purposes—as in deciding whether the House should impeach a justice and the Senate should remove that justice from office—those speculations may indeed be highly relevant. The principal problem with engaging in the motive inquiry at that level remains the impossibility of ascertaining the relevant motives of any one judge, much less a collective judicial body, with anything approximating the requisite degree of confidence. Moreover, when we are talking not of something relatively straightforward like bribery but of something as elusive as partisan bias, the danger is great that the bias will be as much in the eye of the accuser as in the heart of the accused. And the wound inflicted on the credibility and legitimacy of the entire Court on which the accused sits may be wholly out of proportion to the force of the evidence adduced. Particularly when the accuser's proclaimed motive is to restore a judicial institution's tarnished reputation in order that it may better serve the nation,[201] that is not a wound lightly to be ignored.

For all these reasons, asking whether a justice's vote in *Bush v. Gore* would have been the same had the Democratic and Republican candidates switched sides would be a fool's errand. The search for the "real" motive of any justice's undoubtedly overdetermined vote takes us on a wild-goose chase. And the chase is a harmful one, for in pursuing a truth that cannot be proven—and that, if proven, would not really establish what its proponents seek to establish—the proponents of "bad motive" theories tend to discredit other, more substantive criticisms of *Bush v. Gore* through guilt by association. Every attack on a target that misfires reinforces the belief that the target is undeserving of attack. And that belief, in this case, would be tragically wrong.

The Least Dangerous (Argument)

This brief meditation on why the motive inquiry is an irrelevant distraction may have a valuable spin-off: When a judicial decision spawns an endless fusillade of attacks less on the analysis it contains than on the improper political motive it suggests; when the assaults give no evidence of diminishing over time; and when a virtually surefire predictor of who launches these assaults (as well as who finds them at all persuasive) is whether the attacker or listener was on the losing side of the decision, that should serve as a clue that the underlying question was, by its very nature, one in which legal and political considerations were inextricably intertwined, underlining the probable futility of any attempt to render a legal judgment in a way that will be—and that will be *seen* to be—untainted by improper political motives. Recognizing as much in advance, the Court should perhaps have trusted itself less and the people more. It should have realized that, although those in whose favor it would rule might believe it was driven by law rather than partisan desire, those against whom it would rule would be likely to harbor lasting distrust of the tribunal in which they once placed so much hope.

Had there been no textual basis for saying that the Constitution committed the decision in question to the political branches, one might argue that the Court was nonetheless duty-bound to plunge ahead—although, even then, one should not forget the "passive virtues." [202] But there was, of course, just such a basis—in the language of the Twelfth Amendment and the process it creates for congressional resolution of disputes among competing slates of electors. In these circumstances, given the predictable way the decision was sure to polarize the polity, it becomes painfully clear that the Court should never have entered the thicket at all.

The Exceptionality of *Bush v. Gore*

It would be easy to confuse the refusal to condemn the Court in an ad hominem and *ad feminem* way with a willingness to treat *Bush v. Gore* as just another mistaken decision. But the character of the "mistake" renders the case unique. After all, the Court was deciding a case in which the Constitution's text pointed to an overtly political decision-maker and in which the Court's seizure of authority would determine the outcome of a presidential election—in all likelihood shaping the future of its own composition and thus shaping the law for decades to come. Given how breathtakingly strange it is for *any* judicial body willingly to accept so compromising a conflict of interest, not one major constitutional scholar—not even those of us who for years had been criticizing the Court for its arrogance with respect to matters constitutional—predicted before November 26 that it would intervene. We all sounded *positive* that the Court would sit this one out.

But that was not to be. Instead, the justices took their "unsought responsibility" to a new level and, in so doing, did more than simply defy our predictions. By plunging ahead in the face of such overwhelming institutional reasons to stay out, and by rationalizing its action in such painfully weak terms, the Court seemed to dishonor a legal tradition to which most of us had devoted our lives, leading many of us to question, at least momentarily, our long-held "constitutional faith." [203]

But, of course, the passage of time has assuaged that deep disappointment, and has helped us to recall that "the Court" as an institution is much more than the nine justices who sit on it at any one time. In fact, from the perspective of a teacher of constitutional law, the ruling serves as a tremendously illuminating lens through which to examine the intersection of numerous lines of doctrine and to explore the character of the current Court: Its notion that a political crisis was afoot, that the crisis touched our constitutional order, and that therefore only it could come to the rescue, was of a piece with so much else this Court has done of late that *Bush v. Gore,* for all its drama and absurdity, becomes sadly easy to teach.

Although I have gained perspective on the decision in my role as an instructor of constitutional law, appearing before the Court in the wake of *Bush v. Gore* has been another matter. I did so twice within the several months following the decision.[204] A sense of potential solidarity, of shared pride, that I used to feel each time I got up to argue in that marble building—now more than thirty times in all—seemed to have slipped away, replaced by a grim realism of a sort to which I have not grown—and hope never to grow—entirely accustomed. I had often disagreed with the Court's decisions, sometimes in cases I had argued (most notably, probably, *Bowers v. Hardwick*[205] and *Rust v. Sullivan*[206] as well, of course, as *Timmons v. Twin Cities*[207]), but neither those disagreements, nor the cases where in hindsight I agreed with the Court's rejection of a position I had pressed (*Heffron v. ISKCON*[208] comes to mind), had left me with a strong feeling of disconnection, of alienation from a core enterprise that in significant part defines the Court and its sense of its constitutional role.

Understanding even more clearly the nature of the beast, as it were, could comfort me as an academic. But, given the beast's nature, understanding it more clearly offered cold comfort indeed each time I joined in its enterprise by entering its arena as gladiator rather than as spectator, not simply as an observer and a critic, but as a participant and virtual coconspirator.

Cognitive dissonance has no doubt already done its work both on the dissenting justices and, less importantly, on me. Who, after all, would want to be part of, or to argue in front of, a tribunal whose vision of political reality and of the imperative of democratic participation is so stunted? So one gradually accepts excuses, explanations. I am reminded again that "as a general rule, people, even the wicked, are much more naive and simple-hearted than we suppose." [209] Yes, the tribunal's vision was stunted, but the circumstances were so exigent, so confusing, the advocacy so compromised by the political matrix from which it arose. Maybe. But once all the excuses have been set forth and assimilated, there is likely to remain, for me at least, a sad lump in the throat that will, stubbornly, never go away.

LESSONS FOR THE FUTURE

This isn't to say that I regard the trajectory of judicial attitudes and approaches of which *Bush v. Gore* was a kind of distillate as somehow predestined, with an indefinite series of similar future conservative aggressions by the Court being taken as a given. On the contrary, the eventual meaning of *Bush v. Gore* will depend on contingencies, both political and legal, beyond our current capacity to foretell, not least among them how the Court reconfigured in part by forces *Bush v. Gore* unleashed comes to treat it. My own hope is that future Courts see *Bush v. Gore* as a counsel against judicial intrusion into cases where the Constitution points toward resolution of the dispute by the political branches; where there is no clearly threatened violation of any constitutional right that the political branches are structurally incapable of—or indisposed toward—protecting; where taking over the matter would yield no coherent remedy; where the contemplated judicial action would serve to entrench the power of the group seeking such action, rather than protecting relatively powerless individuals or groups from the entrenched power of others; or where the judicial action in question would in some way advance the interests of the controlling majority on the Court in some *extrinsic* way, such as attempting to assure the nomination of like-minded replacements.

Bush v. Gore strikes out on all five criteria.

The idea of *Bush v. Gore* as a kind of "negative object lesson," which to me is more plausible than the idea of *Bush v. Gore* as the seed for some wonderfully flowering tree of doctrine that reveals the Constitution in a yet brighter light, brings to mind an occasion several years ago when my wife and I were having dinner in a Chinese restaurant in Cambridge. After dinner, we were served two fortune cookies, each on its own oval dish. After opening the first, which we had agreed in advance to treat as applicable to us both, we decided not to open the second. We saved the "fortune" that cookie contained: *May your life serve as an example to others how not to lead theirs.* Gulp. From time to time, we were tempted to give the fortune away, but we could never find quite the right recipient. That problem was solved for us by *Bush v. Gore.*

But to draw a reason to doubt the majesty of law and of the Constitution from the Court's smug assurance that it and it alone could rise to this constitutional occasion and evoke the better angels of our nature would be tragically misguided. That the Court's distressing decision to rescue democracy from itself was no isolated misstep but a manifestation of pathologies evidenced in all too many other ways is hardly a basis to diagnose either judicial review or the rule of law as moribund or even mortally wounded. I especially lament the tendency of some to draw from the seemingly Herculean pretension that marked *Bush v. Gore* the ironically immodest lesson that judicial modesty and incrementalism are always the path of wisdom—that the Court that decides the least decides the best. How much the Court should decide and when depends on the constitutional principle to be vindicated, the political setting in which a controversy is embedded, and the social, cultural, and historical forces at play. And the arguments over when the Court does well to act more boldly—when the time and circumstances are right for a *Brown v. Board of Education,*[210] a *Gideon v. Wainwright,*[211] a *New York Times v. Sullivan,*[212] a *Baker v. Carr,*[213] a *Roe v. Wade*[214]—are too complex and multifaceted to be squeezed into any simplistic generalization that would treat *Bush v. Gore* as the right wing's answer to *Roe v. Wade.* The danger of always fighting the last war is too real for us to succumb to any version of the syndrome that would make *Bush v. Gore* our judicial Vietnam.

With that in mind, the main teaching I would extract from *Bush v. Gore* is a teaching addressed more to future Courts than to this one. It is that, when a generation comes to one of those few moments in which a confluence of legal and political factors creates a challenge of historic proportion—I say a *challenge,* not a crisis, for crisis there was none—the Court should take a long, hard look in the mirror of its own past and at the past of the politics we have lost, and recognize in that challenge opportunities for both political and intellectual greatness—opportunities in which the other branches, if the matter is one best understood as left to them by the Constitution, may, without rescue by the Court, summon the better angels of our nature to the work of achieving a "more perfect Union."

4. Constitutionalizing Democratic Politics

Richard H. Pildes*

Bush v. Gore,[1] for all its uniqueness, is not an isolated event. It is best understood, instead, as the most dramatic crystallization of a deeper, more enduring pattern in the contemporary relationship between democratic politics and constitutional law. This pattern might be called the "constitutionalization of democracy." Over the last decade or so, powerful litigants—the major political parties, incumbent officeholders, candidates for the presidency—have increasingly raced to the courts and sought to subject the fundamental structure of democratic processes and institutions to constitutional constraint. And they have succeeded: Whether the issue is what kind of election primaries we are to have, or how we are to finance political campaigns, or how effective a role third parties and independent candidates will play, or whether disputed presidential elections will be resolved through political processes (such as in Congress), constitutional law in the last decade has come to play a central—often the dominant—role. Constitutional law now sharply constrains the possibilities for experimentation with the forms of democratic politics; constitutional law now limits the structural changes through which disaffection with the current practices of democratic politics can be given institutional expression.

That constitutional law plays *some* role in overseeing the structures and processes of democracy is not, in itself, a surprise. Since the Supreme Court first held in 1962 that claims involving "political rights" could be resolved in the courts,[2] constitutional law has regulated certain aspects of democratic politics. Representative institutions must be designed in accord with one person, one vote; the right of adult, resident, non-felon citizens to vote has achieved the status of a fundamental constitutional right; electoral structures cannot be designed to minimize or "dilute" the voting power of certain identifiable groups, such as racial minorities. But these foundational principles from the Court's initial foray into issues of democracy all rested, as I will show here, on a specific, relatively precise, and quite convincing set of functional justifications for why the Court had come to view constitutional over-sight as necessary on selected, discrete issues. What *is* surprising over the last decade is that the Court now routinely deploys constitutional law to cir-cumscribe the forms democracy can take in situations that bear no relation-ship to those that had originally justified constitutional intervention. As this essay will show, the Court now almost reflexively acts as if it were appropriate for constitutional law always to provide ready answers as to what makes democracy "best"—without the Court asking any longer whether there are appropriate reasons that democratic politics itself is not the proper forum in which to address those questions.

This judicial constitutionalization of democratic politics is, perhaps, the single most important development in constitutional law over the last de-cade. But this development has attracted little academic or popular notice. Instead, as Judge Richard Posner rightly observes, scholarship on constitu-tional law and the Supreme Court has remained obsessed for several de-cades with issues of individual rights and equality.[3] Issues concerning the structures of democratic governance, by contrast, have met with indifference at best, disdain at worst—as if sophisticated thinking has moved beyond for-mal politics to more "essential" issues of rights and equality.[4] But the kind of democracy we experience is not some pure distillation of organic cultural and political forces. Democratic experience is a product, more than is often realized, of the institutional frameworks and legal rules that structure current democratic arrangements. Nor can we move "beyond" formal democratic politics to some other, more essential domain. For politics and these other domains—be they culture or economics—mutually influence each other. Many people, for example, are aware of the history of racial segregation and of *Plessy v. Ferguson.* Many fewer, however, understand the history of the massive disfranchisement of black citizens (and poor whites) in the South from 1890–1965 and the importance of *Giles v. Harris.*[5] Yet for the brief window of time in which Southern blacks could vote, interracial political coalitions emerged; much about political culture and law, as well as social re-lations, differed in the era in which formal politics was open to black citizens. Segregation would not have endured for so long had black citizens not been expelled in the South, throughout most of the twentieth century, from demo-cratic politics.

After *Bush v. Gore,* the structures, institutions, and ground rules of democracy—and the role of constitutional law in assessing them—can no longer be avoided. If nothing else, *Bush v. Gore* will shape the agenda of discussion on constitutional law and the Supreme Court for some time. But if we analyze the election decision in isolation from the emerging jurisprudence of democracy of which it is but one piece, we will miss what is least singular—and hence most likely lasting—about *Bush v. Gore* and the vision of democracy it represents.

In this essay, I set the stage initially with a description of the broader political and cultural moment in which we seem to exist. I then turn to how the Supreme Court has responded to the challenges to existing democratic practices that this moment has spawned. My aim is first to chronicle this emerging jurisprudence of democracy, then to understand and explain what appears to be driving it. We will then be in a position to assess analytically what the relationship of constitutional law to democratic politics has become—and what it ought to be.

Democratic Challenges to Traditional Forms of Democracy

We live in an era of disaffection for and disinterest in the conventional forms of electoral politics. I mean this not as a matter of abstract opinions expressed in opinion surveys (though it is true there too[6]), but as a matter of actual political behavior. This disaffection is revealed through tangible, concrete forms of action. Significant popular effort to change some of the basic features of current democratic structures is increasingly common; efforts to abandon or transform the conventional two-party structure now take many forms, and a general rejection of the long dominant two parties can be identified in several ways.

Take the dramatic rise in support for third parties over the last three decades. Third parties stand little chance of actually winning elections in the United States; as political scientists have long appreciated, the first past the post election system we use creates overwhelming incentives for voters to stay with one of the two dominant parties. In the hundred years from 1864–1964, only three presidential elections resulted in a minor party candidate receiving more than 5 percent of the vote. Yet since then, despite the enormous disincentives voters have to "waste votes" on third-party candidates, that 5 percent threshold has been eclipsed by George Wallace, then by John Anderson, and recently in two straight elections by Ross Perot. Perot's candidacy resulted in a third-party candidate receiving more than 5 percent of the vote in two consecutive elections for the first time in the long history of two-party competition between Democrats and Republicans: a remarkable 19 percent in 1992 (the largest third-party popular vote since the Civil War other than Theodore Roosevelt's Bull Moose party run in 1912) and 8 percent in 1996.[7]

In the 2000 presidential election, two significant minor-party presidential candidates achieved ballot status in nearly all fifty states.[8] While the Reform party candidate, Pat Buchanan, was unable to overcome intra-party dissension, Ralph Nader, the Green party candidate, gained enough support in key states to have likely deprived the Democratic candidate, Al Gore, of the presidency.[9] At the non-presidential level, the 1996 election stood out as one of the most significant elections in the twentieth century for minor parties. Almost 600 minor-party candidates ran for both houses of Congress, a figure almost three times the number of candidates who ran in the watershed 1968 election and nearly twice as many as in 1980. In total, two-thirds of all districts in 1996 featured at least one alternative candidate.[10] The 2000 Congressional elections included 587 third-party candidates from thirty-one different parties.[11] Since then, there has also been the momentous disaffiliation of Vermont Senator James Jeffords from the Republican party and his embrace of the status of political independent.

Taken as a whole, this rise in third-party politics and independent candidacies is a telling search among significant numbers of voters for ways out of the existing two-party structure. Moreover, this current upsurge in minor-party activity is particularly striking because—unlike other swells in third-party activity—this one has emerged at a time "filled by neither burning issues nor economic stagnation."[12] Traditionally, minor parties rise in eras of social or economic crisis; often minor parties are seen to be addressing, albeit narrowly, a single momentous issue that the major parties have been neglecting.[13] The Republican party emerged on the eve of the Civil War around the issue of slavery and the territories.[14] Numerous minor parties, such as the

Grangers, the Greenbackers, the Farmers' Alliance, and most importantly, the People's Party, flourished in response to postwar and Reconstruction turmoil during the turbulent years of the 1870s and 1880s. Roosevelt's Progressive Bull Moose party split from the Republican party over specific social issues and labor reform.[15] The Dixiecrat party arose in protest over the Democratic party platform on Civil Rights.[16] Yet while survey data had shown strong support for the two-party system from the forties until the early eighties, that changed in the mid-nineties; for the first time, only a minority of voters thought the two parties were doing "an adequate job" and a majority thought there should "be a major third party."[17] And if there is anything that might be said to characterize and unite the recent invigoration of third parties, it is not a specific issue, but simply disaffection with the dominant parties and the conventional processes of politics itself.

Given the extreme disincentives to third-party voting built into American electoral structures, this defection from the two major parties is striking. Other patterns of voting behavior similarly reveal widespread resistance to the long-standing conventional forms of partisan politics; the routinization of divided government is the most visible result of this transformation. Thus, split-ticket voting was relatively rare until the sixties, but since then it has risen to the point where 20–25 percent of voters split their vote in national elections. A majority of voters now split their ballots for state and local elections.[18] Divided government, with different branches in different partisan hands, then follows. A dramatic rise in divided government has taken place over the last two decades or so, to the point at which it has become the standard form at both the national and state level. Thus, from Lincoln's presidency until 1969, the same party held both houses of Congress and the presidency between 70–80 percent of the time; since then, the figure has been around 20 percent.[19] Whatever the specific reasons for these results, we are living in an era in which voters want something different—manifested in the examples of third parties and divided government—out of democratic politics.

The other unmistakable expression of demand for fundamental structural change is the flourishing of voter initiatives. The mid-seventies and since have witnessed "a tremendous upsurge in usage" of the voter initiatives in those states that permit this device.[20] Between 1977 and 1996, there was a

164 percent increase in use of the initiative compared to between 1941 and 1976.[21] Many of these direct democracy ventures seek to restructure the forms in which politics is practiced. Whether it is efforts to reform the campaign finance system, or to restructure the rules of participation in political primaries to increase choices for voters, or to impose term limits on national, state, and local officials, much of the rise in direct democracy can be traced to voter-initiated efforts to change the terms in which democratic politics is currently practiced. In California, for example, voters before 1980 faced an "institutional reform" initiative—meaning one dealing with campaigns, elected officials, terms limits, elections, or reapportionment—once every four years; since 1980, there have been six such initiatives every four years.[22] In some sense, of course, any voter-initiated act of direct democracy reflects dissatisification with how existing institutions are addressing certain issues. But what is most remarkable in recent years is how many direct democracy initiatives seek to restructure the forms of politics itself. Initiatives and referendum that seek to change the political process have passed at the highest rate in recent years of any category of voter-initiated legal change.[23]

Some of the developments I have described, such as the rise of divided government, are symbols of contemporary disaffection with conventional democratic politics (I have left aside familiar concerns about declining voter turnout rates, given uncertainty about how to interpret what that decline means). Other developments seek to implement direct changes in the structures of American democracy. Challenges of these sorts therefore confront the legal system with concrete pressures for structural change. The rise in third-party support, for example, has led to challenges to existing rules that make it especially difficult to mount such challenges. Voter initiatives have sought to diminish what voters perceive as the extreme partisanship of candidates; consistent with the declining attachment to the two major parties, California voters, for example, sought to open political primaries to all voters, of whatever party, in an effort to bring about more centrist candidates. Other voter initiatives have sought to force greater rotation of public offices through term limits.

The disaffection with conventional politics in our era, in other words, is expressed in a dramatic array of efforts to change the ground rules under which politics is practiced. The question, then, is what role—if any—the

Supreme Court and constitutional law should play in responding to these efforts. Whatever one thinks of any particular measures, there is a more transcendent general question at stake to which this essay now turns: What should the relationship be between democratic politics itself and constitutional law when efforts are made to challenge the conventional forms of politics in which democracy has been practiced? To gain some purchase on that question, I will turn to an account of how the current Supreme Court has responded to these challenges. In doing so, I will approach *Bush v. Gore* obliquely, for the suggestion here is that the current justices divide in recurring, yet perhaps surprising, ways in cases involving democracy. Once we can see the broad tapestry of the Court's democracy decisions, we will better be able to understand *Bush v. Gore* as well.

THE SUPREME COURT RESPONSE TO THE ERA OF DEMOCRATIC DISAFFECTION

Primary Elections

Political parties in the United States are more heavily regulated than their counterparts in any other Western European democracy.[24] This has been true since the era—roughly between 1882 and World War I—in which legislation on myriad issues was enacted to shift control of party affairs from party leaders to the electorate.[25] This "democratizing" legislation imposed mandatory nominating procedures on parties, including the imposition of mandatory direct primary elections, first for delegates to nominating conventions, then for the choice of candidates themselves. State laws also mandated the internal governance structure of parties; central and county committees were required, for example, and state law specified the terms of election, office, and duties for such party members. Similarly, state laws regulated what could be required to become a party member; states typically required election-day "oaths of affiliation" to establish party membership and barred parties from imposing more demanding requirements. In upholding New York's typical party-regulation laws, the chief judge of the prestigious New York court of appeals characterized such laws as designed to constrain the "not unnatural desire" of party majorities to "perpetuate their power" at the expense of ordinary voting members of the party whose "views were not congenial to the majority." [26] Chief Judge Parker went on to add that "the [regulatory] scheme is to permit the voters to construct the organization from the bottom upwards, instead of permitting leaders to construct it from the top downwards." [27]

This history of the deep-rooted, extensive regulation of all phases of political party life affords perspective on current efforts to experiment with the structure of political parties. So too does the judicial response to this wave of regulation that created the modern American party structure. Not surprisingly, those who controlled the parties in the late 19th and early 20th centuries, and against whom this "democratizing" regulation was directed, vehemently resisted these efforts. Among other forms, that resistance was expressed through constitutional litigation in which representatives of the parties argued that these regulations violated the parties' freedom of association as well as state constitutional guarantees of "free and equal elections." [28] Party leaders also analogized parties to private corporations; as such, they argued that parties had associational rights insulating them from state regulation. Yet the state courts disagreed overwhelmingly. As the Wisconsin Supreme Court put it, state law had made parties "a state agency;" as the Missouri Supreme Court said, state regulation was justified "to prevent factional oppressions and outrages in politics, and to lift party management to a plane where it will assist, rather than hinder, the expression of the will of the people;" as the Nebraska court concluded, state law could determine conditions on party membership, for "the right to participate" in candidate nominations had been "taken from the party and placed in the control of the Legislature." [29] This elaborate regulatory structure that forms the modern American party—which has essentially remained in place throughout the twentieth century—has led one of the leading scholars of parties to conclude that American law treats political parties, not as private associations, but more as "public utilities." [30]

Shift now to the present. In 1996, by a margin of 60 percent to 40 percent, with nearly identical support among Republican and Democratic voters, over three million voters in California replaced the state's "closed" political primaries with the "blanket primary." In a blanket primary, voters can choose, office by office, the political party in whose primary they want to vote—the Republican primary for governor, the Democratic primary for attorney general, the Libertarian primary for treasurer. This system contrasts most sharply with what are called "closed" primaries, which is what California had used before voters endorsed the blanket primary. In closed primaries, participation is limited to voters who have registered as members of that party a specified time in advance of the primary.[31] That California voters would want to abandon their closed primary is not a surprise: California now has roughly 1.5 million independent voters, who were excluded altogether from the closed primary system.[32] Nor is the blanket primary structure novel; Washington has used it since 1935, Alaska since 1947.[33]

The structure of primaries is often critical to the nature of those who hold office. Once primaries are over, voters can often have little meaningful choice, particularly in one-party jurisdictions. Regulation of primaries is therefore often a focal point of reformers, and in upholding such regulations long ago, the Oregon Supreme Court colorfully put its rationale: "Once the stream is polluted at its source, access to its waters, however free, will not serve to purify it."[34] Supporters of blanket primaries argue that this is what has happened in states like California. Closed primaries are dominated by each party's most activist wings; as a result, general elections become contests between two extremist candidates. By the time of the general election, moderate voters face a "polluted stream," for centrist candidates have been swept aside in the torrents of party zealotry. Advocates argued that replacing the closed primary with the blanket primary would increase voter turnout and participation; voters would have more choices, candidates closer to the median voter—more moderate candidates—would make it to the general election, and elected officials would then be more responsive to the state's median voter. Voters who turned out for the initiative contest apparently agreed.

I do not purport to know whether the effects of a blanket primary, short-term or long-term, are desirable. Along some dimensions, "democracy" might be enhanced; along others, it might be diminished; there might well be complex trade-offs between different aims we think democracy ought to try to realize. Instead, the question this essay explores is what role, if any, *consti-*

tutional law ought to play in addressing these questions. In addition, what does the way in which the Supreme Court *did* address that question tell us about how the current Court envisions democracy and the relationship between constitutional law and democratic processes when it comes to structuring democracy itself? Thirteen federal judges addressed the question whether blanket primaries are constitutional. Six judges concluded they were, seven judges concluded they were not. But because all seven judges who rejected the blanket primary were on the Supreme Court, the decision in *California Democratic Party v. Jones*[35] held the blanket primary an option that California voters did not have the constitutional power to choose.

In exploring this case and others, my aim is to tease out the cultural ideals about democracy that seem to inform the current Court's "democracy" cases. By cultural ideals, I mean the empirical assumptions, historical interpretations, and normative visions of democracy that seem to inform and influence the current constitutional law of democracy. Thus, my focus is not on the analytical structure of the legal arguments in these cases. Nor is it whether, as a matter of public policy, one electoral form or another is likely to produce a "better" democratic system. Instead, my concern is the role that democratic politics itself should be understood to have in addressing these kinds of questions—and how judges, particularly Supreme Court justices, approach that question. Let us examine, therefore, how different judges portray, describe, and imagine democracy when deciding such cases.

The district court put great weight on expert empirical evidence—exceptional expertise in political science was presented at trial, though the experts divided sharply—regarding the possible effects of blanket primaries on voter behavior and the strength of political parties. But at the same time, the imagery of the district court's opinion celebrated "experiment[s] in democratic government"[36] and cast the blanket-primary issue against that narrative background. As the district court told the story: "Proposition 198 is the latest development in a history of political reform measures that began in the Progressive Era."[37] Reading the opinion, one is struck by how much the district judge emphasized the significance of long-standing and widespread popular support for blanket primaries in California. And because "[t]he history of election law is one of change and adaptation as the States have responded to the play of different political forces and circumstances," the district court expressed confidence in a future in which, whether the blanket primary turned out well or not, democratic politics would be self-correcting enough to respond.[38]

The seven justices on the Supreme Court who reversed—the *Bush v. Gore* majority plus Justices Souter and Breyer—project a strikingly different image of the case. The Court consistently casts the active agent in the case as "the State," an abstract entity, which becomes pitted against the "rights" of political parties.[39] While the voters are active and present throughout the district court opinion, the Supreme Court majority makes bare legal reference to popular adoption of the blanket primary—and none to the level, breadth, or history of popular support. The most dramatic instance of this silence occurs when the Court rejects any appeal to the democratic interest in enhancing voter participation: "The voter's desire to participate does not become more weighty simply because the State supports it."[40] What is the separation between the state and the voters in an initiative contest imagined in such a sentence? Moreover, the Court pictures democratic politics and political organizations as fragile and potentially unstable entities that require judicial protection, for as the Court worries, a single election in a blanket primary "could be enough to destroy the party."[41] Without strong, well-ordered political organizations, enforced by constitutional law that denies popular majorities the power to shape the electoral process in the service (benighted or not) of enhanced participation, the Court sees threats to the stability of the democratic order. A vision further from that of democratic experimentalism and a self-correcting, adaptive democratic system is hard to imagine.

Contrast, now, Justice Stevens's dissent, which Justice Ginsburg joined. This opinion, like the district court's, makes "the people" and "citizens" and "the electorate" the actor behind the blanket primary, not "the State."[42] At work in this case, for the dissent, are "competing visions of what makes democracy work"—and for this very reason, "[t]hat choice belongs to the people."[43] As in the district court's opinion, the image of a resilient democratic system, not a fragile one, reappears; states "should be free to experiment with reforms designed to make the democratic process more robust. . . ."[44] Moreover, the value of voter participation is central in Justice Stevens's dissent; indeed, if that opinion gives one value priority in the justification of democracy over any other, it is the value of participation. Thus,

Justice Stevens *defines* the case as one about voter participation,[45] and his dissent would make the entire structure of constitutional analysis turn on whether regulations of politics expand or constrict voter participation: Regulations that expand participation should not face the same close judicial scrutiny as regulations that constrict participation. For Justice Stevens, once a new political structure can plausibly be justified as expanding participation, any further debate about its overall policy effects should be left to democratic processes to debate—rather than to be analyzed juridically and resolved by courts.[46]

What determines how judges decide crucial cases involving democracy, such as this one, that will directly shape the kind of democratic politics we experience? Though the various opinions confront each other with social-scientific facts and predictions, it seems unlikely that these facts—tentative and disputed as they were—could have determined judicial judgment. Even if we somehow knew exactly how much blanket primaries would weaken political parties, change governing behavior, and affect voter participation, how ought those effects be traded off against each other? Debates cast in empirical terms often masquerade for deeper, underlying disagreements about cultural assumptions and normative ideals.[47] The rhetoric, imagery, and narrative interpretations infusing these opinions, and others involving democratic politics, are a window into those conceptions. Is American democracy fragile, so that relatively novel political structures require aggressive constitutional evaluation? Or is American democracy experimental and self-revising, so that such structures are to be celebrated—or at least judicially tolerated—as contemporary, popular manifestations of a healthy democratic impulse? Should such popular, direct participation in addressing these questions itself be a preeminent value, to be weighed heavily in any judicial judgment? Or is such participation legally irrelevant, so that all regulation of politics, whether emerging from state legislatures or, by contrast, voter initiatives to which the party-dominated state legislature is affirmatively hostile, should be conceived as the action of a singular, undifferentiated entity, "the state?" The cultural attitudes judges bring toward these kind of questions surely influence, if they do not completely dominate, how judges respond to empirical claims and open-ended precedents—which is why, perhaps, it turns out that most justices on the current Supreme Court end up consistently on the same side of these cases (as this essay will show), despite differences in facts, partisan consequences, and precedents among the various issues involving democracy that have recently been before the Court.

For that reason, the way the Court responds to open primaries[48] will be particularly revealing. This is a question the Court will now find hard to avoid, and its resolution will have dramatic effects on democratic politics—especially in an era in which so many voters reject affiliating with any one party. Blanket primaries may seem a novelty, in use in only a few places, and precisely the kind of political innovation voters in a place like California, with their muscular initiative process, might choose. But twenty-nine states use open primaries; many have done so since primary elections themselves were mandated early in the twentieth century. Is it now to be unconstitutional for states to require parties to use open primaries, in which at least independents can choose to vote? Precisely because the open primary has been around for so long and in so many states, it is hard to believe that the American democratic system's health and stability is threatened by such electoral structures. On the one hand then, the open primary might viscerally seem traditional, unthreatening, and consistent with the stability and strength of American democratic culture. For the Court to invalidate it would itself produce a massive and radical restructuring of a central feature of twentieth-century American democracy. On the other hand, there does not appear to be any meaningful distinction,[49] in legal principle or in empirical fact, between the open and the blanket primary. The legal reasons the Court offers for invalidating blanket primaries appear equally applicable to open primaries. Thus, if the Court upholds open primaries, it will have to invoke largely formalistic distinctions;[50] doing so would signal it is the novelty of the blanket primary, and cultural attitudes among the justices toward such popularly adopted innovations, not any deep-rooted matter of substantive legal principle or empirical fact, that divides the conventional open primary from the now unconstitutional blanket primary.

The larger question is why should these issues be settled through constitutional law? Why should we have to speculate about whether the Court, having struck down blanket primaries, will now shift its appetite toward open primaries—and whether any (essentially artificial) distinctions can be found to save this common and longstanding political structure against the claim that it interferes with the "free associational" rights of political parties? For generations, democratic politics has been the arena in which disaffection with existing politics has expressed itself through experimentation with new structures through which to channel electoral competition. For generations, courts have stepped aside to permit these popular efforts, however healthy or misguided in particular instances. But there was no sense that courts had to "constitutionalize democratic politics" to save us from ourselves. Democratic politics itself was judicially viewed as resilient enough to permit this kind of trial-and-error pragmatism, without formalistic legal principles—such as the associational rights of parties—being obstacles to such experimentation.

If there were some defect in the political process itself to which the Court could point in justifying a role for constitutional law in cases such as this, that would be a different matter. If one party, for example, had temporary control over the legislature and adopted laws whose aim and effect was to substantially weaken competitor parties, constitutional doctrines might well be appropriately deployed to curb such manipulations.[51] But that, ironically, was the opposite of the situation in the recent California blanket-primary case. There was no legislative majority that had captured the California legislature and enacted anticompetitive election laws to stifle other parties. As noted above, it was the voters who imposed this primary system *over* the objection of the political parties; and a majority of voters in each of the dominant parties had apparently voted for the change. Even more significantly, the parties themselves refused to make their case in the democratic arena itself against these primaries; the parties spent virtually nothing to fight the issues out in the initiative contest itself.[52] Instead, they sat out the democratic forum, then rushed immediately to the courts and to constitutional litigation to have the voters' preferred primary structure overturned. Nothing could better exemplify the contrast between how these issues of democracy had long been addressed and the current Supreme Court's routine "constitutionalization" of struggles over the forms of democracy.

Third Parties

Almost the exact inverse situation was presented to the Court in another recent case involving the essential structures of democratic politics. This time it was relatively weak, minor parties who sought constitutional assistance; this time, it was the two major parties, through their control over state legislation, that had erected barriers to keep the minor parties from competing as effectively as they otherwise could for votes. This is precisely the kind of case likely to arise in an era characterized by disaffection from the major parties and the search for different forms of politics, such as third parties. The New Party, formed in 1992, is a national party that seeks to build from the local level up and claims to have won 300 of its first 400 local races. One of the New Party's central devices for building up its electoral competitiveness was to use "fusion" candidacies, but Minnesota law made such candidacies illegal. In *Timmons v. Twin Cities Area New Party*,[53] the question was what set of assumptions about democracy, and what theoretical understandings about the relationship between constitutional law and democratic politics, the Court would bring to efforts of emerging organizations, like the New Party, to enhance the competitiveness of American democracy.

"Fusion" politics flourished in the late nineteenth century.[54] Fusion candidacies entail joint nomination by two parties—typically a minor party and one of the two major parties—of the same candidate. The candidate appears on the ballot under both party lines; voters can choose either party line in voting for the candidate. The ability to form fusion candidacies was critical to the existence of a vibrant third-party politics that existed in late nineteenth century America, with parties like the Populists, Greenbackers, Laborites, Prohibitionists, and others successfully challenging the two major parties. In 1878, for example, the Greenback-Labor Party won fourteen congressional seats. In 1892, the Populists won about 10 percent of the popular votes in the presidential election; by 1898, the Populists held twenty-five seats in the House and six (of ninety) in the Senate.

Deep structural features of the American system, of course, make it unlikely that third parties will displace a major party; not since the 1850s has this happened at the national level. One should not, therefore, romanticize the extent to which new parties in America are likely to displace one of the two major parties. But cross-endorsement does enable third parties potentially to influence the positions that the two major parties adopt. Cross-endorsement also gives organizational expression to dissenting voices within the major parties. Most importantly, stringent ballot-access rules in the United States require parties to achieve a fairly high level of support to be included as of right on the ballot in subsequent elections, rather than having to devote scarce resources to signature gathering. Yet if fusion is banned, voters who would otherwise support a third party decline to do so because such a vote seems wasted; with fusion, voters can support both the party of their choice and a major-party candidate who has a realistic chance of winning.

Fusion had played a significant role in making possible the era of robust multiparty politics in late nineteenth-century America. Precisely for this reason, many state legislatures (controlled by the major party most likely to be hurt by fusion candidacies) banned fusion candidacies at the turn of the twentieth century. These bans applied even when both a minor and a major party voluntarily endorsed fusion candidates; anti-fusion laws banned such candidacies regardless of the preferences of all the political parties involved.[55] These fusion bans (along with similar laws) devastated third parties. In particular, they were passed in state after state where the Populist party threat was great, and the laws played a role in ending the Populist party—the last important minor party to sustain a working national, state, and local organization over several election cycles.[56]

With the attempted reemergence of third parties today, these fusion bans were finally challenged in the Supreme Court in *Timmons*. Again, as in *Jones*, a divided Supreme Court (this time 6–3) reversed an unanimous court of appeals.[57] Again, what I want to call attention to here is not the analytical structure of the formal First Amendment analysis, but the dramatically different cultural images of democracy that inform the views of different judges.

To the lower federal court, the Eighth Circuit Court of Appeals, fusion candidacies invigorate the democratic process. While Minnesota argued that protecting the integrity of elections justified its ban on fusion, the court of appeals conjured up just the opposite imagery: "[C]onsensual multiple party nomination may invigorate [democracy] by fostering more competition, participation, and representation in American politics. As James Madison observed, when the variety and number of political parties increases, the chance for oppression, factionalism, and non-skeptical acceptance of ideas decreases."[58] For empirical debates about the effects of fusion, the court of appeals turned to historical experience and interpreted that experience this way: "History shows that minor parties have played a significant role in the electoral system where multiple party nomination is legal, but have no mean-ingful influence where multiple party nomination is banned."[59] Like lower court judges in California, the eighth circuit also envisioned self-correcting internal mechanisms in democratic politics itself if fusion made for bad poli-tics; major parties could simply refuse to consent to fusion.[60]

Now consider how democracy appeared to the decisive Supreme Court—this time, the *Bush v. Gore* majority plus Justice Breyer. The central image in this opinion is not that of invigorated democracy through "political competition," but that of a system whose crucial "political stability" is easily threatened.[61] The word *stable* (and variations of it) appears a remarkable ten times in the brief majority opinion. The central fact about fusion candidacies is the risk to political stability they are pictured to pose; thus, states must surely be able to "temper the destabilizing effects of party splintering and ex-cessive factionalism."[62] Far from seeing the 10th Federalist as supporting fusion candidacies, the Supreme Court sees such candidacies as the very embodiment of the factionalism Madison sought to avoid. Where the court of appeals saw the historically significant role of minor parties in American democracy, the Supreme Court worried about "campaign-related disor-der."[63] Rather than looking at historical experience to assess whether fusion candidacies had actually generated these concerns, or at contemporary em-pirical facts from states that permit fusion, like New York, the Court majority did not require "empirical verification of the weightiness of the State's as-serted justifications" for banning fusion candidacies.[64] Indeed, because the risk of political instability was so high, the Court expressly concluded—for the first time in its history—that the states' interest in political stability justi-fied electoral regulations that "favor the traditional two-party system."[65]

Once again, Justice Stevens led the dissent, joined by Justice Ginsburg. In contrast, his unifying metaphor is "robust competition," not political stabil-ity. Indeed, he calls this concern the "central theme" of the Court's democ-racy jurisprudence: "[T]hat the entire electorate, which necessarily includes the members of the major parties, will benefit from robust competition in ideas and governmental policies" is, in his view, the idea "at the core of our electoral process."[66] Were empirical facts relevant? Then Justice Stevens viewed historical experience as showing that the majority's fears for stability were "fantastical."[67] Fusion, in fact, was "the best marriage"[68] of the virtues of minor parties with the level of political stability democracy required; fusion offered a means by which major parties would be responsive to the view of minor party adherents, without actually threatening to divide a legislature. Interestingly, Justice Souter—who, with Justice Breyer, moves across the voting line in the quadrology of cases I consider in this essay—also dissented, but in a more equivocal way. Writing in the double negative, he thought "it may not be unreasonable to infer that the two-party system is in some jeopardy" today.[69] If it were, he would not be prepared to reject the majority's constitutional enshrinement of that system, as a necessary means toward political stability. But for Justice Souter, the state had simply not yet argued this point adequately enough to permit judgment.[70]

What explains decisions like *Timmons?* What accounts for the bases on which the justices divide, or on which the current Supreme Court divides from lower federal courts, here as in the blanket-primary case? Is the debate over fusion an empirical debate in any meaningful sense; are judges dividing over what "the evidence" shows? If history is one source of such evidence, when different judges look back to historical moments at which fusion flourished, how do those judges interpret that past? Do they see a time of political instability, excessive factionalism, campaign disorder, and party splintering? Or a time of vibrant democracy, robust competition, more responsive government (to those eligible to vote), and more engaged democracy? If the choice about fusion cannot be determined by empirical inquiry, can the internal logic of doctrinal analysis do so? Does the First Amendment protect the right of voters and parties to the seemingly expanded choice fusion facilitates? But surely political stability is a value against which constitutional doctrines must be assessed? If neither facts nor doctrine compel a particular constitutional judgment, and if partisan political stakes point in no particular direction, yet federal judges divide so evenly over questions like this, what explains those differences? Perhaps, the suggestion is here, it is different cultural assumptions about how important order and stability, as opposed to competition and tumult, are to democracy.

Access to Public Campaign Forums

Consider one final example, before we turn to *Bush v. Gore,* of the current Court's approach to assessing the practices of democracy. The case centers on the following question: How specific must the legal norms be that regulate various aspects of democracy—voting and the counting of votes, for example, or getting one's name on the ballot as a candidate, or gaining access to participation in publicly sponsored candidate debates?

Procedural judgments of this sort depend upon evaluations of the particular aspect of democracy at stake. Those judgments can depend on views of how a decision one way or the other will affect the values justifying the particular feature of democracy; on how much a requirement of greater specificity will compromise countervailing values (and by how much); and similar considerations. In addition, the specificity of a legal norm can be generated through two alternative sources. The most obvious is the relevant legal text itself. In theory, a norm can always be made more specific if the enacting body is willing or required to provide greater determinate content *ex ante* as to how that norm is to be applied in a range of contexts, at least to the extent those contexts are foreseeable. An alternative source through which legal norms can potentially gain sufficient precision and specificity is through institutional structures and processes that give post-enactment content to a more general norm in the process of applying it. "Intent of the voter" is a statutory norm, for example, that could be assessed against questions of this sort, questions which, with respect to the vote, are now grounded on the equal protection clause in the wake of *Bush v. Gore.*[71]

In another signal case for the law of democracy, the Supreme Court recently confronted the process by which public television stations are constitutionally permitted to make judgments about which ballot-qualified candidates to include and exclude in publicly sponsored candidate debates. In Arkansas, the state-owned public television station sponsored congressional debates; in one of the state's four congressional districts, an independent candidate had qualified for the ballot. But the station refused to permit him to join the Democratic and Republican candidates in the debate. Lacking a previously established policy, the station excluded him based on its conclusion that he was not "a serious candidate." A jury found that he had not been excluded because of his political views. But a central question was not whether this particular judgment was legitimately based. The question was whether government actors had to make such judgments in advance, through more clearly specified norms, that would protect against potentially inconsistent or biased judgments if the norms were left *ex ante* at a high level of generality and specified only at the moment that specific decisions were being made. "Not a serious candidate," in other words, is a legal norm that can be assessed against constitutionally mandated procedural standards, such as whether the criteria for access to public debates must be specified in advance rather than developed ad hoc on a case-by-case basis.

Again, we have a challenge, typical of our times, to conventional modes of politics. This time the challenge came to the Court in the form of a ballot-qualified independent candidate seeking to participate in debates. The outcome in the case might also, by now, be familiar. In *Arkansas Educational Television Commission v. Forbes,* a divided Supreme Court—the *Bush v. Gore* majority plus Justice Breyer—reversed a unanimous Court of Appeals.[72] Justice Stevens penned the dissent, joined again by Justice Ginsburg, and, less equivocally this time, by Justice Souter. As in the previous two cases, no distinctly mainstream partisan stakes seem apparent in the issue; neither the Republicans nor the Democrats appear likely to benefit systematically from broad or narrow rules of candidate inclusion and exclusion.

What images of democracy form the backdrop for judges in such procedural disputes about how specific legal norms must be? Do multiple-candidate debates raise the prospect of robust, competitive exchange, or the threat of disorder, tumult, and confusion? Here is the Court majority's vision: Public broadcasters would be faced with "the prospect of cacophony, on the one hand" if Forbes's First Amendment claim were accepted; or, on the other hand, public broadcasters would likely withdraw from the role of sponsoring debates at all if confronted with the senseless and chaotic prospect of too many candidates in a debate. The striking image is that of "cacophony," about which we might ask several questions. Is cacophony itself a factual or normative matter? We can all agree that, at some point, too many speakers can frustrate the point of a debate. But is a six-candidate debate "cacophonous?" In the 1992 Democratic presidential primary, six candidates debated in early debates; so too in the 1988 Republican primary.[73]

Yet at stake in *Forbes* was whether a third candidate, qualified to be on the ballot, would be permitted into the public debate.

But more interesting than when exactly a debate becomes mere noise is the way the *image* of cacophony seems to have obscured from the Court other legal possibilities, as well as competing cultural images. Those other procedural possibilities, rather than any profound difference of principle, are what the dissenters emphasized. Thus, the dissents did not require public debate sponsors to open debates to all candidates, nor even to all ballot-qualified candidates. Instead, the dissent would have required greater specificity in advance, through objective, preestablished criteria, of the bases for candidate inclusion—rather than what the dissent called the "ad hoc" and "standardless character of the decision to exclude" that was actually made.[74] Indeed, several debate-sponsoring entities, such as the Commission on Presidential Debates, filed briefs arguing that they had developed precisely such preestablished, transparent, objective allocative criteria and thereby managed to avoid cacophony, or withdrawal from debate sponsorship, while ensuring consistent and uniform treatment.[75] Thus, it seems an exaggerated fear of the *image* of disordered, chaotic debates, rather than meaningful factual evidence, that leads the Court to worry that requiring procedural protections for access will cause public stations to flee the debate-sponsoring role.

How much preestablished specificity judges demand, of course, depends in part on how valued the particular activity is. Here, too, what divided federal judges so evenly might well have been whether multi-candidate debate itself was viewed as a benefit or as a cost to "democracy." Thus, Justice Stevens emphasized that a third candidate who was not likely to win might nonetheless change electoral outcomes by taking votes from a dominant party candidate; in this sense, even if Forbes himself were properly characterized as "not a serious candidate," excluding him from the debate "may have determined the outcome of the election."[76] For Justice Stevens, the power to affect electoral outcomes self-evidently makes a candidate's participation a benefit to democracy. But while the Court's opinion says nothing about that issue, one wonders whether a group of justices who, in *Timmons,* expressed fear of the "destabilizing effects of party splintering and excessive factionalism,"[77] would not consider an independent candidate's outcome-determinative effects on elections a *cost* to democracy, rather than a self-evident benefit.

Because many aspects of elections implicate constitutional values—the vote, access to the ballot, participation in public debates—legal issues will inevitably arise concerning the levels of specificity required of electoral regulation. Whether that specificity must be provided in advance through a formal legal text, whether it can be generated through institutional processes, or whether it is required at all are questions judges will confront repeatedly. That empirical facts could in themselves resolve these issues seems unlikely; does Jesse Ventura's victory in Minnesota, made possible partly by his third-party participation in debates, enhance or threaten appropriate democratic politics?[78] That narrow partisan concerns could explain or motivate results in cases like *Forbes* seems equally implausible. That constitutional doctrine is itself specific enough to determine the level of specificity required of state actors in *Forbes* is also challenged by the divisions, again, among a large group of federal judges. That cultural assumptions and images of ideal democracy play a significant role in explaining differences in cases like *Forbes*—assumptions and images not falsifiable as facts, nor provable through internal legal analysis—is the alternative explanation I mean to suggest here. If we are to recognize and understanding the emerging constitutional law of democracy, it is necessary, I believe, to see the central role that these cultural assumptions play.

BUSH V. GORE: CONSTITUTIONALISM'S APOTHEOSIS

Bush v. Gore can now be seen to exemplify, not narrow interests uniquely tied to the 2000 presidential election (or not just such interests alone), but a broader, recurrent approach in the current Supreme Court to cases involving democracy. Whether this will make the decision less troubling—or more—I leave to the reader. But in two respects, *Bush v. Gore* expresses characteristic practices and assumptions of the current Court. First, *Bush v. Gore* represents the ready invocation of constitutional law to supplant or replace democratic arenas for determining the essential structures of the most fundamental political processes. *Bush v. Gore* is in the same spirit as *California Democratic Party v. Jones,* only more so: *Bush v. Gore* reflects constitutionalism's ultimate transcendence of democratic politics. Resolution of a disputed presidential election is the most political, the most incendiary issue that the American electoral system can confront. In no earlier era would it have even seemed it imaginable that constitutional law and Supreme Court adjudication would be the final mechanism for such a resolution. Indeed, over a hundred years ago, Congress created a congressional mechanism for resolving disputed presidential elections—and recoiled in bipartisan horror at the prospect of the Supreme Court resolving such disputes. In the Electoral Count Act of 1887, much discussed during the 2000 election but not ultimately employed, Congress adopted a mechanism for congressional resolution, with ultimate default rules, for ending disputed presidential contests. In explaining the deliberative choice of a political mode for resolving such disputes, Senator Sherman, a leading supporter of the statute, asserted that the proper means to resolve a disputed presidential election was "a question that is more dangerous to the future of this country than probably any other."[79] In justifying congressional rather than Supreme Court resolution, he went on to argue:

> Another plan which has been proposed in the debates at different times and I think also in the constitutional convention, was to allow questions of this kind to be certified at once to the Supreme Court for its decisions in case of a division between the two Houses. If the House should be one way and the Senate the other, then it was proposed to let the case referred directly to the prompt and summary decision of the Supreme Court. But there is a feeling in this country that we ought not to mingle our great judicial tribunal with political questions, and therefore this proposition has not met with much favor. It would be a very grave fault indeed and a very serious objection to refer a political question in which the people of the country were aroused, about which their feelings were excited, to this great tribunal, which after all has to sit upon the life and property of all the people of the United States. It would tend to bring that court into public odium of one or the other of the two great parties. Therefore that plan may probably be rejected as an unwise provision. I believe, however, that it is the provision made in other countries.[80]

Yet in an era in which it has become routine for the Court to conclude that constitutional law should determine the basic institutional arrangements of democracy, it was no great leap for the Court to conclude that presidential election contests too could appropriately be resolved through Supreme Court decision.

The second way in which *Bush v. Gore* is characteristic of the emerging law of democracy lies in the reasons, assumptions, and visions of democracy upon which the Court seemingly relied. These reasons and assumptions reflect those that the Court has come routinely to invoke in other cases involving democratic politics. Both these points—the fact that the Court has constitutionalized aspects of democracy and the apparent reasons the Court has done so—have general implications for the future of the law of democracy. I will elaborate briefly on each.

1.

I mean the first point in a more minimal way than do many critics of *Bush v. Gore*. These critics make a superficially similar, but more sweeping, point. Many argue (including some dissenting justices) that the Supreme Court should not have gotten involved, in any way, in the 2000 election dispute.[81] On this view, the legal issues should have been left to the Florida courts; if further consideration were appropriate, the place for that would have been Congress when it played its constitutionally specified role of receiving Florida's electoral vote count. Perhaps. But once the state courts become involved in a presidential-election dispute, it becomes more difficult to conclude that there should be no role at all, even a limited oversight role, for the United States Supreme Court. Should a rational structuring of the federal-state judicial relationship preclude all federal court oversight, in any form, of how state courts resolve determinative legal issues in presidential elections? I am skeptical of such a position.[82]

There is certainly room to dispute how the Court should exercise its role of constitutional oversight of state-court decisions in national-election disputes. But the view that the Court has no constitutional authority, in principle, to oversee state judicial decisions, even ones purporting to interpret state law, is hard to square with the constitutional structure and with the constitutional status of the right to vote itself.

A more limited critique, then, of the Court's intervention would start with an acceptance that Supreme Court oversight of state courts in national elections is, at least in principle, justified. Instead, the criticism of *Bush v. Gore* would then be, not that the Court was wrong to intervene at all, but that its substantive basis for resolving the contest was wrong. That substantive basis rested on the procedural and substantive protections the constitutional right to vote ought to require during manual recounts of a disputed election contest. The substantive violation of equality, according to the Court, was that different counties in Florida were free to use different standards as to what counted as a legal vote, even though the contest involved a statewide election. Ballots marked identically might be a legal vote in Palm Beach County but not in Broward County. Critics of the Court's equal protection holding have tended to focus primarily on this purported defect. One form this criticism takes is the argument that, if different counties are permitted to use different voting technologies—which have different levels of effectiveness in recognizing and tabulating "votes"—why is the equal protection clause then violated if different counties choose different substantive rules as to what makes for a legal vote? But even if one accepts this criticism, this is a response that fails to engage the Court's procedural objections to the way Florida's recount was conducted. And ultimately, these procedural objections seem to me the ones that critics of the Court must engage, for these procedural concerns are the strongest basis for the equal protection (or due process) principles that inform *Bush v. Gore.* County officials possessed vague, essentially standardless discretion to decide what standard to adopt in determining whether a ballot contained a valid vote. The concern is that such open-ended discretion, particularly in the hands of partisan, elected officials, would enable them to engage in partisan discrimination against the opposing party's candidate; indeed, with so much at stake, it would be easy to imagine that the manipulation of the counting process toward partisan ends could occur both intentionally and even de facto if not consciously intended. If there are no clear, relatively objective standards specified in advance as to what counts as a valid vote, proving that this discrimination has taken place can be difficult, even if it does occur. As in other areas of constitutional law where the Court adopts prophylactic rules because it is difficult to prove in individual cases whether constitutional violations are taking place, so too with the right to vote: to prevent partisan officials from acting on the obvious temptation to adopt rules or counting practices in the middle of an election dispute that will favor their own partisan purposes, constitutional law might require that the rules be specified in advance in clear enough form to prevent partisan officials from exercising standardless discretion at all.

Florida law did, of course, require that the determination be made based on "the intent of the voter," but if there are constitutional concerns when vote counting is manipulated for partisan purposes, then that "intent of the voter" command might not, in and of itself, provide a clear enough rule, specified in advance, as to what would appropriately manifest that intent. Had Florida law or prior administrative practice filled in the "intent of the voter" standard in advance of the disputed election—or perhaps even if the Florida Supreme Court had given more determinate content to that standard at an early stage of the dispute—perhaps that ought to be sufficient to satisfy the procedural requirements surrounding the constitutional right to vote. In theory, judges would be available to oversee the recount process at the last stage. But if county boards were engaging in partisan manipulation in either the standards they adopted or the way they applied those standards to specific ballots, any possibility that judges would have been able to re-visit that count to bring uniformity and consistency to it, under the exceptional time pressures involved, seems speculative at best. That is not to say that the Court was right in its procedural equal protection concerns; I cannot do justice to that debate here. But I do want to suggest that these are serious concerns, not to be dismissed lightly. That is what Justices Breyer and Souter, along with five other Justices, concluded. And the prospect of partisan officials, free to adopt and apply different and highly subjective standards in a context in which everyone knew (or thought they knew) which way those standards would cut on an issue in which all were intensely interested did, at the least, send a chill down my equal protection bones.

But it matters not, for present purposes, whether we think the Court right or wrong about how it resolved the equal protection issue. For the point of this essay would hold even if the Court were right on that question; even conceding that, *Bush v. Gore* would still exemplify an extraordinarily aggressive constitutionalization of struggles long considered, appropriately, best left to political rather than judicial processes. The central question the election dispute poses would still remain, even if the Court's equal protection principles are accepted. That question is what the relationship should be be-

tween constitutional law and courts, on the one hand, and politics and legislative institutions, on the other.

And here the Court bypassed the obvious answer—even assuming the
Court should have intervened, and even assuming its equal protection analysis is correct. The Court could have gone so far as to specify the processes
and rules required for a constitutional recount; doing so would have fully
protected the constitutional right to vote. But even having gone this far, the
Court could then—as it likely would have in an ordinary case—sent the case
back to have that constitutional recount process carried out under the supervision of Florida judicial and executive officials. We do not know what would
have ensued. It might soon have become apparent that a recount under the
constitutional standards the Court had laid out in *Bush v. Gore* could not be
completed by the day the electoral college was to meet (December 18); if so,
it is plausible that the Florida Supreme Court, already divided 4–3 about
whether to permit further counting *before* the Supreme Court's decision in
Bush v. Gore, would itself then have terminated the counting. But if not (if a
constitutional recount were completed before December 18 or if one were
permitted to go after that date) Congress would ultimately then have resolved the election when it met in January to count the electoral votes—and
Congress would have decided, as well, whether it has power to accept votes
after the electoral college has met. We must keep in mind—whether the justices did or not—that Congress would have faced these issues not in a vacuum, but in a post–*Bush v. Gore* world that the Court itself would have
helped to structure. That is, any recount totals presented to Congress would
have resulted from a recount process overseen by Supreme Court standards,
one in which consistent, uniform, clearly specified vote-counting standards
would have been required.

The choice, then, need not have been an all-or-nothing one between constitutional law and democratic politics. Had the Court been concerned to
preserve as much space as possible for democratic politics, except where
strong constitutional reasons justified a judicial role, solutions were at hand
that would have respected a role for both constitutionalism and democracy.
These solutions were also legally well-supported; as most scholars have suggested, the most widely criticized part of *Bush v. Gore* is the Court's reason
for declining to send the case back to the Florida courts regarding what

Florida law required in the wake of *Bush v. Gore.* The Court could have specified the constitutionally required process for a recount; yet the ultimate decision about what to do with the vote totals and ballots could also have been left to the United States Congress, the institution most widely accountable democratically for any choice about how to resolve the election. But instead the Court specified the constitutional process for a recount, then in the same moment terminated that process altogether (and on the basis of reasons that the strongest defenders of *Bush v. Gore* find hard to credit[83]). Constitutional law overwhelmed any role for democratic politics; the Supreme Court displaced Congress entirely from the process. The contest did become an all-or-nothing one between constitutional law and democratic politics. Not surprisingly, in light of the larger pattern of the current Court's cases, constitutional law dominated. The question, now, is why.

2.

How does one get at the deeper explanations, reasons, and assumptions that might motivate judicial decisions in particular cases, especially a case as freighted as *Bush v. Gore?* Not surprisingly, given the press of time, the decision itself is brief and unrevealing. If one believes that the formal legal reasons expressed do not exhaust the considerations that might have been at work in a case of this magnitude, how can one gain insight into what those other considerations might have been?

One method is to situate a particular case in a pattern of decisions, decisions that themselves are more revealing and self-consciously articulate. By looking at the images, metaphors, and rhetoric that emerge in these decisions, it can become possible to obtain glimpses of the worldviews that inform the Court's decisions. That is what I have tried to do here. In case after case, a majority of the current Court—the five justices who voted to end the election litigation, joined at times by Justices Breyer and Souter—has worried about the "stability" of American democracy and the risk of "excessive fragmentation" of American politics. Where other judges have seen competitive practices that ensure a robust and vital democratic system, the current Court has seen threats to orderly democratic processes. The suggestion here is that it is these kind of concerns, assumptions, beliefs, and values played a contributing role in *Bush v. Gore*. When the Court stared at other institutions that might have settled the election, particularly Congress, it did not see a healthy democratic mechanism for political struggle and stable resolution. Instead, the Court saw the specter of disorder, constitutional "crisis," and dangerous instability.

This fear that democratic institutions would be unable to ensure their own stability, and the perceived need for constitutionally imposed order, would be consistent with each of the Court's interventions into the election. The Court acted with surprising alacrity to assert control over the dispute, a haste suggested by its choice to hear the election litigation the first time, in *Bush v. Palm Beach County Canvassing Board*,[84] followed by its conclusion that no substantive issue of law was yet ready to be decided at that point. The Court's stay order too is indicative of a perceived need to intervene to establish order and control even before the moment of final decision. Whatever the true reasons for these actions, individually and as a whole, the Court's actions seem to manifest anxiety about the capacity of other institutions, including political ones such as Congress, to avoid unleashing what the Court might well have perceived as "the furies of civil commotion, chaos, and grave dangers."[85]

Another method of getting at the assumptions about democracy behind *Bush v. Gore,* and therefore, possibly behind the current Court's other democracy cases, is to look at the justifications that others have offered for the decision. And here, we owe a debt of gratitude to Judge Richard Posner, the leading academic defender of the decision. Freed from the conventions that hamstring judicial opinions, and with his usual relish for exposing cant, Judge Posner has put before us his candid, realist's account of why *Bush v. Gore* was right. He nods towards a possible legal foundation for the decision, based on Article II of the Constitution (and rejects all other legal arguments for *Bush v. Gore*), but he hardly hides his own view that this legal argument plays little role in his endorsement. As Posner forthrightly admits, "there was sufficient play in the legal joints to enable either side to write a professionally respectable opinion justifying its preferred outcome."[86] Acknowledging, therefore, that the legal argument is hardly compelling, Judge Posner goes on to say the decision is one whose most convincing justification is pragmatic.[87] Pragmatic in what sense? In that the failure of the Court to intervene "might have precipitated a constitutional crisis"[88]—a crisis that, in Posner's view, would "place *Bush v. Gore* with the Emancipation Proclamation and *Korematsu*"[89] as cases in which the relevant constitutional text "could be stretched"[90] to "enable a national crisis to be averted by constitutional means."[91] (Posner does not think that "the crisis" over election 2000 was as ominous as the Civil War, only that it was ominous enough.)

In defending *Bush v. Gore,* Posner articulates precisely the cultural assumptions that I see running throughout the Court's recent cases involving the relationship between constitutional law and democratic politics. Posner too sees opposing visions of democracy—and the need for the Court to police democracy—as the decisive consideration in *Bush v. Gore.* As he says, "[o]n one side [his side] was a preference for order—for an orderly transition, an orderly succession, an avoidance of protracted partisan wrangling, or an awkward interrgenum, and of a diminished presidency."[92] The opposing side, which would involve congressional resolution of the election, Posner characterizes and disparages as "a preference for a more populist, perhaps even carnivalesque, but certainly less orderly and legalistic conception of American democracy. . . ."[93] Those more charitably disposed toward this approach might simply call it a preference for democratic practices, period.

LAW, ORDER AND DEMOCRACY

The structures and ground rules through which American democracy is constituted will continue to come under pressure in the coming years. Whether through third-party challenges, uses of the voter initiative, efforts to impose structural changes like term limits, regulation of campaign financing, or other vehicles, efforts to criticize and revise conventional modes of politics seem likely to continue. Whether one agrees with any measure in particular, the larger issue is how much latitude courts will give democratic arenas to confront and respond to these challenges. What role should constitutional law play in constraining the ongoing self-revision of democratic processes?

To argue that constitutional law should play no role would be historically naive. Experience has shown that a central pathology of democratic institutions is the tendency of those who currently hold power to use the law to entrench their power more permanently. There is an important role for constitutional law to play in ensuring that existing officeholders not use their political power to insulate themselves from political competition. That is the lesson on which much of modern constitutional law and theory has been built. From the rise of the one-vote one-person doctrine, in response to generations of legislative malapportionment,[94] to John Hart Ely's famous statement in *Democracy and Distrust* that the Supreme Court's quintessential role is to ensure that the channels for political change remain open, modern constitutional law has properly recognized circumstances that justify constitutional oversight of democratic politics.

But the current Court now constrains democratic options routinely, almost reflexively, in circumstances that bear no relationship to those that had previous justified a more focused, discrete role for constitutional law. Indeed, the Court has turned this previous understanding of the boundary between democracy and constitutional law on its head in two ways. First, the Court has created constitutional constraints on democratic processes when there is no risk that political insiders are manipulating democratic structures to perpetuate their own power. To the contrary, it is often dominant political insiders who run to the Court these days to seek protection against change. The blanket-primary case, *Jones,* illustrates this phenomenon. This transformation is what I call the all-too-ready "constitutionalization of democratic politics." Second, the reasons the Court appears to be constitutionalizing democracy themselves invert the justifications for constitutional oversight of politics. Before, the Court had acted to keep the channels of political change open, in the face of the temptations insiders faced to use legislative power to insulate themselves from competition. But now, it is robust political competition itself that the Court perceives to be the problem. To hear the Court, or its defenders like Judge Posner tell it, American democracy is fragile, on the brink of fragmentation and disarray, in danger of getting out of hand, and hence in need of judicially imposed order to ensure sufficient political stability.

The election decision is over. But the cultural assumptions about democracy that lie behind it will shape how the Court responds to the coming challenges to existing forms of democratic politics. Whether democracy requires order, stability, and channeled, constrained forms of engagement, or whether it requires—and even celebrates—relatively wide-open competition that may appear tumultuous, partisan, or worse, has long been a struggle in democratic thought and practice. The stark opposition, of course, is false: Democracy requires a mix of both order (law, structure, and constraint) and openness (politics, fluidity, and receptivity to novel forms). But whatever the analytical truth about the necessity of both order and openness to democracy, different actors will perceive the greatest threat to come from one direction rather than the other. The current Supreme Court consistently now acts as if the greatest threat is that democracy will become too unstructured, too excessive. The Court believes constitutional law is necessary to help save us from that prospect. *Bush v. Gore* is only the most visible expression of those beliefs. The question we are left with is whether that is the cultural attitude toward democracy we want our judges—including our Supreme Court Justices—to take. Is the democratic order fragile and potentially destabilized easily? Or is the democratic order threatened by undue rigidity, in need of more robust competition and challenge? Does democratic politics contain within itself sufficient resources to be self-correcting? Or must legal institutions carefully oversee political processes to ensure their continued vitality?

The current Court decidedly shows, in Judge Posner's words, "a preference for order." At the same time, we live in an era of significant disaffection with the existing order of politics. In response, the Court has invalidated experiments with new forms of democracy while refusing to require that the system be open to emerging sources of challenge. The Court has done so not because political insiders are manipulating the rules of democracy for self-interested reasons. The Court has done so because it believes, or fears, or assumes that American democracy requires judicial constraint to ensure that stability and order are maintained. Given the resilience and endurance of American democracy, including its capacity for self-revision and correction, is that fear the right stance to stake? Should democracy be constitutionalized to this extent?

5. *Bush v. Gore* as Pragmatic Adjudication

Richard A. Posner*

I have undertaken a tough brief—to defend pragmatic adjudication in the context of the most execrated modern decision of the Supreme Court, a decision widely and I think correctly regarded as defensible, if at all (which most critics of *Bush v. Gore* deny, some considering the decision not only manifestly unsound but actually corrupt[1]), as a pragmatic solution to a looming national crisis.

I have already published a book about the election deadlock and the ensuing court battles,[2] and I want to repeat as little of it as possible beyond what is necessary to set the stage for a discussion of pragmatic adjudication with reference to the Supreme Court's handling of the matter. I will therefore not discuss the causes and character of the deadlock and the rich statistical issues involved in those questions, the issues of democratic theory that the deadlock and its judicial resolution raised, the need for electoral reform that the deadlock and the cases highlighted, the performance of the lawyers, and the criticisms of the Court by law professors—all matters discussed at length in the book.

What I cannot avoid is a fairly full discussion of the legal setting in which the cases arose, which unfortunately is complex. But I will cut some corners. I refer the reader to the relevant chapters of my book for additional detail.[3]

There are two statutes, and several constitutional provisions, that have to be understood. I will introduce them in the order in which they appeared in the unfolding controversy that began early in the morning of November 8, when it became clear that the presidential election would be determined by the winner of the popular vote in Florida and that the vote was so close that, under the Florida election statute, a recount was automatic unless the loser (Gore) didn't want it; and he did want it. The recount involved running the ballots through the tabulating machinery again and when it was completed, Bush's lead had shrunk from 1,782 votes to only 327, though overseas absentee ballots had yet to be counted. The Florida statute entitles a candidate to demand that a county's election board conduct a recount, by hand, of a sample of the ballots cast in the election. If this recount reveals an "error in the vote tabulation" that may have affected the outcome, the board is authorized to undertake various remedial measures, including a hand recount of all the ballots cast.

Gore demanded the sample recount in four heavily Democratic counties (Miami-Dade, Palm Beach, Broward, and Volusia). These recounts revealed numerous instances in which voters, by not punching cleanly through the chad of a presidential candidate,[4] had failed to cast a vote for the candidate that the tabulating machines would record. Gore requested a full hand recount. The election statute requires, however, final submission of the county vote totals to the state division of elections within seven days of the election (with an exception for overseas ballots), and only Volusia County completed a full hand recount by then and so was able to include the results in the final vote totals that it submitted to the state election division. Katherine Harris, who as secretary of state was Florida's highest election official, refused to extend the statutory deadline, as she could have done; she ruled that it could be extended only in exigent circumstances—such as a natural disaster that had interfered with vote counting or recounting—that were not present. The state's election statute authorizes the state election officials both to interpret and to apply the statute. The statute neither sets forth grounds for an extension of the statutory deadline nor defines "error in the vote tabulation." Nor does it specify the criteria to be used in a hand recount to recover votes from ballots spoiled by voter error, although it does say that in the case of "damaged" or "defective" ballots a vote shall be recorded if there is a "clear indication of the intent of the voter."[5] The head of the division of elections, Harris's subordinate Clayton Roberts, ruled that voter errors are not errors in the vote "tabulation," and so there was no basis for the full hand recounts in any of the four counties, for none had based their request for a waiver of the statutory deadline on defects in the design, maintenance, or operation of the tabulating machines.

Had these rulings stood, Bush would on November 18, 2000, after the addition of the late-arriving overseas ballots to the total, have been declared the winner of the popular vote in Florida by 930 votes. But before this happened, Gore brought suit to extend the statutory deadline for counting the votes.

The trial judge held that Harris had not abused her discretion (the canonical standard for judicial review of administrative action) by refusing to extend the deadline. But the Florida Supreme Court, on November 21, reversed the trial court and ordered the deadline extended to November 26. The court relied in significant part on a provision of the Florida constitution that states, though without mention of voting, that "all political power is inherent in the people." The court not only extended the deadline to a date of its choosing, but it ruled that in any recount conducted during the enlarged period voter-spoiled ballots should be counted as valid votes as long as the voter's intent was discernible.

Within the extended deadline, Broward County completed a full hand recount, which produced many new votes for Gore. After inclusion of Broward's results, and other adjustments, on November 26 Harris proclaimed Bush the winner of the Florida popular vote by only 527 votes.

Florida's election statute authorizes the bringing of a suit to contest the election result certified by the secretary of state. One of the grounds for such a suit—and the only one relevant to the 2000 presidential election—is that not all "legal votes," a term characteristically left undefined by the statute, were included in the result. Gore brought a contest suit, complaining principally about the fact that the Miami-Dade election board had abandoned its hand recount because it couldn't complete it within even the extended deadline. He also contended that the results of the recount by the Palm Beach board (which showed a net gain of either 176 or 215 votes for Gore—probably the former, but this has never been determined), completed only a few hours after the extended deadline expired, should have been included in the final vote totals. In addition, Gore complained that the Palm Beach board, whose recount had recovered far fewer votes for Gore than Broward's recount, had used too stringent a standard for recovering votes from voter-spoiled ballots. In particular it had refused to count dimpled ballots[6] as votes unless the ballot had at least three dimples, a pattern that the board thought suggested that the voter had indeed been trying to vote in this fashion as distinct from having dimpled a chad inadvertently or having failed to punch it through because of a last-minute change of mind about voting for that candidate.

The trial judge found that the Miami-Dade board had not abused its discretion in deciding to abandon the recount, because there was no reason to think that a fair hand recount would produce a large enough gain for Gore to make him the winner of the popular vote in the state, and that the criteria used by the Palm Beach board in its recount were not an abuse of discretion either. The trial confirmed that the spoiled ballots were indeed owed to voter errors, or to errors in which the voter was complicit (for example, for failing to seek assistance from polling-place personnel if unable to punch through a chad because of chad buildup in the tray of the punch card voting machine), rather than errors in the tabulating machinery. The trial also revealed that there was no agreed-upon standard on when to count dimples as votes.

Meanwhile, the Florida Supreme Court's decision of November 21 extending the deadline for submission of final county vote totals had been appealed to the U.S. Supreme Court, which agreed to hear the appeal and on December 4 rendered a unanimous decision vacating the Florida court's decision and sending the case back to that court for further consideration. The decision relied on a provision of Article II of the Constitution, which says that a state shall appoint its presidential electors in the manner directed by the state's legislature. The Court interpreted the "manner directed" clause as forbidding a state court to usurp the legislature's prerogative of determining the criteria of appointment. The Court thought the Florida court might have done this in using the "all political power is inherent in the people" provision of the state constitution to support its decision overriding the judgments of the state election officials. But it wasn't sure, so it sent the case back to the Florida court for clarification that was not immediately forthcoming. Eventually, on December 11, that court issued its "clarifying" opinion, in which it said that its decision of November 21 had actually been based on the "plain language" of the election statute, although it did not explain why, if so, it had placed so much weight on the "people power" provision of the state constitution. Moreover, what it seemed to mean by its reference to "plain language" was not, as is the usual understanding of the "plain meaning" standard of statutory interpretation, that the statute on its face dictated the decision, but rather that the decision did no violence to the statute's language because the language was vague. If it was vague, however, the court should have deferred to the interpretation adopted by the state election officials. The fact that they were partisan Republicans did not disentitle them to the usual deference that reviewing courts grant to administrative decisions interpreting vague statutes that the administrative agency is responsible for enforcing. The Florida legislature had decided to make the secretary of state an elected official; elected officials are entitled to at least as much judicial deference as bureaucrats, and probably—because of their greater democratic legitimacy—more. And the election board in Miami-Dade County that had decided to abandon the hand recount was dominated by Democrats, not Republicans.

The trial judge's decision throwing out Gore's contest suit had also been issued on December 4 and on December 8 the Florida Supreme Court reversed, though this time by a vote of 4–3 (the November 21 decision had been unanimous). The court rejected the central thesis of the trial judge's decision, which was that the determination whether the certified vote totals had excluded enough "legal votes" to make a difference in the outcome of the election was one for the state and local election officials to make, not judges, subject to judicial review only for abuse of discretion. The Florida Supreme Court ruled further that the judgments of the election officials were entitled to *no* weight. The consequence was that the election outcome certified by the secretary of the state, even though it was the outcome produced by the court's own extension of the statutory deadline, had not even presumptive significance in the contest proceeding. (But if so, why had the court bothered to extend the deadline, thereby compressing the period for completion of the contest, including any further recount that a judgment in the contest suit might direct?)

Unsatisfied that all "legal votes" had been counted, the state supreme court directed that the Palm Beach recount results, along with the partial results of the interrupted Miami-Dade recount, be added to the candidates' totals, a step that pushed Bush's lead below 200 votes. It ordered that all the undervoted ballots in the state, some 60,000, be recounted by hand (including the balance of the Miami-Dade ballots) but by judicial personnel throughout the state rather than by the county election boards or state election officials. The Florida court refused to establish criteria for recovering votes from spoiled ballots more specific than the intent of the voter; and refused to authorize a recount of overvoted ballots (of which there were about 110,000), which are ballots that contain votes, or markings interpreted or interpretable as votes, for more than one candidate for the same office.

This decision the U.S. Supreme Court stayed the next day and reversed on December 12 in *Bush v. Gore*. A five-justice majority (Rehnquist, O'Connor, Scalia, Kennedy, and Thomas) held that the recount order was a denial of the equal protection of the laws. The decision specified the first two and the last two of the five rulings listed in the preceding paragraph as creating arbitrary differences in the treatment of different voters' ballots. Normally, the remedy for such a violation would be to return the case to the lower court with instructions to purge its order of the unconstitutional features. Alternatively, the Court might have specified the terms of a recount order that would satisfy the requirements of equal protection. Instead, it declared that Florida law forbade resumption of the recount because it could not be completed by December 12 (of course not—the U.S. Supreme Court's decision was not issued until the night of December 12), which is the "safe harbor" deadline under Title III of the U.S. Code, the electoral count act. The act specifies procedures for counting electoral votes. Each state is to vote on December 18, and the votes are to be counted on January 6.[7] But if a state appoints its electors by December 12, they can't be challenged when Congress meets to count the electoral votes. The Florida Supreme Court's opinions in the election litigation had seemed to treat December 12 as the deadline for determining the state's electors, lest the determination be rejected by Congress. These intimations were the basis for the five-justice majority's ruling in *Bush v. Gore* that as a matter of Florida law the recount could not resume.

Two justices, Souter and Breyer, agreed that the recount order raised problems of equal protection that required a remedy, but thought the proper remedy would be to send the case back to the Florida court for the design and conduct of a proper recount. Three of the justices in the majority (Rehnquist, Scalia, and Thomas) opined that in addition to violating equal protection, the recount order violated Article II. Souter and Breyer disagreed; the remaining two justices, Stevens and Ginsburg, disagreed that the recount order violated any constitutional provision.

The dissenters had to consider what might happen if the case did not end on December 12. This was and is extremely unclear. Here is a worst-case scenario that is by no means fantastic, or even highly improbable:

The recount is resumed, and it results in a determination that Gore is the winner of the Florida popular vote. The state supreme court upholds the determination and directs Jeb Bush, the governor of Florida, to cast Florida's 25 electoral votes for Gore. By now, however, since the statewide recount and judicial review of it could not be completed within a week, December 18 has come and gone; and it happens to be unclear whether electoral votes cast after that day can be counted at all, because the Constitution provides that all the electoral votes must be cast on the same day. Meanwhile, the Florida legislature, dominated by Republicans, has appointed a slate of electors pledged to Bush, relying on a provision of the electoral count act that authorizes the state legislature to select the electors if the normal state procedure (the popular election held on November 7) has failed to do so.

The act provides that Congress shall convene on January 6, the first day of the new Congress, in joint session for the counting of the electoral votes. The two houses of Congress are to meet separately, however, to resolve any challenges to any of the electoral votes that the states have cast. The House is Republican, but the Senate is divided 50–50, and until January 20 is controlled by the Democrats by virtue of the vice president's authority to vote to break ties; for Gore retains his office until then. The electoral count act provides that if the two houses cannot agree on the resolution of a dispute involving rival slates of electors—a likely outcome given the split control of Congress—the electoral votes certified by the state governor shall be counted. The Florida Supreme Court has ordered Jeb Bush to certify the Gore slate, but he has refused and certified the George W. Bush slate. The court has responded by holding him in contempt and declaring his certification a nullity and the Gore slate the slate legally certified by the governor. The governor remains defiant, so there are two slates of electors that have purported to cast Florida's electoral votes.

The houses of Congress can no more agree on the resolution of this dispute between Governor Bush and the Florida Supreme Court than it could agree on the resolution of the original dispute between the two slates. Nor can the houses agree on what happens if *no* electoral votes from Florida are counted because the impasse remains unresolved. Does Gore win because he has a majority of the electoral votes that are counted, or does the candidates' lack of an absolute majority throw the election into the House of Representatives, where Bush would win? (The Constitution is unclear, and the electoral count act silent, on the point.) The U.S. Supreme Court refuses to intervene, invoking the "political questions" doctrine. The core of that doctrine is judicial refusal to resolve issues the resolution of which has been confided to another branch of government and which lack the characteristics of a justiciable controversy.[8] The Constitution puts the counting of electoral votes in the hands of Congress with no hint of a judicial role and with no indication of a standard that a court might use to resolve a dispute over those votes.

On January 20, the deadlock still unresolved, an acting president is appointed, probably Lawrence Summers, the secretary of the treasury.[9] The order of appointment is speaker of the House, president pro tempore of the Senate, secretary of state, and secretary of the treasury (there is no need to dip further into the list, which goes on and on), but anyone who accepts the appointment must resign his office, including membership in Congress, in the case of the speaker and the president pro tempore. Neither the speaker of the house (Hastert) nor the president pro tempore of the Senate (Thurmond) would be likely to accept the appointment under these conditions, the latter because his resignation from the Senate would give control of the Senate to the Democrats. Madeleine Albright, the secretary of state, is ineligible for the appointment because she is foreign born.[10]

It is true that the scenario that leads to the appointment of Summers assumes that a vice president has not been selected, since, if he has been, he becomes acting president.[11] But it is extremely unlikely that a vice president would have been picked by January 20. The Twelfth Amendment provides that if no candidate for vice president receives a majority of electoral votes, the Senate shall choose the vice president—but to win, a candidate must receive a majority of the entire Senate, and the 50–50 split in the Senate would prevent this. (The vice president is not a member of the Senate, and so he couldn't vote to break this tie.) And this is on the assumption that it has somehow been resolved that neither candidate obtained a majority of the electoral votes, an issue likely in fact to be deadlocked.

But who becomes acting president is actually a detail from the standpoint of resolving the deadlock over who is to become president. There is no constitutional or statutory provision authorizing the appointment of an acting vice president, and so there would be no one to break Senate ties, making it unclear, therefore, how or when the deadlock over the presidency would be resolved. Not a happy situation, all agree; and the significance of this fact for *Bush v. Gore* is at the heart of the issue of pragmatic adjudication in relation to the Court's decision.

But I have to say something about pragmatic adjudication before I can apply the concept to the decision. And I have to say something about pragmatism before I can define and evaluate pragmatic adjudication.

Pragmatism has two distinct meanings, a philosophical and an everyday. The latter—which is usually in the adjectival form, *pragmatic*—means practical and businesslike; "no nonsense," disdainful of theory and intellectual pretension, and contemptuous of moralizers and utopian dreamers. It shades into "hard-nosed," and in some circles is viewed negatively. John F. Kennedy and his advisors were said to be "pragmatists" because they rejected moralism and ideology (as embodied in such Democratic figures as Adlai Stevenson and Chester Bowles) in the conduct of governmental affairs both foreign and domestic,[12] and some people think the Vietnam War was a legacy of this kind of thinking. Everyday pragmatism of the hard-nosed variety could be said to descend from Machiavelli, though he is better regarded not as an amoralist (the popular sense of "Machiavellian") but as a realist about politics who thus understood that public morality, which is the kind required for the performance of political tasks, not only differs from private morality but should not be judged by its proximity to the latter.[13]

Philosophical pragmatism is sharply different from everyday pragmatism, though a family resemblance is discernible, and in some versions of philosophical pragmatism fairly close. Philosophical pragmatism comes in two varieties, which I'll call *orthodox* and *recusant*.[14] Both are critical of the central philosophical tradition of the West, the tradition that begins with Plato and continues with Aristotle, Aquinas, Descartes, Locke, Kant, and Russell (the last a particularly bitter foe of pragmatism), among many others. The tradition is concerned to the point of obsession with establishing the conditions that make it possible (or impossible—for philosophical skepticism is part of the tradition) to regard truth and knowledge as objective (meaning, basically, observer-independent) entities—scientific truth but in many versions moral, political, legal, and even aesthetic truth as well. The quest is for conditions that will enable us to know with confidence, to prove even—and to people who don't share our own values or presuppositions—that there is an external world, that the universe didn't spring into existence last week, that other people have minds, that science can provide correct descriptions of reality, that $2 + 2 = 4$, that cats don't grow on trees, that no human being has ever eaten an adult hippopotamus at one sitting, that the Nuremberg tribunal was legal, and that torturing innocent children is wrong. Orthodox pragmatism, illustrated by the classical American pragmatists—Peirce, James, and Dewey—but also by the later Wittgenstein, by Quine, Davidson, Hilary Putnam, and Richard Rorty, even perhaps by Hegel, Nietzsche, and Habermas, disagrees with the way the central tradition handles these questions. These philosophers believe that many of the traditional problems of philosophy can be dissolved by being shown to be pseudo-problems, or even ignored completely.

Consider Wittgenstein's criticism in *On Certainty* of G. E. Moore's attempt to prove that he had a body. Wittgenstein argues that the knowledge that one has a body is firmer than any method of proving the fact could be, since a proof can be doubted but no sane person doubts that he has a body. To prove what we cannot doubt, in order to dispel skepticism (doubt, for example, whether there is an external world or whether I am simply dreaming it), is thus a pointless, futile undertaking. Similarly, although the fact that no human being has ever eaten an adult hippopotamus cannot be verified directly, any more than the existence of the external world can be, it is a good deal more certain than many of the phenomena of which we have direct sensory perception; this suggests the pointlessness of prescribing conditions, such as verifiability, for certifying knowledge as true. Even logic does not deliver such assurance. Suppose that a swan is defined as a bird that has various characteristics, including being white. And then one day someone sees a bird that has all the same characteristics except the color. We can either change the definition of *swan* to include this new bird, or we can stick with the old definition and call it something else. Neither response to the new observation is superior to the other, and this means that logical truths can be dislodged empirically, and also that the decision whether to respond to a new experience by altering a logical or an empirical belief is an expedient one.

As these examples suggest, orthodox pragmatism is continuous with the central tradition, because it accepts the centrality of the issues with which that tradition is preoccupied, though it thinks it can do better with them. Orthodox pragmatism is not a rupture with the central tradition (hence my term for it), and indeed draws heavily on philosophers in that tradition, such as Hume and Mill and the logical positivists (whom the pragmatists claim to refute, as in the last two examples in the preceding paragraph—yet to an outsider to academic philosophy, the affinities between these two schools are greater than the differences). The recusant pragmatists, in contrast, a group well illustrated by some of the same philosophers, notably Dewey and, again, the later Wittgenstein (for the gap between the orthodox and recusant schools is not as great as I am pretending), and also by Marx and Richard Rorty, don't think the epistemological and ethical questions that have largely defined the classical tradition worth asking, because they don't think that anything of consequence other than to a career in academic philosophy turns on the answers; the questions are just a distraction from the business of helping us to understand and improve the world, whether the physical or the social. The recusants don't think that anything of moment is at stake, for example, in asking whether science provides us with true descriptions of reality. Science has dramatically increased our ability to control our environment, and nothing more is necessary to establish that it's a useful method of inquiry. Whether it's successful because its theories accurately describe the actual structure of the universe is irrelevant to any practical human interest. We now think Euclidean geometry, Ptolemaic astronomy, and Newtonian physics are all false descriptions of our universe, and yet each of them had and retains enormous utility in practical ventures (sailors still navigate by the Ptolemaic map of the universe).

And similarly if somewhat less clearly, if asked to accept a utilitarian or a Kantian or a religious approach to moral questions, the recusant pragmatist will want to know what the likely consequences of the various approaches are for the things that he's interested in. If his moral intuitions clash with the teachings of moral theory, he will be inclined to go with his intuitions. He will not be impressed, for example, by the utilitarian arguments for infanticide or euthanasia, or the Kantian argument for never lying, or Catholic arguments that abortion violates natural law. He'll want to know what's in it for him to believe in any of these things.

I called the impotence of moral theory less clear than that of epistemology because, while debates over the foundations of knowledge have no power to change people's behavior (no one doubts that he has a body and can't swallow a hippo), debates over morality can, because people sometimes act from a sense of duty or from fear induced by belief in a punitive deity. Moral philosophy, however, seems to have very little power to change people's behavior, hence, few consequences in the real world as opposed to the theory world of the academic philosopher. So the recusant pragmatist is apt to think moral philosophy a useless—or at least a distinctly peripheral—activity.

While the orthodox pragmatist is firmly within the modern philosophical mainstream, battling over the traditional questions with the traditional rhetorical and dialectical weapons, only reaching different conclusions from the classics, the recusant pragmatist is hostile to the mainstream, tempting one to describe this type of pragmatism as anti-philosophical. I have yielded to this temptation on occasion. But I was mistaken. It is one thing to ignore mainstream (or indeed all) philosophy, as most people do; it is another thing to attack it, which is a move within philosophy, however heterodox. Philosophy has no fixed boundaries; if someone spends his career writing against philosophy, what else might one usefully call him but a philosopher? If Rorty and the other recusant pragmatists are not philosophers, what are they? Another way to put this is that the recusants don't want to abandon philosophy, but to redirect it; their hope is "of substituting a less professionalized, more politically oriented conception of the philosopher's task for the Platonic conception of the philosopher as 'spectator of time and eternity.' " [15]

What has all this to do with pragmatic adjudication? Orthodox pragmatism has nothing to do with it. It is a part of technical philosophy, in which few judges take any interest. It is not entirely unrelated to what judges do, because philosophical issues occasionally crop up in litigation. [16] And for the few judges who happen to have some acquaintance with philosophy, orthodox pragmatism might undermine whatever belief those judges may have picked up from their philosophical reading that law might have an autonomous logical structure, enabling the correctness of judicial decisions to be determined with certainty. In other words, orthodox pragmatism might clear the decks. But it wouldn't put anything on them; it would not give the judge an alternative conception of the judicial role to replace the discredited logical one.

Recusant pragmatism has at most a mood or atmospheric effect. It is mainly about refusing to take canonical philosophy seriously, which judges generally refuse to do anyway. Yet the recusant pragmatists don't want to annul philosophy; they want to redirect it, put it in the service of life. (Dewey and Rorty are clearest about this.) They want to encourage a mind-set that will be more conducive than the traditional philosophical outlook to constructive engagement with the world's problems, a mind-set skeptical of abstraction and disdainful of certitude (of coming to rest—the dogmatic slumber), regarding knowledge as a tool for coping rather than as a glimpse of eternity, science as a process of inquiry rather than a pipeline to ultimate reality, and morality as a set of useful rules for getting along rather than an imperative duty either imposed upon us by God or necessarily implied by our nature as reasoning beings. Dewey, much taken with Darwinism, thought that since we're animals, our minds must have evolved not in order to put us into contact with a transcendent realm of truth, beauty, and goodness—the hope that Plato had for us—but to enable us to control our environment better. We believe things when it's useful to believe them and so we demand evidence of the likely consequences before according belief to a proposition.[17]

All these points can be made just against the mainstream philosophers who reject them, but there also may be a spillover of this style of thinking into nonphilosophical fields, and even into the activity of judging. John Dewey thought so. He wrote (and in a law review, no less, so he was trying to reach—and teach—the legal profession), that what law needed was "a logic *relative to consequences rather than to antecedents.*" This would be a logic (he means a method) that would treat general rules and principles as "working hypotheses, needing to be constantly tested by the way in which they work out in application to concrete situations."[18] He concluded that "infiltration into law of a more experimental and flexible logic is a social as well as an intellectual need."[19] This conclusion, however, was not an *implication* of pragmatism; there is no intrinsic incompatibility between any version of philosophical pragmatism and a belief that a judge should *not* consider the consequences of what he's doing. That is the position of Friedrich Hayek, for example, and he defends it, in part anyway, on a ground congenial to a pragmatist—that judges will produce better results if they just enforce existing rules and understandings, come what may, leaving any improvements to legislation or the slow workings of custom.[20] There is nothing in any version of philosophical pragmatism to enable a choice between Dewey's and Hayek's approach to law; the choice is an issue in the design and operation of political institutions.

This point is connected to the lack of any political valence to pragmatism. Richard Rorty's belief that the pragmatic outlook favors social democracy is contradicted by the powerful vein of pragmatic thinking in German jurisprudence during the Weimar and Hitler eras. Carl Schmitt, the most influential German legal thinker of that period, grounded his rejection of liberal legal theory in his belief that the real logic of the law was a logic of consequences rather than one of antecedent principles.[21] Structurally, his view of law was quite similar to Dewey's; as for law's content, pragmatism was and is silent.

Formalism as a pragmatic strategy (roughly Hayek's approach) puts one in mind of rule utilitarianism, which can be understood as a recognition that the means to an end needn't have the same structure as the end. A rule against the knowing punishment of an innocent person accused of crime, come what may, does not aggregate and compare pains and pleasures, yet it may be the best means of promoting that aggregation and comparison. And similarly we might think that responsibility for considering and if necessary adjusting the consequences of judicial action are best lodged elsewhere than in the judiciary. That is a far cry from rejecting pragmatist philosophy in favor of some classical philosophy such as utilitarianism or Catholic natural law or the political morality of Kant or Rawls and deriving from the chosen philosophy a philosophy of adjudication.

This "what works" mentality that the recusant pragmatist seeks to encourage is pretty close to the everyday meaning of *pragmatic*. In fact, if you're as skeptical as I am that philosophy has any resources for making practical proposals for human betterment,[22] or that it has any purchase on the judicial mind, the constructive side of pragmatic philosophy falls away, and (if the destructive is accepted) there is no longer anything *in philosophy* to help the judge decide cases.

So if judges are pragmatic, as I think they largely are (in our system, at any rate) it can only be in the everyday sense of the term. So let's consider what it might mean for judges to be pragmatic in that sense. I will approach the question mainly through *Bush v. Gore*, but a few preliminary remarks will help frame the inquiry.[23] First, while legal formalism *could* be a sound pragmatic strategy, it is unlikely to be, at least for a very powerful court like the United States Supreme Court. The consequences of its decisions can be momentous, and—especially when a decision is premised on the Constitution—they are very difficult to undo. Had the Court decided not to stop the Florida recount, there is very little that I can see that would have headed off the worst-case scenario that I sketched earlier. There was nowhere else to shop for a resolution of the deadlock. The scenario was not inevitable; but given the weirdness of recent U.S. political competition, it could not be thought phantasmal.

Second, pragmatic adjudication does not mean ad hoc decision-making; that is, always deciding in such a way as to bring about the best possible consequences somehow determined. Such an approach would be unpragmatic in its disregard of the systemic, or long-range, consequences of ad hoc adjudication. Those consequences are summarized in the expression *rule of law*. To a pragmatist this connotes not legal formalism in the sense of blind conformity to preexisting norms—*ruat caelum ut fiat iustitia*—but a due regard for the political and social value of reasonable certainty, continuity, and predictability of legal rights and duties and so for the circumscription of judicial discretion. This in turns implies a respectful attitude on the part of the judges toward constitutional and statutory text, and precedents, as the most important materials of judicial decision, for those are the materials on which the community necessarily places its principal reliance in trying to figure out what the "law" is; that is, what the judges will do with a legal dispute if it arises. What the good pragmatist judge tries to do, therefore, is to balance the good effects of steady adherence to the "rule of law" virtues, which tug in favor of standing pat, against the bad consequences of failing to innovate when faced with disputes to which the canonical texts and precedents are not well adapted. (This adaptionist perspective is emphasized in Dewey's essay on law, echoing Darwinian thinking.)

There is no algorithm for striking this balance, and really there is very little to say to the would-be pragmatic judge except that he or she should try to make the decision that is reasonable, all things considered, where *all things* include the standard legal materials and the desirability of maintaining the values of impartiality, impersonality, and predictability that are summed up in the term *rule of law,* but also include the consequences so far as they can be discerned of the decision in the case at hand. The approach is nebulous and banal, and will horrify most legal professionals as a belittlement of legal reasoning and hence an insult to their mystery; but law could do with some demystification.

But at the very least the pragmatic approach is an improvement over legal positivism in H. L. A. Hart's influential account. In that account judges "legislate" but only in the open area where the conventional materials of decision run out. In other words, the judge's discretion is limited to filling gaps in "the law;" he employs a logic of antecedent principles until he encounters a gap and then he switches to a logic of consequences. The pragmatic approach effaces this sharp boundary between the closed and open areas, and in doing so it tracks the actual psychology of judges, for whom the duty to decide is primary and obscures any sharp line between applying and creating law. Judges don't say to themselves, "I've run out of law to apply, so now it's time for me to put on my legislator's hat."

Another way to put this is that the pragmatic approach permits the judge to open the closed area, though cautiously, upon a careful weighing of the consequences of doing so, of somewhat unsettling the law in order to achieve an important practical goal. In thus giving due weight to the rule-of-law values, the pragmatic approach is less nakedly political than that of the political scientists who write about courts, some of the legal realists of yore, and the members of the fast-fading critical legal studies movement. So it is a via media of sorts, though it can still be criticized as giving judges too much room to roam around in, as well as denying that legal reasoning differs significantly from ordinary reasoning; for it enjoins the judge simply to be reasonable. The reply to this criticism is that it's impossible to pen judges in by persuading them to adhere to the traditional formalist rhetoric, which is anyway just a mask rather than the vocabulary of some cogent method of professional analysis. We'll see this point illustrated in *Bush v. Gore,* to which I now turn.

The single most arresting feature of the litigation to a pragmatist is the worst-case scenario that it avoided. Had that scenario been enacted, the forty-third president would have taken office after long delay, with no transition, with greatly impaired authority, perhaps amidst unprecedented partisan bickering and bitterness, leaving a trail of poisonous suspicion of covert deals and corrupt maneuvers, and after an interregnum unsettling to the global and the U.S. domestic economy and possibly threatening to world peace. (How would the crisis over the Chinese seizure of our surveillance plane been resolved by Acting President Summers? And would other hostile foreign powers or groups tried to test us during the interregnum?) The second most arresting feature of the litigation is the conflict of interest of the Supreme Court justices, which arises from the fact that judges are not indifferent to who their colleagues and successors are and know that the identity of the president is likely to make a difference—nowadays, given the dependence of the candidates on the extremists in their parties, a big difference—in who is chosen to fill a vacancy on the Supreme Court. The third most arresting feature, though arresting primarily because of its interaction with the second, is the lack of an obvious handle in the Constitution for stopping the recount.

The first feature of the case, the adverse consequences for the nation of permitting the election deadlock to drag on into and maybe even after January, is the easiest for the pragmatist to work with. The threat of national crisis aligned *Bush v. Gore* with a host of earlier Supreme Court cases in which actual or impending national crises seem to have influenced the outcome. One is *Korematsu v. United States*,[24] the case that upheld the military order, issued a few months after the Japanese attack on Pearl Harbor, that excluded persons of Japanese ancestry, even if they were U.S. citizens, from the west coast of the United States. The Supreme Court held that the order, though unquestionably a species of racial discrimination, was a permissible exercise of the war-making powers that the Constitution grants to Congress and the president. The Court noted that the fear of possible sabotage by persons affected by the order was supported by the reported refusal of thousands of American citizens of Japanese ancestry to swear unqualified allegiance to the United States. Justice Jackson dissented in an opinion—surprising in one of the most distinguished pragmatic justices in the history of the Supreme Court—in which he said that because a court is in no position to determine the reasonableness of a military order, the order's reasonableness could not be a defense to a charge of racial discrimination: "a civil court cannot be made to enforce an order which violates constitutional limitations even if it is a reasonable exercise of military authority."[25] This is the same justice who famously said that the Constitution is not a suicide pact,[26] which could well be the slogan of pragmatic Supreme Court justices. While stating that "defense measures will not, and often should not, be held within the limits that bind civil authority in peace,"[27] Jackson would have forbidden the courts to back up the military order by convicting Korematsu for violating it, pursuant to a statute that made such violations criminal. But if the statute punishing violations of the order were unenforceable, the efficacy of the order, and of "defense measures" taken in time of war generally, would be weakened.

Liberals detest *Korematsu,* just as they do *Bush v. Gore.* Yet they believe that the prohibition against racial discrimination can be bent, without violation of the Constitution, if the race discriminated against, under the rubric of affirmative action, is white rather than yellow. The cases are different, of course, though the net effect of the differences is unclear. Affirmative action is not stigmatizing; on the other hand there was a greater perceived urgency to taking defensive measures in World War II than there is to perpetuating affirmative action, a highly controversial policy now rather long in the tooth. *Bush v. Gore* is analytically similar to *Korematsu,* and *Korematsu* to cases allowing affirmative action, only—but it is not a trivial respect—in showing that powerful norms of legal justice, such as the non-discrimination principle, can bend to practical exigencies, whether it is winning a war or improving race relations.

A closer liberal counterpart to *Korematsu* than affirmative action, because it too involved a national emergency, is *Home Building and Loan Association v. Blaisdell,*[28] the case that fileted the contracts clause in the Constitution. In 1933, in the depths of the Great Depression, Minnesota passed a law that gave relief to debtors by declaring a moratorium on foreclosures. Although Article I of the Constitution forbids the states to pass laws impairing the obligation of contracts, and Minnesota's law did precisely that, the Supreme Court upheld the law. The Court reasoned ingeniously that "the policy of protecting contracts against impairment presupposes the maintenance of a government by virtue of which contractual relations are worth while—a government which retains adequate authority to secure the peace and good order of society." [29] This is a fancy way of saying that a state can impair the obligation of contracts, notwithstanding the constitutional provision (a provision aimed at debtor relief laws, which had flourished after the Revolution, frightening the commercial class and providing impetus to the enactment of the Constitution), provided it has a compelling reason to do so.

An emergency of another kind was presented by *Clinton v. Jones,*[30] the case in which the Supreme Court refused to give the president immunity during his term of office from being sued civilly for acts committed before he became president. The Court's notably unpragmatic decision, full of "no man is above the law" rhetoric, overlooked the potentially disastrous effect of making the president defend himself in a sex case prosecuted by his political enemies. Not only is the decision increasingly criticized as out of touch with reality, but it has incited calls for appointing to the Court people with more political experience than the present justices. The criticism and proposal attest to the vitality of pragmatic thinking in American law.

But now I must consider the second and trickier pragmatic issue presented by *Bush v. Gore,* the significance (if any) that the justices should have given to the conflict of interest inherent in their deciding, in effect, who would be making (though subject of course to Senate confirmation) appointments to the Supreme Court during the next four years. The existence of this conflict meant that if the conservative justices threw their weight behind Bush, as they did, they would be accused of partisanship, as they have been, and the prestige and hence authority of the Supreme Court would suffer, as it has, though we cannot say yet how much. The damage would have been lessened had the conservative justices managed to write a convincing opinion in defense of their position, but they did not. Neither the per curiam majority opinion nor the concurring opinion of Rehnquist, Scalia, and Thomas is convincing. The majority opinion adopts a ground (equal protection) neither persuasive in itself nor consistent with the judicial philosophy of the conservative justices, particularly the three just named, who joined the majority opinion without reservation while writing separately. Neither opinion discusses the pragmatic benefit of ending the deadlock, though without that benefit it is hard to see why the Supreme Court agreed to take the case, let alone why it decided it as it did. The Court's self-inflicted wound was worsened by Justice Scalia's action in writing an unconvincing opinion in support of the stay of the Florida Supreme Court's December 8 decision—an action that cast Scalia, the justice praised by name (along with Thomas) during the presidential campaign by Bush and denounced by name (again along with Thomas) by Gore as a "code word" for opposition to abortion rights, as the ringleader of a conservative cabal determined to elect Bush. The wound was also made worse by the tone of the dissents, particularly Stevens's.

Should the justices have worried not only about the harm that the decision might do to the Court's authority but also that future controversies over appointments to the Court would be embittered by the perceived partisanship of the decision? I think not, because bitter confirmation battles are likely for other reasons. They happen to be reasons connected to the inescapably pragmatic character of the Supreme Court's constitutional decisions. Pragmatic adjudication has regard to consequences but does not in itself determine their weight or valence. It accepts that each judge within the bounds of permissible judicial discretion (that is, with due but not excessive regard to the rule-of-law virtues) will make his own or her own determination on the basis of personal values, temperament, unique life experiences, and ideology. Long before *Bush v. Gore,* it was understood that the law crafted by the Supreme Court—especially but not only when the Court was interpreting vague or open-ended provisions of the Constitution—is not stabilized by text or precedent or the other tools of formalist judging. Supreme Court justices have and exercise broad discretion, legislative in character, however much they deny it. The only practical means of stabilizing law is to maintain a diverse judiciary, by analogy to stabilizing one's investment portfolio through diversification, and by being realistic at the time of nomination and confirmation about the likely course of the candidate's judging, a course that cannot be predicted from the disclaimers of "activism" that are a routine part of the confirmation ritual. *Bush v. Gore,* a notably pragmatic decision joined by several justices of distinctly formalist pretensions (particularly Scalia and Thomas), is just a reminder of what we should have known all along: that pragmatism is the secret story of our courts.

Suppose the conservative justices, first setting aside as improper or trivial their interest in who might be filling any vacancy in the Court in the next four years, had decided that, on balance, the damage to the Court from a decision perceived as partisan would exceed the damage to the nation from leaving the deadlock unresolved; would that determination have justified them in refusing to intervene? I think it would have, provided, however, that one distinguishes between the decision to grant certiorari, that is, to hear a case, and the decision of the case on the merits. The Court's jurisdiction is discretionary and by tradition it gives no reasons for granting or denying certiorari; nor is there a law that limits or guides the Court's exercise of its discretion. The absence of legal standards fairly invites a pragmatic approach, as Alexander Bickel argued.[31] Had the Court ducked the election crisis by simply refusing to grant any of the petitions for certiorari that were filed in the election litigation, it would not have been criticized as lawless or partisan, especially since—and this brings me to the third pragmatic issue—the Constitution had to be stretched to provide a remedy for Bush. Denial of certiorari would have been interpreted to mean that the Court didn't think Bush had a case; and this, as I'm about to argue, would have been a plausible though not a compulsory reading of the relevant texts and precedents.

But before I turn back to the case, I want to consider the following hyperpragmatic question: Had one of the conservative justices believed that the election of Gore as president would be a national calamity, would this have justified him or her in voting to stop the Florida recount? This question is perhaps the ultimate challenge to pragmatic adjudication. But fortunately the answer is no.[32] The systemic consequences of allowing partisan politics to influence Supreme Court decisions would be worse than the harm of having to put up with a bad president, of whom we have had many. Justices who thought it a part of their job description to overturn an election in order to annul a bad choice by the electorate would be deranging the balance of powers among the branches of government. If this is right, it suggests that a sound theory of pragmatic adjudication will incorporate elements of "rule pragmatism," that is, will rule *completely* out of bounds for judges certain consequential considerations. This is implicit in the rules forbidding judges to sit in cases in which they have a financial interest. The financial implications of a decision for the judge are among the consequences of adjudication that judges are—rightly—*never* permitted to consider.

Back to *Bush v. Gore.* There were two possible federal grounds for invalidating the recount ordered by the Florida Supreme Court. The first, and the one the majority of the justices embraced, was that the recount would deny the equal protection of the laws by distinguishing arbitrarily among voters in the Florida presidential election. Undervoted ballots would be recounted but not overvoted ones—the Florida court did not even try to give a reason for this distinction. And undervoters in Broward County (and perhaps other counties) would be treated much more favorably than undervoters in Palm Beach County (and perhaps other counties), because the election board in Broward County had used a more liberal standard for recovering votes from undervoted ballots than the Palm Beach board had used. The recounts in those two counties were at least completed; but the court declined to specify a uniform standard for the recount of the additional 60,000 undervotes throughout the state that it was ordering, except the "voter's intent" standard, which seems hopelessly vague when it comes to counting dimpled chads. And it made additional disparities inevitable by assigning the recounting to inexperienced judicial personnel, by truncating the right of the candidates to make objections to the counters' decisions, and by imposing unrealistic deadlines, though understandably so in light of the looming December 12 safe-harbor deadline.

The recount order was farcical. But did it violate equal protection? The objection to supposing that it did is that while the recount would have been a farce, the election itself had been a farce in the same sense; it had been administered in an arbitrary manner that had produced large differences across and probably within counties in the percentage of ballots that had actually been recorded as votes. It is doubtful that the recount would have produced a result closer to what a well-administered election would have produced; but it is difficult to say that it would have produced a worse result than the actual election. The underlying problem is the decentralization of election administration to the county and even the precinct level, which, along with a generally insouciant attitude on the part of election officials toward the details of election administration, causes arbitrary disparities in the likelihood that a person's vote will actually be counted as a vote, rather than rejected. This problem had not previously been thought to rise to the level of a denial of equal protection, and, as I have said, the recount would not have aggravated the problem, though it probably wouldn't have ameliorated it either.

So if the recount was a denial of equal protection, the implication was that our system of decentralized election administration is a denial of equal protection too. Unwilling to embrace this far-reaching implication of the ground of the decision, the majority opinion as much as said that the decision was not intended to have precedential significance in future election litigation.[33] This made the opinion seem thoroughly unprincipled, as did the remedy of stopping the recount. If the vice of the recount order was that its terms denied equal protection, the natural remedy would have been to direct the Florida Supreme Court to redo the order. To rule that Florida law, implicitly Florida case law (for there was nothing in the election statute on this point), forbade a recount after safe-harbor day was thoroughly unsound because there was no case law either, only hints by the Florida Supreme Court that December 12 was indeed the deadline for any recounting, hints properly regarded as alluding not to any rule of Florida law but to judicial discretion in the formulation of an appropriate remedy for the botched election.

The majority opinion must have been a particular embarrassment to the three most conservative justices (Rehnquist, Scalia, and Thomas), since while it is false that they never support claims of denial of equal protection, they could not be expected to be sympathetic to a ground of decision that implied that the nation's traditionally decentralized election administration is unconstitutional. But here pragmatic considerations come into play again. Had these justices refused to join the majority opinion, there would still have been a majority to stop the recount, because these three justices in their concurring opinion stated that the recount would violate Article II. But there would have been a majority to reject both grounds for stopping the recount: The three conservative justices, plus Stevens and Ginsburg, would have been voting to reject the equal protection ground, and all but the three conservative justices would have been voting to reject the Article II ground. The moral authority of the decision, at best limited because of the justices' conflict of interest, would have been further weakened by the fact that a majority of the justices had rejected the only available grounds for the decision.

So did those three conservative justices join an opinion they actually disagreed with? I don't know. But if they did, it would bring to the fore one of the unsettling features of judicial pragmatism, a kind of amoralism that connects it with the everyday sense of the word. If all that matters are consequences, then dishonesty, which might seem the correct term for subscribing to a judicial opinion that one thinks all wrong, while no doubt regrettable becomes just another factor in the calculus of decision. But maybe this *is* the right way to think about judicial honesty, or more precisely candor (for *honesty* has financial connotations that are irrelevant to the subject under discussion). A judge will often join an opinion with which he doesn't agree, because he doesn't think a dissent will have any effect, or because he thinks a dissent would merely draw attention to a majority opinion otherwise likely to be ignored, or because he doesn't think the issue important enough to warrant the bother of writing a dissent and doesn't want to encourage other judges to dissent at the drop of a hat. These are pragmatic judgments, and such judgments suffuse the writing of a judicial opinion as well, where tact and candor are frequent opponents. Are these bows to the practical to be regarded as tokens of dishonesty, of a subtle form of corruption brought about by yielding to the pragmatic Sirens? If not, perhaps the decision of the conservative justices to join the majority opinion in *Bush v. Gore,* a momentous decision, is defensible even if they had to hold their breath to do so.

The Article II ground for stopping the recount was far stronger than the equal protection ground, and the failure of Justices O'Connor and Kennedy to adopt it seems to me a major failure of judicial statesmanship. Article II is explicit that the setting of the ground rules for the selection of a state's presidential electors is the prerogative of the state's *legislature.* It is true that there is no evidence that the choice of this word (rather than simply of *state*) was deliberate, or that the framers of the Constitution foresaw the use of this provision of Article II to limit the scope of state judicial intervention in the selection of a state's electors. But constitutional provisions have traditionally been treated more as resources than as commands, resources that judges use to craft solutions to problems unforeseen by the framers. The problem at hand is a state court's intervening to change the result of an election of the state's presidential electors by changing the ground rules under which the election was held. Such intervention sets the stage for an interbranch struggle within the state over the choice of the electors, and such a struggle is likely to lead to the appointment of rival slates of electors and hence to the kind of crisis that

Bush v. Gore headed off. Article II establishes a clear line of demarcation between state judicial and legislative prerogatives in the selection of a state's presidential electors, and in doing so prevents the state courts from hijacking an election by changing the rules after the outcome of the election is known.

The Article II ground has been criticized as implying that state courts have no power to interpret the state's election statute so far as bears on presidential elections no matter how ambiguous or riddled with gaps the statute is, or to declare it unconstitutional no matter how blatantly its terms violate settled constitutional principles, whether federal or state. But that is not what the ground implies. The state courts retain their ordinary powers; the Supreme Court is authorized to intervene if, in the guise of interpretation, the state courts in effect rewrite the state election law, usurping the legislature's authority. The difference between interpretive and usurpative judicial "work" on statutes is subtle, but is illuminated by comparison to the settled distinction in the law of labor arbitration between an arbitrator's interpreting a collective bargaining agreement, on the one hand, and, on the other, importing his own views of industrial justice in disregard of the agreement. The former is legitimate interpretation, and is insulated from judicial review; the latter is usurpative, and is forbidden.

The interpretation of Article II that I have just sketched actually commanded the support of all nine justices in the first opinion in the election litigation, that of December 4. A unanimous decision by the Supreme Court may well be wrong, but it is unlikely to be so far wrong as to impair the Court's authority. The issue that divided the Court later was whether the Florida Supreme Court had stepped so far out of the line of the statute as to bring down the bar of Article II. That is a difficult issue, but as I have argued at length[34] and continue to believe, resolving it in favor of invalidating the court's rulings and hence stopping the recount would have been a plausible application of Article II. A majority opinion so finding with emphasis on the pragmatic justifications for this application of Article II would have been a defensible specimen of pragmatic adjudication, a vindication, even, of the merits of the pragmatic approach.

And it would have deprived critics of the Court of much of their ammunition. The justices could not have been accused of betraying their settled convictions, because none of them had ever written or joined an opinion dealing with the "manner directed" clause of Article II, which was last (and first) before the Supreme Court in 1892[35] and because views of the clause do not divide along "liberal" and "conservative" lines, as views of the equal protection clause do. The justices would have eluded other criticisms as well, because there would have been no need for the opinion to say that the decision had no precedential effect, since the ground of the decision would have had no implications for election administration generally. The Article II ground, being esoteric, would not have provided a handle for criticisms that the general public could understand. That ground has a clear textual basis in the word *legislature* in Article II. The ground could be persuasively related to the avoidance of the looming crisis. Overriding the Florida Supreme Court on the basis of Article II would not be an affront to states' rights (which the conservative justices of the U.S. Supreme Court have tended to favor in recent years), since it would be vindicating the authority of state legislatures. And there would be no awkwardness in the remedy of stopping the recount, since if the recount order should never have been issued, rather than should merely have been configured differently, there would be no occasion for a remand of the case to the Florida court, rather than an outright reversal.

The failure of the majority to adopt the Article II ground was a particular embarrassment for the Court's most conservative justices, Scalia and Thomas, who have gone out of their way in opinions and (in Scalia's case) in speeches and articles, to embrace a concept of adjudication that is inconsistent with the majority opinion that they joined. *Bush v. Gore*'s severest critic, Alan Dershowitz, delights in being able to quote Scalia's statement that when he writes a majority opinion, he limits his freedom of action:

> If the next case should have such different facts that my political or policy preferences regarding the outcomes are quite the opposite, I will be unable to indulge those preferences; I have committed myself to the governing principle. In the real world of appellate judging, it displays more judicial restraint to adopt such a course than to announce that, "on balance," we think the law was violated here—leaving ourselves free to say in the next case that, "on balance," it was not. . . . Only by announcing rules do we hedge ourselves in.[36]

How does this square with the statement in the majority opinion in *Bush v. Gore,* which Scalia joined however reluctantly, that "Our consideration is limited to the present circumstances, for the problem of equal protection in election processes generally presents many complexities?" It doesn't, inviting charges of hypocrisy, or worse—the charge of rank partisanship leveled against Scalia by Dershowitz on insufficient evidence, but plausible enough to resonate with the millions of Americans who already profoundly distrust the good faith of all government officials.

6. How to Democratize American Democracy

ARTHUR SCHLESINGER, JR.

The true significance of the disputed 2000 election has thus far escaped public attention. This was an election that made the *loser* of the popular vote the president of the United States. But that astounding fact has been obscured: first by the flood of electoral complaints about deceptive ballots, hanging chads, and so on in Florida; then by the political astuteness of the court-appointed president in behaving as if he had won the White House by a landslide; and now by the effect of September 11 in presidentializing George W. Bush and giving him commanding popularity in the polls.

"The fundamental maxim of republican government," observed Alexander Hamilton in the 22nd Federalist, ". . . requires that the sense of the majority should prevail." A reasonable deduction from Hamilton's premise is that the presidential candidate who wins most votes in an election should also win the election. But four times in the history of the American republic the people's choice has been denied the presidency. The ever-present possibility of crowning the popular-vote *loser* is surely the great anomaly in the American democratic order.

Yet the National Commission on Federal Election Reform, a body appointed in the wake of the 2000 election and co-chaired (honorarily) by former Presidents Gerald Ford and Jimmy Carter, virtually ignored it. Last August, in a report optimistically entitled *To Assure Pride and Confidence in the Electoral Process,* the commission concluded that it had satisfactorily addressed "most of the problems that came into national view" in 2000. But nothing in the ponderous 80-page document addressed the most fundamental problem that came into national view: the constitutional anomaly that permits the people's choice to be refused the presidency.

How did this anomaly arise? The answer, of course, is that the Constitution awards the presidency to the winner not of the popular vote but of the state-by-state electoral vote as registered in the electoral college. The electoral college, a last-minute addition to the Constitution, is a mystic agency hovering between the electorate and the presidency—impossible to explain to foreigners; even most Americans don't understand it.

Why the electoral college? Little consumed more time in the Constitutional Convention than debate over the mode of choosing the chief executive. The question was brought up, Professor Shlomo Slonim has calculated, on twenty-one different days and occasioned over thirty distinct votes. James Wilson, next only to James Madison in his influence on the proceedings, said, "The subject has greatly divided the House, and will also divide people out of doors. It is in truth the most difficult of all on which we have had to decide."

The Framers, determined on the independence of the executive and on the separation of powers, rejected the proposal that Congress elect the president. Though both Madison and Wilson argued for direct election by the people, the convention, fearing the parochialism of uninformed voters, also rejected that plan. "The extent of the country," said George Mason, "renders it impossible that the people can have the requisite capacity to judge of the respective pretensions of the candidates." In an age of great distances and difficult communications, voters would tend to go for people they know at the expense of national figures they had barely heard of.

In the end, the Framers agreed on the novel device of an electoral college. Each state would appoint electors equal in number to its representation in Congress. The electors would then vote for two persons. The one receiving a majority of electoral votes would become president; the runner-up, vice president. And in a key sentence the Constitution stipulated that of these two persons, one at least should not be from the same state as the electors.

Presumably the electors would be cosmopolitans who would know, or know of, eminences in other states. This does not mean that they were created as free agents authorized to ignore or invalidate the choice of the voters. This was not the Framers' intention. Electors were expected, though not legally required, to express the will of the voters. The Framers, with their talent for ambiguity, were hazy on the question of the electors' freedom to choose. Perhaps they were making tactical concessions in order to win the acquiescence of those who thought Congress should elect presidents. But the Framers did not expect electors routinely to contravene the popular will. The electors, said John Clopton of Virginia, are the "organs . . . acting from a certain and unquestioned knowledge of the choice of the people, by whom they themselves were appointed, and under immediate responsibility to them."

"The president," as Madison summed it up when the convention finally adopted the electoral college, "is now to be elected by the people." The president, he assured the Virginia ratifying convention, would be "the choice of the people at large." In the First Congress, he described the president as appointed "by the suffrage of three million people." "It is desirable," Hamilton wrote in the 68th Federalist, "that the sense of the people should operate in the choice of the person to whom so important a trust was to be confided." As Lucius Wilmerding, Jr., concluded in his magistral study of the electoral college, "The Electors were never meant to choose the president but only to pronounce the votes of the people."

The electoral system set the contours of American politics on a state-by-state basis. The electoral college's role was slightly modified in 1804 when the Twelfth Amendment required separate votes for president and vice president. Though unknown to the Constitution and deplored by the Framers, political parties were remolding the presidential election process. By 1836 all the states except South Carolina had decided to cast their votes as a unit—winner-take-all, no matter how narrow the margin. This decision minimized the power of third parties and created a solid foundation for a two-party system.

"The mode of appointment of the Chief Magistrate of the United States," wrote Hamilton in the 68th Federalist, "is almost the only part of the system, of any consequence, which has escaped without severe censure." This may have been true when Hamilton wrote it in 1788; it was definitely not true thereafter. The electoral system, though reluctantly accepted as part of the constitutional procedure, has had an uneasy existence. According to the Congressional Research Service, legislators since the First Congress have offered more than a thousand proposals to alter the mode of choosing presidents.

No one after the Constitutional Convention has advocated the election of the president by Congress. Some have advocated modifications in the electoral college—to change the electoral units from states to congressional districts, for example, or to require a proportional division of electoral votes. The latter approach received some congressional favor in the 1950s in a plan proposed by Senator Henry Cabot Lodge, Jr., and Representative Ed Gossett. The Lodge-Gossett amendment would have ended the winner-take-all electoral system and divided each state's electoral vote according to the popular vote. In 1950 the Senate endorsed the amendment by more than the two-thirds required by the Constitution, but the House turned it down. Five years later Senator Estes Kefauver revived the Lodge-Gossett plan and won the backing of the Senate Judiciary Committee. A thoughtful debate ensued, with Senators John F. Kennedy and Paul H. Douglas leading the opposition and defeating the amendment.

Each state, however, retains the constitutional right to appoint its electors "in such manner as the legislature thereof directs." In 2000, two states, Maine and Nebraska, split their electoral votes—two going to the winner of the statewide vote; the rest to the popular-vote winner in each congressional district. The other states kept the unit rule.

But neither the district plan nor the proportionate plan would prevent a popular-vote loser from winning the White House. To correct this great anomaly of the Constitution, many have advocated the abolition of the electoral college and its replacement by direct popular elections.

The first minority president was John Quincy Adams. In the 1824 election, Andrew Jackson led in both popular and electoral votes but, with four candidates dividing the electoral vote, failed to win an electoral college majority. The Constitution provides that, if no candidate has a majority, the House of Representatives must choose among the top three. Speaker of the House Henry Clay, who came in fourth, threw his support to Adams, thereby making him president. When Adams then made Clay his secretary of state, Jacksonian cries of "corrupt bargain" filled the air for the next four years and helped Jackson win the electoral majority in 1828.

Jackson was the first president to confront the constitutional anomaly and call for direct popular elections. "The first principle of our system," Jackson told Congress in 1829, is that *"the majority is to govern* . . . To the people belongs the right of electing their Chief Magistrate." "Experience proves," he continued—the experience in his own mind no doubt that of his 1824 defeat in the House of Representatives—"that in proportion as agents to execute the will of the people are multiplied there is danger of their wishes being frustrated." He asked for the removal of all "intermediate" agencies preventing "the expression of the will of the majority . . . It is safer for them to express their own will." The winner of the popular vote had the overriding claim to democratic legitimacy.

Jackson added in tacit verdict on Adams's failed administration, "A President elected by a minority can not enjoy the confidence necessary to the successful discharge of his duties." History bears out Jackson's point. Indeed, Adams himself came close to conceding it when he said in his inaugural address, "Less possessed of your confidence in advance than any of my predecessors, I am deeply conscious of the prospect that I shall stand more and oftener in need of your indulgence."

The next two minority presidents—Rutherford B. Hayes in 1877, Benjamin Harrison in 1889—had, like Adams, ineffectual administrations. All suffered setbacks in their midterm congressional elections. None won a second term in the White House.

The most recent president to propose a direct-election amendment was Jimmy Carter in 1977. The amendment, he said, would "ensure that the candidate chosen by the voters actually becomes president. Under the electoral college, it is always possible that the winner of the popular vote will not be elected." This had already happened, Carter said, in 1824, 1876 and 1888.

Actually, Carter placed too much historical blame on the electoral system. Neither J. Q. Adams in 1824 nor Rutherford B. Hayes in 1876 owed his elevation to the electoral college. The House of Representatives, as we have seen, elected Adams. Hayes's anointment was more complicated.

In 1876, Samuel J. Tilden, the Democratic candidate, won the popular vote, and it appeared that he had won the electoral vote too. But the Confederate states were still under military occupation, and electoral boards in

Florida, Louisiana, and South Carolina disqualified Democratic ballots in order to give Hayes the electoral majority.

The Republicans controlled the Senate, the Democrats the House. Which body would count the electoral votes? To resolve the deadlock, Congress appointed an electoral commission. By an 8–7 party-line vote, the commission gave all the disputed votes to Hayes. This was a supreme election swindle, and there was a season of great bitterness. But the compromise of 1877 appeased Democrats by terminating Reconstruction and turning the South over to the ex-Confederates. Three days before the inauguration, the electoral college by a single vote declared Hayes the next president. But it was the rigged electoral commission, not the electoral college, that denied the popular-vote winner the presidency.

In 1888 the electoral college did deprive the popular-vote winner, Grover Cleveland, of victory. But 1888 was a clouded election. Neither candidate received a majority, and Cleveland's margin was only 95,000 votes. The claim was made, and was widely accepted at the time and by scholars since, that white election officials in the South banned perhaps 300,000 black Republicans from the polls. In the North, as the chairman of the Republican National Committee observed, Harrison would "never know how close a number of men were compelled to approach the gates of the penitentiary to make him president." Fraud tainted the result both north and south. The installation of a minority president in 1889 took place without serious protest.

The republic went through several further elections in which a small shift of votes would have given the popular-vote loser an electoral college victory. In 1916, if Charles Evans Hughes had gained 4000 votes more in California, he would have won the electoral college majority, though he lost the popular vote to Woodrow Wilson by more than half a million. In 1948, a shift of fewer than 30,000 votes in three states would have given Thomas E. Dewey the electoral college majority, though he ran more than two million votes behind Harry Truman. In 1976, a shift of 8000 votes in two states would have made Gerald Ford president, though he ran more than a million and a half votes behind Jimmy Carter.

Many eminent politicos and organizations have joined Jackson and Carter in advocating direct popular elections—Presidents Richard Nixon and Gerald Ford, Vice Presidents Alben Barkley and Hubert Humphrey,

Senators Robert A. Taft, Mike Mansfield, Edward Kennedy, Henry Jackson, Robert Dole, Howard Baker, Everett Dirksen; the American Bar Association, the League of Women Voters, the AFL-CIO, the United States Chamber of Commerce. Polls showed overwhelming public support for direct elections. The Gallup poll in June 1944 recorded 65 percent in favor, 23 percent opposed (the rest had no opinion); in 1967, it was 58 to 22 percent.

In the late 1960s the direct-election amendment achieved a certain momentum. The campaign was led by Senator Birch Bayh, an inveterate and persuasive constitutional reformer, and it was fueled by the fear that Governor George Wallace of Alabama might win enough electoral votes in 1968 to throw the election into the House of Representatives. In May 1968 Gallup recorded 66 percent in favor of direct elections and in November an astonishing 80 percent.

In 1969 the House of Representatives approved a direct-election amendment by the impressive vote of 338–70. But the next year a filibuster killed the amendment in the Senate. Wallace's forty-six electoral votes in 1968 had not been enough to deny Nixon a majority, and an unjustified complacency soon took over. "The decline in one-party states," a Brookings Institution study concluded in 1970, "has made it far less likely today that the runner-up in popular votes will be elected president."

Polls continued to show popular support for direct elections—73 percent in 1977, 67 percent in 1980. But because the danger of electoral college misfire seemed academic, abolition of the electoral college became once again a low-priority issue: "Nobody has a kind word for the outmoded electoral college," wrote Robert Bendiner, "but only professors and cartoonists get really worked up about it."

Then came the election of 2000. Here was a flagrant example of the structural anomaly in the American polity. For the fourth time in American history, the winner of the popular vote was denied the presidency. And Albert Gore, Jr., had won the popular vote—not by Grover Cleveland's dubious 95,000—but by more than half a million. Another 2.8 million votes had gone to the third-party candidate Ralph Nader, making the alleged victor George W. Bush more than ever a minority president.

Nor was Bush's victory in the electoral college unclouded by doubt. The electoral vote turned on a single state, Florida. Five members of the Supreme Court, forsaking their usual deference to state sovereignty, stopped the Florida recount and thereby made Bush president. Critics derided the Court's decision. They wondered whether, if the facts had been the same but the candidates reversed, with Bush winning the popular vote (as indeed observers had rather expected) and Gore hoping to win the electoral vote, the gang of five would have found the same legal arguments to elect Gore that they used to elect Bush.

I expected an explosion of public outrage over the rejection of the people's choice. But there was surprisingly little in the way of outcry. In July 2001 the Oregon Democratic central committee, spurred on by former congressman Charles O. Porter, passed a resolution petitioning Congress to determine whether the gang of five on the Supreme Court should be impeached for their partisan intervention in the election. The proposal got nowhere.

For one thing, the new president, avoiding J.Q. Adams's acknowledgment of a deficit in public confidence, acted as if he had won a mandate. This was politically astute, and voters, weary after the prolonged electoral agony and eager to get on with their lives, accepted Bush's claim to legitimacy.

Another factor was the tepid reaction to the Gore candidacy. It is hard to imagine such popular acquiescence in a popular-vote loser presidency if the popular-vote winner had been, say, Adlai Stevenson or John F. Kennedy or Ronald Reagan. Such leaders attracted do-or-die supporters, voters who cared intensely about them and who would not only have questioned the result but would have been ardent in pursuit of fundamental reform. After a disappointing campaign, Vice President Gore simply did not excite the same impassioned commitment.

Justice Stephen Breyer, part of the Court's dissenting minority, suggested another factor in remarks before the American Bar Association in August 2001. The absence of outrage, Breyer was reported as saying, was evidence of the faith of Americans in their system of justice. The acceptance of the Court's 5–4 presidential choice, Breyer said, demonstrated "that losers as well as winners will abide by the result, and so will the public."

Of course there was no alternative to abiding by the result. But the absence of outrage made the search for reform technical rather than constitutional. Diverse commissions, official and unofficial, focused their reform interests on such topics as voting machines, ballot design, voter registration, access to the polls, absentee ballots, media reporting of election results, and uniform national standards for these and other matters. They did not focus at all on the most vital question posed by the 2000 election: the role of the electoral system as a subversion of democracy.

The modernization of electoral technology will no doubt produce a more accurate and efficient expression of voters' preferences. But it will not touch the great anomaly of the Constitution. Nothing in the technical reforms will prevent the rejection of the people's choice once again in the future.

Yet surely the 2000 election put the republic in an intolerable predicament—intolerable because the result contravened the theory of democracy. Many expected that the election would resurrect the movement for a constitutional amendment mandating direct election of presidents. Since direct elections have obvious democratic plausibility and since few Americans understand the electoral college anyway, its abolition seems a logical remedy for our intolerable predicament.

The resurrection has not taken place. Constitutional reformers seem intimidated by the argument that the direct-election amendment will antagonize the small states and therefore cannot be ratified. It would necessarily eliminate the special advantage conferred on small states by the two electoral votes handed to all states whatever their population. Small-state opposition, it is claimed, would make it impossible to collect the two-thirds of Congress and the three-fourths of the states required for ratification.

This is an odd argument because political analysts argue that the electoral college in fact benefits large states, not small states. Far from being hurt by direct elections, small states, they say, would benefit from them. The idea that "the present electoral college preserves the power of the small states," write Lawrence D. Longley and Alan G. Braun in *The Politics of Electoral College Reform,* ". . . simply is not the case." The electoral college system "benefits large states, urban interests, white minorities, and/or black voters." So too the Brookings report: "Advocates of the existing system approve of the power it gives to populous states. . . . The decline of the metropolitan bloc would be the most important change [brought about by direct elections]. For several decades liberal, urban Democrats and progressive, urban-suburban Republicans have tended to dominate presidential politics; they would lose influence under the direct-vote plan."

Minorities holding the balance of power in large states agree that the abolition of the electoral college would be disadvantageous. "Take away the electoral college," said Vernon Jordan as president of the Urban League, "and the importance of being black melts away. Blacks, instead of being crucial to victory in major states, simply become 10 percent of the electorate, with reduced impact."

And it is an odd argument too because the small vs. large state lineup has practically vanished since the constitutional convention. "None of the great battles of American political history—in Congress or in Presidential elections," Neal Pierce has pointed out, "has been fought on a basis of small versus large states."

The debate over whom direct elections would benefit—large states? small states? urban interests? rural interests? whites? blacks? Latinos?—has been long, wearisome, contradictory, and inconclusive. Even computer calculations assume a static political culture. They do not take into account, nor can they predict, the changes wrought in voter dynamics by candidates, issues, and events.

As Senator Kennedy said during the Lodge-Gossett debate, "It is not only the unit vote for the presidency we are talking about, but a whole solar system of governmental power. If it is proposed to change the balance of power of one of the elements of the solar system, it is necessary to consider all the others. . . . What the effects of these various changes will be on the federal system, the two-party system, the popular plurality system and the large-state-small-state checks and balances system, no one knows."

Direct elections have at least the merit of correcting the great anomaly of the Constitution and providing an escape from the intolerable predicament. The arguments for the direct-election plan are indeed powerful. "The electoral college method of electing a president of the United States," said the American Bar Association, "is archaic, complex, ambiguous, indirect, and dangerous." "Direct popular election of the president," said Birch Bayh, "is the only system that is truly democratic, truly equitable, and can truly reflect the will of people."

The plan meets the moral criteria of a democracy. It would elect the people's choice. It would ensure equal treatment of all votes. It would reduce the power of sectionalism in politics. It would reinvigorate party competition and combat voter apathy by giving parties the incentive to get out their votes in states that they have no hope of carrying.

The abolition of the electoral college would also solve the problem of the "faithless elector"—the person who is sent to the electoral college to vote for one candidate and then votes for another. This has happened from time to time in the past, could happen again, and might even change the outcome when the electoral vote is closely divided.

The direct-election plan sounds reasonable. Its objectives are excellent. But direct elections raise troubling problems of their own, especially their impact on the party system and on JFK's "solar system of governmental power."

In the nineteenth century, visiting Europeans were awed by the American commitment to politics. Alexis de Tocqueville in the 1830s thought politics "the only pleasure an American knows." James Bryce half a century later was impressed by the "military discipline" of American parties. Voting statistics justified transatlantic awe. In no presidential election between the Civil War and the end of the century did turnout fall below 70 percent of eligible voters.

The dutiful citizens of these high-turnout years did not rush to the polls out of uncontrollable excitement over the choices they were about to make. The dreary procession of presidential candidates moved Bryce to write his famous chapter in *The American Commonwealth* on "Why Great Men Are Not Chosen President." But the party was supremely effective as an agency of voter mobilization. Party loyalty was intense. People were as likely to switch parties as they were to switch churches. The great difference between then and now is the decay of the party as the organizing unit of American politics.

The modern history of parties has been the steady loss of the functions that gave parties their classical role. Civil-service reform largely dried up the reservoir of patronage. Social legislation reduced the need for parties to succor the poor and helpless. Mass entertainment gave people more agreeable diversions than listening to political harangues. Party loyalty became tenuous; party identification casual. As Franklin D. Roosevelt observed in 1940, "The growing independence of voters, after all, has been proven by the votes in every presidential election since my childhood—and the tendency, frankly, is on the increase."

Since FDR's day, a fundamental transformation in the political environment has further undermined the shaky structure of American politics. Two electronic devices—television and computerized polling—have had a devastating impact on the party system. The old system had three tiers: the politician at one end; the voter at the other; the party in between. The party's function was to negotiate between the politician and the voter, interpreting each to the other and providing the links that held the political process together.

The electronic revolution has substantially abolished this mediatorial role. Television presents politicians directly to voters who judge candidates far more on what the box shows them than on what the party organization tells them. Computerized polls present voters directly to politicians, who judge the electorate far more on what the polls show them than on what the party organization tells them. The political party is left to wither on the vine.

The last half century has been notable for the decrease in party identification, for the increase in independent voting and for the number of independent presidential candidacies by fugitives from the major parties: Henry Wallace and Strom Thurmond in 1948, George Wallace in 1968, Eugene McCarthy in 1976, John Anderson in 1980, Ross Perot in 1992 and 1996, Ralph Nader and Pat Buchanan in 2000.

The two-party system has been a source of stability. FDR called it "one of the greatest methods of unification and of teaching people to think in common terms." The alternative to the party system would be a slow, agonized descent into an era of what the political scientist Walter Dean Burnham has termed "politics without parties." Political adventurers might roam the countryside like Chinese warlords, building personal armies equipped with electronic technologies, conducting hostilities against some rival warlords, forming alliances with others, and, if they win elections, striving to govern through ad hoc coalitions. Accountability would fade away. Without the stabilizing influences of parties, American politics would grow angrier, wilder, and more irresponsible.

There are compelling reasons to believe that the abolition of state-by-state, winner-take-all electoral votes would hasten the disintegration of the party system. Minor parties have a dim future in the electoral college. Unless third parties have a solid regional base, like the Populists of 1892 or the Dixiecrats of 1948, they cannot hope to win electoral votes. Millard Fillmore, the Know-Nothing candidate in 1856, won 21.6 percent of the popular vote and only 2 percent of the electoral vote. In 1912, when Theodore Roosevelt's candidacy turned the Republicans into a third party, William Howard Taft carried 23 percent of the popular vote and only 1.5 percent of the electoral vote.

But the direct election plan, by enabling minor parties to accumulate votes from state to state—impossible in the electoral college system—would give them a new role and a new influence. Direct-election advocates recognize that the proliferation of minor candidates and parties would drain votes away from the major parties. Most direct-election amendments therefore provide that, if no candidate receives 40 percent of the vote, the two top candidates would fight it out in a runoff election.

The runoff would offer potent incentives to radical zealots (e.g., Ralph Nader), freelance media adventures (e.g., Pat Buchanan), eccentric billionaires (e.g., Ross Perot), flamboyant characters (e.g., Jesse Ventura) to jump into presidential contests; incentives too to green parties, senior citizen parties, nativist parties, right-to-life parties, pro-choice parties, anti–gun-control parties, homosexual rights parties, prohibition parties, and so on down the single-issue line.

Splinter parties would multiply not because they expected to win elections but because their accumulated votes would increase their bargaining power in the runoff. Their multiplication would very likely make runoffs the rule rather than the exception. One national election is alarming enough; a double national election is a fate almost too grim to contemplate.

Splinter parties would aim to extract concessions from the runoff candidates in exchange for their pledges of support. Think of the finagling that would take place between the first and second rounds of a presidential election! Like J. Q. Adams in 1824, the victors would become a new target for "corrupt bargains."

Direct elections would very probably bring to the White House candidates who do not get anywhere near a majority of the popular votes. The prospect would be a succession of 41-percent presidents or else a succession of double national elections. Moreover, the winner in the first round might often be beaten in the second round, depending on the deals the runoff candidates made with the splinter parties. This result would hardly strengthen the sense of legitimacy the presidential election is supposed to provide. Nor have I mentioned the problem in close elections of organizing a nationwide recount.

In short, direct elections promise a murky political future. They would further weaken the party system and further destabilize American politics. They would cure the intolerable predicament, but the cure might be worse than the disease.

Are we therefore stuck with the great anomaly of the Constitution? Is no remedy possible?

There is a simple and effective way to avoid the troubles promised by the direct-election plan and at the same time to attain its objectives—that is, to prevent the popular-vote loser from being the electoral-vote winner. The solution is to award the popular-vote winner a bonus of two electoral votes for each state and the District of Columbia. This is the national bonus plan proposed in 1978 by the Twentieth Century Fund Task Force on Reform of the Presidential Election Process.[1]

Under the bonus plan, a national pool of 102 new electoral votes would be awarded to the winner of the popular vote. This national bonus would balance the existing state bonus—the two electoral votes already conferred by the Constitution on each state regardless of population. This reform would virtually guarantee that the popular-vote winner would also be the electoral-vote winner.

At the same time, by retaining state electoral votes and the unit rule, the plan would preserve both the constitutional and practical role of the states in presidential elections. By insulating recounts, it would simplify the consequences of close elections. By discouraging multiplication of parties and candidates, the plan would protect the party system. By encouraging parties to maximize their vote in states they have no chance of winning, it would reinvigorate state parties, stimulate turnout, and enhance voter equality. The national bonus plan, combining the advantages of the historic system with the assurance that the winner of the popular vote would win the election, would contribute to the vitality of federalism.

The problem of the "faithless elector" can be easily solved by abolishing individual electors while retaining the electoral vote and the unit rule. There is the further problem, affirmed by the Supreme Court in *Bush v. Gore,* that the individual citizen "has no federal constitutional right to vote for electors for president unless and until the state legislature chooses statewide election." Individuals in 135 nations enjoy the constitutional right to vote, but, Professor Jamin B. Raskin tells us, the United States joins Iran, Iraq, Libya, Pakistan, Chechnya and a few other backward countries in neglecting to recognize that fundamental right in their constitutions. This should have been corrected long since.

The national bonus plan would be a basic but a contained reform. It would fit comfortably into the historic structure. It would not derange or unbalance JFK's "solar system of governmental power." It would vindicate "the fundamental maxim of republican government . . . that the sense of the majority should prevail." It would make the American democracy live up to its democratic pretensions.

How many popular-vote losers will we have to send to the White House before we finally democratize American democracy?

7. And to the *C* Students: The Lessons of *Bush v. Gore*

LANI GUINIER*

To loud boos as well as cheers, George W. Bush spoke at Yale University's 2001 commencement, to use his phrase, about his own college daze. According to the *New York Times* report, "He alluded to a tendency to nap. He alluded to activities that sometimes blotted out memory. He alluded, again and again, to an academic record of limited achievement."[1] "To those of you who received honors, awards and distinctions, I say, well done," Mr. Bush said. "And to the *C* students, I say, you too can be president of the United States." Someone yelled "barely" when he reminded his audience that he had received his first degree from Yale in 1968. Barely making it through college, Bush also barely made it to the presidency of the United States.

Just as his pedigree ensured his admission to Yale, so did it contribute to Bush's election. He campaigned, without apology, as the candidate of the rich. At one appearance with several hundred well-heeled contributors Bush said, not quite tongue-in-cheek, "This is an impressive crowd. The haves and the have-mores. Some people call you the elite. I call you my base."[2] And his friends in high places came through for him even before the legal maneuvering over Florida's twenty-five electoral college votes reached the highest court.[3] He raised more money than Al Gore and his voters were more educated and better-off than those who voted for the Democratic candidate.

Although Bush was certainly the candidate of the rich in 2000, to see the presidential election as a contest between the elites and ordinary Americans is not entirely accurate. Bush's elevation to the presidency was merely one manifestation of the way elitist assumptions about democracy still hover over our entire political process. From my perspective, better public policy decisions would have been likely had the wishes of the majority of all of Florida's voters, rather than a majority of the Supreme Court Justices, been heeded.[4]

Yet, the public policy differences between George W. Bush and his Democratic opponent Al Gore pale by comparison to what they had in common. Aided by our country's historic flirtation with a democratic aristocracy, each manifested a preference for hierarchy concealed in the guise of equality.

Both enjoyed the benefits of an elite education and a politically established family. They simply justified and used their privileged status differently. One served his pedigree and status in a relaxed west Texas accent; the other projected a confident and paternalistic rationality. One seemed to think that an elite should rule by virtue of its intellectual prowess; the other operated comfortably from the unspoken premise that generations of property holding (both public and private) constituted a legitimate credential.

Their personal characteristics and mannerisms tracked their politics. For Gore, the campaign was about the rich vs. "working families," and he was against the rich. But as a policy wonk, it was *his* plans and expert opinions that counted. Because he was even more learned and informed than his opponent, his perch atop a merit-based hierarchy entitled him to lead. George Bush drew an explicit contrast by presenting himself as a man with character and values that were less snobbish than his intellectually privileged opponent. His was a strategic effort to capitalize on the resentment such intellectual elitism can breed. For Mr. Bush, "the war is between the meritocracy and everyone else," and he was for everyone else.[5] Bush's goal was to distance himself from the operating assumptions of the reigning "meritocracy" that raw intellect was the key to the White House. This strategy effectively played upon the fact that there is something deeply alienating about paternalism, even when well-meaning or well-informed. As national security advisor Condoleezza Rice says in explaining her choice as a black woman to be a Republican, "I would rather be ignored than patronized."[6] Moreover, while Bush stood for and with the rich he offered an important concession. Come join us and we will try to help you become rich too.

Of course, Bush's effort to distinguish his you-too-can-be-rich populism from Gore's I-am-so-smart elitism involved the creation of a false dichotomy. The meritocracy, as reenacted by Al Gore and reinterpreted by George Bush, merely arrogated power to itself in a pattern that replicated more obvious forms of elitism. By limiting opportunities to those who succeed through ranking and sorting, the meritocracy fails to supply our citizens with equitable access to gain the necessary expertise to rule, and more important for the purposes of this essay, fails to involve ordinary people in the processes of democratic decision-making. As David Lebedoff writes, a big problem with the meritocracy is "that it doesn't really believe in majority rule, because if we already know who the smartest people are, why should we bother to solicit the opinion of anyone else?"[7]

In a similar display of arrogated power and off-putting presumptions of unique expertise, the Supreme Court halted the recounting of votes in Florida and thus handed George Bush the presidency. The Court's conservative majority claimed that only meritorious votes—meaning those that passed the Court-invented baseline of uniformity—were legal. As a close examination of the Supreme Court's jurisprudence makes clear, a preference for the supposedly uniform and neutral standards of meritocracy ultimately became a preference for a governing aristocracy in slightly more egalitarian guise.

Indeed, the Court's analysis underscores the evolving symmetry between meritocracy and aristocracy more generally. Some may still believe in what Nick Lemann calls an "Episcopacy" based on wealth and birth. Others prefer its liberal counterpart, a meritocracy based on testable mental aptitude that controls access to expertise. In either case, hierarchy trumps democracy.

Nevertheless, our democracy is not in danger just because Bush won the White House primarily through the intervention of our highest court. While that is certainly a troubling sign, the responsibility does not rest entirely with the legal system or what many legal academics term the ideological hypocrisy of the five Supreme Court justices who handed him the presidency.[8] The premise of this chapter is that the debacle of election 2000 was less surprising than inevitable given what we have come to accept in the name of democracy.

The unfortunate reality is that the first president of the twenty-first century embodies, in his personal as well as political biography, the odd way that terms like *democracy, meritocracy,* and *reigning plutocracy* have come to mean the same thing. The convergence of Bush's elite background and the hierarchical features of an electoral system that assured his victory is not mere serendipity. That a natural aristocracy should rule in a democracy was, in fact, the founding premise of many of our framers. As the second Justice

Harlan wrote in the late sixties, "it was probably accepted as sound political theory by a large percentage of Americans through most of our history, that people with some property . . . are consequently more responsible, more educated, more knowledgeable, more worthy of confidence, than those without means, and that the community and Nation would be better managed if the franchise were restricted to such citizens."[9] The country's founders implemented the idea of a democratic aristocracy by granting the vote almost exclusively to wealthy white male property holders and excluded white women, blacks, illiterates, and the landless. In fact, the chance to participate in the new republic was originally extended to just 120,000 of the two million free Americans (not counting the more than one million slaves and indentured servants). At the time, about 6 percent of the population was entitled to vote.[10]

Renowned for his lack of engagement with issues of policy, scholarship or the lives of ordinary Americans, George W. Bush rode this historical reality into the present. Yet Bush was not alone as a beneficiary of our civil union of democracy and aristocracy. Gore's embrace of the conventional assumptions of the meritocracy—its reification of a superior knowledge and special expertise—illustrates in the political realm the adverse, antiegalitarian effects that so-called uniform measures of "merit" demonstrate in the educational arena, a matter to which I will soon return. These practices elevate a few at the expense of the many and then, under the misleading claim that the criteria are "merit-" rather than wealth-based, justify the continued power and control of certain families. Because these people's claim to power is now legitimated by supposedly objective indicia of ability, they "deserve" to govern. Yet their very claim of "desert" has led to a crisis of confidence in two foundational ideas of democracy for a multiracial society: That the people themselves are capable of governing and that such capacity requires an interactive, engaging, and egalitarian space in which the people can become informed, deliberate, and influence public decision-making.

In response to this crisis in American democracy, we must raise our expectations and remember that democracy can involve more inclusive forms of self-government that create space for local organizing and collective action. In addition, as Ian Shapiro notes, "opposition rights" are important for democratic politics independently of the value of inclusive participation.[11]

We should begin to acknowledge that democracy is a system for structuring power relations and reconceptualize our own approach to value the interests and voices of the losers, not just those of the winners. We need to fortify the greatest resource of any functioning democracy—the people themselves—by building intermediate institutions that restore the link between the people and the act of political decision-making. In other words, it is time to confront the paradox of aristocracies based on inherited wealth or its liberal counterpart, inherited talent, governing our democracy.[12]

Section I explores a few of the more salient assumptions surrounding the Court's decision in *Bush v. Gore* in greater detail. I suggest that this decision, as flawed as it was, must be understood as one of a series of Court judgments that privilege hierarchical rules over more participatory and engaged forms of democratic decision-making. I argue that the continued institutionalization of aristocratic preference at the ballot box is only the tip of the iceberg in understanding the antidemocratic forces that plague our polity. The American political system has not shaken its roots in oligarchy—a problem for which the Supreme Court is only partially responsible. This crisis involves several elements, but mostly it centers on the stories both liberals and conservatives tell that reward and then justify rule by the most privileged Americans. Section II then examines ways to reconceptualize democratic citizenship to benefit all Americans. I argue that the experience of black voters in Florida showcases the need for such a reconceptualization, but this movement must ultimately tie the experiences of Americans of color to poor and working-class whites. It is only by creating intermediate institutions that can engage groups of citizens throughout the political process that we will begin to see what a richly participatory and more egalitarian democracy might look like.

I

Supplementing his individual charm and his efforts to put a different spin on the principal issues at stake, George W. Bush got a boost from many of the antidemocratic features of the electoral process that reflect our nation's complex heritage. For example, Bush lost the popular vote and only "won" the electoral college vote once the Supreme Court stopped the recounting of votes in Florida. As Yale law professor Akhil Amar argues, the electoral college was established as a device to boost the power of southern states in the election of the president. The same "compromise" that gave southern states more House members by counting slaves as three-fifths of a person for purposes of apportioning representation (while giving the slaves none of the privileges of citizenship) gave those states electoral college votes in proportion to their Congressional delegation. Treating nonvoting slaves as a political asset shifted power to the southern states; not surprisingly, Southern slaveholding presidents governed the nation for roughly fifty of the first seventy-two years of our country's existence. As a result, the institution of slavery and the concept of black inferiority on which it depended defined the institutions of democracy itself. As Henry Wiencek writes, "With their eyes open, the founders traded away the rights of African-Americans, many of whom had fought bravely in the revolution, so that the national enterprise could go forward." [13] That George W. Bush lost the popular vote yet gained the Oval Office through this very same electoral college is a depressing reminder that the legacy of racism distorts our governing structures to reinforce a tradition of hierarchy.

The conjunction of a reigning meritocracy with ideas of a natural aristocracy further bolsters this tradition. Both approaches limit opportunity to a small group of winners who then claim they can legitimately monopolize the processes of self-government. This tradition is complex, however, in that concepts that structure and institutionalize inequality coexist with values of democratic opportunity. That five justices of the United States Supreme Court ultimately decided the closely contested presidential election of 2000 on the grounds of equal protection of the law simply highlights these contradictions between our rhetoric and our practice. The Court, elsewhere unwilling to enforce a broad view of the rights of individuals of color to equal protection, took an expansive view of the equal protection claim in *Bush v. Gore.* Evoking the fulsome language of the more liberal Warren Court writing in the early one-person, one-vote cases of *Reynolds v. Sims* and *Harper v. Virginia,* the current Court majority ruled—in the name of George W. Bush's rights to equal protection of the laws—that the recounting of Florida's closely divided votes could not continue. In stark contrast to much of its own recent precedent, the Supreme Court boldly entered the political thicket to declare the right of a political candidate—and only one political candidate at that—to have all the votes counted using a single standard.[14]

The Court extended the equal protection of the right to vote to an entirely new terrain—to the operation of the ballot counting machinery. Instead of protecting equal and meaningful access to the ballot for all voters, it focused on "the formulation of uniform rules" to determine each voter's intent after the ballots were already cast. Only at the moment of tabulating votes ballot-by-ballot were specific, uniform standards prudentially required; they were, the Court concluded, "necessary" to ensure "equal application" of the law.[15] Ignored in this formula were idiosyncratic local rules that made it hard for some voters even to cast a ballot reflecting their real choices; such disparate procedures at the county level caused some who showed up to vote to be effectively disenfranchised. But the enormous county-by-county differences in the accessibility or the accuracy of voting technology did not—at least for the Court majority—disturb the "confidence all citizens must have in the outcome of elections."

As a result, black Americans—the people the equal protection clause was designed to protect—had their ballots disqualified at shockingly high rates in Florida. Antiquated voting technology, lack of trained clerks, and confusing instructions in many counties adversely affected black voters' ability to cast a "legal vote," meaning a vote worth counting. Difficulty reading or interpreting the ambiguous rules was counted against them by not counting their ballots at all.

The Court's use of the equal protection clause was limited to the moment of recounting ballots. According to many scholars, the Court's failure to examine the widespread inequality in ballot access and technology, while invoking the equal protection clause at the moment of recounting ballots, created nothing more than a "false patina of legitimacy."[16] In reality, meaningful democratic equality was not a concern. Rather, a set of antiegalitarian premises apparently provided the philosophical foundation for the decision to enjoin the democratic process altogether and thus hand Bush the presidency.[17] Black voters, elderly Jewish voters in Palm Beach, and poor people throughout the state were disenfranchised but left without a remedy. Principles of meritocracy justified their disenfranchisement. Essentially they had to pass a test to have their ballots counted, and the implicit suggestion was that only those who passed this test actually deserve to participate in the democratic process.

For example, during oral argument in *Bush v. Gore,* Justice Sandra Day O'Connor grilled Al Gore's lawyer David Boies about what vote-counting standard could properly be used in terms of determining the intent of the voter:

> Well, why isn't the standard the one that voters are instructed to follow, for goodness sakes? I mean, it couldn't be clearer. I mean, why don't we go to that standard?[18]

Those voters who were unable to follow "the rules" simply failed to file a legal vote when they attempted to cast their ballot. Their citizenship rights were only as strong as the voting machine's ability to discern their intent.

That our constitutional democracy would permit the disenfranchisement of thousands—perhaps millions—of voters is a function of two converging phenomena. One is the Court's ambivalence toward the principles of democracy itself. The second is the way the Court's rhetoric of democracy confuses uniformity with equality, and tests of merit with democracy. I will address these two themes in reverse order.

The Merits of Democracy

It was on the presumption that they could discern a merit-based approach to voting, an approach that ironically combines elements of both Gore's and Bush's rhetoric, that the conservative majority stopped the recounting of votes in Florida. Yet, a "merit-based" approach to democracy—just like the "merit-based" approach to admissions in other institutions—systematically privileges wealthy, white Americans over poor people and people of color. The Court found in 1970, for example, that the use of tests or devices to "discern merit" can perpetuate racialized inequities in educational opportunity; they can and did also depress voter registration and participation by poor whites. Indeed, the Voting Rights Act of 1965 explicitly prohibited the use of literacy tests as a precondition to voting, a ban extended nationwide in 1970 and unanimously upheld by the Supreme Court.[19]

Nevertheless, the current court seems in thrall to the illusion that merit is easily testable and an acceptable basis on which to distribute democratic opportunity. This is consistent with the story the term *meritocracy* was designed to tell. The term was coined in 1958 by a British sociologist, writing a parody of privilege and power.[20] A meritocracy was a device by which those who already had power defined a system that enabled them to retain their status, encouraging the winners to believe they earned their victory and the losers to believe that they too deserved their lot in life. Admissions to elite colleges are a perfect example: Although the original application of the meritocracy concept to the college admissions process was done in the name of extending access to students beyond the confines of the New England private preparatory schools, it too has become a vehicle for codifying and camouflaging social hierarchy.[21] Our preoccupation with meritocracy has become a preoccupation with the sorting-and-ranking behavior that awards scarce places in higher education on the basis of timed tests that favor those possessing the resources to prepare for the test.[22] The resulting test scores become the building blocks of a testocracy, and are then deemed the most important evidence of an individual's visible, rankable worth or "merit."[23]

Originally it was thought that those from humble origins whose test scores propelled them forward would bring with them a commitment to public service that was less noblesse oblige and more egalitarian.[24] But it turns out that, over time, the testocracy has replicated a chief characteristic of the old system: it rewards those already privileged. In the old boys network, access to higher education and good jobs was passed from one generation to another through exposure to boarding schools and other institutions in which one's merits (that is, proof of belonging) were observed and finely honed. In the "the new meritocracy," privilege is passed on through a new kind of club: a testing system that allows those with resources to show that they too belong. They belong because they are able to learn the rules of the test either through explicit coaching, private school, or an upper-middle-class, resource-rich suburban education. They then successfully play the testing game to their own advantage. Studies show that within each race and ethnic group, aptitude test scores rise substantially with parental income.[25]

At the University of California at Berkeley, for example, in 1997, 42 percent of the white freshmen came from families who earn more than $100,000 a year, even though this is a public institution financed by all taxpayers.[26] At the University of Texas, when a standardized test-centered approach determined admission, 75 percent of the freshman class came from 10 percent of the state's 1500 high schools. The middle- and upper-middle-class suburban high schools dominated the admissions process at Texas's public universities and some poor, predominantly white rural counties did not send a single resident to either of the state's two flagship schools. The use of standardized tests, in other words, disadvantages poor whites as well as blacks and Latinos.

As it has evolved, the notion of contributing to the community has also taken a backseat in the equation. Many of those admitted based on their test scores come to believe that their merit justifies their continued privilege. Thus, they are not burdened even by notions of noblesse oblige in terms of public service, self-sacrifice for the common good or acts of public charity. Indeed, 75 percent of college students report that one of the main things they want to get out of college is to make a lot of money. And 70 percent think it is not important even to be informed about politics. When the admissions process strongly favors white, upper-middle-class students, very few of whom pursue careers devoted to the public interest, it is not surprising that the new meritocracy breeds resentment among those who are excluded.

What is surprising, however, is that despite significant evidence that aptitude tests fail to predict anything beyond first-year college grades (and even then the relationship is extremely modest), an array of explanations justifies the exclusion of those who do not do as well on what have become "class-based" criteria for determining merit. In fact, studies show that the aptitude tests more accurately measure parental socioeconomic status than first-year college grades. The resulting inequities are justified in the name of merit, even though the correlation between performance on these tests and future academic success is exceedingly tenuous.[27]

This phenomenon of normalizing inequitable outcomes applies in politics as well. Tracking conventional forms of "meritocratic" selection, the baseline for "admission" is a single uniform standard. The only difference is whether the applicant's performance, as measured by that standard, entitles her to admission to college or deems her capable of casting a legal vote. Such a standard purports to be objective and fair in identifying who deserves admission. Just as entrance to Yale or other highly selective colleges is supposedly based on visible, rankable merit, participation in a democracy becomes synonymous with measurable ability—arbitrarily evaluated at the micro level of ballot counting, not ballot voting—to cast a "legal vote."

But as the 2000 election made painfully clear, such purportedly merit-based tests contain a bias toward existing privilege, which has a major impact at the earliest stage of the voting process—at the ballot box. Rules that limit time in the voting booth to five minutes fail to provide adequate help to illiterate voters, and deny voters a chance to cast a ballot for their first-choice candidate without jeopardizing their second-choice candidate's election all combine to privilege participation by the better-educated members of the electorate. Presumably fair and objective, these voting rules define the "legitimate" or deserving voters, restricting ballot access to those who are educated—and, for that matter—who can afford to take time off from work to vote. Yet, this type of inequality (inequality in access to the ballot) is apparently constitutionally irrelevant, while inequality during a recount is dispositive evidence of a constitutional violation. Even worse, in Florida and many other states, disparate ballot technology makes the process the most complicated for the poorest and least well-educated members of society, especially those who are also descendants of slaves or treated as such.

The racial effects of applying a so-called merit-based approach to voting in Florida were striking: Automatic machines rejected 14.4 percent of ballots cast by African Americans, but only 1.6 percent of ballots cast by others.[28] Although blacks made up 16 percent of the voting population, they cast 54 percent of the machine-rejected ballots.[29] Ballots cast by African Americans were almost ten times more likely than the ballots of whites to be rejected.[30] Furthermore, counting machines rejected punch card ballots in predominantly African-American precincts in Miami-Dade County at twice the rate they rejected ballots in predominantly Latino precincts, and four times the rate they rejected ballots in predominantly white precincts.[31] Black precincts also lacked the technology that helped handle overflow crowds in white and some Latino (Cuban/Republican) precincts. Compounding the problem were flaws in the registration lists and state law prohibiting from voting those who have served their time in prison and repaid their debt to society.[32]

Indeed, this merit-based approach to ballot counting (that ignores blatant inequities in access to the act of voting itself) is hauntingly reminiscent of devices, like literacy tests and grandfather clauses, imposed systematically throughout the South following Reconstruction to disenfranchise black voters. Just as in the Jim Crow South, the realities of Florida balloting demonstrate that, despite its purported objectivity, this merit-based approach primarily benefits those already enjoying power. These practices continue, even in the effort to remedy the botched procedures of 2000. A law enacted by the Florida legislature in 2001 includes a ten-point list of voter responsibilities that must be posted in all polling places. The list says voters should "study and know candidates and issues." Such language, civil rights advocates maintain, could be misconstrued by voters and polling officials as a requirement for voter eligibility and not just a suggestion, and it could intimidate the poor and uneducated.[33] While obsessing about partisan motives that potentially compromise the integrity of the ballot, the proponents of a merit-based system elevate concerns about fraud over concerns about participation. In the name of "ballot integrity," the legacy of race-based disenfranchisement continues to haunt our nation.

But no matter. In *Bush v. Gore,* the conservative majority reminded us that "the individual citizen has no federal constitutional right to vote for electors for president of the United States unless and until the state legislature chooses a statewide election as the means to implement its power to appoint members of the electoral college."[34] While the state cannot overtly fence out a group of voters arbitrarily to deny them an opportunity to cast their ballots, the state may establish voting rules that covertly accomplish the same exclusion.[35] This means that those who are functionally illiterate (as are more than 40 million adults in this country),[36] or who live in poor counties without access to the technology necessary to confirm registration status and ease lines at the polling place, simply do not enjoy the same "ability" to cast legal votes. Even when such citizens manage to cast their ballots—because of the vagaries of state law, antiquated voting technology, as well as the delegation of enormous discretion to local polling officials—some citizens' votes are still not counted.

The Order of Democracy

The Court's impatience with nonuniform vote counting standards stands in marked contrast to its tolerance of chaotic balloting mechanisms in the voting booth. The vast disparity from county to county between the voting technology available to poor and rich voters discourages many less-educated voters from even attempting to cast a ballot. Yet this Court has not shown the same solicitude to assure uniform access to the ballot for the voters themselves. This is consistent with its long-standing preference for order rather than participation. In her concurring opinion in a political gerrymandering case, *Davis v. Bandemer,* Justice O'Connor suggested as much when she asserted that a commitment to stability and measured change is the sine qua non of a functioning democracy: "The emergence of a strong and stable two-party system in this country has contributed enormously to sound and effective government. The preservation and health of our political institutions, state and federal, depends to no small extent on the continued vitality of our two-party system, which permits both stability and measured change."[37] This preference for mechanical or tradition-bound rules that privilege stability and measured change over genuine and broad-based democratic participation also informs the Court's recent jurisprudence in its decisions to (1) tolerate extreme political gerrymandering that essentially predetermines electoral outcomes when districts are drawn, thus rendering elections virtually meaningless;[38] (2) yet apply strict scrutiny to majority-minority districts designed to provide people of color a fair opportunity to elect candidates of their choice;[39] (3) rule that the First Amendment prohibits campaign expenditure limits and certain other measures designed to limit the role of private money in politics;[40] (4) privilege the associational rights of the two major parties at the expense of broad-based participation in primaries;[41] and (5) uphold various devices, such as strict ballot access requirements, that inhibit the possibility of third parties playing a significant role in the political process.[42]

Reflecting upon this pattern, both Professors Heather Gerken and Spencer Overton conclude that *Bush v. Gore* is part of the Court's long-standing failure to interrogate our democratic principles to develop legal rules that foster an energetic and inclusionary vision of democracy.[43] The elevation of stability and measured change as *the* primary goal of politics disconnects democracy from its participatory ideal. The combination of a thin and mechanistic view of democracy governed by a similarly thin and mechanistic view of equality simply reinforces the ability of the elite within the two major parties to compete among themselves for the reigns of power, while manipulating elections to assure the desired outcome. The Supreme Court's role in *Bush v. Gore* must be assessed in the light of this phenomenon, which has deep roots in our country's jurisprudential tradition.[44]

Professor Richard Pildes, for example, writes about a Supreme Court case early in the twentieth century in which Justice Oliver Wendell Holmes ruled that the Court was helpless in the face of the elimination of black citizens from political participation in Alabama. Jackson Giles, a literate black man and Republican-party activist who had a federal patronage job as janitor in the federal courthouse in Montgomery, Alabama, had registered and voted in Montgomery from 1871 to 1901. Giles, represented by a lawyer hired by Booker T. Washington, challenged the handiwork of the 1901 Alabama constitutional convention that disenfranchised him (and countless others) with, in the words of the convention's president, the explicit purpose "to establish white supremacy in this State."[45] In a classic catch-22, Holmes concluded that the very wrong Giles complained of made impossible the relief he sought. If the statute were a fraudulent scheme, as Giles suggested, then were the Court to order Giles's name added to the list the Court would itself be party to the very fraud at issue. The Court also refused, on the grounds of institutional competence, to intervene. It lacked the enforcement authority to protect Giles's rights "when the great mass of white people" in Alabama were opposed to his voting.[46]

It is striking how similar the effects of the Supreme Court's decision in *Bush v. Gore* are with those of *Giles v. Harris,* even as Holmes's opinion in *Giles,* in Pildes's words, "has been airbrushed out of the constitutional canon."[47] The Court's ruling in *Bush v. Gore* also upheld the rights of a majority of white people to choose the president of the United States while blacks were simultaneously disenfranchised in Florida.[48] Despite his many friends in high places both at Yale and on the Supreme Court, Bush's bona fides as a member of the "ruling class" did not discourage many in the white working class from voting for him.[49] Indeed, Bush was able to poll a majority of the votes cast by whites to make the contest in Florida close. This was also true nationwide. Even the so-called gender gap is only apparent when the votes of black women are also included. When only white women's voting pattern is observed a small plurality preferred Bush.[50]

Holmes's putative commitment to majority rule was hardly democratic since it failed to consider the protection and inclusion of the minority; this same lesson is clearly still relevant in the context of the Court's failure in *Bush v. Gore* to value the discarded votes of Americans of color. Similarly, Holmes's contorted (or in Pildes's term, *repellant*) logic and the *Bush v. Gore* per curiam's opinion both value disingenuous uniformity and the appearance of stability over genuine equality in democratic participation. In these ways, the five-member majority in *Bush v. Gore* continues the benighted trajectory of opinions in which the Supreme Court "remov[es] democracy from the agenda of constitutional law."[51]

As the political scientist Alex Keyssar points out, "the very unpretty election of last November emerged from deep currents in American political life. Although we don't like to acknowledge it, there have always been strong antidemocratic forces in the United States. Large numbers of Americans, throughout our history, have not believed in universal suffrage and have acted accordingly."[52] Keyssar emphasizes elsewhere in his treatise on the right to vote a factor crucial to understanding our democratic ambivalence: those opposed to universal suffrage were members of the founding elite. Their influence disenfranchised vast numbers of our population from the very beginning of our constitutional democracy; their assumptions that the elite should rule helped contract not only the right to vote but also the right to cast an effective vote. The Americans who harbored such ambivalence continued beyond the early years of our country's history to include at different stages the leadership of both the Democratic and Republican parties. Both political parties have cooperated—some might even say conspired—to constrict the electorate in order to insure their own dominance.

This highly antidemocratic impulse has had devastating consequences for disadvantaged individuals of all races. Few among us are familiar with the way the leaders of the Democratic party, for example, orchestrated the disenfranchisement of blacks as well as masses of poor whites throughout the South during the late 1800s and early 1900s.[53] According to Professor Pildes, the framers of disenfranchisement were "typically the most conservative large landowning, wealthy faction of the Democratic party, who were also seeking to entrench their partisan power and fend off challenges from Republicans, Populists, other third parties, as well as the more populist wings of the Democratic party."[54] Their goal was to remove the less educated and impoverished whites who might be inclined to join forces with even more impoverished blacks to challenge the Democrats' one-party rule.[55] The Democratic party was "the organized vehicle of white supremacy" and it "regained control of the legislature and governor's office by framing politics around issues of race rather than economics or class."[56] The Democratic party aimed to thwart the conditions that made for genuine multiparty competition and greater participation by poor and uneducated whites as well as blacks.

The unseemly role of the Democratic party in the South at the beginning of the twentieth century foreshadowed more contemporary complaints that some in the Republican party orchestrated—or at least benefited from—the massive disenfranchisement of Florida's voters in election 2000. Efforts to disenfranchise votes, in other words, are not limited to idiosyncrasies of either the current conservative Supreme Court majority or one political ideology.

What is significant, therefore, is not simply the disconcerting parallel between the disenfranchisement of blacks at the turn of the twentieth and twenty-first centuries. The consequences for blacks in Florida and elsewhere of Supreme Court decisions that avoid engaging basic democratic principles affect our larger understanding of democracy itself. The real significance of the aftermath of the 2000 presidential election is the way that the disenfranchisement of blacks in Florida highlights the country's history of tolerating disenfranchisement across-the-board. Florida simply made visible an ongoing pattern of disenfranchisement within a larger pattern of exclusions based on race, class, and gender.

Indeed, the United States is exceptional in the degree to which the privileged dominate politics. The most striking statistic about our political system is how poorly it fosters participation in democracy's most basic act: voting. Of the 172 countries in the world that profess to be democracies, 81 percent have higher levels of voter participation than the United States.[57]

This extraordinarily low turnout is especially disturbing since it is fueled by even lower rates of working-class participation. In Europe, the difference between turnout levels among the affluent and low-income voters ranges from 5–10 percent. In the United States, more than two-thirds of people with annual incomes greater than $50,000 vote, compared with one-third of those with incomes under $10,000.[58] Moreover, in part owed to the aforementioned bias in voting technology, even when poor people (and people of color) do go to the ballot box, their votes are three times more likely to go uncounted than the votes of their affluent white counterparts.[59] And if this differential participation rate were not enough, the exceptional importance of private money in American politics by international standards provides the country's elites with an additional lever to influence policy-making.

Poor people are not the only group that is badly underrepresented in American politics. Despite having one of the world's most active women's movement, our democracy also has a very poor record of promoting the political representation of women. Women comprise only 13.8 percent (a record) of the 107th Congress. In western Europe, women make up 23.9 percent of the average national parliament. For the five Scandinavian countries, this figure reaches 37.7 percent.[60] In fact, the U.S. ranks forty-fifth in its representation of women in national legislatures or parliaments worldwide.[61] Considering its long history as a multiracial, poly-ethnic society, the U.S. also continues to be exceptionally poor at including people of color in politics. African Americans, the country's largest racial minority, comprise slightly over 12 percent of the population but only 6.7 percent of the 107th Congress. In New Zealand, people of Maori descent—whose situation "in terms of demographics and socioeconomic status . . . is remarkably similar to that of African Americans in the United States"[62]—represent 14.5 percent of the population and hold 13.3 percent of the seats in parliament.[63] In South Africa, the white minority represents 15 percent of the population and a full 32 percent of the national legislature.[64]

It was because of our country's extraordinary failure to involve racialized minorities and others who were historically left out that George W. Bush became president. Certainly, the Supreme Court's decision in *Bush v. Gore* serves as a continuing reminder that some of the nation's most powerful institutions are governed by disturbingly elitist principles. But *Bush v. Gore* is really just the tip of the iceberg in this nation where, in stark contrast to our liberal democratic collective self-image, the voices of those less privileged are systematically discounted and half of the population does not vote at all. In a country where deep, structural inequities prevent everyone from succeeding on tests of "knowledgeable voting," the importation of meritocracy into the electoral arena fundamentally undermines the values of democratic participation. The Supreme Court's role, though key, is not alone responsible for our nation's reliance on thin views of equality to camouflage widening gaps of inequality. After all, both liberals and conservatives seem to share the idea of rule by an elite. Their elite is differently defined: It is a meritocracy for most liberals; a plutocracy for many conservatives. Yet in both versions egalitarian terminology increasingly substitutes for meaningful representation or popular involvement in our democratic experiment. What is missing is a tradition that emphasizes broad-based participation throughout the political process and a set of institutional practices that actively encourages it.

II

A few days after the Supreme Court's decision in *Bush v. Gore,* I received the following message on my voicemail:

> I hope you remember me. I was one of your students at U. Penn Law School back in 1990–91. I am calling because Tony, president of the class and one of my buddies, suggested I call you. I am deeply disturbed about the Supreme Court decision [in *Bush v. Gore*] that came down. I am trying to make sense of it. I just find it unbelievable. Tony was telling me maybe if I talked to you for a few minutes one day I could emerge with something to hold onto that would make it easier for me. . . . Above all I believed in the Constitution and that the Supreme Court justices had to have some semblance of objectivity with respect to it. Never before in my life have I been more offended by something that has happened in this country than this decision at this level.[65]

Justice Stevens had predicted this crisis of legitimacy as a result of the *Bush v. Gore* fiasco. He anticipated that "although we may never know with complete certainty the identity of the winner of this year's presidential election, the identity of the loser is perfectly clear. It is the nation's confidence in the judge as an impartial guardian of the rule of law." [66]

Yet the crisis of confidence that has emerged, particularly within the black community, extends beyond the feelings of legal scholars who report a "shaken constitutional faith." [67] A CBS News poll, made public on the eve of the inauguration, attested to that. Although 51 percent of the respondents said they considered Mr. Bush's victory a legitimate one, only 19 percent of Democrats and 12 percent of blacks said so. [68] A survey released December 7, 2000 from the Harvard vanishing voter project indicated that large majorities of the American people believed the election procedures have been "unfair to the voters." Not surprisingly, nationwide those most likely to feel disenfranchised were blacks. Moreover, one out of ten blacks reported that they or someone in their family had trouble voting according to a national report produced by Michael Dawson and Lawrence Bobo, of the Center for the Study of Race, Politics and Culture and the W.E.B. Du Bois Institute. The alienation of the black community was also evident in the reaction of the congressional black caucus, which alone raised formal objections in the House of Representatives to Florida's slate of Bush electors. In a poignant column for the *Boston Globe,* James Carroll asked: "What does it say that even the most left-wing of white congressmen and senators have apparently adjusted themselves to the problematic Bush election, while the congressional black caucus has not?" He concluded: "Those who sit atop the social and economic pyramid always speak of love, while those at the bottom always speak of justice." [69]

One thing is certain to those of us who have studied the structure, not just the mechanics, of our election system: Reforms for the tabulation of ballots alone will not resolve the deep alienation that pervades our democracy and causes people not even to vote. Turnout in 2000 was up in Florida and other contested states, primarily as a result of grassroots efforts to increase participation. But a report from the Committee for the Study of the American Electorate, a nonprofit research organization, suggested that such efforts will not increase turnout in future elections. As more and more power gravitates to a permanent set of political elites, a process that discourages their active involvement has increasingly marginalized many Americans. Last year, the registration of Democrats continued a thirty-six-year decline and registration for third parties and independents streamed upward. Upgrading voting equipment and creating uniform ballot counting procedures will not do much to alter these demographic changes, which suggest the withdrawal of many citizens from our current two-party system. "The root of the turnout problem is motivational" and not technical, the report said.[70] In other words, the skewed incentive structure of our current two party duopoly with its candidate-centered, elite-driven set of rules discourages a large number of people from participating in the most basic aspects of our political process.

It is the political process itself that needs fixing. And on this point, John Dewey had it exactly right: "The cure for ailments in democracy is more democracy."[71] We need to imagine systems that encourage greater levels of voter participation, lead to a higher degree of confidence in election results and the related policy outcomes, and encourage ordinary citizens to join together more effectively to play a role in the process of self-government beyond just voting. As Professor Overton notes, "Although the Court's facially neutral merit-based criteria focus on individual responsibility, they interfere primarily not with individual rights, but with the ability of groups of voters like African Americans to identify with one another as a political community, to create alliances with others of different backgrounds, and to use the vote to enact political change."[72]

What Overton identifies is the way that the rhetoric of democratic equality has obscured structures of disadvantage by focusing the Court's attention on abstract claims of uniform sameness. The populist promise of this rhetoric is cabined by a commitment to election structures that discourage grassroots collective action and dissuade multiracial political activity by organized groups. To unearth the potential for a broader multiracial progressive coalition at the beginning of the twenty-first century we need to revive something comparable to the budding black/white populist coalition that led to the Democratic shenanigans in Alabama and North Carolina at the beginning of the twentieth century. While working-class whites often support a conservative political agenda in clear contrast to what some might term their "objective" material interests, workers who belong to unions—where they have the opportunity to participate in politics—show a marked preference for Democratic candidates. In the most recent election, members of union households (13 percent of the workforce) were more likely to vote and also to vote Democratic. The key explanatory factor was not the political preferences of union leaders who announced early for Gore. It was the grassroots organizing of the rank and file. By returning to the on-the-ground leafleting, phoning, and door-knocking of the past, union workers become democrats with a small *d* and thus overcome Republican efforts to divide working-class voters by race. Were unions in a position to organize within a multiparty democracy where presidential choices were not limited to a "compassionate" conservative and a moderate Democrat, they might be even more effective at changing the demographic skew of the electorate.

Our often-duplicitous rhetorical commitments could be rechanneled away from ideas that encourage ranking and sorting were we to consider alternative democratic arrangements that promote collective activity, engaged struggle, and greater contingency of outcomes. These reforms would require an alternative sense of collective ethics. Such consideration necessitates a certain suspension of disbelief that a system as ingrown as ours can change. It also means that we have to deconstruct the "American dream" narrative of radical individualism that draws many white working-class voters into racially polarized voting blocs and conservative coalitions. Making a commitment to have equality work requires more than lip service to ideas of simple sameness.

We need to look beyond our own backyard to understand the forms that a more robust democracy might take. Indeed, we can possibly jump-start a different kind of conversation by examining the systems adopted by other mature democracies as well as by those countries that had the benefit of building on other's mistakes. For example, a 1995 survey of twenty industrialized democracies reveals a number of practices other countries have implemented to restrict the role of private money in legislative elections. Canada and Great Britain, for instance, both limit legislative candidates' campaign spending to under $25,000. Perhaps more practically, the United States could follow other democracies in providing greater public financing of elections and requiring media organizations to provide equal, free advertising access. It is worth noting that fifteen of the twenty democracies surveyed "prohibit paid political advertisements as a way of keeping the playing field even."[73] A comparative analysis also supplies insights to revitalize American democracy in other areas. Turnout could be increased by voting on a week-end or holiday rather than a workday,[74] as most democracies do, and weighing the benefits of mandatory voting,[75] as a few countries have. The most important lesson other countries have to teach the United States, however, involves proportional representation.

Before describing a range of comparative examples that might help inspire a broad, multiracial, and progressive coalition committed to reviving American democracy, let me set forth several assumptions on which this exploration proceeds. First, blacks already possess a high level of group consciousness and understand many of the systemic biases that render the country more oligarchic than meritocratic, which means they must play an active role for any pro-democracy movement to be successful. But this movement would obviously also reach out to other people of color, poor whites, young people, organized labor and, of course, other potential allies such as the middle- and upper-class progressives that currently form the backbone of support for the Green Party. Its members would be identified by their politics and their willingness to link their fate to those currently most disadvantaged. Second, a pro-democracy movement might start with basic reforms, such as twenty-four-hour voting on a national holiday. But it must not stop there. Uniform national standards, imposed top-down, do little to change the incentive structure for participation. Giving people a reason to vote is by far the most vital element of a democracy movement. And yet, merely voting is not even enough. People need to be given opportunities to participate and contribute between elections for the seeds of meaningful democratic change to take root. Such opportunities require intermediate institutions that help educate, organize, and mobilize grassroots involvement in the conversation of democracy.

Finally, the short-term prospects for fundamentally transforming American politics along the lines I outline are admittedly quite low. The recent experience of the Greens suggests that without structural changes in our winner-take-all rules, it is difficult to field candidates at the national level who will alter the debate and gain an institutional foothold in the forums of representative democracy. After all, many accuse Ralph Nader of simply losing the election for Al Gore, because the 92,000 votes cast for Nader in

Florida would have changed the close election into a decisive Gore victory.[76] The Greens experience is not unique. Many third parties have tried and failed to become legitimate contenders in American politics over the last hundred years. On the other hand, alternative strategies for advancing a progressive political agenda have also failed in the electoral arena where efforts to move the Democratic party leftwards have often had the opposite effect.[77]

The goal of this thought experiment is, therefore, much more modest. I hope simply to demonstrate once again just how poorly the country currently represents the interests of poor and working-class people of all races— both by normative and comparative standards. With that lesson in mind, committed reformers working in various institutional settings could redouble their efforts to start with the experience of people of color in order to effect the fundamental change necessary to provide all Americans with equitable political and social citizenship. Here are three approaches to reinvigorate, at the very least, a deeper discussion of the failings of our democracy so that the reforms pursued in the wake of election 2000 go beyond cosmetic changes merely involving the mechanics of voting.

The Emergence of Grassroots and Locally-Based Parties

First, a new party could seek political influence to mobilize and organize at the grassroots level rather than to start out as a force in national politics. What might set such a new political party apart from past attempts along these lines is that it would begin by fielding candidates primarily in majority-minority districts, where electorates would likely respond favorably to its efforts to build a new political movement based on the experiences and interests of people of color and other underrepresented groups.[78] Such a strategy would likely depend upon the party persuading at least some of the current (Democratic) representatives of these districts to switch party affiliation. The feelings of profound alienation voiced by many black and Latino elected officials—even in relation to their fellow Democrats—suggests this is not an entirely implausible scenario.[79] Moreover, as the example of the British Labour party proves, progressive third parties can achieve electoral breakthroughs even in winner-take-all electoral systems such as ours.

In the late 1800s, two parties, the Conservatives and the Liberals, dominated British politics. The Liberals were the more progressive of the two parties, and they had enjoyed strong union support as well as the electoral backing of most workers. However, by the turn of century, many union activists became dissatisfied by their inability to influence the Liberal platform to any significant degree. Moreover, labor organizations questioned the Liberal party's inclination to promote their interests in the face of judicial decisions unfavorable to unions and an employer offensive against union privileges. After all, wealthy employers dominated the Liberal leadership.

In 1899, these developments helped prompt Britain's Trade Unions Congress to create the Labour Representation Committee (LRC), an organization designed to further working-class representation in government. By 1906, in the aftermath of the government's refusal to overturn the effects of the Taff Vale judgment that held unions financially liable for losses employers sustained owing to strikes, the LRC gained the affiliation of most unions and formally became the Labour party.

The Labour party wisely coordinated its efforts closely with the Liberals in its early years. Eager not to divide the "progressive" vote in Britain's electoral system that, like our own, is based on single-member plurality district elections, the Liberals gave Labour a free hand against the Conservatives in a number of constituencies. By 1910, Labour won 6 percent of the nationwide vote and forty seats in the House of Commons. The Labour party gained more and more votes as Britain's political structure continued to be transformed in the wake of technological advancement, social movements, and the dislocations and reforms that resulted from two world wars. Within a half century of its creation, Labour stormed to an impressive electoral victory that allowed it to implement dramatic sociopolitical reforms.[80]

The experience of British Labour is far from unusual internationally. Indeed, although a number of countries conduct elections based on winner-take-all districts, G. Bingham Powell reports in his comparative study of twenty industrialized democracies that the complete two-party dominance in the U.S. is unique. "[O]nly in the United States did the two largest parties consistently win more than 90 percent of the vote in legislative elections."[81] While Supreme Court decisions mentioned in Section I of this essay place additional barriers on the formation of politically significant third parties in the U.S., they certainly do not create insurmountable obstacles. In the mid-sixties—despite tremendous legal and political discrimination—the Mississippi Freedom Democratic party mounted an impressive challenge to the Democrats and Republicans. This progressive party, dedicated to promoting the full citizenship rights of black Americans, fielded candidates in elections for the U.S. Congress who won the support of a majority of black voters.[82] Imagine the potential such a party could have now with the advent of majority-minority districts.

However, another equally important question remains. Even if a progressive party were to overcome the admittedly significant barriers to entry in our current political system and won as many as say two-dozen seats in Congress, could it really have enough influence to foster significant advancements in social and political citizenship in this country? There are at least three reasons why the answer might be a plausible *yes*. First, a political organizing effort that began in communities of color could rectify the extreme alienation felt by poor and young voters of all races who care little about the major issues emphasized in recent campaigns, such as tax relief for the middle and upper classes and prescription drug plans for the elderly. As Mary Eakle, twenty-five, a $7-an-hour assistant deli manager put it during the 2000 presidential contest: "None of what they're saying is about us."[83] Local political organizations, developed in conjunction with issues of concern in the community, would encourage participation through local forums, door-knocking campaigns, and face-to-face contact on issues of concern as defined by the people in the communities themselves. Second, the party could use municipalities, counties, or even states where it gained sufficient influence as laboratories of democracy in promoting individuals' social and political rights through the implementation of policies ranging from a living wage to proportional representation. Successful experiments would serve as models and encourage the two major parties to promulgate similar national (or statewide) reforms. The experience of Canada's National Democratic Party (NDP)—the country's only significant party advocating social democracy—teaches relevant lessons in this respect. While never winning more than 20 percent of the vote in a federal election, NDP provincial governments implemented progressive labor and health care reforms that were so popular that the federal government eventually extended their basic principles throughout the nation. This was most notably the case in the development of

Canada's universal, single-payer health care system, which was first promulgated by the NDP provincial government of Saskatchewan.[84]

Third, the existence of a locally initiated third party might pressure the Democratic party to advocate more progressive policies, since Democrats could no longer take the support of progressive voters for granted.[85] However, the experience of the initial alliance between the Liberals and Labour in Britain suggests that local, progressive political parties would have to work with—rather than against—the Democrats. Such a strategy would avoid splitting the progressive vote and throwing elections to conservative Republicans—a danger few are likely to underestimate after the 2000 presidential election.[86]

In other words, a third-party might force the Democrats to alter their policies; it might also force them to become advocates for citizens to exercise their political clout. On the other hand, incumbents of all races generally have a vested interest in the hierarchical status quo. Many black incumbents have had to work hard to curry favor with wealthy (black and white) constituents and businesses in order to accumulate the war chests necessary to run for office. As a result, they have an important disincentive to joining a new grassroots political organization. Thus, a scenario that seeks to disrupt hierarchy or at least to minimize it may need to be accompanied by more dramatic structural changes that elevate the role of political issues and political engagement rather than rely solely on the sympathies of political candidates. It is to these structural changes that I now turn.

Proportional Representation

Some might say that 225 years after the American Revolution, it is time for the United States to consider the advantages of democratic models that do not stem from the history of the British Isles. Democratic reformers interested in learning from the present would be wise to think about the political systems of other developed nations throughout the world. A second thought experiment is to imagine that a pro-democracy movement generates activity around the issue of structural reform, including the adoption, via referenda or initiative, of proportional representation (PR) systems starting at the local level and then expanding statewide. Such reforms would certainly reinforce the plausibility of the first scenario previously discussed.

The most common type of PR is the party-list system. The basic principle behind party-list systems is that each party offers a list of candidates in each constituency. Seats are then awarded to each party in proportion to its support in the constituency, and individuals fill the available seats based on their position on the list—e.g., if a party wins 30 percent of the vote and earns 3 of 10 city council seats, only the top three persons on that party's list will gain places in the council. How the order of the list is determined is just one of the several important variations possible in party-list systems.[87]

Since list systems tend to use districts with large numbers of seats, they are generally the best arrangements to ensure proportionality between votes cast for, and legislative seats won by, political parties. By placing emphasis on parties rather than individual candidates, party-list systems also promote campaigns based on issues and platforms. This helps to ensure that the substantive needs of more citizens are addressed in the political arena. Party-list systems also encourage grassroots social movements to spawn electorally oriented political parties, because such parties need capture a far smaller share of the electorate than their counterparts in a winner-take-all system to win a council or school board seat. But PR also promotes greater grassroots mobilization within the confines of the major political parties. Since PR encourages parties to emphasize policies rather than candidates, different constituencies have a strong incentive to organize their supporters in order to influence the party platform on the issues that matter most to them. Moreover, the order of names on party lists is an issue around which constituencies can mobilize and negotiate without resulting in all-or-nothing victories of one faction or another—as occurs in political systems in which each party runs just one candidate per contest. As a result, women and racial minorities often fare better in party-list systems.[88]

Cross-national comparisons of west European nations reveal that roughly twice as many women are elected to parliament in countries that use party-list systems.[89] Similarly, the use of party-list systems in democracies with deep racial divisions like South Africa and Namibia has resulted in impressively diverse national legislatures, even when race continues to shape voting preferences and party affiliation.[90]

But PR is considered a radical alternative here in the U.S., even though most western democracies—other than former colonies of Great Britain—use some form of it and, in a modified form, it was used for 100 years in Illinois. Among the most common criticisms of party-list systems are that their high level of proportionality results in an excessive number of parties and thus legislative gridlock. These concerns reflect our preference for election systems that promote stability and measured change over robust, participatory forms of democracy. Critics depend upon supposedly paradigmatic cases, which conclusively illustrate the havoc that PR can wreak on political systems. Some students of both present-day Israel and Weimar Germany have suggested that the PR systems used in these two states fostered an excessive number of parties that in turn promoted high levels of government instability and paralysis, and ultimately—at least in the case of interwar Germany—devastating consequences. A deeper analysis of the two cases, however, challenges the idea that they offer a general indictment against all electoral systems based on proportional representation.

Israel and Weimar Germany both conducted elections using particular variants of PR that allow a great number of parties to be represented in the national legislature. The type of PR used in Weimar Germany promoted the multiplication of political parties since a seat in the national legislature (the Reichstag) was allocated for every 60,000 votes cast nationwide—less than .2 percent of the average electorate. As long as a party won at least 30,000 votes in one of the thirty-five constituencies, it could count on roughly proportional representation in the Reichstag.[91] A 5 percent threshold of exclusion would have consistently reduced the number of parties with Reichstag representation in Weimar Germany.[92] What the critics really object to was the combination of PR with a tiny entry threshold that permitted very small parties to enjoy disproportionate power. Our winner-take-all system, however, might have made matters even worse. In 1933, in the last "free" election of interwar Germany, the Nazis were by far the largest party, with 44 percent of the vote, yet they only won 288 of the 647 parliamentary seats. "Goering said at his trial that under the British [winner-take-all] system that election would have given the Nazis every seat in the country, and he cannot have been far wrong."[93]

In Israel, the entire country serves as one district to elect 120 members of

parliament, and the threshold of exclusion is a mere 1.5 percent.[94] Simply in-
stituting a 5 percent threshold of exclusion would reduce the number of parties in the current legislature from fifteen to seven.[95] Israel also is a
problematic case for comparison because it is a religious rather than a secu-
lar democracy, which increases and intensifies the social cleavages that underlie Israeli politics.[96] On the other hand, PR does allow the number of
political parties in the Israeli parliament to be more fully representative of the
range of opinions within the country. In an ironic but revealing paradox,
Palestinians rate Israeli democracy higher than American winner-take-all
democracy. "The reason," says Jon B. Alterman, an analyst at the United
States Institute of Peace, "is that they see American democracy as beholden
to interest groups, whereas Israeli democracy reflects what the Israeli people
want."[97]

Critics of party-list systems also contend that the system does not nourish
close ties between constituents and their representatives based on easily observed geographic proximity or identity.[98] This issue is clearly a problem
for many citizens in the United States, with its deep traditions of territorial-
based plurality elections.[99] However, there are many different types of
proportional representation, each of which has different strengths and
weaknesses.[100]

There is, for example, a representational system that combines the numerous advantages of party-list systems while simultaneously promoting
strong geographic ties between constituents and their representatives; it is
called mixed-member proportional voting (MMP). Under MMP, voters
make two choices. Their first vote is used to elect individual candidates in
single-member district plurality contests, just as in most elections in the
United States. The second vote is for a party, and the remaining legislative
seats (in general roughly one half) are allocated through a party-list system to
ensure that each party that meets the system's minimum threshold of support has proportional representation in the legislature.[101] In recent years, the
clear advantages of MMP, first implemented in 1949 by West Germany, has
made it quite popular among new democracies and states considering major
electoral reform. Even by the elevated standards of Western Europe, under
MMP postwar Germany has witnessed high turnout, high levels of proportionality between votes cast and candidates elected, and large numbers of

women in Parliament.[102] Germany's 5 percent threshold of exclusion has also helped prevent a multiplicity of tiny parties, and the government has enjoyed stability without gridlock.[103] The "German system," as MMP has come to be called, has been adopted in Hungary, New Zealand, and the new regional parliaments of Scotland and Wales.[104]

New Zealand is an especially interesting case for our purposes since the country shifted from an electoral system almost identical to our own to MMP.[105] Proportional representation, after two election cycles in New Zealand, has stemmed the tide of declining turnout and has had a positive impact on representation and public policy influence for the Maori—the country's indigenous population group—progressive voters, and women.[106] The two major party leaders are now both women, and seven of the twenty current cabinet members are women. The Maori, who represent 14.5 percent of New Zealand's population,[107] now hold over 13 percent of the seats in the national legislature, double their level of representation in the 1993 parliament.[108]

MOVING TOWARD THE TWENTY-FIRST CENTURY

The creation of locally based but politically networked third or fourth parties and the use of proportional representation are both important sites for engagement and reform. However, they cannot by themselves guarantee the type of grassroots organization I have argued is crucial to reinvigorating American democracy. For instance, women and people of color who gain office under PR can still be token representatives without substantive policy-making influence. Facilitating the electoral success of parties with progressive public policy agendas is a good thing, in my view, but fails to nurture the crucial connections between the voters, and the decision-making process may lapse without ongoing opportunities for citizen participation. It is helpful, therefore, to imagine the role that local and interactive grassroots experiments can play in promoting broad-based democratic participation independent of the political structure or party system in place.

Perhaps the most unlikely examples of alternative forms of popular engagement come from Brazil. The work there of a Brazilian dramatist illustrates that it is possible to provide all citizens not just with a voice to be heard, but also with a real role to play in the democratic decisions that are most important to them.

When his theater company lost its funding, Augusto Boal moved to dismantle it in style. He wanted to showcase his troupe in the event that attracted large numbers of local residents—the annual carnival. To secure a place he had to find a political party that would share its space with him. One party agreed to give him space if one of his members ran for office on the party list. Boal agreed and ran on the platform, Vote for me, and Elect My Theater Company. He won two terms as a city councilman. Rather than hiring legislative aides, he hired members of the company to organize his constituents into issue-oriented groups. These groups worked through local public policy concerns using techniques of forum theater and role-plays. Each of the seventeen constituent groups then enacted an improvisational play at a theater festival that demonstrated their view of important problems they faced and presented possible solutions. The productions were critiqued and revised based on audience feedback. Several of the proposals were then drafted into bills, which Boal introduced. Some became law. Yet because Boal played his formal role with a more transitive understanding of the representational relationship between him and his constituents, he never once introduced a bill of his own.[109]

The work of Augusto Boal is novel, and it moves us to the beginnings of an alternative vision of democracy—one that does not fetishize the role of a meritorious or otherwise deserving representative but views the representative as one member of an interactive community. It is a radically unfamiliar vision to most Americans, yet it is grounded in the same despair that millions of Americans experienced after the 2000 election. Boal asked a simple question of the other supporters of a Brazilian presidential candidate who won thirty-one million votes and lost by a narrow margin: "We Are Thirty-One Million: Now What?" Rather than simply rely on technical solutions to fix the winner-take-all character of Brazil's presidential elections, Boal turned to a local form of citizen engagement.[110] His experiments in what he calls "legislative theater" illustrate the dual power of organizing local residents. He invited their participation in ways that continued even after his election. He also facilitated opportunities for his constituents to generate innovative solutions to long-standing public policy dilemmas.

CONCLUSION

This country's emphasis on promoting political stability above all else—fostered by Supreme Court decisions such as, but certainly not limited to, *Bush v. Gore*—has meant that the same win-lose binaries, self-perpetuating protocols, and limited participation that characterize many academic meritocracies have become fundamental elements of our democracy as well. The meritocracy and the judiciary share an apparent preference for hierarchy based on access to expertise. This preference then defines important features of our political process, as revealed by the voting fiasco in Florida and the Supreme Court's dramatic intervention. Indeed, the defiant confidence behind the Supreme Court's decision in *Bush v. Gore*—a confidence it shares with other believers in the regime of meritocracy—resulted in the exclusion of Florida voters who did not pass a certain test in terms of precisely following balloting procedures, and/or who simply had the misfortune to live in poor areas with antiquated voting systems. In other words, seemingly neutral, meritocratic rules can hide systematic inequalities that advantage certain citizens over others in the public as well as private sphere.

Consistent with the original terms of our democracy, the debacle in Florida and its unseemly denouement at the hands of our highest court were surprisingly inevitable. They grew from the seeds planted early on in our history in which the capacity of the many was compromised to protect the rights of the few. If we want to build a democracy upon a set of more participatory and egalitarian premises, we have to come to terms with the legacy of slavery as it has shaped our fundamentally unfair current political structures. But we also must let go of notions that a more liberal or egalitarian-sounding elite can be trusted with this task. The idea of democracy is the idea that the people shall rule. Draping elitism in meritocratic clothing does not a democracy make. This is not about changing the couture of democracy to a more pedestrian, soft brown-toned wardrobe. This is about embracing a fundamentally participatory role for the people themselves. We will know we have shifted paradigms when the grandsons and great-granddaughters of former slaves assume their rightful place, not just as members of a ruling elite, but as respected members of a democratic polity where votes are counted, voices are heard, and people are encouraged to participate even after the election.

As Henry Wiencke wrote in the *New York Times*, "This country was founded upon a bargain for which we continue to pay the price. We compound the mistake by draping a veil of innocence over the transaction. The true beneficiary of the presentism defense is not the past but the present—it guards and preserves our fervent wish to have sprung from innocent origins." Black Americans understand this all too well, and they therefore have much to contribute to the reinvigoration of our democracy.

After all, despite George W. Bush's rhetorical winks upon receipt of his honorary degree, his claim that the *C* students can become president is highly misleading, and this applies to individuals of all racial backgrounds. Only his wealth and political connections got him into both Yale and the Oval Office. For those who do not excel at traditional forms of educational evaluation (who are disproportionately poor and people of color), the bastions of higher education and higher political office remain out of reach. But there is something even worse about the misleading rhetoric of meritocratic democracy. The structural shortcomings of our democracy, grounded in the original bargain that transitioned slavery from an economic to a political institution, also insure that the voices of individuals marginalized by the current testocracy are discounted. In short, Bush's ascension to the presidency—just as his admission to Yale—makes clear that we are living in an era of democracy morphing into "meritocracy" and meritocracy becoming primarily a means for imposing order without truly representative opportunity.

There are contrasting approaches to democracy that have, as yet, untapped potential to create something egalitarian, issue-oriented, and participatory through innovation and collaboration both among the people and between people and their representatives. Not only is this presumably the normative goal of democracy, it is a model that has been adopted to at least some degree by many nations throughout the world. It is not implausible to imagine such alternative forms finding their way to our shores.

Yet, even within our current winner-take-all system, if poor and working-class whites joined with blacks and Latinos and other people of color, someone outside the governing elite (defined by the meritocracy or the plutocracy) may yet become president. And even more, that person may be elected by a genuine majority of all the people, not just those whose education or parentage assured their franchise and influence. Such an outcome depends upon our coming together to create a vibrant multiparty democracy that considers the voices of the losers as well as the winners, and that builds toward a society governed by a vigorous combination of ideas and engaged citizens rather than an entrenched oligarchy dependent upon pedigree, paper credentials or money.

8. Holy Cow! Preliminary Reflections on the 2000 Election

NELSON W. POLSBY

A famous American newspaper editor is reliably alleged to have said (approximately), "When readers look at the front page of the *Washington Post* at breakfast each morning, I want them to exclaim, 'Holy Cow!' " He must have been delighted with the presidential election of 2000, which provided a barnyard full of holy cows to breakfast-time thrill seekers. This essay will take another look at a few of the issues that the election raised in an attempt to answer the pressing question: What can we say once we have said "Holy Cow?"

A CLOSE ELECTION IS NOT A CONSTITUTIONAL CRISIS (NECESSARILY)

We might begin with the observation that it was a close election. An election in which the electorate as a whole is narrowly divided around 50 percent ought not *ipso facto* to provoke great alarm. Indeed, on many occasions the existence of a strong two-party system, with two strong parties, is accounted to be rather a good thing. This seems worth saying because so much of the news coverage of the election projected an atmosphere of crisis, in which, for example, the erroneous classification of Florida by the networks as a win for Gore early election evening—and the retraction later on—were portrayed as momentous. But I know of no evidence that the premature call selectively deterred Bush voters, as was alleged, or anybody else from casting their votes in the Florida panhandle, where the polls stayed open an hour later.[1] Sooner or later, the result—some result—was bound to come out. There is no particular handicap, no particular benefit in an early call, right or wrong, as far as the general population is concerned.

A close election is not a crisis, and need not cause a crisis. A proper crisis, it seems to me, comes into being when circumstances exist in which there are no clear constitutional guidelines about how to proceed. But as it happens, the U.S. Constitution—especially after the Twelfth Amendment patched up the problem created by the Burr-Jefferson standoff of 1800—provides in detail for close calls, including instances when the electoral college does not identify a clear winner. As a matter of fact, this machinery was not needed once the disposition of Florida's electoral votes was determined, since there was little doubt about the proper allocation of the electoral votes of all the other states.

Of course, there was quite a bit of turmoil over the results in Florida. And no wonder. The Florida results were close too, and a very large number of defects in Florida electoral administration were uncovered in time to serve as the foundation of legal objections to the certification of electors for George W. Bush. These objections were raised in courts of law, and ultimately resolved—at least for the purpose of certifying a winner—by the U.S. Supreme Court, which chose to intervene rather than allowing the course of action laid out in law to proceed.[2] A new president was duly sworn in, and he now exercises all of the prerogatives of office.

There was enough irregularity in all of this to stimulate the adrenalin of onlookers, not to mention partisans. But this does not add up to a crisis by world standards. Tanks did not rumble in the streets. There were no shootouts at polling places. Nobody stormed the TV stations. The armed forces went about their usual business. Americans are accustomed to peaceable transfers of power, and the election of 2000 provided no exception. It would be complacent to leave the discussion there, however, without some consideration of the discomfort generated by the Florida outcome.

While there was not a lot of convincing evidence of fraud in the administration of the election in Florida—at least not at first—there is a great deal of evidence of defective administration.[3] The now infamous butterfly ballot in use in Palm Beach County but not elsewhere generated a large number of votes for Pat Buchanan that obviously were intended for Al Gore.[4] There is evidently no practical remedy in law for a situation of this kind short of a new election; whatever voters intended to do, their actual vote—no matter how deceptively elicited—is all that was available to count. One might think of this as an instance in which the election was administered unevenly but, because there seems to be no requirement that ballots in different Florida counties be uniform in their design, no issue of equal protection arises. An innocent bystander, not learned in the law, might wonder why not. After all, the rubric of equal protection was invoked by the Supreme Court to shield a presidential candidate in advance from hypothetical, anticipated harm arising from possible unevenness from place to place in judgments by electoral officials following Florida law if they were to be permitted to hand count ballots for one reason or another uncounted or improperly counted by machines. To the untrained eye, both sets of circumstances look like consequential nonuniformities in electoral administration. What neutral principle forbids the one and permits the other to fall under the umbrella of equal protection?

The heat of the moment and the adversarial structure of the American legal system required questions of this sort to be considered at the time almost entirely in light of their expected partisan impact. Thus, judging from what the parties were saying at the time the view that votes should be hand counted was considered simply a pro-Gore position and strenuously resisted by representatives of George W. Bush. A great deal was made of Gore's alleged tactical errors in not asking for hand counts everywhere rather than only in counties where he believed he could pick up votes. The Bush camp's similar tactical selectivity with respect to military ballots went largely unremarked at the time.

The tactical second-guessing may or may not be right. Unfortunately, it deflects attention from a significant interest that is nonpartisan in character: Voters not committing fraud (e.g., voting twice) regardless of their preferences are entitled to reasonable assurance that appropriate effort is made to see that their votes are counted. Each and every discarded ballot (overvotes, undervotes, military ballots without legible postmarks, votes partially mutilated by defective machinery) encoded the preferences of a citizen of Florida. It seems clear enough to an onlooker that the state of Florida owed these voters its best effort to decode and register their preferences even if in some instances that effort would not be enough to arrive at a conclusion about the voter's intent. Any participant taking a contrary view owes a better explanation to Floridians and to the rest of us than has been forthcoming.

We were all witnesses, via television, to varied attempts to thwart the exercise of this effort. The worst such attempt occurred on November 23, 2000, when a rent-a-mob of Republican congressional staffers who were sent down from Washington, D.C., for some such purpose evidently succeeded in halting a hand count of ballots in Miami-Dade County. This was not thuggish misbehavior merely because it was aimed at keeping Al Gore from the presidency. Gore's interests, though obviously not trivial, are nevertheless not the central issue. It was misbehavior because citizens of Florida were entitled to have their votes counted. Florida law says so, and the presumption in advance that hand counts cannot be done fairly constitutes a leap of faith easily construed in the circumstances as a highly partisan political judgment. Much the same comment applies to legal appeals to stall hand counting of votes until deadlines were safely reached. In the end, the view prevailed that such a count could not proceed in a timely fashion using the criteria provided for by Florida law. But nagging doubts persist that this decision by what looked like a Supreme Court caught in the grip of partisan calculations short-circuited a system that could have been made to work. Americans are unfamiliar with contests in which the referee holds the ball until time runs out.

The Theory and Practice of a Presidential Mandate

Given the unique properties of the decision-making that put him in office, a number of commentators were taken by surprise by the manner in which George W. Bush commenced the conduct of his presidency during the early months while Republicans controlled both the House and the Senate. The self-proclaimed "uniter not divider" made little or no allowance for the circumstances of his arrival in office and plowed ahead with his plans for a tax cut, missile defense, and other controversial programs. This approach to governing was not only consistent with some of his campaign promises, but it was also consistent with a reasonable—indeed a time-honored—construction of what a mandate amounts to in American presidential politics.

To be sure, George Bush received no mandate in the sense of a message from voters about what public policy should be. American presidents rarely do; indeed, arguably, they never do. Mandates must be inferred from electoral results since American presidential elections are not fought over single issues, and the mandate thus varies according to who is doing the inferring. Voters may have all sorts of issues in mind or no issues at all when they make their choices. The mechanisms of vote counting, as in the case of the electoral college, can thwart the expression of a plurality vote for a particular candidate, even assuming that all those who vote for a candidate want everything a candidate is promising.

So while is it traditional for winning candidates (or in special circumstances, even candidates who actually lose the popular vote) to claim they have a mandate to do whatever it is they want to do, the claim is usually little more than partisan propaganda. And fatuous though a claim of a mandate may be in any non-referendum, multiple-issue election, it is even more so in the American political system in which precisely these sorts of complicated elections simultaneously bring to office presidents, senators, members of Congress, and countless others, each with their commitments, promises, and campaign slogans, and, therefore, mandates to claim.

Thus, as a practical matter, a president's mandate can rarely be culled directly out of the multiple, mixed, and equivocal messages that electorates send on election day. But, indirectly, the story is different. By virtue of taking and holding office, a president is entitled to use the powers of the office to set a direction for government. These powers are shared and constrained. Presidents especially are required to adapt to the constraints placed on presidential discretion by the Constitution, notably the need to seek and secure the agreement of Congress for legislation and appropriations, and the advice and consent of the Senate on important appointments to the executive branch and the judiciary. As a practical matter, therefore, presidential mandates must be inferred not only from the results of presidential elections but also from the results of the elections that populated the Congress with which he serves.

This means that like all his predecessors George W. Bush is entitled to seek to be whatever sort of president he wants to be, but of course it also means that the failure of his administration to keep Senator James Jeffords under the Republican tent is likewise an expression rather than a repudiation of the mandate the American political system actually confers. The rules of our electoral system permit a president to assume office if he wins in the electoral college, even if he receives fewer popular votes than his main rival.

The rules also permit a sitting senator to change party affiliations, as Republicans were happy to acknowledge when changes went in their direction in the cases of Richard Shelby of Alabama and Ben Nighthorse Campbell of Colorado, both elected to the Senate not so long ago as Democrats.

In short, the only mandate the American system actually confers is the entitlement, under complicated rules, to assume office. After that, public officials must manage their relations with one another, and with public opinion, and prepare for future elections in which there will also be no mandate in the conventional sense on offer.

The Acceptability of Electoral Machinery: The Electoral College and Some Alternatives

Close presidential elections, those in which the president-elect has only a narrow margin in the total popular vote, always lead to renewed public discussion of the merits of the electoral college, since close elections remind people of the possibility that the candidate with a plurality of all the individual votes will not necessarily become president. The election of 2000 reminded us that such an event can actually happen. Reform interest surges even higher when a regionally based third party, such as the party George Wallace led in 1968, or a conspicuous independent candidate, such as Ross Perot in 1992, becomes strong enough conceivably to prevent any candidate from having an electoral vote majority. The Constitution is ready for such an eventuality, but that is a story for some other year. This was the year the electoral college picked the loser of the popular vote.

The mechanics of the electoral college are set forth in Article II of the Constitution with admirable simplicity: "Each state shall appoint, in such manner as the legislature thereof may direct, a number of electors, equal to the whole number of Senators and Representatives to which the state may be entitled in the Congress." This plain text has misled more than a few otherwise careful students of the Constitution to think that the electoral college gives special advantage to small states. Electors equivalent to the number of each state's representatives in Congress would of course yield numbers roughly proportional to each state's population; the two added Senatorial electors allocated to each state regardless of population presumably puts a thumb on the scale favoring the small states. And so it would be if the legislatures of virtually all states had not long since directed that the appointment of electors take place on a winner-take-all basis. Only Maine and Nebraska currently direct otherwise, providing that two votes be cast according to statewide results and that the vote in each congressional district determine a single electoral vote.

Since Maine casts four electoral votes and Nebraska five, the dilution of their vote in this fashion is of little consequence. Larger states have more at stake. The casting of all their electoral votes for a single winner means that voters within the larger states have a much greater opportunity to participate in a winning coalition than voters in small states.[5] So it is the large states (holding competitiveness constant) that benefit the most. Politicians know this and respond accordingly. They realize that winning California—or any other large state—by a single vote produces more in the electoral college than winning nearly all the small states put together by any margin. Somebody should have explained this to the new junior senator from New York before she advocated the abolition of the electoral college soon after the election of 2000 was decided. In any event, whether from motives of self-interest, misguided self-interest, idealism, or misguided idealism, the election put the reform of the electoral college once again on the agenda.

The number of plans to reform the electoral college that have been proposed over the years is legion. These can readily be boiled down to three basic alternatives to the present system, the rest being variations. One would abolish the electoral college outright and weigh individual votes equally, everywhere. The net effect of such a proposal would be to undermine slightly the current strategic advantage enjoyed by populous, two-party, urbanized states. As we will see in a moment, it might also have some long-run effects on the two-party system itself. The second proposal would retain the apportionment of the electoral college (which as indicated gives a numerical advantage to the smaller, less populous states) but abolish the winner-take-all electoral option (which operates strongly in favor of larger states). This proposal is quite extreme in its potential import, because it confers an additional political advantage to states that over much of American history have been overrepresented in positions of congressional power. A third, quite similar, proposal enacts the Maine and Nebraska formula everywhere, retaining the apportionment of the electoral college but distributing one electoral college vote to the plurality vote winner in each congressional district and two additional electoral votes to the winner in each state. Since this system enhances the strength of one-party states, it would also work to realign the presidential coalition in fundamental ways.

Now let us take a brief plunge into some numbers. The Constitution provides that each state, regardless of its population, shall be represented in the Senate by an equal number of senators. This means that the eight largest states, with just under half of all of the voters in the United States in the year 2000, are represented by 16 percent of the senators. In the course of proceedings in the Senate, these sixteen senators' votes can be canceled out by the sixteen votes of the senators from the eight least populous states, with 2.4 percent of the voters in the 2000 presidential election.[6] In 2000, an average vote in Wyoming was worth about fifty-four times as much as a vote in California in elections for the Senate. This imbalance contrasts with the advantage that more populous, urbanized, two-party states enjoy in the electoral college, and thus in access to the presidency.

2000 Electoral Votes (Top and Bottom 14 States)

State	2000 Electoral Votes[a]	2000 Census Population	2000 Presidential Votes
California	54	33,871,648	10,965,856
Texas	33	20,851,820	6,407,637
New York	32	18,976,457	6,821,999
Florida	25	15,982,378	5,937,705
Illinois	22	12,419,293	4,739,935
Pennsylvania	23	12,281,054	4,912,185
Ohio	21	11,353,140	4,701,998
Michigan	18	9,938,444	4,232,501
New Jersey	15	8,414,350	3,187,226
Georgia	13	8,186,453	2,583,208
North Carolina	14	8,049,313	2,914,990

Virginia	13	7,078,515	2,736,640
Massachusetts	12	6,349,097	2,698,994
Indiana	12	6,080,485	2,199,302
Nevada	4	1,998,257	605,655
Idaho	4	1,293,953	501,615
Maine	4	1,274,923	651,790
New Hampshire	4	1,235,786	567,795
Hawaii	4	1,211,537	367,951
Rhode Island	4	1,048,319	409,112
Montana	3	902,195	410,986
Delaware	3	783,600	327,529
South Dakota	3	754,844	316,269
North Dakota	3	642,200	288,256
Alaska	3	626,932	284,492
Vermont	3	608,827	293,794
District of Columbia	3	572,059	201,894
Wyoming	3	493,782	213,726
United States	538	281,421,906	105,337,933

Note: States are ranked according to their 2000 census population. The California vote total reflects the amended total submitted by the state after the electoral vote took place.

ª2000 electoral votes were apportioned on the basis of the 1990 census of population.

Sources: U.S. Census Bureau, Census 2000 Redistricting Data (P.L. 94–171) Summary File and 1990 Census. Voting data come from the secretary of state Websites for the respective states.

The present electoral college system yields a nominal advantage to the smallest states, since their overrepresentation in the Senate guarantees them overrepresentation in the electoral college; after the 2000 census, the seven states with three electoral votes each had a ratio of 301,000 or fewer citizens per electoral vote, while the dozen states with thirteen or more electoral votes had a ratio of 534,000 or more citizens per electoral vote. But this is a secondary advantage.[7]

It is primarily the larger states, through the winner-take-all principle, which benefit from the electoral college. A candidate who can get a narrow majority in California alone can bag almost as many electoral votes (fifty-four) as he could by carrying each and every one of the sixteen smallest states (fifty-eight). He can carry California by only one vote and not receive any votes at all in those sixteen states and do just as well. This fact suggests as a matter of strategic prudence that a presidential candidate should spend his energy in the larger states and tailor his programs to appeal to voters there, provided that energy expended there has any decent political chance of yielding results. It also constitutes a standing incentive to both major political parties to choose their candidates and write their platforms so as to appeal to the people who vote in the larger states.

The large states are the home of many organized minorities, especially racial and ethnic minorities, and this has traditionally tempted presidential candidates to pitch their appeals to attract these groups, or at least not to drive them off. This feature of the current system has in the past led to criticism from politicians and others who do not especially wish to gratify urban minorities. In recent years, however, critics have concentrated their fire on the possibility of the "wrong winner" that turned up this year.

Allowing a majority (or plurality) of individual voters to choose a president has a great deal to commend it. At first blush, it looks like the simplest method of doing business. It would be most easily understood by the greatest number of people; it is a plan generally favored by the majority of Americans when they are asked; and it comes closest to reflecting intuitive notions of direct popular sovereignty through majority rule.

The outright abolition of the electoral college, and the substitution of the direct election of the president, would reduce the importance of the larger states. It would mean that the popular vote margin for a given side that a state could provide—not the total number of its electoral votes—would determine its importance. For example, under the present system a candidate who carries California by 144,100 votes (as Ronald Reagan did in 1980) has garnered one-sixth of the support he needs to win, while under the direct-vote system, states such as Massachusetts or Alabama can sometimes generate three and four times that margin. In the two-party states, in which category most of the larger states fall, voters are cross-pressured in many ways, and a candidate can not always count on defeating his opponent by a very large margin as Al Gore did in California in 2000. The reason, then, that the large states lose influence under the direct vote is not that the direct vote makes them less large but because this system switches influence from the close states to one-party states. In some states where one party's organization is weak, it is easier for the other party to achieve a large turnout at election time, and special rewards might be forthcoming for interest groups particularly strong within states that could provide a large margin of victory for their candidate. As candidates currently look with favor on those who can bring them support in the large states so might they be expected to look with favor on those who can bring them large popular margins in the one-party states, should that become the preferred strategy for winning. The emphasis would not be on which candidate was going to win the state—already a foregone conclusion—but by how many votes he was going to win. The small states do not gain, however, because even when they are controlled by one party, they are not large enough to generate big numbers of voters. Direct election thus changes the advantage from the biggest and the smallest two-party states to the medium-sized one-party states. These, in recent elections, have frequently been located in the South. How one feels about direct elections thus ought to depend in part on how one feels about the diminution of large-state influence and the gain by one-party states.

Now let us consider how much of a plurality a newly elected president should have. If the rules of the game stipulated that whoever came first in a wide-open race would win, what would prevent the winner of, let us say, 25 percent of the vote in a crowded field from being elected president? Simple first-past-the-post rules can act as attractive nuisances, drawing in more and more candidates, siphoning more and more support away from front-runners. Such a system could produce a wrong winner by electing a candidate with an enthusiastic middle-sized following whom everybody else hated. We can call this the George Wallace scenario. Two mechanisms can guard against this eventuality. The number of candidates can somehow be restricted or discouraged; or a minimum vote can be required for election.

Reformers have generally agreed that the winner should be required to win by at least a substantial plurality; for example, the electoral college reform amendment that passed the House in 1969 provided for a runoff between the top two candidates if no one secured as much as 40 percent of the popular vote in the initial election. This arrangement still delivers influence to splinter parties. If voters are going to have a second chance to express their preferences anyway, there is an incentive for any sizable organized minority to take a chance at getting in the runoff and therefore to contest the first election on its own and without seeking alliances. That the runoff would likely be used if it were provided for is suggested by 1992, when there was a fairly strong third-party candidate in the race. A fourth candidate would have needed only 6 or 7 percent of the national total to keep either major-party candidate from gaining the required 40 percent (Clinton won with 43 percent, although he had 68.8 percent of the electoral vote). Once this becomes even a plausible expectation, there is an incentive for various other intense minorities to put up their own candidates. Thus, direct election—even with a runoff—might well encourage the flying of a lot of kites: a white supremacist party, a labor party, a Hispanic party, a peace party, an environmentalist party, a right-to-life party, an African American party, a farmers' party, and parties serving as vehicles for the vanity of assorted millionaires, celebrities, activists, ideologues, saints, icons, nutcases, and so forth. One of the strong features of the present system is that it enforces compromise by making it hard for groups that will not align with a major party or that lack a regional base to win much of anything. A direct election system would encourage a situation Americans associate with continental Europe, in which numerous groups contest the first election and then get together for the second. Should such an arrangement occur in the future, the alleged simplicity, ease of comprehension, and inherent majoritarian rightness of the direct election solution would quickly evaporate as voters engaged in an unknown combination of tactical and sincere voting. One of the hidden effects of the electoral college is to restrict the number of parties seriously contesting for the presidency. Because it requires organizing to contest fifty separate states, the electoral college system helps focus the electorate in each state on a limited menu of choices. In turn, this increases the chance that winners will have the backing of a sizable number of voters and the legitimacy to lead Congress and the nation.

The direct election plan passed by the House in 1969 received a warmer reception in the Senate than in 1956, when it was voted down 66 to 17. There were, not surprisingly, two major opposition groups. The first was the bloc of liberal senators from the biggest states, who in those days realized they had the most to lose. The second was composed of some of the conservative senators from the smallest states, the group deriving second-greatest benefits from the current system. They argued that direct election would be a complete break with the federalism underlying our Constitution, since it would de facto abolish state boundaries for presidential elections.

Another proposal, embodied fifty years ago in the unsuccessful Lodge-Gossett resolution, was touted by some reformers as an acceptable "compromise" between outright abolition of the electoral college and its retention. In this scheme, the electoral vote in each state is retained, and split between the candidates according to their proportion of the state's popular vote. This may seem to be a procedural compromise, but it is a rather extreme reform in political terms.

Under proportional allocation of electoral votes, campaigning presidential nominees would have to give special attention to those states in which they felt a large difference in electoral votes could be attained. Once again, the proposed reform emphasizes not absolute numbers but the difference within the state between the winner and the loser. In this case, however, the electoral votes of the states are divided, rather than the popular votes. This effectively cancels out the advantage of the large state electorates entirely, since electoral college numbers underrepresent the large states. The beneficiaries are again the one-party states, as well as the smaller states, since in any particular election West Virginia and Arizona, for example, may have more to contribute to the difference in electoral votes than the more evenly divided Illinois, New Jersey, Ohio, or Florida.

There are two versions of this plan, one that divides electoral votes to the nearest vote and one that divides them to the nearest tenth of a vote. Most proponents favor the plan to divide them to the nearest tenth, since the nearest whole vote in many cases still would understate the closeness of the vote in a large number of states, especially those with few electoral votes to divide, and "representatives" is the primary theoretical advantage of the plan. Since preventing deadlock is supposed to be one of the goals of electoral college reform, it is interesting to note that with the majority-vote victory required by both plans, either the whole or the tenth-vote system would have thrown the 1968, 1992, 1996, and the 2000 elections into the House of Representatives and the system allotting electoral votes to the nearest tenth would have deadlocked the election of 1960.[8]

A third plan, the district plan, has been proposed as still another "political compromise" between the other two major reform proposals. The district plan would give a presidential candidate one electoral vote for every congressional district he carried, plus two more for every state. As mentioned, this is how electoral votes are now distributed in the states of Maine and Nebraska. It has been pushed largely by conservative senators; it is clearly the most radical of all the reform proposals in its effect on the U.S. political system, because it is least advantageous to the big states. This system would have given Nixon victory in 1968, but if it had already been in effect, he probably would not have been running, since it would also have reversed the results of the election of 1960. George W. Bush—still without a popular majority—would have won in 2000 with a 286–252 majority using this method.

This "compromise" seems to me a nonstarter. Since the goals of electoral college reform are supposedly to prevent the wrong candidate from winning, to avoid deadlock, and to do away with winner-take-all arrangements, it is hard to see what is offered by a system that frequently gives the less popular candidate victory, provides no more guarantee against deadlock than the present system (George Wallace in 1968 got forty-five electoral votes under the prevailing system, but would have received fifty-seven under this one), uses a winner-take-all principle, and has the incidental feature of ending the activist character of the American presidency and giving policy control to one-party areas for the foreseeable future.

The election of 1988 would have come out the same way under all the plans for counting votes so far mentioned. Under proportional allocation, the 1992 and 1996 elections would have been thrown into the House of Representatives, but Clinton would still have won under district representation. Plans to abolish the electoral college, by damping down even large landslides, would bring stronger splinter parties and more of them into the electoral competition, thus changing the climate of electoral competition altogether.

Under the present electoral college system, there has been no time since 1876 when any splinter group has been able to make good its threat to throw the election into the House. Even in 1948 Harry Truman won an electoral college majority despite sizable threats from both a third (Henry Wallace, Progressive) and a fourth (Strom Thurmond, States' Rights) party. Obviously, under the current system the loser of the popular vote can become president. But it doesn't happen very often. A direct election plan that required a 40 percent plurality might well have forced a runoff in 1968 and 1992. The proportional plan would have created deadlocks in two recent elections; and the district plan would have thrown the election to the popular vote loser in at least one recent case. There are no foolproof systems.

There are no doubt situations of social polarization that no electoral system can paper over. And there are evidently no systems much better than the current one from the standpoint of the professed goals of most reformers. However, one minor change might help. Under the present plan the actual electors who make up the electoral college are in fact free to vote for whomever they wish. These electors are usually party faithful who are chosen in each state by party leaders or the organizations of winning presidential candidates. As an almost invariable rule, they vote for the winner in their state, but abuses are possible, and two within recent memory come to mind. The unpledged electors chosen by citizens in Mississippi and Alabama in 1960 decided for whom they would vote only well after the election, treating the expressed preferences of citizens as advisory, not mandatory. This clearly thwarts popular control and allowed George Wallace to hope in 1968 that by running for president, he could create an electoral deadlock and then bargain with one of the other candidates for policy concessions in exchange for his electors. An amendment abolishing the office of elector and making the casting of electoral votes automatic would dispel both these possibilities.

A final idea deserves consideration, the creation of a private commission set up by the Twentieth Century Fund (now the Century Foundation) some years ago. The commission came up with a proposal for a national bonus plan, which would award 102 electoral votes en bloc (two for each state plus the District of Columbia) to the plurality winner of the nationwide popular vote. This plan would more or less guarantee that no president could be elected who did not get more votes than his nearest rival. An additional feature is that candidates would be encouraged to get as many popular votes as they could, and campaign even in states where they were pretty sure to lose, because these could add on to the candidate's national popular vote total. The bonus plan would guard against a minority president, preserve the form and the spirit of the constitutional structure, and do all this without encouraging splinter parties. It did not attract much interest.

I have raised a number of considerations that may or may not disturb thoughtful readers. Splinter parties, for example, are undoubtedly enemies of a strong two-party system, but voters may not like a two-party system. They may find splinter parties an attractive method for expressing the varied shades of political opinion that undoubtedly exist in the large, diverse population that comprises the U.S. electorate. This relaxed view of splinters comports well with a conception of elections primarily as occasions for the venting of expressive behavior rather than as more workaday instruments for arriving at a final result that voters can live with. Elections must in part perform both functions, and reasonable people may well prefer different emphases.

Similarly, not everyone will want to go to great lengths to protect the interests most frequently to be found in the big, politically competitive states. In the days before the line of reapportionment court cases that started with *Baker v. Carr* (1962) the interests of urban minorities and large states were seriously underrepresented in state legislatures, in the apportionment of congressional seats that then prevailed, and therefore in the leadership of the committee structure of Congress. This gave urgency to the argument that the electoral college provided a necessary political check and balance in the system. But as reapportionment has proceeded over the last forty years, and cities and suburbs have increased their influence in state capitals and in Congress, the extra clout that the electoral college gives large states may come to seem obsolete—and not only to observers hostile to large state interests on other grounds.

A glance at the table also shows that not all states that are alike in size are alike in sheltering the same sorts of interests. Arguably, Hawaii, the District of Columbia, and Rhode Island among the small states have more in common with New York than any of them has with Wyoming or Idaho. So some analysts may conclude that protecting the political influence of large states in the electoral college is an inefficient way of protecting interests no longer structurally handicapped in Congress.

A further consequence of disturbing the electoral college arrangement has to do with the extent to which alternative systems of vote counting rely upon the enhanced productivity of political parties in turning out the vote. If high productivity—that is, turning out voters beyond the minimum necesary to win a state's electoral votes under a winner-take-all rule—becomes necessary to win, presumably those parties that produce more votes will gain influence with candidates. As a first approximation the assumption has been that dominant parties in one-party states would be best positioned to reap this advantage, but this may or may not be true over the long run. Conceivably putting a premium on vote productivity would encourage more state parties to connect effectively with voters and potential voters and thus stimulate electoral politics at the grass roots. Such a regime might in due course shift influence toward successful state party leaders of productive parties in their dealings with candidates and to a degree attenuate the overwhelming candidate-centricity of the current presidential nominating process.

These, at any rate, are some of the matters that one would hope to see discussed in any serious deliberation over the fate of the electoral college. Although the electoral college in 2000 failed to pick the winner of the popular vote, the sky did not fall. I do not know that we would have predicted in advance of the event that there would be so little objection to the anomalous result that thoughtful analysts for years had been anticipating with great apprehensiveness. In fact, Americans seem to have been reasonably content with the outcome. The accident that was waiting to happen finally happened with less damage than expected.

POLITICAL CONSEQUENCES?

If the electoral college result proved to be less damaging to the overall acceptability of the outcome than anticipated, other aspects of the process in play during 2000 came off less well. For example, the best that can be said of the intervention of the Supreme Court is that the sky did not fall on them, either—at least not yet. But the reputation of the Court for doing business in a manner that rises above crass partisanship took a powerful hit. This is not the first such hit in recent years. It has to be conceded that the Court is in many fundamental ways a political body, and cannot escape evaluation on a political basis. Even so, many observers thought the activities surrounding the failed Supreme Court nomination of Robert Bork in 1987 took the Court further into partisan politics than was good for its maintenance as a high-level umpire bringing important principles to bear on decisions governing the system. If anything, this election was worse. It is only sensible to suppose that it too will have repercussions in the way all high judicial nominations of President Bush will be received.

It has in the past been respectably argued, for example, that a judicial nominee's views of public policy ought not to figure prominently in their evaluation for confirmation. Since Bork was rejected for alleged deviation from "mainstream" judicial philosophy, nominees have had to endure more and more elaborate scrutiny, and in some cases been subjected to very long delays before being confirmed or without being confirmed. Recalling Thomas Hobbes, Anthony Lake described the process as nasty and brutish without being short.

The manner of the Court's intervention in *Bush v. Gore* seems likely to provide a basis for more—perhaps a lot more—delay and sharp partisan combat in the judicial confirmation process. Some commentators have gone so far as to recommend that all Supreme Court nominations from President Bush be rejected without the intervention of a less irregular election. There may partially in consequence be no Supreme Court vacancies for a while to test the strength of the sentiment behind this rather stringent recommendation, but vacancies in the appellate courts already exist and since the defection of Senator Jeffords from the Republican party, the Senate is no longer available as a presidential rubber stamp.

Under present circumstances, it is hard to see how setting an extremely high bar for judicial nominees in the confirmation process can plausibly be attacked as excessively partisan. No doubt some defenders of the president and, presumably defenders of the (we are assured) non-precedential manner of his arrival in office, will make some such arguments, but who will believe them?

The argument here is that the disposition of the election of 2000 can be seen in the context of a more general loosening of constraints on partisan competition that has become more and more evident in the political system over the last eighty years. There is a theory that overlapping cleavages hold down extreme partisanship. As the major political parties evolve toward more coherence ideologically, with liberal northern Republicans like Jeffords and conservative Southern Democrats disappearing from the scene, the parties became more serviceable as organizational weapons in more and more arenas. This, arguably, is how impeachments become possible instruments of partisan combat, and why we see increasing rancor between the parties on Capitol Hill.

It might reasonably have been expected that the Supreme Court would lag somewhat behind these developments in American party politics. But it is now a historical fact that despite the plentiful availability of doctrines to the contrary—all of them familiar to the justices—the Court jumped into the thickest political thicket that the American political system possesses. I have no idea whether its expressed wish that this intervention have no precedential value will prove to be constraining on the behavior of future courts. One imagines, however, that in other arenas there will be political repercussions. Surely, these were intended in the case of the executive branch of government, but one somehow doubts that they will be confined merely to what now seems to be the abrupt and extraordinary selection in the year 2000 of a president and vice president by judicial action.

Notes

INTRODUCTION

1. He does not deny that a respectable case can be made, on traditional legal grounds, for the Court's decision. He believes that the Article II argument I discuss later in this introduction does constitute a respectable argument. But he thinks that the interpretation of Article II that the dissenting justices proposed is just as reasonable as the interpretation on which the Article II argument depends, and that the decision can therefore be justified only on the consequentialist grounds he proposes.

2. 3 U.S.C. Section 5 (1887).

3. See Fried, "An Exchange," *New York Review of Books,* February 22, 2001.

4. *United States v. Virginia,* 518 U.S. 515, 596 (1996).

5. In some circumstances, to be sure, the mere fact of different treatment constitutes a harm, or is suggestive of an official intention to create or perpetuate genuine inequality. The Supreme Court, in its famous decision in 1954 to end official racial segregation in state schools, declared that separate schools were, just in their separation, unequal schools. But that ruling presupposed the special background of long eras of explicit racial discrimination and victimization: It held that in those circumstances segregation, without more, imposed an injury. As I argue in the text, no comparable claim is even intelligible in the case of the Florida recount.

6. *U.S. v. Hays,* 515 U.S. 737 (1995).

7. See, e.g., *Reynolds v. Sims,* 377 U.S. 533 (1964).

8. Samuel Issacharoff, Pamela S. Karlan, and Richard H. Pildes, *When Elections Go Bad* (revised edition) (New York: Foundation Press, 2001).

9. *Roe v. State of Alabama,* 43 F.3rd 574 (11th Cir. 1995).

10. See Tribe's argument to the same effect in Chapter 3 and my own argument in Chapter 1.

11. See David Barstow and Don Van Natta, Jr., "How Bush Took Florida: Mining the Overseas Absentee Vote," *New York Times,* July 15, 2001.

12. See Fla. Stat. Section 101.67 (2000); Fla. Admin. Code, Section 15-2.013 (2000).

13. See Fla. Const. Art. 1, Sec. 1.

14. The Supreme Court's December 4 decision cited only one, very old, decision in support of its surprising reading of Article II. In *McPherson v. Blacker,* 146 U.S. 1 (1892), the then Supreme Court considered whether the Michigan legislature had the power to allocate two of its presidential electors to districts, so that each of these two electors would be elected by the people of only half the state. In his opinion in that case, Chief Justice Fuller, in order to show that Article II did not prevent the state legislature from adopting that

arrangement, said that Article II "does not read that the peoples or the citizens shall appoint [all the electors, as a whole], but that 'each State shall,' and if the words 'in such manner as the legislature thereof may direct' had been omitted, it would seem that the legislative power of appointment could not have been successfully questioned in the absence of any provision in the state constitution in that regard. Hence the insertion of these words, while operating as a limitation upon the State in respect of any attempt to circumscribe the legislative power, cannot be held to operate as a limitation on that power itself." As the contemporary Court conceded, this language is not precedent for the proposition that a state constitution cannot constrain a state legislature in designing the manner of elections, because that issue was not before the 1892 court. At best, the remark is an offhand suggestion to that effect, and it is a sign of the weakness of the Article II argument that this is as close as the Court could come to finding authority for that argument. But Fuller's suggestion that Article II limits the state's power to "circumscribe the legislative power" can in any case easily be read to state the more sensible proposition I called the natural reading of Article II in the text: That Article prevents a state constitution from assigning the general power to design elections to any body other than the state legislature, but does not extinguish the citizens' normal power to protect their rights through constitutional limits on what the legislature, in the exercise of that general power, can do.

15. Fla. Stat. Section 102.166(5). The three justices also mentioned, as a further error in the Florida court's interpretation, its reading of "legal votes" in Fla. Stat. Section 102.168(3)(c), but their argument that the Florida court misread the latter section is parasitic on its argument that it misread the former one. "It is inconceivable," they said, "that what constitutes a vote that must be counted under the 'error in the vote tabulation' language of the protest phase is different from what constitutes a vote that must be counted under the 'legal votes' language of the contest phase."

16. Posner, in his book about the election, to which he refers in his contribution to this volume, offers a different way of defending the idea that Article II qualifies the judges' normal authority to interpret election statutes. He distinguishes between courts exercising "the normal judicial power to fill statutory gaps and resolve statutory ambiguities" and their "exercising a plenary power of 'interpretation.' " See Posner, *Breaking the Deadlock: The 2000 Election, the Constitution and the Courts* (Princeton: Princeton University Press, 2001), 155. Article II, he suggests, permits a state court to fill gaps and resolve ambiguities in a state election statute, but not to engage in any more substantial kind of interpretation. But what can that distinction mean? What can he have in mind as "plenary" interpretation? *Gaps* and *ambiguities* do not exhaust the categories of semantic features that provoke interpretation: Interpretation is also required when words are vague (like *heap*) or abstract (like *unreasonable*), and also when it is unclear how a statute should be read even though no particular word can be described, on its own, in any of these ways. Surely Posner does not mean that it would be permissible for the Florida court to resolve ambiguities in the Florida election law, but not to make vague terms or abstract standards more concrete. Perhaps he means that when judges are confronted with a problem arising out of a presidential election, they are permitted to interpret state election statutes by searching history for some direct evidence of legislators' mental states, but not by engag-

ing in any of the other familiar techniques of interpretation. But, as I say in the text later in this section, historical evidence of mental states is almost never available, and is rarely pertinent to statutory interpretation when it is available. Perhaps he really means that judges should not interpret election statutes in presidential cases at all, but just enforce the statute as it is actually written. But there is no such thing as the statute as it is actually written: What counts as a statute is determined by interpretation, not before interpretation begins.

17. Florida Statutes, Section 97.012.
18. Florida Statutes, Section 106.23.
19. I expand on and defend this account of statutory interpretation in Chapter 9 of my book, *Law's Empire* (Cambridge: Harvard University Press, 1986).
20. See Florida Election Reform Act of 2001.
21. Posner, *Breaking the Deadlock, supra,* at 171.
22. Posner, id, at 185-6.
23. I do not agree with Posner's analysis of the history or content of philosophical pragmatism, but since that analysis does not bear on his argument in Chapter 5 I will not defend my disagreement here. His account of non-philosophical judicial pragmatism, on the other hand, seems to match my own description of judicial pragmatism in my book, *Law's Empire, supra.*
24. Posner, Chapter 5, page 201.
25. Posner, Chapter 5, page 192.
26. Posner, Chapter 5, page 201.
27. It would make no difference to this point whether the imagined pragmatist judge intended to decide, on the merits, not on the equal protection grounds Posner thinks fallacious but on the Article II grounds he thinks somewhat more respectable. The pragmatic judge would still have had to compare, on December 9, the results of refusing any further intervention then with the results of declaring, somewhat later, that the Florida court had violated Article II, and he would have had no reason to assume, on December 9, that the recounters would in any case stop recounting then and, for some inexplicable reason only take it up again on December 13.
28. Anthony Lewis, "Bush the Radical," *New York Times,* July 21, 2001.
29. Posner, *Breaking the Deadlock, supra,* at page 180.
30. Suppose we assume, as Posner imagines some justice believing, that a Gore presidency would be "a national calamity." (See Posner, Chapter 5, page 207.) Suppose we also assume, as Posner supposes, that the "systemic consequences" of allowing such an opinion to influence a Supreme Court decision would be very bad. If the badness of those systemic consequences outweighs the calamity of a Gore presidency, in the consequentialist scales, in the long run, then a pragmatic judge would not be tempted to follow his political opinion. But if, on the contrary, the calamity outweighs the systemic consequences, even in the long run, then why should he hesitate to do what is, all things considered, the best? Posner's apparent nervousness at this point suggests that he is, at best, a halfhearted pragmatist.
31. Posner, Chapter 5, page 207.
32. We might even add to that proposition, if we think it relevant and true, that it will in

fact have the best consequences in the long run if judges decide such cases only on principle.

33. See Dworkin, "Thirty Years On," 115 *Harv. L. Rev.* 1655 (2002).

34. Pildes and Tribe point out that Justices Breyer and Souter, the two more moderate justices who joined the five conservative justices in accepting the equal protection argument in *Bush v. Gore,* also joined the five conservatives in some of those decisions.

35. See the discussion of the case by Pildes and Tribe in Chapters 4 and 3.

36. For an exploration of the role of money in politics, see Chapter 10 of my book, *Sovereign Virtue* (Cambridge: Harvard University Press, 2000).

37. Posner, *Breaking the Deadlock, supra,* at 203.

38. I expand on the argument of this paragraph in my book, *Freedom's Law: The Moral Reading of the Constitution* (Cambridge: Harvard University Press, 1996).

1.   EARLY RESPONSES

 *   This article first appeared in *The New York Review of Books* on December 21, 2000.

 1.   See "Americans Patiently Awaiting Election Outcome," *New York Times,* November 14, 2000, p. A1.

 2.   For a sample analysis, see the article posted on the Web at madison.hss.cmu.edu.

 3.   *Beckstrom v. Volusia County Canvassing Board,* 707 So. 2d 720 (1998).

 4.   See, for example, *Craig v. Wallace,* 2 Fla. L. Weekly Supp. 517a (1994), *Ury v. Santee,* 303 F. Supp. 119 (N.D. Ill. 1969), *Akizaki v. Fong,* 461 P.2d 221 (Haw. 1969), and *Adkins v. Huckabay,* 755 So. 2d 206 (La. 2000).

 5.   Republicans charged illegality in the vote count in Illinois and Texas in the 1960 election, and switching the electoral votes of those two states would have changed the result. Some commentators hail Nixon's decision not to challenge as an act of patriotism, though others say he feared discovery of Republican as well as Democratic fraud in Illinois.

 6.   Would the result of a new election in that county be closer to original intentions than the recorded first vote was? Professor Laurence Tribe of Harvard suggested in the *New York Times* of November 12 that any new election be limited to those who voted in the first one, and that the votes for Bush and Nader should be held at their initial totals, so that only the votes for Gore and Buchanan could change.

It would also help to limit a possible Gore vote to his original total plus the number of initial Buchanan and double-punched ballots. That would not in fact prevent Nader voters from switching to Gore, perhaps making his total larger than it would have been the first time but for the confusion, but it would reduce the impact of any such switches.

 †   This article first appeared in *The New York Review of Books* on January 11, 2001.

 7.   For a detailed account of this conservative activism, see Larry Kramer, "No Surprise. It's an Activist Court," *New York Times,* December 12, 2000.

 8.   Scalia also said that since "it is generally agreed" that further handling of the ballots might degrade them, Bush might suffer irreparable harm if that degradation made a further, more accurate, recount impossible. But there is no evidence (only Republican allegations) that a recounting of ballots by judges is likely to injure those ballots, no request

by the Bush team for any further recounting, and no real prospect of the Supreme Court ordering one.

9.   The *New York Times* suggested that they agreed in hopes, which failed, of constructing a compromise decision to send the case back to allow the Florida court to set more concrete counting standards. See Linda Greenhouse, "Bush Prevails," December 13, 2000, p. A1.

10. The Florida Supreme Court had adopted the "clear voter intent" standard from the Florida statutes. In his dissenting opinion, Souter said that he could see no rational basis for using such an abstract test for inspecting ballots. But a state might rationally decide that accuracy would be improved overall by using a general standard rather than trying to anticipate in detail all the evidence that a ballot might present: a set of concrete tests might not have allowed, for example, for the Florida voter who wrote "I vote for Al Gore" across his otherwise unmarked and unpunched ballot.

11. This interpretive question asks not whether the present Florida legislature, dominated by Republicans who seemed anxious to deliver their state to Bush in any way possible, would make that choice, but whether it would be justified by sound legal interpretation of existing Florida law, which cannot appeal to partisan political motives of that character.

12. When on December 4 the Court vacated the Florida Supreme Court's initial decision extending the time for manual recounts, and asked for clarification of the ground of that decision, several commentators praised the Court for a minimally interventionist decision, noting that the liberal justices could join in that minimal opinion to achieve unanimity. But it was not a minimally interventionist decision: It laid the ground for a dubious understanding of the constraints on state judges interpreting their state's election law that might well have accounted, as Breyer noted in his dissent, for the Florida Supreme Court's reluctance to stipulate more concrete counting standards, for fear that the Supreme Court would declare that it was making new law.

13. See Don Van Natta, Jr. and Dexter Filkins, "Contesting the Vote: Miami-Dade County," *New York Times,* December 1, 2000.

14. Advanced electronic voting devices might, of course, malfunction, though it seems unlikely that they would be subject to as many of the failings that have now been documented in machines and ballots now used, and software could be designed to detect malfunction immediately.

2 .   LAWLESS ORDER AND HOT CASES

*   I am grateful to Richard Posner and Mary Anne Case for helpful comments on an earlier draft. This is a significantly revised and expanded version of an essay that first appeared in 68 *U. Chi. L. Rev.* 757 (2001).

1. *United States v. Morrison,* 529 US 598 (2000) (striking down the violence against women act as beyond the power of Congress under the commerce clause); *City of Boerne v. Flores,* 521 US 507 (1997) (holding that the religious freedom restoration act exceeded Congress's remedial powers under the Fourteenth Amendment); *United States v. Lopez,* 514 US 549 (1995) (holding that the prohibition of firearm possession near schools was outside the power of Congress).

2. For a general discussion of judicial minimalism, see Cass R. Sunstein, *One Case at a Time* (Cambridge: Harvard University Press, 1999).

3. See *Romer v. Evans,* 517 US 620 (1996) (holding law forbidding special government protections for homosexuals to be invalid under the equal protection clause, without fully explaining its consistency with earlier decisions).

4. 121 S Ct 471 (2000).

5. 121 S Ct 525 (2000).

6. See *Reynolds v. Sims,* 377 US 533 (1964) (holding an apportionment decision violative of the equal protection clause because of the different weight given to different votes); *Baker v. Carr,* 369 US 186 (1962) (holding state apportionment decision not to present nonjusticiable political questions).

7. Of course, such terms as *liberals* and *conservatives* can be defined however we want. In saying that there are no liberals, I mean that no one on the Court would like to follow in the path set by Justices William Brennan, Harry Blackmun, Earl Warren, and Thurgood Marshall; none of the justices is a "liberal" in the sense that those justices were.

8. *Bush v. Palm Beach Canvassing Board,* 121 S Ct 510 (2000) (granting first writ).

9. *Bush v. Palm Beach Canvassing Board,* 121 S Ct 471 (2000).

10. *Bush v. Gore,* 121 S Ct 512 (2000).

11. *Bush v. Gore,* 121 S Ct 525 (2000).

12. See *Palm Beach Canvassing Board v. Harris,* 772 S2d 1220, 2000 Fla LEXIS 2311, *11 (Nov. 21), vacated and remanded as *Bush v. Palm Beach County Canvassing Board,* 121 S Ct 471 (2000) (per curiam).

13. *Palm Beach Canvassing Board v. Harris,* 2000 Fla LEXIS 2311 at *57.

14. Petition for Writ of Certiorari, *Bush v. Palm Beach County Canvassing Board,* 2000 US Briefs 836 (Nov. 22, 2000).

15. Id at *12–18, US Const Art II § 1, cl 2.

16. Petition for Writ of Certiorari, 2000 US Briefs 836 at *18–20; 3 USC § 5 (1994).

17. Petition for Writ of Certiorari, 2000 US Briefs 836 at *19–20.

18. Id at *20–26.

19. *Bush v. Palm Beach Canvassing Board,* 121 S Ct at 510 (granting certiorari).

20. See *Bush v. Palm Beach County Canvassing Board,* 121 S Ct 471, 475 (2000).

21. Id at 474.

22. Id.

23. *Gore v. Harris,* 772 S2d 1243, 2000 Fla LEXIS 2373 (Dec. 8), revd and remd as, *Bush v. Gore,* 121 S Ct 525 (2000).

24. *Bush v. Gore,* 121 S Ct 512 (2000) (granting certiorari and staying the implementation of the Florida Supreme Court's decision).

25. As emphasized by Justice Scalia, see *id* (Scalia concurring).

26. *Cuomo v. NRC,* 772 F2d 972, 974 (DC Cir 1985).

27. 121 S Ct 525 (2000).

28. Id at 525. Technically the two arguments are not identical, but they are very close.

29. Id.

30. 121 S Ct. at 529–30.

31. Id. at 529.
32. Id.
33. Id. at 531.
34. Id.
35. Id.
36. Id at 531.
37. Id.
38. Id.
39. Id.
40. Id.
41. See Cass R. Sunstein, *One Case at a Time* (1999).
42. As urged in Cass R. Sunstein, *Legal Reasoning and Political Conflict* (New York: Oxford University Press, 1996).
43. *Harper v. Virginia Board of Elections,* 383 US 663 (1966); *Reynolds v. Sims,* 377 US 533 (1964).
44. One of the real oddities of the majority opinion is that it was joined by two justices—Scalia and Thomas—who have insisted in their commitment to "originalism" as a method of constitutional interpretation. There is no reason to think that by adopting the equal protection clause, the nation thought that it was requiring clear and specific standards in the context of manual recounts in statewide elections. In fact, it is controversial to say that the Fourteenth Amendment applies to voting at all. The failure of Justices Scalia and Thomas to suggest the relevance of originalism, their preferred method, raises many questions.
45. Henry E. Brady, *Equal Protection for Votes* (unpublished manuscript, Dec. 11, 2000).
46. See Pamela Karlan, "The Newest Equal Protection," in *The Vote,* ed. Cass R. Sunstein and Richard A. Epstein (Chicago: University of Chicago Press, 2001), 77, 90.
47. *Bush v. Gore,* 121 S Ct at 533.
48. Id.
49. *Gore v. Harris,* 2000 Fla LEXIS 2373 at 9.
50. Id. at 31–37.
51. See 3 USC § 15 (1994).
52. See this volume; see also Richard A. Posner, *Breaking the Deadlock* (Cambridge: Harvard University Press, 2001).
53. Consider another illustration. Judge Posner thinks that the Court should have held that the president of the United States has immunity against civil suit, in order to avoid "the potentially disastrous effect of making the president defend himself in a sex case." I tend to agree that as a matter of policy, the president should be immune from such suits. But where is the constitutional basis for creating the immunity? I do not believe a solid basis exists, and Judge Posner seems to find it unnecessary to identify one. In the absence of a solid basis for immunity, the Court was right to decide *Clinton v. Jones* as it did, even though the consequences were not very good.
54. See Adrian Vermeule, "Interpretive Choice," 75 *NYU L Rev* 74 (2000).
55. See Ronald Dworkin, *Law's Empire* (Cambridge: Harvard University Press, 1985), for a general account.

56. This is the basic theme of Kenneth Culp Davis, *Discretionary Justice: A Preliminary Inquiry* (Louisiana State University Press, 1969).

57. A possible answer is that no more rule-bound approach would be better, all things considered. This is a difference from *Bush v. Gore,* where it was easy to imagine a rule-bound approach that would add constraints on discretion without sacrificing any important value.

58. *Hornsby v. Allen,* 326 F2d 605 (5th Cir 1964); *Holmes v. NYCHA,* 398 F2d 262 (2d Cir 1968).

59. For examples of unsuccessful attempts to challenge unconditioned discretion violative of equal protection in these contexts, see *Phelps v. Housing Authority of Woodward,* 742 F2d 816 (4th Cir 1984); *Atlanta Bowling Center, Inc v. Allen,* 389 F2d 713 (5th Cir 1968).

60. See *The Vote,* ed. Cass R. Sunstein and Richard A. Epstein (Chicago: University of Chicago Press, 2001).

61. See Jon Elster, *Alchemies of the Mind* (New York: Cambridge University Press, 1999); Martha Nussbaum, *Upheavals of Thought* (New York: Cambridge University Press, 2001).

62. See Roger Brown, *Social Psychology* (2d ed.) (New York: The Free Press, 1986); Cass R. Sunstein, "Deliberative Trouble? Why Groups Go To Extremes," *Yale LJ* (2000).

63. Linda Babcock and George Loewenstein, "Explaining Bargaining Impasse: The Role of Self-Serving Biases," 11 *Journal of Economic Perspectives* 109 (1997).

64. Charles Lord et al., "Biased Assimilation and Attitude Polarization," 37 *Journal of Personality of Social Psychology* 2098, 2102–2104 (1979).

3 · FREEING EROG V. HSUB FROM ITS HALL OF MIRRORS

* This chapter is drawn from thoughts I had formulated and conclusions I had reached as of late August 2001, before the terrible events of September 11 and the government's responses to them so painfully punctuated our national life. It perhaps goes without saying that this watershed raised anew a host of issues about the rule of law, about the sources of power's legitimacy in a time of crisis, and about the circumstances in which one can truly say without hyperbole that a crisis is upon us and that pragmatic considerations must for a time prevail over doing business as usual, whether in the realm of elections or in the realm of homeland security. Rather than attempting to expand or alter anything I had written as of August to reflect the cataclysm of September, I decided to leave the chapter unchanged, just as I left unchanged another essay I wrote more or less simultaneously with this one dealing with the same matters, which appears as a comment entitled "eroG v. hsuB and its Disguises: Freeing Bush v. Gore From Its Hall of Mirrors," 115 *Harvard Law Review* 172–304 (November 2001). My Tanner Lectures (Oxford University, May 2002) mean to explore at some depth matters I might have addressed here had this book gone to press after the date of those lectures. That said, I want to emphasize that nothing that has happened since I wrote this chapter would lead me to abandon any of the constitutional arguments it presents or to reach any different conclusions about what I continue to regard as the profound wrongness of Bush v. Gore.

† I am grateful to Bruce Ackerman, Mike Dorf, Heather Gerken, Dan Geyser, Tom Gold-

stein, Mike Gottlieb, Tara Grove, Pat Gudridge, Ben Hatch, Jonathan Massey, Joel Perwin, Rick Pildes, Ben Souede, and Kevin Walsh for helpful suggestions. All errors are my own.

1. 121 S. Ct. 525 (2000).

2. I served as counsel to Vice President Gore in the lawsuit brought by then-Governor Bush in the federal courts to enjoin the recounts in Florida, and as his counsel of record in all of the Supreme Court proceedings.

3. Judge Richard Posner has argued that the Court's intervention in *Bush v. Gore* was necessary in part to ensure that the crisis would be decided before Christmas. Pamela Karlan and Richard Posner, "Forum, The Triumph of Expedience: How Americans Lost the Election to the Courts," *Harper's* (May 2001); 31, 32.

4. See, e.g., *The Vote: Bush, Gore and The Supreme Court,* eds. Cass R. Sunstein and Richard A. Epstein (Chicago: University of Chicago Press, 2001).

5. See e.g., *Democracy in Crisis* ed., Bruce Ackerman, forthcoming in Yale Press, 2001.

6. See e.g., Richard A. Posner, *Breaking the Deadlock: The 2000 Election, the Constitution, and the Courts* (Princeton, NJ: Princeton University Press, 2001).

7. See e.g., Vincent Bugliosi, *The Betrayal of America: How the Supreme Court Undermined the Constitution and Chose our President* (New York: Thunder's Mouth Press/Nation Books, 2001), and Alan M. Dershowitz, *Supreme Injustice: How the High Court Hijacked Election 2000* (New York: Oxford University Press, 2001).

8. See Ronald Klain, "The Labor of Sisyphus: The Gore Recount Perspective," in *Overtime! The Election 2000 Thriller,* ed. Larry J. Sabato (New York: Longman, 2002), 157, 159–60.

9. See 3 U.S.C. §5. This "safe harbor" provision, enacted in 1887 after the Hayes-Tilden debacle, promises that Congress will entertain no challenges to the electoral slate selected by a state that concludes its election contests, using procedural rules in place on Election Day, at least six days before the meeting of the electors, a date fixed as the "first Monday after the second Wednesday in December." 3 U.S.C. § 7.

10. The principle echoed the one I'd pressed over a decade earlier in the Supreme Court on behalf of Pennzoil, when I argued the lower federal courts had no place preventing Texas from forcing Texaco, as required by state law, to post a multi-billion dollar bond in the state's courts if it wished to protect its assets pending appeal. I thought it plain that the same arguments that produced a unanimous Court in Pennzoil would apply in spades to Governor Bush's position. See *Pennzoil v. Texaco,* 481 U.S. 1, 16–18 (1987).

11. U.S. Const., art. II, § 1, cl. 2 provides that each state shall choose its presidential electors in the manner directed by its legislature.

12. *Siegel v. LePore,* 120 F. Supp.2d 1041 (S.D. Fla. Nov 13, 2000), aff'd *Siegel v. LePore,* 234 F.3d 1163 (11th Cir. Dec 6, 2000), reh'g denied *Siegel v. LePore,* 234 F.3d 1218 (11th Cir. Dec 9, 2001), cert. denied *Touchston v. McDermott,* 531 U.S. 1061 (Jan 5, 2001).

13. *Bush v. Palm Beach County,* 121 S. Ct. 471 (2000).

14. *Palm Beach County Canvassing Board v. Harris,* 772 So.2d 1220 (Fla. November 21, 2000), vacated and remanded, *Bush v. Palm Beach County Canvassing Bd.,* 121 S.Ct. 471 (December 4, 2000), reinstated w. explanation *Palm Beach County Canvassing Bd. v. Harris,* 772 So.2d 1273 (Fla. Dec 11, 2000).

15. See *Bush v. Gore,* 121 S. Ct. at 533.

16. Id. at 536–538 (Rehnquist, C.J., joined by Scalia and Thomas, JJ. concurring).

17. *NCAA v. Tarkanian,* 488 U.S. 179, 192–93 (1988).

18. Cf. *U.S. Term Limits v. Thorton,* 514 U.S. 779 (1995) (invalidating a provision of the Arkansas Constitution, which prohibited incumbents that had served more than a certain number of years from having their names placed on the ballot for that office). Justice Stevens's opinion, which was joined by Justices Kennedy, Souter, Ginsburg, and Breyer, treated a state's U.S. Senators and U.S. Representatives as fully federal officers and rejected the dissent's contention that the "original powers of sovereignty that the Tenth Amendment reserved to the States" included the power to fix the terms of their own members of Congress. Id. at 802; *id.* at 803.

19. Cf. *U.S. Term Limits v. Thornton,* 514 U.S. 779, 845, (1995) (Thomas, J., dissenting). Chief Justice Rehnquist and Justices Scalia and O'Connor joined Justice Thomas's dissent in *U.S. Term Limits,* see id. at 845, which contended that the states at the time of the Constitutional Convention reserved the power to define the qualifications of their own representatives in Congress. See id. at 883. It would seem that the power to allocate decision-making authority among the states' own governmental organs, even with respect to such federal officers as presidential electors, would be at least as fundamental an attribute of a state's sovereignty as the power to set the qualifications of its federal representatives.

20. Supra note 9.

21. The part of the state court decisions (of November 21 and December 11) to which the *Bush v. Gore* per curiam referred in declaring that all recounts had to be completed by December 12. See *Bush v. Gore,* 121 S. Ct. 525, 533 (2000) (December 11) ("The Supreme Court of Florida has said that the legislature intended the State's electors to 'participat[e] fully in the federal electoral process,' as provided in 3 U.S.C. § 5."), did not address what to do if meeting a December 12 deadline conflicted with counting all legal votes and in any event dealt not with deadlines for the recounts, but instead with the limitations on the power of the secretary of state to reject late returns from canvassing boards. See *Palm Beach County Canvassing Bd. v. Harris,* 772 So.2d 1220, 1237 (Fla. 2000) (November 21) ("Ignoring the county's returns is a drastic measure and is appropriate only if the returns are submitted to the Department so late that their inclusion will . . . preclud[e] Florida voters from participating fully in the federal electoral process.") (citing 3 U.S.C. §§1–10) (emphasis added); *Palm Beach County Canvassing Bd. v. Harris,* 772 So.2d 1273 (Fla. 2000) (December 11) ("[W]e conclude that the reasoned basis for the exercise of the Department's discretion to ignore amended returns is limited to those instances where failure to ignore the amended returns will . . . result in Florida voters not participating fully in the federal electoral process, as provided in 3 U.S.C. §5.") (Emphasis added); id. at 1289 - 90 (same). Neither did the state court's opinion of December 8, which ordered the statewide recount, establish December 12 as a deadline mandated by state law. See *Gore v. Harris,* 772 So.2d 1243, 1261 (2000) ("The need for prompt resolution and finality is especially critical in presidential elections where there is an outside deadline established by federal law."). Even the Florida court *dissenters* did not contend that December 12 was mandated by the state election code. Id. at 1268 n. 30 (Wells, C.J., dissenting) ("As the Supreme Court recently noted, 3 U.S.C. §5 creates a safe harbor provision regarding

congressional consideration of a state's electoral votes should all contests and controversies be resolved at least six days prior to December 18, 2000, if made pursuant to the state of the law as it existed on election day. There is no legislative suggestion that the Florida Legislature did *not* want to *take advantage* of this safe harbor provision."); id. at 1272 (Harding, J., dissenting) ("[E]ven if I were to conclude that the appellants' allegations and evidence were sufficient to warrant relief, I do not believe that the rules permit an adequate remedy under the circumstances of this case. *This Court,* in its prior opinion, and *all of the parties* agree that election controversies and contests must be finally and conclusively determined by December 12, 2000.") (emphasis added). Moreover, as we will see later, viewing the Court's opinion in this way ignores the evidence that the legislature most likely would have rejected such a firm deadline. See infra TAN 157–161.

22. See *Bush v. Gore,* 773 So.2d 524, 528 - 29 (Fla. December 22, 2000) (Shaw, J., concurring).

23. 121 S. Ct. 1693 (2001) (holding that the retroactive application of a state supreme court's abolition of its common law "year and a day" rule did not violate the Due Process Clause because the change in the law could have been anticipated by the petitioner).

24. Art. I, §10, cl. 1.

25. Id. at 1697 (quoting *Marks v. United States,* 430 U.S. 188, 191 (1977) (internal quotation marks omitted)).

26. The *Rogers* Court conducted an independent analysis of the application of the "year and a day" rule in prior state court rulings, and, finding that the rule had "never once served as a ground of decision in any prosecution for murder," the Court determined that it was fair to apply the retroactive rule change to Rogers's case. 121 S. Ct. at 1701.

27. Although Justice Breyer dissented in *Rogers,* he agreed "with the majority's basic approach," rejecting only the Court's factual analysis. Id. at 1711 (Breyer, J., dissenting).

28. *Bush v. Gore,* 121 S. Ct. 525, 549 (2000) (Ginsburg, J., dissenting).

29. Judge Richard Posner charges that "what the Florida Supreme Court did with the statute was so freewheeling as to raise a serious question of conformity with Article II of the U.S. Constitution. . . ." See Posner, supra note 4, at 127. See also Einer Elhauge, "Florida's Vote Wasn't 'Irregular.' " *Wall Street Journal,* Nov. 13, 2000, A36; Charles Fried, "A Badly Flawed Election: An Exchange," *New York Review of Books,* Feb. 22, 2001, 8.

30. 501 U.S. 452, 456 (1991).

31. 121 S.Ct. 1693 (2001).

32. 121 S. Ct. at 1704 (Scalia, J., dissenting).

33. Posner, supra note 6, at 175, 185–87.

34. *Palm Beach County Canvassing Bd. v. Harris,* 772 So.2d 1220, 1237 (Fla. 2000).

35. *Gore v. Harris,* 772 So.2d 1243, 1262 (Fla. Dec 08, 2000). "Undervotes" are ballots on which the machine failed to detect a vote for president.

36. Posner, supra note 6, at 148.

37. The party requested recounts in Broward, Miami-Dade, Palm Beach, and Volusia counties. See *Palm Beach Canvassing Bd. v. Harris* (Harris I), 772 So.2d 1220, 1225, 1229 (Fla. 2000).

38. Id. at 1226 (noting trial court's determination that the deadline was "mandatory").

39. Sections 102.111 and 102.112 have since been amended.

40. Florida Division of Elections, "Deadline for Certification of County Results," Advisory Opinion DE 00-10 (November 13, 2000).

41. Palm Beach, 772 So.2d. 1226 n.5 (Fla. 2000).

42. Id. at 1239. The court applied traditional canons of statutory construction, concluding that the code's permissive language ("may") supplanted its mandatory language ("shall"). Id. at 1235-37. Relying on the Florida Constitution and previous case law to determine the bounds of the statutory grant of discretion, the court then concluded that "the authority of the Florida Secretary of State to ignore amended returns . . . may be lawfully exercised only under limited circumstances." Id.

43. See Id. at 1239 (citing State ex. rel. *Chappell v. Martinez,* 536 So.2d 1007 [Fla. 1988] and noting that, under Florida law, "the will of the electors supercedes any statutory requirements").

44. Even supporters of the decision tend to argue that the Florida court liberally construed its election code, prioritizing purpose over text, thereby necessarily provoking the strict textualists on the Court. As will soon become clear, however, the Florida court's opinions adhered both to the precise letter *and* underlying spirit of the election statute. See infra TAN 49 - 53.

45. See *Palm Beach County,* 772 So.2d at 1240.

46. *Bush v. Palm Beach County Canvassing Bd.,* 121 S.Ct. 471, 475 (2000).

47. 772 So.2d at 1288.

48. Michael McConnell, *Two and a Half Cheers for Bush v. Gore,* 68 *U. Chi. L. Rev.* 657, 668 (2001).

49. See Fla. Stat. § 102. 168 (requiring a contest to be filed "within 10 days after midnight of the date the last county canvassing board" certifies its results).

50. Cf. Antonin Scalia, *The Rule of Law as a Law of Rules,* 56 *U. Chi. L. Rev.* 1175 (1989).

51. Fla. Stat. 102.168(3)(c). Gore identified 168 net votes from a partial manual recount in Miami-Dade and 215 net votes from a full manual recount in Palm Beach County that were not included in the certified total. *Gore,* 772 So.2d at 1259.

52. Section 102.168(8) vests the circuit judge hearing the contest with authority to "fashion such orders as he or she deems necessary to ensure that each allegation is investigated, examined, or checked, to prevent or correct any alleged wrong, and to provide *any relief appropriate under such circumstances.*" Fla. Stat. § 102.168(8) (emphasis added).

53. *Gore,* 772 So.2d at 1261.

54. *Gore,* 772 So.2d at 1257.

55. Fla. Stat. § 101.5614(5). The very subject of that provision—instructions for county canvassing boards on how to handle ballots—seems to make it a logical provision from which to seek legal guidance when doing a manual recount.

56. Fla. Stat. § 101.5614(4) (emphasis added).

57. Fla. Stat. § 101.5614(5).

58. Fla. Stat. § 101.5614(5) (emphasis added).

59. Fla. Stat. § 101.5614(8) (emphasis added).

60. The Chief Justice's dissent discusses only the 9000 uncounted ballots in Miami Dade, giving scant attention to §101.5614 in general. See *Gore,* 772 So.2d 1243, 1267 (Wells, C.J., dissenting).

61. Id. (quoting Fla. Stat. § 101.5614(5)) (emphasis added).
62. "[T]here is no basis for reading the Florida statutes as requiring the counting of improperly marked ballots, as an examination of the Florida Supreme Court's textual analysis shows. We will not parse that analysis here, except to note that the principal provision of the election code on which it relied, § 101.5614(5), was, as the Chief Justice pointed out in his dissent from *Harris* II, entirely irrelevant." *Bush v. Gore,* 531 U.S. 98, 112, 120 (Rehnquist, C.J., concurring).
63. Posner, supra note 6, at 97.
64. 707 So.2d. 720 (1998).
65. Id. at 722 n.4. The post–1998 changes in the statute in no way affected this holding.
66. The concurrence refers to *Beckstrom* in its discussion of the length of appeals. See *Bush v. Gore,* 121 S. Ct. 525, 538 (2000) (Rehnquist, C.J., concurring). The case also featured prominently in the parties' briefs and in Secretary Harris's letter to the Palm Beach County Canvassing Board.
67. See Posner, supra note 6, at 107 n.29.
68. *Bush v. Gore,* 531 U.S. 98, 119 (2000) (Rehnquist, C.J., concurring). To stress his point, the Chief Justice quoted in large print the instructions allegedly supplied by counties using punch card ballots: "AFTER VOTING, CHECK YOUR BALLOT CARD TO BE SURE YOUR VOTING SELECTIONS ARE CLEARLY AND CLEANLY PUNCHED AND THERE ARE NO CHIPS LEFT HANGING ON THE BACK OF THE CARD." *Bush v. Gore,* 121 S. Ct. 525, 537 (2000) (Rehnquist, C.J., concurring). But not all punch-card counties provided such precise instructions. For example, entirely different language was used in Broward County: "To vote, hold the stylus vertically. Punch the stylus straight down through the ballot card for the candidates or issues of your choice." *Touchston v. McDermott,* 234 F.3d 1133, 1141 n.19 (11th Cir. 2000).
69. Posner, supra note 6, at 96.
70. Bush v. Gore, 531 U.S. 98, 119 (Rehnquist, C.J., concurring).
71. See John Mintz and Peter Slevin, "Human Factor Was at Core of Fiasco," *Washington Post.,* June 1, 2000, A1 (noting the lack of Spanish ballots in Osceola County).
72. See Fla. Stat. ch. 101.46 (1977) (requiring that "[t]he authorities in charge of elections, where voting machines are used, shall designate suitable and adequate times and places for giving instructions to electors who apply.")
73. Posner, supra note 6, at 96.
74. See Fla. Stat. § 102.141(4). Florida law mandated an automatic recount whenever the margin in the vote totals between any two candidates for a particular office was less than one-half of 1 percent. Id.
75. Fla. Stat. § 102.166(4).
76. Fla. Stat. § 101.5614(4).
77. *Bush v. Gore,* 531 U.S. 98, 121 (2000) (Rehnquist, C.J., concurring).
78. See *Jacobs v. Seminole County Canvassing Bd.,* 773 So.2d 519 (Fla. 2000); *Taylor v. Martin County Canvassing Bd.,* 773 So.2d 517 (Fla. 2000).
79. *Bush v. Gore,* 531 U.S. at 119 (Rehnquist, C.J., concurring).
80. See Fla. Stat. ch. 97.012(1) (1998) (listing, as one of the responsibilities of the secretary of state, the duty to "maintain uniformity in the application, operation, and interpretation

of the election laws."). See also *State ex rel. Chappell v. Martinez,* 536 So.2d 1007, 1008–09 (Fla. 1988) (refusing, in the context of an election for a seat in the U.S. House of Representatives, candidate's request to order the invalidation of 11,000 votes that had been certified by the Florida Elections Canvassing Commission).

81. 102.168(8).

82. Posner, supra note 6, at 120. The contest provisions mention the county canvassing board only in saying "[t]he canvassing board or election board shall be the proper party *defendant."* Fla. Stat. ch 102.168(4) (emphasis added). Moreover, defenders of the "deference" theory also ignore the evidentiary significance the Florida court attached to several key county canvassing board determinations. Consider the court's rejection of Gore's claim that the Palm Beach County canvassing board improperly failed to recover votes from 3300 manually inspected ballots. Because it had refused to register any of those ballots only after conducting a manual recount that the state court found in compliance with an appropriate understanding of a "legal vote," the court, deferring to the board's action (*see Gore,* 772 So.2d at 1260) did *exactly* what Judge Posner accuses it of *failing* to do: it deferred to the board's expertise in administering a manual recount of ballots under a proper legal standard—deference readily distinguishable from the court's independent resolution of legal questions with respect to which it is standard learning, not some Sunshine State innovation, that no deference is due.

83. As the Florida Supreme Court stressed in the first phase of the *Bush v. Gore* litigation, Florida courts should not defer to executive interpretations that are "contrary to law." *Palm Beach County Canvassing Bd. v. Harris* (Harris I), 772 So.2d 1220, 1228 (Fla. 2000). See, e.g., *Legal Environmental Assistance Foundation v. Bd. of County Commissioners of Brevard County,* 642 So.2d 1081, 1083–83 (Fla. 1994) ("When an agency's construction amounts to an unreasonable interpretation, or is clearly erroneous, it cannot stand.").

84. See Molly Ivins and Lou Dubose, *Shrub: The Short but Happy Political Life of George W. Bush* (New York: Vintage Books, 2000) 13.

85. 323 So.2d 259 (Fla. 1975).

86. Id. at 264. *Boardman's* "substantial compliance" rule extends beyond the absentee ballot context to other Florida election cases. See State ex rel. *Chappell v. Martinez,* 536 So.2d 1007, 1008 (Fla. 1988) (relying on *Boardman* "substantial compliance" principle when finding that 11,000 ballots should not be invalidated despite the canvassing board's having improperly certified them telephonically, rather than in writing).

87. See id. at 262.

88. Id. at 267–68.

89. See e.g., *McLean v. Bellamy,* 437 So.2d 737, 744, 745-46 (Fla. App. 1983) (finding that there was no substantial departure from the election code, and thus refusing to invalidate absentee ballots cast in election for the city commissioner that were allegedly defective for a variety of reasons); *State ex rel. Chappell v. Martinez,* 536 So.2d 1007, 1008–09 (Fla. 1988) (finding that a county had substantially complied with statutory requirements by submitting its results telephonically, rather than in writing, by the November 14 deadline, and thus refusing candidate's request that the court invalidate 11,000 ballots in a U.S. House of Representatives race).

90. See, e.g., Matter of Protest Election Returns and Absentee Ballots in Nov. 4, 1997 Election for City of Miami, Florida, 707 So.2d 1170, 1174–75 (Fla. App. 1998) (refusing the trial court's call for a new election, based on uncontradicted statistical evidence of massive fraud in the absentee voting, and instead invalidating the entire slate of absentee ballots); *Bolden v. Potter,* 452 So.2d 564, 567 (Fla. 1984) (invalidating all absentee ballots because of evidence of vote buying).

91. Posner, supra note 6 at 108.

92. Palm Beach, 772 So.2d. at 1237 n.53 (quoting *Boardman v. Esteva,* 323 So.2d 259, 269 [Fla. 1975]).

93. Id. at 1237 n.52 (quoting *State ex rel. Landis v. Dyer,* 148 So. 201, 203 [Fla. 1933]).

94. Id. at 1237 (quoting *State ex rel. Landis v. Dyer,* 148 So. 201, 203 [Fla. 1933]).

95. See, e.g., Posner, supra note 6, at 126 (predicting that the "manual recount [authorized on December 8] would have been both standardless and incomplete, and in the absence of judicial review . . . *tainted with partisanship.*") (emphasis added). But, among other things, the Florida court's December 8 order provided for judicial review by a "single impartial magistrate." *Bush v. Gore,* 121 S. Ct. at 541 (Stevens, J., dissenting).

96. See Fla. Stat. § 101.5614(4) (describing the procedure for manually counting absentee ballots); Fla. Stat. § 101 5614(5) (detailing the procedure for tabulating "damaged or defective" ballots); Fla. Stat. § 102.166(5)(c) (authorizing canvassing boards to decide to "[m]anually recount all ballots" when a candidate or political party files a protest).

97. Fla. Stat. § 102.166(7)(a) ("A counting team must have, when possible, members of at least two political parties.").

98. Fla. Stat. § 102.166(6) ("Any manual recount shall be open to the public.").

99. See Opening Brief for Appellants at 7, *Siegel v. LePore,* 234 F.3d 1163 (11th Cir. 2000) (No. 00-15981) (claiming that, during the protest phase of the election, several of the counting teams in Palm Beach County did not include Republicans); id. (alleging that the canvassing board members in Palm Beach County only asked Democrats to monitor the recount process).

100. David Barstow and Don Van Natta, Jr., "How Bush Took Florida: Mining the Overseas Absentee Vote," *New York Times,* July 15, 2001, 1 ("Judge Anne Kaylor, chairwoman of the Polk County board, said the combination of Republican pressure and court rulings caused it to count some ballots that would probably have been considered illegal in past years. 'I think the rules were bent,' Judge Kaylor, a Democrat, said. 'Technically, they were not supposed to be accepted. Any canvassing board that says they weren't under pressure is being less than candid.' ").

101. The Florida election code requires that a recount team include, "when possible, members of at least two political parties," Fla. Stat. § 102.166(7)(a), and makes no distinction between major and minor parties. Thus, it is possible that members of minor parties could also have participated in the monitoring process.

102. The Federalist No. 51, at 319 (James Madison) ed. Isaac Kramnick (Harmondsworth: Penguin, 1987).

103. Cf. Siegel v. LePore, 234 F.3d 1163, 1211–13 (11th Cir. 2000) (Carnes, J., dissenting) (arguing that the Florida election code on its face violates the equal protection clause, because it permits a candidate or political party to request recounts in particular counties, en-

couraging them to make such requests only in populous counties that tend to support that candidate or party, and thereby diluting the votes of citizens in less populous regions).

104. *Bush v. Gore,* 121 S. Ct. 525, 538 (2000) (Rehnquist, C.J., concurring).

105. 475 U.S. 260 (1986).

106. 520 U.S. 351 (1997).

107. This trend has been noted and perceptively analyzed elsewhere. See, e.g., Richard Pildes, "Democracy and Disorder," 68 *U. Chi. L. Rev.* 695 (2001). See also Professor Pildes's important contribution to this volume.

108. For an insightful analysis of the Justices' inclinations to favor either rules or standards, see Kathleen M. Sullivan, "Foreword: The Justices of Rules and Standards," 106 *Harv. L. Rev.* 22 (1992).

109. Mintz and Slevin, supra note 72 at A01.

110. *Bush v. Gore,* 121 S. Ct. at 541 (Stevens, J., dissenting).

111. Compare, e.g., *Shaw v. Reno,* 509 U.S. 630, 642 (1993) (finding "irregular" appearances in the drawing of congressional voting districts suggestive of racial "segregation" and discrimination under the equal protection clause) with *Hunt v. Cromartie,* 121 S.Ct. 1452, 1466 (2001) (rejecting a district court's finding that the same congressional district at issue in *Shaw* was drawn on impermissible racial grounds because the plaintiffs could not demonstrate that race "predominantly account[ed] for the result."); or *Dawson v. Delaware,* 503 U.S. 159, 166–168 (1992) (reversing the death sentence of an Aryan Brotherhood member because the prosecutor's mention of his membership unnecessarily and discriminatorily injected race into the proceedings) with *McCleskey v. Kemp,* 481 U.S. 279, 292 (1987) (upholding a death sentence despite statistical evidence that the state in question had administered the death penalty in a racially discriminatory manner because such statistics failed to demonstrate the existence of "purposeful discrimination 'ha[ving] a discriminatory effect' on" the defendant).

112. *Bush v. Gore,* 121 S. Ct. at 532 (per curiam).

113. Compare *U.S. R.R. Retirement Bd. V. Fritz,* 449 U.S. 166, 179 (1980) (Rehnquist, J., for the Court) (holding it immaterial whether Congress was deliberately deceived into including a challenged provision in the statute it enacted, on the ground that, were that standard enforced, few laws would survive).

114. Br. for Florida Legislature as Amicus Curiae, *Bush v. Gore,* 531 U.S. 98 (2000) (No. 00–949).

115. Id. at 25, 27.

116. Id.

117. John Mintz and Peter Slevin, supra note 72 at A01.

118. I owe this example to a private communication with Professor Mark Tushnet, professor of law, Georgetown University Law Center, July 2001.

119. See Ronald Dworkin, "A Badly Flawed Election," *New York Review of Books,* Jan. 11, 2001, 53–55.

120. *Bush,* 121 S. Ct. at 531.

121. Id.

122. Fla. Stat. § 102.141(4).

123. Mintz & Slevin, supra note 72 at A01.

124. Id.

125. Id. ("In the fifteen counties in which the technology did not exist, one ballot in seventeen was rejected—5.7 percent.").

126. Robert Pierre and Peter Slevin, "Florida Vote Rife With Disparities, Study Says," *Washington Post,* June 5, 2001, A01.

127. Mintz and Slevin, supra note 72 at A01.

128. Id.

129. Mintz and Slevin, supra note 72 at A01.

130. *Bush v. Gore,* 121 S. Ct. 525, 550 (2001) (Ginsburg, J., dissenting).

131. Id. at 545 (Souter, J., dissenting) (finding that "the Equal Protection Clause does not forbid the use of a variety of voting mechanisms within a jurisdiction, even though different mechanisms will have different levels of effectiveness in recording voters' intentions; local variety can be justified by concerns about cost, the potential value of innovation, and so on."). *Cf. id.* at 551 (Breyer, J., dissenting) (noting that "since the use of different standards could favor one or the other of the candidates, since time was, and is, too short to permit the lower courts to iron out significant differences through ordinary judicial review, and since the relevant distinction was embodied in the order of the State's highest court, I agree that, in these very special circumstances, basic principles of fairness may well have counseled the adoption of a uniform standard to address the problem.").

132. *Bush v. Gore,* 121 S. Ct. 525, 532 (2000) (per curiam) (Emphasis added).

133. Id.

134. Some argue, along these lines, that *Bush v. Gore* can be seen as a bold extension of equal protection doctrine into hitherto uncharted territory: Namely, the application of equal protection to the *counting of votes,* rather than to districting or explicit barriers to voting. See, e.g., Jack Balkin, *Bush v. Gore and the Boundary Between Law and Politics,* 110 *Yale L.J.* 1407, 1427–28 (2001). This argument wrongly assumes that the equal protection doctrines of the Warren Court, the Burger Court, or the early Rehnquist Court would somehow have ignored, or given a "bye" to, state court rules irrationally or invidiously singling out some distinct categories of votes for counting under a less discerning or more error-prone basis than other categories. I see no basis for any such bizarre supposition. The equal protection "innovation" of *Bush v. Gore* lay not in its extension of equality's domain but in its application to yet another context using a superficial notion of equality already well established in the Court's jurisprudence over the past decade and a half.

135. *Cf. Planned Parenthood v. Casey,* 505 U.S. 833, 866 (1992) "[T]he Court's legitimacy depends on making legally principled decisions under circumstances in which their principled character is sufficiently plausible to be accepted by the Nation.").

136. See *Washington County v. Gunther,* 452 U.S. 161, 183 (1981) (Rehnquist, J., dissenting) (quoting *Smith v. Allwright,* 321 U.S. 649, 669 (1944) (Roberts, J., dissenting)). Some ground this type of objection in Article III. See, e.g., *Anastasoff v. U.S.,* 223 F.3d 898 (8th Cir. 2000) (holding that "the doctrine of precedent limits the 'judicial power' delegated to the courts in Article III.") (vacated by 223 F.3d 898 (8th Cir. 2000)); others are more

inclined to ground it in prudential or jurisprudential considerations. See, e.g., Frederick Schauer, *Precedent,* 39 *Stan. L. Rev.* 571, 595–601 (1987).

137. See, e.g., *Thornburgh v. American College of Obstetricians and Gynecologists,* 476 U.S. 747, 819–821 (1986) (O'Connor, J., dissenting). Thus, critics of "judicial legislation" and "activism" praise the Court when it modestly limits its holdings narrowly. See, e.g., Cass Sunstein, *One Case at a Time: Judicial Minimalism on the Supreme Court* (Cambridge, MA: Harvard University Press, 1999).

138. *Miranda v. Arizona,* 384 U.S. 436 (1966).

139. See *Planned Parenthood of Southeastern Pennsylvania v. Casey,* 505 U.S. 833, 966 (1992) (Rehnquist, C.J., concurring in part and dissenting in part) ("Under the guise of the Constitution, this Court will still impart its own preferences on the States in the form of a complex abortion code."). This argument, that the Court often writes decisions as if they were provisions of a code or statute, became increasingly common after *Miranda,* 384 U.S. at 504 (Harlan, J., dissenting) (criticizing the majority for creating a "constitutional code of rules for confessions"); see also *Dickerson v. United States,* 530 U.S. 428, 465 (2000) (Scalia, J., dissenting) (noting that the *Miranda* Court "impos[ed] its Court-made code upon the States").

140. Cf. Willard V. Quine, *Word and Object* (Cambridge, MA: MIT Press, 1984); Willard Van Orman Quine, *The Ways of Paradox and Other Essays* (Cambridge, MA: Harvard University Press, 1976).

141. *Bush v. Gore,* 121 S. Ct. at 531.

142. See, e.g., *Baker v. Carr,* 369 U.S. 186 (1962); *Reynolds v. Sims,* 377 U.S. 533 (1964).

143. See, e.g., *Bishop v. Wood,* 426 U.S. 341 (1976). Chief Justice Rehnquist would have gone further still. See *Cleveland Bd. of Education v. Loudermill,* 470 U.S. 532, 559 (1985) (Rehnquist, J., dissenting).

144. Overvotes are ballots rejected because they appear to contain more than one vote for a given office.

145. *Bush v. Gore,* 531 U.S. 98, 106 (2000) (per curiam).

146. Id. Florida Supreme Court Chief Justice Wells made a similar point in his dissent from that court's December 8 decision. See *Gore v. Harris,* 772 So. 2d 1243, 1264 n.26 (Fla. 2000) (Wells, C.J., dissenting).

147. *Bush,* 531 U.S. at 106.

148. See McConnell, supra note 48 at 658 n. 8 (citing *Gore v. Harris,* 773 So. 2d 524, 535 n.26 (Fla. 2000) (Pariente, J., concurring)); John Mintz and Peter Slevin, supra note 72 at A01 (noting one supervisor's comment that, "if it's the same person, it's a no-brainer" to explain why overvotes were included in the tally despite the technical flaw of marking "two" candidates and that thirty-four counties included such "overvotes").

149. The Court's insistence that there be a uniform standard more specific than the "clear intent of the voter"—and its holding that, so far as equal protection is concerned, any standard sufficiently objective and uniform would do—*assumes that whole classes of certain "ballot markings" may properly be excluded.* One must wonder how the Court could *require* a uniform standard that would undoubtedly exclude a "class" of ballot (say, dimpled chads) and yet find a constitutional violation in the state legislature's decision to exclude a different class of ballot (i.e., overvotes).

150. See *Fla. Stat.* ch. 101.5614(6) (1994) ("If an elector marks more names than there are persons to be elected to an office or if it is impossible to determine the elector's choice, the elector's ballot shall not be counted for that office, but the ballot shall not be invalidated as to those names which are properly marked.").

151. *Bush v. Gore,* 121 S. Ct. at 533, 545, 551.

152. Id. at 533.

153. See p. 6 and n. 21.

154. See id. at 533–35 (Rehnquist, C.J., concurring).

155. Id. at 538 (emphasis added).

156. *Bush,* 121 S. Ct. at 528 (2000).

157. Id. at 538–39 (Rehnquist, C.J., concurring).

158. Richard Serrano and Ricardo Alonso-Zaldivar, "Decision 2000/America Waits," *Los Angeles Times,* December 11, 2000, at A1 ("However the U.S. Supreme Court rules, Bush still enjoys support from the Republican-controlled Florida legislature, where House and Senate committees will convene today to continue a special session . . . The special session is designed to give Florida's 25 electoral college votes to Bush, even if Gore prevails in court.").

159. *Bush,* 121 S. Ct. at 529–30.

160. As we have seen already, the Court's attempt to "read" a firm December 12 deadline rests at best on a shaky construction, and at worst an utterly implausible interpretation, of the Florida Supreme Court's several opinions. See supra note 21.

161. There is no way under the Constitution for one Congress to tell a future Congress how to discharge a constitutionally assigned responsibility. See Laurence H. Tribe, *American Constitutional Law* § 2–3, at 125–126 n.1, 3d ed. (New York: Foundation Press, 2000).

162. *Bush v. Gore,* 121 S. Ct. at 550 (Ginsburg, J., dissenting).

163. The "final" resolution that the December 11 per curiam decision generated did not arise from Florida's use of November 7 rules, but from the U.S. Supreme Court using its (newly minted) version of the equal protection clause. See *Bush v. Gore,* 121 S. Ct. at 551–552 (Breyer, J., dissenting).

164. Id. at 541 (Stevens, J., dissenting).

165. *Bush v. Gore,* 121 S. Ct. 525, 532 (2000) (per curiam).

166. See infra, TAN 109–118.

167. See supra, TAN 122–131.

168. Cf. *Bendix Autolite Corp. v. Midwesco Enterprises,* 486 U.S. 888, 897 (1988) (Scalia, J., concurring) (criticizing meaningless balancing between things that aren't commensurable as "like judging whether a particular line is longer than a particular rock is heavy.").

169. *Bush v. Gore,* 121 S. Ct. 525, 533 (2000) (per curiam).

170. Id. (Emphasis added).

171. Id.

172. Id.

173. *Gore v. Harris,* 772 So.2d. 1243, 1270 (Fla. 2000) (Wells, C.J., dissenting) (quoting Philip Gailey, "The Election Is a Tie, So Let's Get On With It," *St. Petersburg Times,* Dec. 3,

2000, 3D (quoting David Remnick, "Comment: Decisions, Decisions," *The New Yorker,* Dec. 4, 2000, 35)).

174. *Gore v. Harris,* 772 So.2d at 1263.

175. *Bush v. Gore,* 121 S.Ct. 525, 529-30 (2000) (per curiam).

176. See supra notes 18–24 on same point.

177. See *Baker v. Carr,* 369 U.S. 186, 217 (1962) (holding that courts should avoid deciding an issue when there is "a textually demonstrable constitutional commitment of the issue to a coordinate political department; or a lack of judicially discoverable and manageable standards for resolving it . . .").

178. *Nixon v. United States,* 506 U.S. 224, 234 (1993) (dismissing as a nonjusticiable political question whether the Senate had held a "trial" as required by the Constitution when a federal judge was being removed).

179. *Bush v. Gore,* 121 S. Ct. 512 (2000) (Scalia, J., concurring) (mem.).

180. The image of Hercules is invoked with apologies to Ronald Dworkin, whose ideal of the omniscient Hercules as judge is never confused with the reality of judges who are mere mortals. See "Hard Cases," 88 *Harv. L. Rev.* 1057, 1083–1109 (1975).

181. See, e.g., Michael W. McConnell, "Comment: Institutions and Interpretation: A Critique of *City of Boerne v. Flores,* 111 *Harv. L. Rev.* 153, 177 (1997).

182. See also Laurence H. Tribe, *American Constitutional Law* § 5-16, at 949–51 n.121, 998–99, § 5-19 n. 74 (3d ed. 2000).

183. See Robert C. Post and Reva B. Siegel, "Equal Protection By Law: Federal Antidiscrimination Legislation after" Morrison and Kimel, 110 *Yale L. J.* 441, 521 (2000) (urging such pluralism and arguing it had been respected by the Court until the nineties).

184. See *City of Boerne v. Flores,* 521 U.S. 507 (1997).

185. See *Fla. Prepaid v. College Savings Bank,* 527 U.S. 627 (1999).

186. See *College Savings Bank v. Fla. Prepaid,* 527 U.S. 666 (1999).

187. See *Kimel v. Fla. Bd. of Regents,* 528 U.S. 62 (2000).

188. See *Bd. of Trustees of Univ. of Ala. v. Garrett,* 121 S. Ct. 955 (2001).

189. 410 U.S. 113 (1973).

190. 505 U.S. 833 (1992).

191. Id. at 868.

192. Mary Ann Glendon, *A Nation Under Lawyers: How the Crisis in the Legal Profession Is Transforming American Society* (Cambridge, MA: Harvard University Press, 1994), 112 (quoting Terry Carter, "Crossing the Rubicon," *California Lawyer,* October 1992, pp 39, 40).

193. Antonin Scalia, "The Rule of Law as a Law of Rules," 56 *U. Chi. L. Rev.* 1175 (1989).

194. *Brown v. Bd. of Education,* 347 U.S. 483 (1954).

195. See Robert C. Post and Reva B. Siegel, "Equal Protection By Law: Federal Antidiscrimination Legislation after" Morrison and Kime, 110 *Yale L. J.* 441, 521 (2000).

196. *United States v. Nixon,* 418 U.S. 683, 715–16 (1974).

197. Fyodor Dostoyevsky, *The Brothers Karamazov* 4, Ralph Matlaw, ed. and Constance Garnett, trans. (New York: Norton, 1976).

198. See, e.g., Alan M. Dershowitz, *Supreme Injustice: How the High Court Hijacked Election 2000* (New York: Oxford University Press, 2001). Vincent Bugliosi, *The Betrayal of*

America: How the Supreme Court Undermined the Constitution and Chose Our President (New York: Thunder's Mouth Press/Nation Books, 2000).

199. See Laurence Tribe, "The Mystery of Motive, Private and Public; Some Notes Inspired by the Problems of Hate Crime and Animal Sacrifice," 1993 *Sup. Ct. Rev.* 1, 19–22.

200. I readily admit that the Court's own efforts to cabin the reach of its precedent underscore just how different this judgment was from the promulgation of a "general rule." Yet neither was the decision comparable to the kind of ruling against an individual or group with respect to which it makes sense to ask, "Why did the court do that to *me*?"

201. See Dershowitz, supra note 2 at 203–06.

202. Alexander M. Bickel, *The Least Dangerous Branch* (2d. ed.) (New Haven, CT: Yale University Press, 1986).

203. Cf. Sanford Levinson, *Constitutional Faith* (Princeton, NJ: Princeton University Press, 1988).

204. See *New York Times Co., Inc., v. Tasini,* 121 S. Ct. 2381 (2001); *United States v. United Foods,* Inc., 121 S. Ct. 2334 (2001).

205. 478 U.S. 186 (1986).

206. 500 U.S. 173 (1991).

207. 520 U.S. 351 (1997).

208. 452 U.S. 640 (1981).

209. Supra note 195.

210. 347 U.S. 483 (1954).

211. 372 U.S. 335 (1963).

212. 376 U.S. 254 (1964).

213. 369 U.S. 186 (1962).

214. 410 U.S. 113 (1973).

4. CONSTITUTIONALIZING DEMOCRATIC POLITICS

* This is a substantially expanded and recast version of an essay that first appeared in 68 *U. Chi. L. Rev.* 695 (2001). I am grateful to a research paper written by Marie Gillen for information in Part I of this essay. I should also have expressed my debt in that earlier piece to Richard Parker, whose work long ago taught me to look at judicial decisions through the lens I employ here.

1. 531 U.S. 98 (2000).

2. The fount of this jurisprudence is *Baker v. Carr,* 369 U.S. 186 (1962).

3. See Richard A. Posner, *Breaking the Deadlock: The 2000 Election, The Constitution, and The Courts* (Princeton, NJ: Princeton University Press, 2001), 210 ("The leftward drift [of legal academics] has deflected professorial attention from the structural provisions of the Constitution (such as those regulating the election of the President) to the provisions that create individual rights against government, leaving the professoriat unprepared to address the issues thrown up by the Florida deadlock."). My coauthored casebooks are an effort to bring systematic study of the law of democracy to classrooms in law schools and elsewhere. See Samuel Issacharoff, Pamela S. Karlan, and Richard H. Pildes, *The Law of Democracy: Legal Structure of the Political Process,* 2d. ed. (New York: Founda-

tion Press, 2001) and Samuel Issacharoff, Pamela S. Karlan, and Richard H. Pildes, *When Elections Go Bad: The Law of Democracy and the 2000 Presidential Election* rev. ed., (New York: Foundation Press, 2001). One other casebook similarly focuses on structures of democratic governance. See Daniel H. Lowenstein and Richard L. Hasen, *Election Law—Cases and Materials,* 2d. ed. (Carolina Academic Press: 2001). Ironically, while Posner's basic observation is important, Posner fails to recognize that an entire field of study—the law of democracy—has emerged in recent years.

4. This point can be illustrated by considering the single most canonical yearly assessments of the Supreme Court's work product, which are the *Harvard Law Review*'s annual forewords to its Supreme Court issue each November. Professor Erwin Chemerinsky, for example, wrote that our age was one of "the vanishing Constitution. See Erwin Chemerinsky, "The Supreme Court, 1988 Term—Foreword: The Vanishing Constitution," 103 *Harv. L. Rev.* 43 (1989). More recently, Professor Mark Tushnet argued that we live with the "chastened aspirations" of a "new constitutional order" in which constitutional law plays an increasingly minor and reactive role. Mark Tushnet, "The Supreme Court, 1998 Term—Foreword: The New Constitutional Order and the Chastening of Constitutional Aspiration," 113 *Harv. L. Rev.* 29. 108 (1999). But if the Constitution has vanished, or our age is chastened, it has only been with respect to the issues of individual rights and equal protection that defined the Warren Court era and that have remained the preoccupation of many constitutional scholars. Professor Amar's recent foreword concerning the 1999 term footnotes constitutional cases involving democracy but provides no analysis of them. See Akhil Reed Amar, "The Supreme Court, 1999 Term—Foreword: The Document and the Doctrine," 114 *Harv. L. Rev.* 26, 89 n. 212 (2000). In my review of recent Forewords, the more familiar issues of federalism or individual rights appear again and again, yet there is almost no notice taken of this emerging jurisprudence of democracy. Professor Morton Horwitz's foreword is a slight exception; in a provocative quantitative analysis of Supreme Court opinions, he notes that appeals to the words *democracy* and *democratic* as legitimating concepts began only in the forties and exploded in the seventies, eighties, and nineties. Morton J. Horwitz, "The Supreme Court, 1992 Term—Foreword: The Constitution of Change: Legal Fundamentality Without Fundamentalism." 107 *Harv. L. Rev.* 30, 57 (1993). But Professor Horwitz did not develop this insight into a normative assessment of the Court's work, nor did he purport to analyze any of the specific legal issues in democratic politics that the Court actually confronted. The Forewords are exemplary, not peculiar, in what they reveal about the traditional focus of constitutional scholarship: Constitutional scholarship has typically left to the background legal issues involving the constitutional structure of democratic processes.

5. For the history of disfranchisement and the evidence of its absence from constitutional scholarship, see Richard H. Pildes, "Democracy, Anti-Democracy, and the Canon," 17 *Const. Comm.* 295, 319 (2000) ("Even today, the canon of constitutional law barely touches upon issues of democratic governance, let alone giving those issues the systematic, sustained, and central attention they require.").

6. For example, the public opinion literature reports that the percent of Americans who said they trusted government "about always or most of the time" peaked at 70 percent in 1964 but has ranged between 20–40 percent since the Watergate era of the early seventies. See

Nathaniel Persily, "The Right To Be Counted," 53 *Stan. L. Rev.* 1077, 1100 (2001); see also Seymour Martin Lipset and William Schmeider, *The Confidence Gap: Business, Labor, and Government in the Public Mind* (1987).

7. See Martin P. Wattenberg, *The Decline of American Political Parties, 1952–1996* (Cambridge, MA: Harvard University Press, 1998), 233. See generally Christian Collet, "Taking the Abnormal Route: Backgrounds, Beliefs, and Political Activities of Minor Party Candidates," in *Multiparty Politics in America,* 103 (1997).

8. Pat Buchanan was on the ballot in all states but Florida, Michigan and D.C.; Ralph Nader qualified to be on the ballot in all states except Georgia, Idaho, Indiana, North Carolina, Oklahoma, South Dakota, and Wyoming. Additionally, less well-known third party candidates like Howard Philips (Constitution Party), John Hagelin (Reform-Independent), and James Harris (Socialist Workers) appear on a good percentage of state ballots. See Ballot Access News, November 16, 2000, 4.

9. In Florida, for example, Nader received 96,837 votes, around 180 times the number of votes that gave George W. Bush victory in Florida and hence the presidency. See Michael Powell, "Scared But Unwilted: Democrats See Red. But Green Party Faithful Say They Made Their Point," *Washington Post,* December 27, 2000.

10. See Christian Collet and Martin P. Wattenberg, "Strategically Unambitious: Minor Party and Independent Candidates in the 1996 Congressional Elections," in *The State of the Parties: The Changing Role of Contemporary American Parties,* John C. Green and Daniel M. Shea, eds.

11. "The 2000 Election," *New York Times* On The Web (visited November 9, 2000) <http://www.nytimes.com/specials/election2000/states.html>.

12. Samuel J. Eldersveld, *Political Parties in American Society* (1982), 245. For a summary of the history of third-party politics in the United States, see Steven Rosenstone, et. al., *Third Parties in America* (Princeton University Press: 1996).

13. See Eldersveld, id., at 387; V.O. Key, *Politics, Parties, and Pressure Groups,* (4th ed., 1963), 183–218.

14. See Samuel Eliot Morison, *The Oxford History of the American People,* (1965), 590–93.

15. See Key, *supra,* at 186–214.

16. See Morison, *supra,* at 1053.

17. Christian Collet, "Third Parties and the Two-Party System," 60 *Pub. Opinion Q.* 431, 433 (1996).

18. Aldrich *supra,* at 267.

19. These figures are taken from the 1998 edition of Wattenberg, supra, at 224.

20. Larry J. Sabato, et al., eds., *Dangerous Democracy? The Battle Over Ballot Initiatives in America* (New York: Rowman & Littlefield Publishers, Inc., 2001), 22.

21. Id. at 21.

22. Shaun Bowler and Todd Donovan, "Proposition 198: Political Reform Via the Initiative Process," in Bruce E. Cain and Elisabeth R. Gerber eds., *Voting at the Political Fault Line: California's Experiment with the Blanket Primary* (Berkeley, CA: University of California Press, 2002).

23. For the data, see Elisabeth R. Gerber, *The Populist Paradox: Interest Group Influence and The Promise of Direct Legislation* (Princeton, NJ: Princeton University Press, 1999), 118.

(Twenty-three percent of initiatives and referendum dealing with "government and political process" pass.)

24. The comparative perspective is developed in one of the leading contemporary studies of American parties, Leon Epstein, *Political Parties in the American Mold* (Madison, WI: University of Wisconsin Press, 1986), 156. (parties outside the United States are not "ordinarily subject to most of the other regulations imposed on the internal affairs of American parties.")

25. For the history of these reforms, and the state judicial response to them, see the important article by Adam Winkler, "Voters' Rights and Parties' Wrongs: Early Political Party Regulation in the State Courts, 1886–1915," 100 *Colum. L. Rev.* 873 (2000), on which I draw heavily.

26. *People ex rel. Coffey v. Democratic General Committee,* 58 N.E. 124, 125–26 (N.Y. 1900).

27. Id. at 126.

28. Winkler, supra, at 878. For various historical reasons, this litigation was overwhelmingly in the state courts under state constitutional provisions.

29. For the cases, see Winkler, supra, at 879, 880, 889.

30. Epstein, supra, at 7.

31. Primary election structures can crudely be classified as closed, open, or the kind of blanket primary California adopted. In a "closed" party primary, eligibility is limited to voters who have registered as members of that party a specified period of time in advance of the primary. Fifteen states employ closed primaries. In an "open primary," a registered voter may choose an election day in which party primary he or she prefers to vote, whether or not the voter has registered previously as a member of that party; but the voter may vote only in that one party's primaries on election day. Twenty-one states use this structure. In addition, eight more states permit participation to independents as well as party members; these are sometimes called "semi-open" or "semi-closed" primaries. After the California vote, four states would have used blanket or nonpartisan primaries. 984 F. Supp. at 1291–92. According to purportedly reliable exit polls, 61 percent of Democrats, 57 percent of Republicans, and 69 percent of independents supported the blanket primary in California's Proposition 198 contest. Id. at 1291.

32. Bowler and Donovan, supra, at .

33. From 1960–66, Alaska temporarily shifted back to an open primary.

34. *Ladd v. Holmes,* 66 P. 714, 721 (Or. 1901).

35. 530 U.S. 567 (2000).

36. 984 F. Supp. at 1303.

37. 984 F. Supp. at 1301.

38. 984 F. Supp., at 1301. The Court of Appeals panel unanimously adopted the district court's opinion. 169 F. 3d 646 (Ninth Cir. 1999).

39. Contrast the opening lines, for example, of the Court's opinion with the concurrence of Justice Kennedy. Compare 120 S.Ct. 2405 ("This case presents the question whether the State of California may [adopt a blanket primary]") with 120 S.Ct. 2414 (Kennedy, J., concurring) ("Proposition 198, the product of a statewide popular initiative, is a strong and recent expression of the will of California's electorate."). Justice Kennedy's interesting concurrence, which cannot be explored here, is noteworthy because, in partial spirit with

the dissenters and unlike the majority, he puts considerable stress on an image of "a strong, participatory democratic process" but not enough to change the outcome.

40. 120 S. Ct. at 2413.

41. 120 S. Ct. at 2410.

42. See, e.g., 120 S. Ct. at 2416, 2422.

43. 120 S. Ct. at 2421.

44. Id. at 2422.

45. Id. at 2416.

46. Id. at 2419.

47. A theme masterfully developed in Dan Kahan, "The Secret Ambition of Deterrence, 113 *Harv. L. Rev.* 413 (1999).

48. For the differences among types of primaries, see supra note 31.

49. Other scholars have reached similar views. See, e.g., Richard L. Hasen, "Do the Parties or the People Own the Electoral Process," 149 *U. Pa. L. Rev.* 815, 830–31 (2000). In an open primary, the only act of "affiliation" with a party that is required is to ask for that party's ballot on election day—compared to a closed primary in which the voter must be registered some period of time in advance as a party member. If the formality of asking for the party ballot is enough to distinguish open from blanket primaries, the distinction is hard to see as meaningful. See, e.g., Samuel Issacharoff, "Private Parties with Public Purposes: Political Parties, Associational Freedoms, and Partisan Competition," 101 *Colum. L. Rev.* 274 (2001) ("The Court fastens on a factual difference between the blanket primary and open primaries, the fact that voters in an open primary are 'limited to one party's ballot,' without specifying the constitutional principle that informs why the 'right not to associate' is breached when voters are allowed to vary party affiliation moment by moment as they traverse the ballot, but not hour by hour as they temporarily 'join' a party for potentially adventitious reasons."). In addition, open primaries require a voter to vote only in one party's primary for all offices that particular election day; if there is a meaningful distinction here from blanket primaries, it would have be that the power to pick and choose among party primaries for various offices leads, as an empirical matter, to greater rates of actual, undesirable (unconstitutional) crossover voting—for which there is no convincing empirical support, as far as I am aware. Indeed, Professor Issacharoff argues the Court fails to explain convincingly why, if blanket primaries are unconstitutional, the very existence of state-mandated primaries is not itself also unconstitutional—apart from the fact that mandated primaries began about a generation before the first mandatory blanket primary.

50. See supra note 49.

51. That was precisely the situation in the one case before *Jones* in which the Court had held unconstitutional a state's effort to impose a primary structure; in *Tashjian v. Republican Party of Connecticut,* 479 U.S. 208 (1986), the Democratic-dominated legislature had refused to change state law to permit the Republican party to allow independents to vote in Republican party primaries.

52. Richard L. Hasen, "Parties Take the Initiative," 100 *Colum. L. Rev.* 731, 745–751, 747 (2000) ("Republicans spent $48,899 opposing the measure; Democrats spent a mere $4,630.").

53. 520 U.S. 351 (1997).

54. The classic treatment is Peter H. Argersinger, " 'A Place on the Ballot' Fusion Politics and the Antifusion Laws," 85 *Am. Hist. Rev.* 287, 288 (1980). For greater context on the legal questions discussed here, see Samuel Issacharoff and Richard H. Pildes, "Politics as Markets: Partisan Lockups of the Democratic Process," 50 *Stan. L. Rev.* 643, 683–88 (1998).

55. Argersinger, supra, at 288–290, 303–304.

56. D. Mazmanian, *Third Parties in Presidential Elections* (1974), 115–135. Argersinger, supra, at 304; S. Rosenstone, supra, at 75 (on the significance of the Populist party).

57. A different Court of Appeals in a 2–1 decision had upheld another state's fusion ban, *Swamp v. Kennedy,* 950 F.2d 383 (7th Cir. 1991), *cert. denied,* 505 U.S. 1204 (1992), with Judges Easterbrook, Posner, and Ripple dissenting from the en banc court's refusal to review the case. 950 F. 2d at 388, 389 ("A state's interest in political stability does not give it the right to frustrate freely made political alliances simply to protect artificially the political status quo.")

58. *Twin Cities Area New Party v. McKenna,* 73 F.3d 196, 199 (Eighth Cir. 1996).

59. Id. at 199.

60. Id. at 199.

61. See, e.g., 520 U.S. at 366 ("States have a strong interest in the stability of their political systems.").

62. 502 U.S. at 367.

63. Id. at 358.

64. 520 U.S. at 364.

65. Id. at 366. For the demonstration that the Court has never previously invoked just a justification, see Richard L. Hasen, "Entrenching the Duopoly: Why the Supreme Court Should Not Allow the States to Protect the Democrats and Republicans from Political Competition," 1997 *Sup. Ct. Rev.* 331.

66. 520 U.S., at 382 (Stevens, J., dissenting) (quotation omitted).

67. Id. at 375 n.3

68. Id. at 380–81.

69. 520 U.S. at 384 (Souter, J., dissenting). Ironically, Justice Souter cites a 1992 *New York Times* essay by Professor Theodore J. Lowi, which asserts that 1992 will be historically viewed "as the beginning of the end of America's two-party system" although Lowi celebrates this purported fact precisely because he believes the demise of the two-party system will enhance, not threaten, American democracy. See Theodore J. Lowi, "Toward a Responsible Three-Party System," in John C. Green and Daniel M. Shea, eds., *The State of the Parties: The Changing Role of Contemporary American Parties,* 1994, 45. ("One of the best kept secrets in American politics is that the two-party system has long been brain-dead—kept alive by support systems such as state electoral laws that protect the established parties from rivals and by public subsidies and so-called campaign reform.")

70. 520 U.S. at 384.

71. Along with whether equal protection requires statewide uniformity in the substantive issue of what counts as a legal vote.

72. 523 U.S. 666 (1998)

73. Jamin B. Raskin, "The Debate Gerrymander," 77 *Tex. L. Rev.* 1943, 1973 (1999). Of course, early primaries might be viewed differently than general election debates, but the Court's opinion relies not at all on these kind of distinctions.

74. Id. at 684.

75. See Brief of Amicus Curiae Commission on Presidential Debates in Support of Petitioner, *Arkansas Educational Television Commission v. Forbes,* No 96-779 (filed May 30, 1997) (available on Lexis at 1996 US Briefs 779). See also 11 CFR Sec. 110.13(c) (2000); New York City Admin Code Sec. 3-709.5 (1999); Commission on Presidential Debates, Nonpartisan Candidate Selection Criteria for 2000 General Election Debate Participation, available online at <http://www.debates.org/pages/candsel.html>. (visited Apr 10, 2001). Even once preestablished, objective criteria are specified, those criteria might of course be challenged substantively.

76. Id. at 685.

77. 502 U.S. at 367.

78. For discussion of the crucial role that less restrictive electoral laws and debate practices played in enabling Ventura's success, see Richard H. Pildes, "A Theory of Political Competition," 85 *U. Va. L. Rev.* 1605, 1617–18 (1999).

79. 17 Cong. Rec. 815 (1886) (Sen. Sherman).

80. 17 Cong. Rec. 817–18 (1886) (Sen. Sherman).

81. This was the consistent position taken throughout the dispute by Jeff Rosen's writings in *The New Republic.* See *Bush v. Gore,* 531 U.S. 98 (2000) (Souter, J., dissenting, joined by Justices Breyer, Stevens, and Ginsburg) ("The Court should not have reviewed either *Bush v. Palm Beach County Canvassing Bd.I,* or this case. . . .)

82. Drawing on how federal courts have handled oversight of previous election disputes, including for state office, I have argued elsewhere that there is a justifiable, limited federal constitutional role in ensuring that state courts do not change election rules in the middle of an election dispute under the guise of merely interpreting those laws. But I also argue that this federal oversight role should be circumscribed by the need to find particular factors present to justify the dramatic conclusion that a state court has improperly changed the rules in the middle of the game, and that the evidence to support such a conclusion in *Bush v. Gore* is thinner than in other cases in which federal courts have found state courts unconstitutionally to have created "new law" while resolving election disputes. Richard H. Pildes, *Judging "New Law" in Election Disputes,* 29 *Florida State University Law Review* 691 (2002)

83. Professor Michael McConnel, for example, defends the substantive finding in *Bush v. Gore* that the recount process violated the Constitution, but believes the Court's failure to allow the process to continue in the Florida courts was not legally correct. Michael W. McConnell, "*Two-and-a-Half Cheers for Bush v. Gore,*" in Cass. R. Sunstein and Richard A. Epstein eds., *The Vote: Bush, Gore, and the Supreme Court* (Chicago: University of Chicago Press, 2001), 98, 117.

84. 121 S. Ct. 510 (2000).

85. These are the terms in which defense of the Court's decisions are cast in Gary C. Leedes, "The Presidential Election Case: Remembering Safe Harbor Day," 35 *U. Rich. L. Rev.* 237 (2001).

86. Posner, *Breaking the Deadlock,* 180.
87. Id.
88. Id. at 152.
89. The Supreme Court decision permitting the United States military to inter Japanese-American residents and citizens during World War II. *Korematsu v. United States,* 323 U.S. 214 (1944).
90. Posner, at 188.
91. Posner, at 188.
92. Id. at 256.
93. Id.
94. The starting point for this doctrine is *Baker v. Carr,* 369 U.S. 186 (1962).

5.   *BUSH V. GORE* AS PRAGMATIC ADJUDICATION

* I am greatly indebted to Brian Leiter for his extensive comments on a previous draft.
1. The charge of corruption is elaborated in Alan M. Dershowitz, *Supreme Injustice: How the Supreme Court Hijacked Election* 2000 (2001). Dershowitz and I debated this charge in "Dialogue: The Supreme Court and the 2000 Election," *Slate,* July 2–3, 6, 9, 2001, http://slate.msn.com/dialogues/01-07-02/dialogues.asp?iMsg=2.
2. Richard A. Posner, *Breaking the Deadlock: The 2000 Election, the Constitution, and the Courts* (Princeton, NJ: Princeton University Press, 2001).
3. See id., chs. 3–4.
4. All four counties used the much-criticized punch card voting technology. The chad is the perforated area (usually rectangular) on the punch card ballot, adjacent to each candidate's name, that the voter uses a stylus to punch out. The ballot is tabulated by being run through a computer that trains a light or other electromagnetic beam on the ballot and records a vote for the candidate whose chad has been punched out, permitting the beam to pass through the chad hole to the sensor that records the vote. See id., introduction and ch. 2.
5. Citations to these and other statutory (and constitutional) provisions, as well as to the various judicial decisions, may be found in id., ch. 3.
6. A dimpled ballot is one in which the chad, though indented or pierced, remains attached to the ballot at all four of the chad's corners.
7. These dates of course are not specified in the act. They happen to be the dates in 2000 picked out by the provisions of the act that set forth the timetable for events specified in it.
8. See Alexander M. Bickel, *The Least Dangerous Branch: The Supreme Court at the Bar of Politics* (2d ed., 1986); 185–186; Posner, note 3 above, at 182–184.
9. See id. at 137–139.
10. I expressed uncertainty whether her ineligibility for the presidency would carry over to the position of acting president, see id. at 138 n. 83, but I was wrong, having overlooked 3 U.S.C. § 19(e).
11. U.S. Const. amend. XX, § 3.
12. See, for a generally favorable view of Kennedy's pragmatism, Kenneth W. Thompson,

"Kennedy's Foreign Policy: Activism versus Pragmatism," in *John F. Kennedy: The Promise Revisited* (Paul Harper and Joann P. Krieg, eds., 1988), 25, 28–33.

13. The distinction loomed large in the debates over the Clinton impeachment. See Richard A. Posner, *An Affair of State: The Investigation, Impeachment, and Conviction of President Clinton,* ch. 4 (1999).

14. The latter a term originally applied to Roman Catholics who refused to attend Church of England services though required by statute to do so.

15. Richard Rorty, "Pragmatism," in *Routledge Encyclopedia of Philosophy* (Edward Craig, ed., 1998), 633, 644.

16. For example, in connection with free-speech issues, as I have argued from time to time, most recently in my unpublished paper "Pragmatism versus Purposivism in First Amendment Analysis" (forthcoming in *Stanford Law Review*). See also Richard A. Posner, *The Problems of Jurisprudence,* ch. 5 (1990), where I consider the use of philosophy to illuminate causation in tort cases and voluntariness in coerced-confession cases.

17. "Pragmatists are committed to taking Darwin seriously. They grant that human beings are unique in the animal kingdom in having language, but they urge that language be understood as a tool rather than as a picture. A species' gradual development of language is as readily explicable in Darwinian terms as its gradual development or spears or pots, but it is harder to explain how a species could have acquired the ability to *represent* the universe—especially the universe as it really is (as opposed to how it is usefully described, relative to the particular needs of that species)." Rorty, note 16 above, at 636 (emphasis in original).

18. John Dewey, "Logical Method and Law," 10 *Cornell Law Quarterly* 17, 26 (1924) (emphasis in original). On legal pragmatism generally, see Thomas F. Cotter, "Legal Pragmatism and the Law and Economics Movement," 84 *Georgetown Law Journal* 2071 (1996).

19. Dewey, note 18 above, at 27.

20. See, for example, F. A. Hayek, *Law, Legislation and Liberty: A New Statement of the Liberal Principles of Justice and Political Economy,* vol. 1: *Rules and Order* 87, 97, 119, 121 (1973), and my unpublished paper "Kelsen, Hayek, and the Economic Analysis of Law," where I note a curious parallel between Hayek's and Dewey's conceptions of knowledge and inquiry.

21. See William E. Scheuerman, *Carl Schmitt: The End of Law,* ch. 1 (1999). Cf. Richard A. Posner, *Overcoming Law* (1995), 155–157.

22. See Richard A. Posner, *The Problematics of Moral and Legal Theory,* ch. 1 (1999); Posner, *Public Intellectuals: A Study of Decline,* ch. 9 (Cambridge, MA: Harvard University Press, 2001).

23. For a more extensive discussion, see Posner, *The Problematics of Moral and Legal Theory,* note 22 above, ch. 4; Posner, *Overcoming Law,* note 21 above, passim; Posner, *The Problems of Jurisprudence,* note 16 above, passim.

24. 323 U.S. 214 (1944).

25. Id. at 247.

26. *Terminiello v. City of Chicago,* 337 U.S. 1, 37 (1949) (dissenting opinion).

27. 323 U.S. at 244.

28. 290 U.S. 398 (1934).

29. Id. at 435.

30. 520 U.S. 681 (1997).

31. Bickel, note 8 above, at 126–127, 132. I do not think he used the term *pragmatic*; he would have said, instead, principle leavened with prudence, but I think it comes to much the same thing. Here it should be noted that the discretionary character of the Supreme Court's jurisdiction is only one of many areas of explicit judicial discretion, where pragmatic considerations dominate virtually by default.

32. Under *American* conditions—for the answer might be different in Germany in 1933, if judicial intervention could have prevented Hitler's being appointed chancellor.

33. "Our consideration is limited to the present circumstances, for the problem of equal protection in election processes generally presents many complexities." *Bush v. Gore,* 531 U.S. 98, 108 (2000) (per curiam).

34. Posner, note 2 above, chs. 2–3.

35. See *McPherson v. Blacker,* 146 U.S. 1 (1892).

36. Antonin Scalia, "The Rule of Law as a Law of Rules," *56 University of Chicago Law Review* 1175, 1179–1180 (1989), quoted in Dershowitz, note 1 above, at 123–132.

6.   HOW TO DEMOCRATIZE AMERICAN DEMOCRACY

1. The task force included, among others, Richard Rovere, Jules Witcover, Jeane Kirkpatrick, Stephen Hess, Patrick Cadell, Thomas Cronin, Neal R. Pierce, who preferred direct elections but found the national bonus plan "infinitely preferable" to the present system, and John Sears, Leonard Garment's nominee for Deep Throat. I must declare an interest: I was a member too, and I first proposed the bonus plan in "The Electoral College Conundrum," *Wall Street Journal,* 4 April 1977. William R. Keech was rapporteur, and the task force owed much to his objective analysis.

7.   AND TO THE *C* STUDENTS: THE LESSONS OF *BUSH V. GORE*

* I would like to thank Samantha Bent, Heather Gerken, Michael Gottlieb, Travis LeBlanc, Spencer Overton, and Rob Richie for helpful comments on an earlier draft. I am indebted to my research assistant, Sam Spital for his many, absolutely invaluable contributions to this essay.

1. Frank Bruni, "Bush Returns to Yale, but Welcome Is Not All Warm," *New York Times,* May 22, 2001, A12.

2. "Quotes of Note," *Boston Globe,* Oct. 21, 2000, A15.

3. See, for instance, David Barstow and Don Van Natt, Jr. "Examining the Vote; How Bush Took Florida: Mining the Overseas Vote" *New York Times,* July 15, 2001, Section 1, 1 and E.J. Dionne Jr. "Dirty Pool in Florida," *Washington Post,* July 17, 2001, A17.

4. I am counting the votes for Ralph Nader in combination with the votes cast and counted for Al Gore to determine that a majority of voters cast ballots "against" George Bush.

5. David Lebedoff, "The Class War Gore Could Lose," *New York Times,* August 27, 2000, Section 4, 15.

6. Dale Russakoff, "Lessons of Might and Right: How Segregation and an Indomitable Family Shaped National Security Advisor Condoleezza Rice," *Washington Post*, Sept. 9, 2001, W23.

7. Moreover, Lebedoff observes, another problem with the meritocracy "is that it believes it's certifiably better at everything. It has demonstrated a proficiency at reasoning skills, and therefore thinks every problem can be solved entirely with that proficiency." Although Gore presented himself as the more liberal candidate, he cooperated with Bush in denying access to the presidential debates to Ralph Nader. Thus we saw two parties and two candidates so afraid of open discourse, and so committed to maintaining mutual hegemony over our nation's political discourse, that they refused to allow a third party candidate to participate in, or even gain entrance to, the debates.

8. See Richard Briffault, "*Bush v. Gore* as an Equal Protection Case" 29 *F.S.U.L. Rev.* 325 (2001); Richard L. Hasen, "*Bush v. Gore* and the Future of Equal Protection Law in Elections," 29 *F.S.U.L. Rev.* 377 (2001). Both authors reflect the conventional view that the decision departed dramatically from prior equal protection jurisprudence.

9. *Harper v. Virginia Bd. Of Elections*, 383 U.S. 663, 685 (1996) (Harlan, J. dissenting).

10. "The Federalist solution is mainly a matter of engineering institutional sclerosis to make all government action difficult and so protect the interest of landed elites." Ian Shapiro, "The State of Democratic Theory" (forthcoming in Ira Katznelson and Helen Milner, eds., *Political Science: The State of the Discipline*), 12. See also Marc Mauer, "Mass Imprisonment and Mass Disfranchisement" (April 2001, draft). Even one of the most celebrated "liberal" dissents of our constitutional jurisprudence, Justice Harlan's dissent in *Plessy v. Ferguson*, valorized the superior expertise of "the white race": "The white race deems itself to be the dominant race in this country. And so it is, in prestige, in achievements, in education, in wealth and in power. So, I doubt not, it will continue to be for all time, if it remains true to its great heritage and holds fast to the principles of constitutional liberty."

11. Ian Shapiro, "The State of Democratic Theory" (forthcoming in Ira Katznelson and Helen Milner, eds., *Political Science: The State of the Discipline*), 6–7, 30.

12. While a hierarchy may be created in democratic ways, "hierarchies have propensities to atrophy into systems of domination, necessitating institutional constraints that shift burdens of proof to those who would defend them." Ian Shapiro, "The State of Democratic Theory" (forthcoming in Ira Katznelson and Helen Milner, eds., *Political Science: The State of the Discipline*), 6–7, 30.

13. Henry Wiencek, "Yale and the Price of Slavery," *New York Times*, August 18, 2001, A15: "If the founders had such misgivings over slavery, how is it that they allowed slavery to continue? The answer is not that they didn't know any better, but that they kept slavery so the Southern states would join the union. It was a transaction, a deal, just like the deal that put the national capital on the Potomac in exchange for the federal assumption of states' debts. . . ."

14. The Court made sure to assert that its ruling applied only to the circumstances surrounding the election of George W. Bush. "Our consideration is limited to the present circumstances, for the problems of equal protection in election processes generally presents many complexities." *Bush v. Gore*, 531 U.S. 98 (2000) (per curiam opinion).

15. Id.

16. "The Court, in announcing a new type of equal protection claim, is simply reverting to one of its worst habits in voting-rights cases: decision-making unmoored from an explicit normative theory." Heather Gerken, "New Wine in Old Bottles: A Comment on Richard Hasen's and Richard Briffault's Essays on *Bush v. Gore*," 29 *Fla. St. U. L. Rev.* 409, 422 (2001) ("The Court's failure to wrestle with these questions—what does equality mean, and how far will we go to attain it when the twin problems of race and poverty permeate our democratic structures?—gives an undeserved patina of legitimacy to the election system.") Id. See Frank Michelman, "Suspicion, or the New Prince," 68 *Chi.L.Rev.* 679, 693 (2001): "The justices of the *Bush v. Gore* majority might be imagined as Machiavelli's new prince, a ruler and savior prepared to sacrifice all to save the imperiled republic—probity, reputation, even the salvation of an honored place in history."

17. Indeed, in his timely and eerily propitious op-ed, "The Class War Gore Could Lose," analyzing the class war in meritocratic terms, Lebedoff suggested in August 2000 that the removal of decision-making from the people has become characteristic of the legal system itself. "Increasingly, too, major decisions are made by judges and administrators virtually immune from electoral reproach, let alone removal."

18. Justice O'Connor's query echoes the position of Joseph Klock (the lawyer arguing on behalf of Florida Secretary of State Katherine Harris). Responding to Justice Souter's question about what a uniform standard would be for counting ballots, Klock said:

> I'll try to answer that question. You would start, I would believe, with the requirements that the voter has when they go into the booth. That would be a standard to start with.
>
> The voter is told in the polling place, and then when they walk into the booth, that what you're supposed to do, with respect to the punch cards, is put the ballot in, punch your selections, take the ballot out, and make sure there are no hanging pieces of paper attached to it.
>
> The whole issue of what constitutes a legal vote, which the Democrats make much ado about, presumes that it's a legal vote no matter what you do with the card. And presumably you could take the card out of the polling place and not stick it in the box and they would consider that to be a legal vote.

19. *Oregon v. Mitchell,* 400 U.S. 112 (1970).

20. Michael Young, *The Rise of the Meritocracy 1870–2033: An Essay on Education and Equality* (London: Thames and Hudson, 1958).

21. Nicholas Lemann, *The Big Test* (New York: Farrar, Straus and Giroux, 1999).

22. Indeed, these standardized test scores tend to correlate better with parental income (and even grandparents' socioeconomic status) than actual student performance in college or graduate school. See Susan Sturm and Lani Guinier, "The Future of Affirmative Action: Reclaiming the Innovative Ideal," 84 *Cal. L. Rev.* 953 (July 1996).

23. The term *testocracy* highlights the ways in which selection policies are heavily dependent on standardized aptitude testing (See Susan Sturm and Lani Guinier, "The Future of Affirmative Action: Reclaiming the Innovative Ideal," *Cal. L. Rev.* 84:953, 968 (1996). By *testocracy* we refer to test-centered efforts to score applicants, rank them comparatively, and then predict their future performance. In this essay I limit the discussion of testing, however, to aptitude tests (as opposed to achievement tests).

24. They were designed to promote a more democratic distribution of opportunity—continuing the democratic impulse behind adopting aptitude tests in the sixties and seventies that especially benefited Jews and recent immigrants previously excluded by the old boy's network. See Lemann for a history of the tests.

25. Susan Sturm and Lani Guinier, "The Future of Affirmative Action: Reclaiming the Innovative Ideal," 84 *Cal. L. Rev.* 953, 956 (1996).

26. See Mindy Kornhaber, *Reconfiguring Admissions to Serve the Mission of Selective Public Higher Education* (January 14, 1999) (typescript on file with author). In 1997, nearly 42 percent of white freshmen at Berkeley had parental incomes over $100,000 a year, as did 27 percent of Asians. In contrast, 14 percent of African Americans and 10 percent of Chicanos had family incomes at that level.

27. The correlation between aptitude test scores and parental income should not surprise us, given the role that high-priced coaching techniques play in raising test scores. But what may surprise some is just how weak the relationship is between high test scores and what the tests claim to predict (i.e., first-year-college or law school grades). Studies suggest that nationwide the aptitude test for law schools (LSAT) is between 9 percent and 14 percent better than random in predicting first-year grades. See sources collected in Susan Sturm and Lani Guinier, "The Future of Affirmative Action: Reclaiming the Innovative Ideal," 84 *Cal. L. Rev.* 953 (July 1996).

28. See Katharine Q. Seelye, "Divided Civil Rights Panel Approves Election Report," *New York Times,* June 9, 2001, (reporting on a study conducted by Allan J. Lichtman, a history professor at American University and an elections expert); see also "U.S. to Look into Possible Irregularities at the Polls," *Chicago Tribune,* Dec. 4, 2000, news 9 ("The *Washington Post* reported Sunday that a computer analysis had found that the more black and Democratic a precinct, the more likely a high number of presidential votes was not counted.").

29. See U.S. Commission on Civil Rights, Voting Irregularities in Florida During the 2000 Presidential Election 2 (2001).

30. See U.S. Commission on Civil Rights, Voting Irregularities in Florida During the 2000 Presidential Election 2 (2001).

31. See Josh Barbanel and Ford Fessenden, "Racial Pattern in Demographics of Error-Prone Ballot," *New York Times,* Nov. 29, 2000, A25 (the potential magnitude of the difference in technology "is evident in Miami-Dade County, where predominantly black precincts saw their votes thrown out at twice the rate as Hispanic precincts and nearly four times the rate of white precincts. In all, 1 out of 11 ballots in predominantly black precincts were rejected, a total of 9,904.") Moreover, "64 percent of the state's black voters live in counties that used the punch cards while 56 percent of whites did so." Id. "U.S. to Look into Possible Irregularities at the Polls," *Chicago Tribune,* Dec. 4, 2000, news 9 ("In Miami-Dade, the state's most populous county, about 3 percent of ballots were excluded from the presidential tally. But in precincts with a black population of 70 percent or more, about 10 percent were not counted."); Kim Cobb, "Black Leaders Want Action on Florida Vote Complaints," *Houston Chronicle,* Nov. 30, 2000, A24 ("U.S. Rep. Corrine Brown, D-Jacksonville, said that 16,000 of the 27,000 ballots left uncounted in Duval County were from predominantly black precincts). But see Stephen Ansolabehere, "Vot-

ing Machines, Race, and Equal Protection," 1 *Election L. J.* 61 (2002) (arguing that na
tionally, no significant correlation exists between race and punch–card machine-rejected
ballots, and that racial disparities are explained by a higher percentage of less reliabl
punch card technology in African-American precincts). By contrast, the voices of certain
groups of (primarily Republican) voters received preferential counting treatment. A
complicated political and legal strategy helped ensure that canvassing boards accepted
41 percent of flawed absentee military ballots compared to 30 percent of flawed absente
civilian ballots. David Barstow and Don Van Natt, Jr., "Examining the Vote; How Bush
Took Florida: Mining the Overseas Vote," *New York Times,* July 15, 2001, section 1, 1.

32. Mireya Navarro and Somini Sengupta, "Arriving at Florida Voting Places, Some Black
Found Frustration," *New York Times,* Nov. 30, 2000, A1. See also Gregory Pabst
"Florida's Disappeared Voters: Disenfranchised by the GOP," 272(5) *The Nation* (Feb
ruary 5, 2001), 20, describing the flawed lists used by the state to purge a disproportion
ate number of blacks in Florida.

33. A lawsuit filed by the American Civil Liberties Union and others alleges that some mea
sures will have the effect of rendering Florida's voting procedures even more like a test, in
violation of the Voting Rights Act, and will thus discourage the participation of poor peo
ple and people of color. JoNel Newman, codirector of the Florida Equal Voting Right
Project, said that instead of moving the state forward, the changes enacted by the legisla
ture earlier this year contain provisions that "are a giant step backward . . . so far back
that it approximates a literacy test." Paul Brinkley-Rogers, "State's New Voting Guidelines Illegal, Rights Lawsuit Charges," *Miami Herald,* August 16, 2001, at http://www.miami
com/herald/content/news/local/dade/digdocs/116068.htm (visited September 8, 2001).

34. *Bush v. Gore,* 531 U.S. 98, 104 (2000). Citizens have no federally mandated or constitu
tionally sacrosanct right to vote. It is up to the various state legislatures to determine
whether to vest the right to vote in the people, and only then does the right become fundamental and protected based on rights to equal protection. This means that the rights of
voters are only triggered once the ballot is made available; when the state accedes to allow
voters to vote, then it is up to the state to establish the rules for voting so that your ballot
is in fact tabulated.

35. "Once the franchise is granted to the electorate, lines may not be drawn which are inconsistent with the Equal Protection Clause of the Fourteenth Amendment," *Harper v. Virginia Bd. Of Elections,* 383 U.S. 663, 665 (1966) as cited in *Bush v. Gore.*

36. For detailed analysis and statistics about illiteracy in the United States, see the National
Institute for Literacy's website at http://novel.nifl.gov/nifl/faqs.html#literacy%20rates
(visited September 10, 2001).

37. *Davis v. Bandemer,* 478 U.S. 109, 145 (1986) (concurring in the judgment).

38. In *Davis v. Bandemer* 478 U.S. 109 (1986), the Court ruled that political gerrymandering
was justiceable, but the Court's threshold is so high that only once have plaintiffs successfully brought a partisan vote dilution claim.

39. See *Shaw v. Reno,* 509 U.S. 630 (1993), *Miller v. Johnson,* 515 U.S. 900 (1995), *Shaw v.
Hunt,* 517 U.S. 899 (1996), and *Bush v. Vera,* 517 U.S. 952 (1996).

40. See *Buckley v. Valeo,* 424 U.S. 1 (1976) and *Colorado Republican Federal Campaign Committee v. Federal Election Commission* 518 U.S. 604 (1996).

41. See *Arkansas Educ. Television Comm'n v. Forbes,* 523 U.S. 666 (1997); *California Democratic Party v. Jones* 530 U.S. 567 (2000).

42. While the Court has struck down some of the most egregious laws attempting to deny fair access to third parties, its concerns about destabilizing threats to the two-party system can also be found in opinions on blanket primaries, fusion candidates, and party raiding. See, e.g., *California Democratic Party v. Jones,* 120 S. Ct. 2401, 2410 (2000); *Timmons v. Twin Cities Area New Party,* 520 US 351, 366–67 (1997) ("destabilizing effects of party splintering and excessive factionalism" from fusion tickets); *Burdick v. Takushi,* 504 U.S. 428, 439 (1992) ("divisive sore-loser candidacies" might emerge from allowing write-in voting in one-party Hawaii), and *Munro v. Socialist Workers Party* 479 U.S. 189 (1986). Justice Antonin Scalia offers a remarkable defense for the Court's tolerance of laws that unfairly promote the existing two-party system and the alienation it brings to large segments of the electorate: "The voter who feels himself disenfranchised should simply join the party." See also Theodore Lowi, "Deregulating the Duopoly" 271(18) *The Nation* (December 4, 2000).

43. Gerken, "New Wine in Old Bottles," 408. "One of the great oddities in the Supreme Court's voting-rights jurisprudence dating back to the Warren Court is that the justices often disavow the notion that they are importing a particular theory of democracy into the decision. Their claim to agnosticism is, of course, implausible. And the Court's self-conscious preference for avoiding any discussion of its normative premises has led to the type of decision-making we see in the *Bush v. Gore* per curiam: An opinion that articulates the injury in an abstract, formal manner; announces a legal rule with no easily discernible limits; defines equality in mechanical, quantitative terms; and fails to address the hard normative issues embedded in the questions it resolves." Id. See also Spencer Overton, supra.

44. Richard Pildes, *Democracy and Disorder,* 68 Chi L. Rev. 695, 707, citing *Timmons* majority opinion and concluding: "The central image in this opinion is not that of invigorated democracy through 'political competition,' but that of a system whose crucial 'political stability' is easily threatened. The word 'stable' (and variations of it) appears a remarkable ten times in the brief majority opinion."

45. Richard Pildes, "Democracy, Anti-Democracy, and the Canon," 17(2) *Constitutional Commentary* 295 (Summer 2000), at 11, citing *Hunter v. Underwood,* 471 U.S. 222 (1985).

46. The Court refused to intervene to protect Giles's rights "when the great mass of white people" in Alabama were opposed to his voting. In fact, there is some evidence that a majority of whites actually voted against the disenfranchising constitution and that it only passed because the votes of blacks, who never appeared at the polls, were nevertheless counted as supporting their own disenfranchisement. Pildes at 29–30 (the disfranchising constitution was approved with only 57 percent of the vote (a margin of 26,879 votes) and in 54 of the state's 66 counties, the total vote was actually against the constitution. Approval only came with the 36,224 to 5,471 votes for the constitution in 12 black-belt counties where three times as many votes were cast for the constitution as the number of white men eligible to vote. The voting was engineered by the elite landowners who used their control of the Democratic party to discourage alliances between poor whites and blacks.

47. For example, Justice Frankfurter cites *Giles v. Harris* in *Colegrove v. Green,* 328 U.S. 549

(1946) where he coined the now infamous terminology *political thicket* and cautioned that the Court must stay out of it. Yet the same case, *Giles v. Harris,* does not receive any mention in four of the leading constitutional law casebooks. Pildes at 3.

48. Of course it is important to note than unlike Mr. Giles's attorney, Mr. Gore's lawyers did not raise the disenfranchisement issue on the grounds of race.

49. Gore did, however, score impressive wins among voters from union households and among working-class people of color. See table accompanying Majorie Connelly, "The Election; Who Voted: A Portrait of American Politics, 1976–2000," *New York Times,* November 12, 2000, Section 4, 4.

50. See table accompanying Majorie Connelly, "The Election; Who Voted: A Portrait of American Politics 1976–2000." *New York Times,* November 12, 2000, Section 4, 4.

51. Pildes at 3.

52. Alex Keyssar, "Reform and an Evolving Electorate," *New York Times,* August 5, 2001 at Section 4, 13.

53. Frances Fox Piven and Richard Cloward, *Why Americans Don't Vote* (New York: Pantheon Books, 1988).

54. Richard Pildes, "Democracy, Anti-Democracy, and the Canon," 17(2) *Constitutional Commentary* 295 (Summer 2000).

55. J. Morgan Kousser, *The Shaping of Southern Politics* 238–265 (New Haven: Yale University Press, 1974).

56. Pildes at 27–28, describing events in North Carolina, where a fusion coalition of Republicans and Populists controlled the state legislature through 1898, with black and white support.

57. See voter turnout window for all elections in all countries between 1945 and 1998 at http://www.idea.int/voter_turnout/voter_turnout2.html (visited July 31, 2001).

58. Lani Guinier, "What We Must Overcome," *The American Prospect,* March 12–26, 2001, 28.

59. David Stout, "Study Finds Ballot Problems are More Likely for Poor," *New York Times,* July 9, 2001, A9. Another study revealed that, in total, poor voting technology contributed to 4–6 million votes being uncounted for the presidential election, and that the incidence of uncounted ballots rose to even higher levels for other contests. See Guy Gugliotta, "Study Finds Millions of Votes Lost," *Washington Post,* July 17, 2001, A1.

60. Calculations from table in Michael Gallagher, Michael Laver, and Peter Mair, *Representative Government in Modern Europe,* third edition, (Boston: McGraw-Hill, 2001), 322.

61. Beverly Neufeld, Executive Director, The White House Project, Sept. 5, 2001, letter to the editor, *New York Times,* Sept. 10, 2001, A30.

62. Susan A. Banducci, Todd Donovan, and Jeffrey A. Karp, "Minority Representation, Empowerment, and Participation in New Zealand and the United States" (revised June 25, 1999), 6 at www.nzes.org (visited March 13, 2002).

63. See www.ps.parliament.govt.nz/educate/indexes/texts/maoirimp.htm.

64. *The International IDEA Handbook of Electoral Design* (Institute for Democracy and Electoral Assistance Handbook Series, Andrew Reynolds and Ben Reilly, eds., 1997), 70.

65. Voicemail message received in December 2000 from Duane Hughes, Univ. of Pennsylvania Law School, 1991.

66. *Bush v. Gore* 531 U.S. 98, 129 (2000) (Stevens, J. Dissenting).

67. See, e.g., Jack Balkin, "*Bush v. Gore* and the Boundary Between Law and Politics," 110 *Yale L. J.* 1407 (June 2001) (quoting Professor Akhil Amar and others).

68. R.W. Apple Jr., "News Analysis: Tradition and Legitimacy," *New York Times*, January 21, 2001, Section 1, 1.

69. James Carroll, *Boston Globe*, January 9, 2001, A19.

70. "Voter Turnout Rose in 2000, But no Lasting Impact Is Seen," *New York Times*, August 31, 2001, A12.

71. Quoted in James A. Morone, *The Democratic Wish: Popular Participation and the Limits of American Government* (New York: Basic Books, 1990), 322.

72. I thank Professor Spencer Overton, "A Place at the Table: *Bush v. Gore* Through the Lens of Race," 29 *F.S.U. L.R.* 473 (2001) for his insightful analysis of the way the conventions of meritocracy apparently inform the court's analysis. "*Bush v. Gore* rejected more inclusionary assumptions about democracy articulated in earlier cases, but . . . the Court embraced merit-based assumptions that conditioned political recognition on an individual voter's capacity to produce a machine-readable ballot." Overton, 5. See also Pamela S. Karlan, "Nothing Personal: The Evolution of The Newest Equal Protection from Shaw v. Reno to Bush v. Gore," 79 *N.C.L. Rev.* 1345, 1366 (2001) ("There is credible evidence that systems that disproportionately reject votes both have a racially disparate impact and are more often used in the populous jurisdictions in which minority voters are concentrated. Thus, the newest equal protection once again vindicates the interests of middle-class, politically potent voters, while ignoring the interests of the clause's original beneficiaries.")

73. Steven Hill, "For Campaign Finance Laws that Work, Look Abroad," *Christian Science Monitor* (February 28, 1995), 19.

74. Indeed, the recent Electoral Reform Commission chaired by former presidents Ford and Carter proposed just such a reform.

75. While this may initially seem to violate personal autonomy, it is no greater civic burden than, for instance, requiring eighteen-year-old-males to register for the draft.

76. Sam Howe Verhovek, "An Unrepentant Nader Unveils a New Grass-Roots Project," *New York Times*, August 6, 2001, A8.

77. Joel Rogers, "The New Party—Now More than Ever: Rogers Replies" 18 *Boston Review* (January/February 1993). On the other hand, it might be useful to study the example of the Christian right, which started at the grassroots level, gradually got elected to school boards and city councils and developed a much louder voice within the Republican party precisely because they provided important local organizing to win elections.

78. An interesting side note is that, according to the Supreme Court's current, confused jurisprudence regarding majority-minority districts, the Progressive party could seek to draw majority-minority districts more easily than the traditional parties because it would clearly be doing so primarily for political rather than racial motives. See *Hunt v. Cromartie et al.*, 532 U.S. 234 (2001).

79. As described above, it is often the black elected officials who stand alone to protest obvi-

ous injustices, while their white Democratic colleagues, though sympathetic, sit back, constrained to follow the rules. James Carroll, "Black Caucus Sends a Message about Justice," *Boston Globe,* January 9, 2001, A19. It is also worth noting that the concept of the Progressive party fits well with the fact that some members of the congressional black caucus already serve as caseworkers for members of marginalized communities in general rather than simply the district from which they are elected. For instance, in 1995, a full 30 percent of all calls seeking assistance from Congresswoman Cynthia McKinney of Georgia came from individuals outside her district; 80 percent of these persons were "low-income minority individuals." (Lisa A. Kelly, "Race and Place: Geographic and Transcendent Community in the Post-Shaw Era," 49 *Vand. L. Rev.* 227, 284, n179 (1996).)

80. There is a rich literature that analyzes the rise of the British Labour party. Readers interested in exploring this topic greater detail might consult the following: Gregory Luebbert, *Liberalism, Fascism or Social Democracy* (New York: Oxford University Press, 1991); Henry Pelling, *The Origins of the Labour Party 1880–1900* (Oxford: Clarendon Press, 1965); Martin Pugh, *The Making of Modern British Politics* (Oxford: Blackwell, 1993); Duncan Tanner, *Political Change and the Labour Party, 1900–1918* (Cambridge: Cambridge University Press, 1990).

81. G. Bingham Powell, Jr. *Elections as Instruments of Democracy: Majoritarian and Proportional Visions* (2000), 90. See also ibid. 28–29.

82. Dan Nicolai, "The Law and the Struggle for the Soul of the Democratic Party," (12/20/00), 26 (unpublished manuscript on file with author).

83. Dale Russakoff, "Cut Out of Prosperity, Cutting Out at the Polls," *Washington Post,* October 24, 2000, A1. See also Dale Russakoff, "Young Voters See Little In It for Them," *Washington Post,* November 2, 2000, A1.

84. Peter Dreier and Elaine Bernard, "Kinder, Gentler Canada," 4 *The American Prospect* 85 (Winter 1993). See also, Elaine Bernard, "The Difference a New Party Would Make" 18 *Boston Review* (January/February 1993). Bernard's piece is in the context of a series of articles about the New Party, a political party founded in the early nineties and with quite similar goals to the objectives of the hypothetical Progressive party. In my view, a crucial difference is that the New Party—while clearly demonstrating an admirable interest in racial justice and working with black elected officials—does not focus to the same degree on the grassroots involvement of poor people of color as the Progressive party would. Nevertheless, the New Party is a step in the right direction that could coalesce with the Progressive party to advocate transformative democratic change.

85. For a theoretical discussion of this point, see G. Bingham Powell, Jr. *Elections as Instruments of Democracy: Majoritarian and Proportional Visions* (New Haven: Yale University Press, 2000), 198.

86. Therefore, this coordination should also appeal to Democrats as long as these locally grounded, grassroots organizations could reasonably threaten to run viable candidates in a number of constituencies. Attracting some black incumbents to the party at the local level would immediately lend credibility to this threat. On the other hand, as Heather Gerken reminds me, third-party candidates would in fact sometimes result in Democratic losses. Indeed, for third parties to have any effect, the threat of defection must be credible, which means that there will be short-term costs.

87. The major variations among party list systems are: (1) the formula used to award seats at the constituency level, (2) if there is a formula to correct any imbalances in the proportionality of representation from the constituency level, (3) whether lists are closed, meaning their order is determined entirely by the party; or open, allowing voters to influence which candidates, not just which parties, gain representation, and (4) the existence and level of a minimum threshold for legislative representation. Gallagher, Laver, and Mair *Representative Government in Modern Europe*, 309.

88. Douglas J. Amy, *Behind the Ballot Box: A Citizen's Guide to Voting Systems* (Westport, CT: Praeger, 2000), 88–89. *The International IDEA Handbook of Electoral Design* (Institute for Democracy and Electoral Assistance Handbook Series, Andrew Reynolds and Ben Reilly, eds., 1997), 62.

89. Gallagher, Laver and Mair, *Representative Government in Modern Europe*, 322. Not only do the countries with party-list systems vastly outperform the single-member district systems used by Britain and France, they also fare vastly better than Ireland and Malta, the two countries that currently use STV to elect their parliaments. Ibid. However, it is worth noting that in Australia, women fare far better in elections to the Senate, which use STV, than they do in contests for the House of Representatives, which are based on single-member districts. (Douglas J. Amy, *Real Choices/New Voices, The Case for Proportional Representation Elections in the United States* (New York: Columbia University Press, 1993), 107.

90. *The International IDEA Handbook of Electoral Design* (Institute for Democracy and Electoral Assistance Handbook Series, Andrew Reynolds and Ben Reilly, eds, 1997), 62–63, 70.

91. E.J. Feuchtwanger, *From Weimar to Hitler: Germany, 1918–1933* (Houndmills, Basingstroke, Hampshire: Macmillan, 1993), 42. That the publication of political parties corresponded to interwar Germany's bitter sociopolitical cleavages was in part a very small threshold for representation of each party. Post-war Italy is another country that opponents of PR often cite as a paradigmatic case of the havoc wreaked by the multiplication of small parties PR supposedly promotes. Like Weimar Germany and Israel, for most of the postwar period, Italy used a system of PR with an extremely low threshold of exclusion.

92. Such a 5 percent threshold would have been enough to keep the Nazis out of the Reichstag as late as the elections of 1928. While a winner-take-all system would have achieved a similar result in 1928, it would have probably grossly *overrepresented* the Nazis in the national legislature beginning in 1930, when, with 18.3 percent of the national vote, the Nazis became the second largest party. Feuchtwanger, *From Weimar to Hitler*, 42, 326.

93. Enid Lakeman, *Power to Elect: The Case for Proportional Representation* (London: Heinemann, 1982), 68. Among other obstacles, the anti-Nazi parties faced press censorship, prohibition of meetings, and police intimidation and violence during this "free" election. Feuchtwanger, *From Weimar to Hitler*, 313–314.

94. Giovanni Sartori, "The Party-Effects of Electoral Systems" in *Parties, Elections and Cleavages: Isreal in Comparative and Theoretical Perspective* (London: Frank Cass, 2000), 15, 27. Before 1992, the threshold of exclusion was one percent. Ibid.

95. Based on data table provided by Moshe Maor and Reuven Y. Hazan, "Parties, Elections and Cleavages: Israel in Comparative and Theoretical Perspective" in *Parties, Elections and Cleavages: Israel in Comparative and Theoretical Perspective* (London: Frank Cass, 2000), 6.

96. On a 7-point scale designed by Lijphart, Bowman, and Hazan to measure the number and intensity of sociopolitical cleavages in thirty-six democracies since World War II, Israel now scores a 5.0 "This is a remarkably high number compared with . . . the other thirty-five democratic party systems in the 1945–1996 period, the highest of which is 3.5 and found in only one country (Finland)." By contrast, the United States receives a score of 1.0. Arend Lijphart, Peter J. Bowman, and Reuven Y. Hazan "Party Systems and Issue Dimensions: Israel and Thirty-Five Other Old and New Democracies Compared," in *Parties, Elections and Cleavages: Israel in Comparative and Theoretical Perspective* (London: Frank Cass, 2000), 33–37, 48. Other info 35–48.

97. Elaine Sciolino, "Who Hates the U.S.? Who Loves it?" *New York Times,* Sept. 23, 2001, week in review 1, quoting Jon B. Alterman who has written extensively on the flow of information in the Arab world. "Whenever there is a survey of Palestinians, they always rate Israeli democracy higher than American democracy." Id.

98. Amy, *Behind the Ballot Box,* 31.

99. Single-transferable voting (STV) is another form of PR that does maintain close constituent-representative ties. However, it remains a candidate-centered system and, in my view, is thus less desirable than PR systems based on party lists.

100. Douglas Amy's admonition should not be lost that, "In the end . . . the primary danger facing any American pro-PR movement is not that it might opt for the 'wrong' one, but that it would waste valuable time and energy squabbling over which system is better." Amy, *Real Choices/New Voices, The Case for Proportional Representation Elections in the United States,* 96.

101. Amy, *Behind the Ballot Box,* 90.

102. Gallagher, Laver and Main, *Representational Government in Modern Europe,* 260, 322. Not surprisingly, German women are three times more likely to win seats through party lists than through single-member districts. This pattern holds in New Zealand and Italy, which recently adopted electoral systems that include the use of both party lists and single-member plurality districts. Richie and Hill, *Reflecting Us All: The Case for Proportional Representation* (Boston: Beacon Press, 1999), 16–17.

103. Rob Richie and Steven Hill, *Reflecting Us All: The Case for Proportional Representation* (Boston: Beacon Press, 1999), 30.

104. Amy, *Behind the Ballot Box,* 90–91.

105. At first glance, the transition to PR does not appear to have greatly increased turnout in New Zealand; at 75 percent of eligible voters, turnout in 1999 was roughly identical to turnout in 1993. This stability, however, must be put in the context of declining turnout in most OECD countries throughout the nineties as well a general pattern of declining turnout in New Zealand itself since the fifties. "Electoral System Opinion and the Evolution of MMP: A Report to the Electoral Commission," New Zealand Election Study, 35, 36. (76.7 percent 1993, 78.4 percent in 1996, 74.9 percent in 1999, but one percent of decline in last election reflects an adjustment for the census undercount of 1996. Ibid.). See

also Jeffrey A. Karp and Susan A. Banducci, "The Impact of Proportional Representation on Turnout: Evidence from New Zealand," 34(3) *Australian Journal of Political Science* 363, 368.

106. Jeffrey A. Karp and Susan A. Banducci, "The Impact of Proportional Representation on Turnout: Evidence from New Zealand," 34(3) *Australian Journal of Political Science* 363; 370–71, 375. See also Susan Banducci and Jeffrey Karp, "Representation Under a Proportional System" in *Voters' Victory? New Zealand's First Election Under Proportional Representation* (Jack Vowles et. al., eds. Auckland: Auckland University Press, 1998), 137. The shift to PR has also influenced the policy positions advanced by New Zealand's parties—as they now have a greater incentive to appeal to all voters since each vote counts towards a legislative seat—and this shift has dramatically improved the chances for the Maori to influence policy-making on issues that are especially important to them. Since the shift from winner-take-all elections to PR, "All parties have moved further to the left on Maori issues: the parties have become more favorable toward compensating Maori for land, increasing the Maori voice in government, and keeping references to the Treaty of Waitangi [enacted in the early seventies to redress Maori grievances] in the law." Susan Banducci and Jeffrey Karp, "Representation Under a Proportional System," in *Voters' Victory? New Zealand's First Election Under Proportional Representation* (Jack Vowles et. al., eds., Auckland: Auckland University Press, 1998), 137, 145. The information about the treaty comes from Anne Sullivan and Jack Vowles, "Realignment? Maori and the 1996 Election" in *Voter's Victory* at 173. At a descriptive level, the proportion of both women and Maori in New Zealand's parliament increased dramatically between 1993 and 1999. Women comprised 21 percent of New Zealand's parliament in 1993 and 31 percent in 1999. Susan Banducci and Jeffrey Karp, "Representation Under a Proportional System," in *Voters' Victory? New Zealand's First Election Under Proportional Representation* (Jack Vowles et al., eds., Auckland: Auckland University Press, 1998), 141. 1999 statistics from <www.ps.parliament.govt.nz/educate/indexes/texts/members. htm>

107. Susan A. Banducci, Todd Donovan, and Jeffrey A. Karp, "Minority Representation, Empowerment, and Participation in New Zealand and the United States" (revised June 25, 1999), 6 at www.nzes.org (visited March 13, 2002).

108. Banducci and Karp "Representation Under," 137, 141. 1999 statistics from www.ps. parliament.govt.nz/educate/indexes/texts/maoirimp.htm. Previously, the Maori won representation almost exclusively from separate Maori electorates that Maori can choose to register for. These separate Maori districts were preserved along even with the adoption of PR in 1993. Susan A. Banducci, Todd Donovan, and Jeffrey A. Karp, "Minority Representation, Empowerment, and Participation in New Zealand and the United States" (revised June 25, 1999), 7–8 at www.nzes.org (visited March 13, 2002). There was also an increase in representation of Asians and Pacific Islanders.

109. Augusto Boal, *Legislative Theatre: Using Performance to Make Politics* (New York: Routledge, 1998). Boal describes his actual experiences running as Vereador in Rio and getting elected for two terms. During that period he successfully introduced thirteen laws that were drafted by constituency groups using forum theater exercises that helped citizens "develop their taste for political discussion (democracy) and their desire to develop

their own artistic abilities (popular art)." Id., 9. Boal hired members of his theater group to function as "jokers" or wild cards who facilitated the development of seventeen constituency groups, each of whom worked through the improvisation of possible solutions to locally generated problems. Those solutions were then converted into bills and introduced into the legislature by Boal.

110. Although Boal's experience may seem improbable by U.S. standards, there are many local examples of similar efforts. See Lani Guinier and Gerald Torres, *The Miner's Canary: Enlisting Race, Resisting Power, Transforming Democracy,* (Cambridge, MA: Harvard University Press, 2002) Chapter 6. See also Tamar Lewin, "One State Finds Secret to Strong Civic Bonds," *New York Times,* August 26, 2001, Section 1, 1. (describing unlikely role that people without a high school education play in local government in New Hampshire).

8. HOLY COW! PRELIMINARY REFLECTIONS ON THE 2000 ELECTION

1. Nobody seems to be able to explain why a premature call by a network would cause late Bush voters to abandon an intention to vote but not late Gore voters, or vice versa. The issue was given close attention when Jimmy Carter conceded the 1980 election before polls closed in California—a somewhat stronger stimulus than a network projection. The scholarly consensus seems to be that even on that unusual occasion the effect of the news on turnout was insignificant if there was any effect at all. See Laurily K. Epstein and Gerald Strom, "Election Night Projections and West Coast Turnout," *American Politics Quarterly* 9 (October 1981), pp 479–491; Raymond E. Wolfinger and Peter Linquiti, "Turning and Turning Out," *Public Opinion* 4 (February/March, 1981), pp 56–60; and Phillip L. Dubois, "Election Night Projection and Voter Turnout in the West," *American Politics Quarterly* 11 (July 1983), pp 349–364.

2. I suppose the law the Court wanted to circumvent was the Electoral Count Act of 1887 (49 *Cong. Ch.* 90; 24 Stat. 373). It is bound to puzzle laypersons when a court steps in to prevent what looks like an applicable law that is already on the books from taking effect. Is this different from changing the rules in mid-contest?

3. I am now not as confident that there was no fraud in Florida as I was before two reports were published. See United States Commission on Civil Rights, "Draft Report: Voting Irregularities in Florida During the 2000 Presidential Election," (June 2, 2001), online at: http://www.usccr.gov/vote2000/stdraftl/main.htm; and David Barstow and Don Van Natta, Jr., "Examining the Vote: How Bush Took Florida: Mining the Overseas Absentee Vote," *New York Times,* July 15, 2001, A1.

4. Henry E. Brady, Michael C. Herron, Walter R. Mebane, Jr., Jasjeet Singh Skehon, Kenneth W. Shotts, and Jonathan Wand, "Law and Data: The Butterfly Ballot Episode," *PS: Political Science & Politics* 34 (March 2001), pp. 59–69.

5. This proposition is backed by a substantial technical literature showing that voters in large competitive states are pivotal in the election of the president. Irwin Mann and Lloyd Shapley (1962) in "Values of Large Games, VI: Evaluating the Electoral College Exactly," *Rand Memorandum,* RM-3158, define "the power of actor A [a state] as the number of

permutations (orderings) in which actor A occupies the pivotal position (that is, orderings in which A can cast the deciding vote) divided by the total number of possible permutations" and show large states to be advantaged because of the large number of electoral votes they control. Building on the Mann and Shapley model, John F. Banzhaf, III, (1968) found that as the size of a state's population increases, the probability that a voter can affect the outcome of the national election decreases at a ratio less than the increase in population ($1/\sqrt{n}$ rather than $1/n$). Again, voters in large competitive states have disproportionate influence. See John F. Banzhaf, III, "One Man, 3.312 Votes: A Mathematical Analysis of the Electoral College," *Villanova Law Review* 14, pp 304–332. For extensions and elaborations of these basic models, see John A. Yunker and Lawrence D. Longley, "The Biases of the Electoral College, Who is Really Advantaged?" in *Perspectives on Presidential Selection,* Donald R. Matthews, ed., (Washington, D.C.: Brookings Institution, 1972), 172–203; Steven J. Brams and Morton D. Davis, "The 3/2's Rule in Presidential Campaigning," *American Political Science Review* 68 (March 1974), 113–34; Claude S. Colatoni, Terrence J. Levesque, and Peter D. Ordeshook, "Campaign Resource Allocation Under the Electoral College," *American Political Science Review* 69 (March 1975), 141–152; George Rabinowitz and Stuart MacDonald, "The Power of the States in U.S. Presidential Elections," *American Political Science Review* 80 (March 1986), 65–87; Lawrence Longley and James Dana, Jr., "New Empirical Estimates of the Biases of the Electoral College for the 1980s," *Western Political Quarterly* 37 (March 1987), 157–175; and J. Nagler and J. Leighley, "Presidential Campaign Expenditures—Evidence on Allocations and Effects," *Public Choice* 73 (April 1992), 319–333.

6. The eight states with the most voters (California, New York, Texas, Florida, Pennsylvania, Illinois, Ohio, and Michigan) had 46.3 percent of the vote and 48.2 percent of the population in 2000. The eight states with the fewest voters (Rhode Island, Hawaii, Delaware, South Dakota, Vermont, North Dakota, Alaska, and Wyoming) had 2.4 percent of the vote and 2.2 percent of the population in 2000. While the District of Columbia casts three electoral votes, it does not have representation in the Senate and is therefore excluded from these calculations.

7. The District of Columbia is included here because of its electoral college representation.

8. The tenth-vote system would have thrown all of the close elections beginning in 1960 into the House of Representatives, including the 1992, 1996, and 2000 elections (John F. Kennedy and Jimmy Carter would have won in 1960 and 1976 using whole votes; the 1976 result using tenth-votes would depend on whether 270 electoral votes were needed, as under the current rules, or only 269.1). Under the tenth-vote plan, elections would wind up in the House so frequently (requiring only a very close election, as in 2000, or a moderately strong third candidate, as in 1996, or both, as in 1968) that the presidency would be primarily dependent on Congress, not on the presidential election.

About the Contributors

RONALD DWORKIN is Sommer Professor of Law and Philosophy at New York University Law School, and Quain Professor of Jurisprudence at University College, London.

LANI GUINIER is Bennett Boskey Professor, Harvard Law School.

RICHARD H. PILDES is Professor of Law, New York University School of Law. He is the author, with professors Samuel Issacharoff and Pamela S. Karlan, of *The Law of Democracy: Legal Structure of the Political Process* (2d ed., 2001) and *When Elections Go Bad: The 2000 Presidential Election and the Law of Democracy* (rev. ed., 2001).

NELSON W. POLSBY is Heller Professor of Political Science at the University of California, Berkeley. He is the author, with the late Aaron Wildavsky, of *Presidential Elections,* first published in 1964 and now in its 10th edition.

RICHARD A. POSNER is Judge, U.S. Court of Appeals for the Seventh Circuit; Senior Lecturer, University of Chicago Law School.

ARTHUR SCHLESINGER, JR., a historian, taught at Harvard and the City University of New York and served as special assistant to President John F. Kennedy.

CASS R. SUNSTEIN is Karl N. Llewellyn Distinguished Service Professor, Law School and Department of Political Science, University of Chicago.

LAURENCE H. TRIBE is the Tyler Professor of Constitutional Law, Harvard Law School.

Index

absentee ballots, 15, 118, 121, 299n100, 317n31
Adams, John Quincy, 218, 219
AFL-CIO, 221
African Americans
  Bush v. Gore decision alienating, 249
  and merit-based voting rights, 241–42, 317nn28, 31, 318n32
  See also minority voters
Age Discrimination in Employment Act, 143
Alabama Supreme Court, 11
Albright, Madeleine, 34, 194, 312n10
Alterman, Jon B., 259, 324n97
Amar, Akhil Reed, 236, 306n4
American Bar Association, 221, 222, 225
American Civil Liberties Union, 318n33
The American Commonwealth, 225
Americans with Disabilities Act, 143
Amy, Douglas, 324n100
Anderson, John, 158, 226
aptitude testing. *See* meritocracy and merit-based democracy
Arkansas Educational Television Commission v. Forbes, 173–76
Article II of the Constitution
  core meaning of, 112
  and electoral college system, 270–71
  and electoral power of legislatures, 17–22, 68–69, 73, 95, 108, 210–11, 212, 293n11
  and Florida legislature, 8, 17, 18, 20–22, 109, 136
  and Florida Supreme Court, 8–9, 16–17, 18–22, 82, 108–12, 136, 190, 295n29

  and Florida Supreme Court
    interpretation of state law, 8–9, 16–17, 109–12, 136, 190
  legitimacy of Supreme Court role in enforcing, 110–12
  Posner on, 93, 95, 183, 285n1, 286n16, 287n27, 295n29
  and pragmatic rationale for majority opinion, 93, 95, 110–12, 210–13
  as reason to stop recount, 8–9, 17, 211–212
  recount as violating, 192
  as "red herring," 109–12
  and remand by Supreme Court, 20–21, 108–9, 190, 211, 285n4
  and state constitutions, 20–22
  and uniform election codes, 73
  weakness of Supreme Court argument, 18–22, 285n14
Article V of the Constitution, 21–22

Baker, Howard, 221
Baker v. Carr, 153, 280
ballot design
  butterfly ballot, 4, 23, 30, 58, 59–60, 107, 129, 266
  "defective" ballots, 116
  dimpled ballots, 5, 189, 312n6
  optical scan ballots, 88–89, 129
  punch-card ballots, 4–5, 23, 30, 65–66, 89, 129, 241, 297n68, 312n4, 317n31
  See also voting machinery
Banzhaf, John F., 326n5
Barkley, Alben, 220
Bayh, Birch, 221, 225

Beckstrom v. Volusia County Canvassing Board, 116, 118, 297n66
Bendiner, Robert, 221
Bernard, Elaine, 322n84
Bickel, Alexander, 207, 314n31
Blackmun, Justice Harry, 290n7
blanket primaries, 162–68, 308n31
Boal, Augusto, 261, 325n109, 326n110
Boardman v. Esteva, 119, 298n86
Bobo, Lawrence, 249
Boies, David, 65, 238
bonus plan, 228–29, 279. *See also* electoral college system
Bork, Robert, 281, 282
Bowers v. Hardwick, 151
Bowles, Chester, 195
Brady, Henry, 88
Braun, Alan G., 223
Brennan, Justice William, 290n7
Breyer, Justice Stephen
    agreement with equal protection ruling, 8, 65, 67, 129–30, 146, 180, 289n9
    Arkansas Educational Television Commission v. Forbes, 174
    and conservative alliance on Court, 124
    on public faith in justice system, 222
    and remedy issue, 8, 63, 135, 192
    on risks of majority opinion, 67
    and *Rogers v. Tennessee,* 295n27
    Timmons v. Twin Cities Area New Party, 171
Brookings Institution, 221, 224
Broward County
    recounts, 188, 189
    vote-counting standards, 84, 89, 128, 208
    voting instructions, 297n68
Bryce, James, 225
Buchanan, Pat
    as independent party candidate, 158, 226, 307n8
    Palm Beach county vote, 4, 23, 58, 59, 107, 266, 288n6
Burnham, Walter Dean, 226

Bush, George W.
    and antidemocratic features of electoral process, 235–36
    assumption of mandate, 268, 269
    early presidency and possible harm to nation, 37–38
    meritocracy and elitism of, 231–34, 263
Bush, Jeb, 70, 193
Bush v. Gore majority opinion
    and Article II, 16–22, 109–12, 210–13, 285n14
    as bringing order to postelection crisis, 9, 31–32, 76, 91–93, 103, 140–42
    Bush arguments, 78–80, 82
    and claim of "unsought responsibility," 139–45
    and the constitutionalization of democracy, 176–85
    and Court's ambivalence toward democratic principles, 243–44, 319n43
    and Court's extraconstitutional motive, 145–50
    and discipline of argument, 54–55
    and equal protection (*see* equal protection and *Bush v. Gore*)
    and errors in vote tabulation, 22–26
    and Florida election law, 112–23
    justifications for hearing case, 139–50
    minimalism of, 76–77, 79–80, 85, 87–88, 90, 104, 289n12
    and "one person one vote" principle, 66
    and "political questions" doctrine, 144–45, 194
    politically and emotionally-charged legal opinions, 99–103
    and pragmatism, 32–43, 91–96
    and recount standards (*see* recount)
    on statutory deadline (*see* "safe harbor" provision)
    summary of events, 4–6, 78–82
    and vote-counting standards, 6, 62–63, 65–66, 83–84, 123, 133–34, 288n8, 302n149

See also Bush v. Gore majority opinion,
  consequences and effects of; *Bush v.
  Gore* majority opinion, problems with
  ruling; equal protection and *Bush v.
  Gore*
Bush v. Gore majority opinion,
  consequences and effects of
  accusations of partisanship in judicial
    confirmation process, 282–83
  damage to Court's reputation, 53–54,
    150–52, 281–82
  destabilizing future political processes,
    44–45
  expansion of voting rights, 76, 96–99,
    103–4
  legacy of, as negative object lesson, 152–
    155
  partisan reactions to decision, 99–100
  and rule-bound decisions, 98–99, 292n57
Bush v. Gore majority opinion, problems
  with ruling, 76–77, 85–90
  absence of precedents, 85, 86–87, 103,
    291n44
  better to remand again, 63, 103, 110, 181,
    209
  claim of "unsought responsibility,"
    139–45
  equal protection problems of stopping
    recount, 135–39, 209
  extraconstitutional motives, 145–50
  Florida Supreme Court's correct
    interpretation of state law, 112–23
  interpretation of recount deadline, 138–39
  limited to present circumstances only,
    9–10, 130–32, 209, 305n200, 314n33,
    315n14
  as minimalist and political, 85, 87–88
  as non-unanimous decision, 76, 77, 103
  not reflecting conservative positions,
    63–64
  risks, 67, 141–42
  similar equal protection problems in
    system Court let stand, 85, 88–90,
    237

weak rationale of equal protection
  principle and poor remedy, 7–8, 76–77,
  96, 209
Bush v. Palm Beach Canvassing Board,
  75–76, 183, 289n12
Butterworth, Bob, 23

California Democratic Party v. Jones,
  164–66, 168, 170, 176, 185, 308n39
Campbell, Ben Nighthorse, 270
Carroll, James, 249
Carter, Jimmy
  election of 1976, 215, 327n8
  election of 1980, 326n1
  and election reform, 215, 219
Center for the Study of Race, Politics and
  Culture, 249
certiorari
  Bush arguments in seeking first grant of,
    78–79
  and halt of recounts, 78, 80–82
Chermerinsky, Erwin, 306n4
Clay, Henry, 218
clear voter intent
  and equal protection, 62, 65–66, 173, 237,
    289n10, 302n149
  in Florida election code, 115
  and Florida Supreme Court, 62, 65–66,
    89, 115–18, 120–23, 189, 289n10
  and machine recounts, 124–27
  and manual recount standards, 120–23,
    124–27, 302n149
  and rights of voters to have their votes
    counted, 267–68
  and vote-counting standards, 120–23,
    124–27, 238, 302n149, 316n18
  and voting machinery, 116–18, 125, 127,
    237, 267
  See also recount
Cleveland, Grover, 220
Clinton, Bill, 101, 278
Clinton v. Jones, 205, 291n53
Clopton, John, 217
Commission on Presidential Debates, 175

Committee for the Study of the American Electorate, 249

Congress
    and best-case scenario of postelection, 34, 181–82
    election of president by, 216, 218
    and electoral votes, 7, 138–39, 141–42, 181, 270–71
    and elimination of electoral college, 70, 72–73
    and establishment of uniform election code, 70–71, 73
    and safe harbor provision, 7, 137, 181, 293n9, 303n161
    and worst-case scenario of postelection, 34, 92, 193–95
    See also House of Representatives

Congressional Black Caucus, 249, 321n79

Congressional Research Service, 217

Constitution
    amendment to eliminate electoral college, 70–73
    Article V, 21–22
    First Amendment, 142
    See also Article II of the Constitution; equal protection and *Bush v. Gore*

constitutionalization of democracy
    academic indifference to democratic governance and attention to rights and equality, 156, 305n3, 306n4
    and access to public campaign forums, 173–76
    Bush v. Gore, 155, 157, 176–85
    challenges to traditional forms of democracy, 157–61
    and constitutional law, 155–57, 180–185
    minor-party presidential candidates, 158, 307nn8–9
    primary elections, 161–68, 309n49
    public disaffection for electoral politics, 157–60, 306n6
    recent pattern of, 155–56, 157–61, 185–186

    and relationship between constitutional law/courts and politics/legislation, 180–85
    role Court should play in democratic processes, 161–76, 184–86
    and split-ticket voting, 159
    and Supreme Court involvement in postelection dispute, 178–80, 311n82
    and Supreme Court majority opinion, 176–85
    third party politics and independent candidates, 157–59, 160, 168–72
    voter initiatives and direct democracy, 159–60
    See also democracy

contest of election, 5, 71–72, 115, 119, 121, 189, 296n52, 298n82

Davis v. Bandemer, 243, 318n38

Dawson, Michael, 249

democracy
    and antidemocratic features of electoral process, 235–36, 315n13
    and antidemocratic impulse in American life, 245–48
    collective rights and, 48–50
    and crisis of confidence in public decision-making, 234–35, 316n17
    current ambivalence toward, 243–48, 318n38, 319nn42–43
    and electoral system, 48–53
    grassroots and locally-based progressive parties, 253–56, 260, 321nn78–79, 322nn84, 86
    hierarchies and, 235, 315n12
    and individual rights, 50–53
    and meritocracy and merit-based democracy, 231–64
    and pro-democracy reforms of system, 251–60
    and problems of election system, 246–48, 249–51, 321n72
    and reforms of system for robust democracy, 251–52

and right to vote, 233, 234, 315n10
Supreme Court ambivalence toward
    order of, 243–45, 318n38, 319nn42–43
and Supreme Court equal protection
    decision, 236–37
See also constitutionalization of
    democracy; meritocracy and merit-
    based democracy
Democracy and Distrust (Ely), 185
Dershowitz, Alan, 212–13
Dewey, John, 196, 199–200, 250, 313n17
Dewey, Thomas E., 220
direct elections, 223–25, 274–79
    arguments against, 223–24
    arguments for, 224–25
    historic calls for, 218–21
    impact on party system, 227–28, 271,
        274–77, 278
    popular support for, 221
    and provision for run-off election, 227,
        275–76, 279
    and right to equality of impact, 52
    as sole criteria, 271, 274–77
    voting blocs and state size, 223–24,
        274–75
Dirksen, Everett, 221
disenfranchisement. *See* voting rights
Dole, Robert, 221
Douglas, Paul H., 218

Eakle, Mary, 255
election procedures
    establishing uniform codes, 70–71, 73,
        125–26, 289n14
    and fraud in Florida, 266, 326n3
    and potentially good effects of *Bush v.
        Gore,* 76, 96–99, 103–4
    reforms of, 70–73
    See also electoral college system; voting
        machinery
electoral college system, 67–73, 270–81
    Article II and, 270–71
    bonus plan, 228–29, 279
    and Congress, 218, 219, 221, 227, 327n8

consequences of disturbing, 280–81
dangers of retaining, 68–70
district plan, 271, 278, 279
electors' roles, 216–17, 225, 229, 279
eliminating, 70–73, 219–21
as elitist and outdated, 67–68, 73
and equality of impact, 51–53
and "faithless elector," 225, 229, 279
how it works, 45–46, 216–17, 272–73,
    327n6
and metropolitan voting blocs, 223–24,
    274
and "one-person-one-vote," 68–69, 217
original plans for, 45–46, 67–68, 216–
    217
and party system, 217
popular vote in, 46, 71, 72, 218–20, 270,
    278–79
popular vote-loser winning election, 270,
    278–79
and postelection challenges and contests,
    71–72
and power to southern slaveholding
    states, 236, 315n13
and proportional representation, 45–47,
    218, 224, 271–72, 277, 278, 279, 327n8
and reapportionment, 280
reforms or modifications, 70–73, 217–21,
    223–24, 228–29, 271, 274–79
and state legislatures, 68–70
and state size, 51–52, 223–24, 270–71,
    273–75, 277, 280, 326n5
third parties and splinter parties, 227–28,
    270, 278–79, 280
and Twelfth Amendment, 217
and 2000 election, 218, 221–23, 281–83
winner-take-all system, 217, 218, 271,
    273–74, 275
See also direct elections
Electoral Count Act of 1887, 6, 141, 177, 192,
    193, 312n7, 326n2
Eleventh Circuit Court of Appeals, 11
Ely, John Hart, 185
Epstein, Richard, 100

equal protection and *Bush v. Gore,* 123–39
absence of precedents for, 9–10, 11, 85, 86–87, 103, 291n44
and African Americans' voting rights, 237
application to voting, 291n44
Bush arguments, 82, 108
and clear voter intent, 62, 65–66, 173, 237, 289n10, 302n149
emergence of belief that violations occurred, 123–30
errors by election officials or machines, 127–28
liberal justices' agreement with, 8, 65, 67, 129–30, 146, 180, 289n9
limited to present circumstances only, 9–10, 130–32, 237, 315n14, 316n16
meritocracy and aristocracy in, 236–37
merits for ruling, 6, 9–15, 62–63, 65–66, 83–89, 128–35, 237, 289n9, 291n44
minimalism in, 85, 87–88
"one-person-one-vote" principle, 11, 65–66, 132–35
and possible legacies of *Bush v. Gore,* 16–17, 97–98, 131, 301n134
recount as violating (final decision), 6, 192
remedy of stopping recount, 135–39, 209
and safe harbor, 136–38
similar problems in system that Court let stand, 85, 88–90, 237
and Supreme Court change of recount rules, 135, 303n163
topsy-turvy nature of, 123–24
underlying count problem, 128–30, 134
unequal treatment of "overvotes" and "undervotes," 13–15, 65, 84, 133–34, 302n149
and vote-counting standards in recount, 6, 8, 13–14, 62–63, 65–66, 83–89, 124–27, 133–34, 208–10, 237, 302n149
and voting machinery/ballots, 65–66, 88–89, 124–25, 130, 237, 267, 301n131
weakness of argument, 7–8, 9–15, 62–63, 76–77, 94–95, 183, 208–10, 285n5
"errors in vote tabulation," 22–31

Fillmore, Millard, 227
First Amendment, 142
Fisher v. City of Berkeley, 123, 124
Florida election law
and absentee ballots, 118
and ballot-design, 59
and clear voter intent, 115–16, 120–23, 180, 188, 267–68
and contest of results, 5, 298n82
and counting of overvotes, 133–35, 303n150
and deference to election officials, 118–19, 298nn82–83
on errors in vote tabulation, 22–26, 29, 31
Florida Supreme Court proper interpretation of, 112–23, 296n44
and "legal votes," 116–19, 189, 191, 286n15, 298n82
mandated recounts, 117, 129, 187–88, 297n74
and manual recounts, 5
protest system, 5, 122
recount standards, 120–23, 299n101
and statutory deadline for election returns (safe harbor), 110, 113–15, 136–38, 188, 294n21
"substantial compliance" and right to vote, 119–20, 298n86
and voting instructions, 117
Florida Equal Voting Rights Project, 318n33
Florida legislature
and Article II, 8, 17, 18, 20–22, 109, 136
and certification of Bush electors, 137, 140–41, 193, 303n158
and errors in vote tabulation, 24, 26–27, 29–31
right to certify electors, 18
safe harbor provision and deadline for recounts, 6–7, 66–67, 90–91, 136–38, 289n11

Florida Supreme Court
  and Article II, 16, 17, 18–22, 82, 108–12,
    136, 190, 295n29
  and clear voter intent standard, 62,
    65–66, 89, 115–18, 120–23, 189, 289n10
  and deference to election officials, 118–19,
    298nn82–83
  and election law, proper adherence to,
    112–23, 296n44
  and errors in vote tabulation, 24–25,
    29–31
  extension of statutory deadline, 113–15,
    189, 190, 296n42
  and final stop of recount, 64–65, 80–82,
    90–91, 135–39
  and initial remand, 63, 76, 78–80, 114,
    190, 289n12
  and "legal votes," 116–19, 189, 191, 286n15
  and partisan recounts, 12–13
  public reactions to decision, 99–100
  on safe harbor provision and deadline for
    recounts, 6–7, 66–67, 90–91, 110,
    136–38, 294n21
  and statewide recount order, 115
  "substantial compliance" and right to
    vote, 119–20, 298n86
  Supreme Court's view of their
    interpretations, 7, 16, 66–67, 78,
    80–81, 82, 90–91, 109–12, 136–38, 190
  Supreme Court's view that they changed
    law, 8, 16, 31, 95
Ford, Gerald, 215, 220
Fourteenth Amendment
  due process clause, 8, 133
  and Rehnquist Court, 133, 143
  See also equal protection and Bush v. Gore
Frankfurter, Justice Felix, 319n47
fraud in Florida, 266, 326n3
Fried, Charles, 9, 126–27
Fuller, Chief Justice Melville, 285n14
fusion politics, 43–44, 169–72, 310n57

Gerken, Heather, 243, 319n43, 322n86
Germany, postwar, 259–60, 324n102

Germany, Weimar, 258, 323nn91–93
Giles v. Harris, 156, 244, 319nn46–47
Ginsburg, Justice Ruth Bader
  and Arkansas Educational Television
    Commission v. Forbes, 174
  Bush v. Gore dissents, 65, 111, 129, 137
  and California Democratic Party v. Jones,
    165
  and Rogers v. Tennessee, 111
  and Timmons v. Twin Cities Area New
    Party, 171
Gore, Al
  effect of stay of recount on, 81
  meritocracy and elitism of, 232, 234
  and popular vote, 50, 221–22
  and public's lack of outrage over election
    results, 222
  and state-wide hand recount, 267
Gossett, Ed, 218
Green Party, 158, 252–53. See also Nader,
    Ralph
Gregory v. Ashcroft, 112

Hagelin, John, 307n8
Hamilton, Alexander, 215, 217
Hand, Justice Learned, 54
Harlan, Justice John Marshall, 234, 315n10
Harper v. Virginia, 236
Harris, James, 307n8
Harris, Katherine
  adherence to statutory deadline for
    recount, 5, 23, 78, 113, 188, 189
  authorization to interpret election code,
    24
  certification of election outcome, 7, 191
  and errors in vote tabulation, 23–25
  Florida Supreme Court overruling of, 20,
    22, 113, 189
  permission to extend statutory deadline, 5
  as political, 24, 70
Harrison, Benjamin, 219
Hart, H. L. A., 202
Harvard Law Review, annual forewords to
    Supreme Court issue, 306n4

Hayak, Friedrich, 200
Hayes, Rutherford B., 219–20
Heffron v. ISKCON, 151
Hispanics
  and merit-based voting, 241, 317n31
  and voting instructions, 117, 125
  See also minority voters
Holmes, Justice Oliver Wendell, 244, 245
Home Building and Loan Association v.
  Blaisdell, 204–5
Horwitz, Morton J., 306n4
House of Representatives
  Congressional Black Caucus, 249,
    321n79
  and electoral college system, 218, 219,
    221, 277, 278, 327n8
  worst-case scenario role, 34, 193–94
Hughes, Charles Evan, 220
Humphrey, Hubert, 220

Israel, 258–59, 323n94, 324nn96–97
Issacharoff, Samuel, 309n49

Jackson, Andrew, 218–19
Jackson, Henry, 221
Jackson, Justice Robert, 203–4
Jeffords, James, 158, 269, 282
Jordan, Vernon, 224
judicial activism, 64, 75–76

Karlan, Pamela, 89, 321n72
Kaylor, Anne, 299n100
Kefauver, Estes, 218
Kennedy, Edward, 221, 224
Kennedy, John F., 195, 218, 327n8
Kennedy, Justice Anthony
  activism of, 64
  and Article II grounds for decision, 210
  and *California Democratic Party v. Jones,*
    308n39
  and conservative alliance on Court, 124
  and *Roe v. Wade,* 143–44
Keyssar, Alex, 245
Klock, Joseph, 316n18

Korematsu v. United States, 184, 203–4,
  312n89

Labour Party (Britain), 254, 256
Lake, Anthony, 282
Latinos. *See* Hispanics
League of Women Voters, 221
Lebedoff, David, 233, 315n7, 316n17
Lemann, Nicholas, 233
Lodge, Henry Cabot, Jr., 218
Lodge-Gossett amendment, 218, 224, 277
Longley, Lawrence D., 223
Lowi, Theodore J., 310n69

Machiavelli, Niccolo, 195
Madison, James, 170, 216, 217
mandates, presidential, 268–70
mandatory voting, 252, 321n75
Mann, Irwin, 326n5
Mansfield, Mike, 221
Marshall, Justice Thurgood, 290n7
Mason, George, 216
McCarthy, Eugene, 226
McConnel, Michael, 311n83
McKinney, Cynthia, 321n79
McPherson v. Blacker, 285n14
meritocracy and merit-based democracy,
  231–64
  and antidemocratic impulse in American
    life, 245–48
  and Bush, 231–32
  and crisis in democratic processes,
    234–35
  and democratic aristocracy, 232–35,
    315nn10, 12
  and disenfranchisement of minority
    voters, 237–38, 241–42, 244–47,
    317nn28, 31; 318nn32–33
  and elitism, 232–34, 248, 315n7
  and Gore, 232, 234
  in higher education and aptitude testing,
    239–40, 316nn22–23, 317nn24, 26–27
  and poor voter participation, 246–48
  and public decision-making, 234–35

and Supreme Court, 238, 242–45, 318nn34, 38; 319nn42–43

and Supreme Court's majority opinion, 233

as term, 239

and "testocracy," 239–40, 316nn22–23, 317n24

and underrepresented voters, 247–48, 320n59

voter participation and representation, 246–48

voting procedures, 241–42, 317nn28, 31; 318nn32–34

Miami-Dade County

abandoning of hand recount, 189–90, 191, 268

Democratic election board, 191

first sample recount, 188

Florida Supreme Court ruling on recount results, 191

rejected punch-card ballots of African Americans, 241, 317n31

military ballots, 267, 317n31

minority voters

disenfranchisement of, 237–38, 241–42, 244–47, 317nn28, 31, 318n32, 320n59

and legacy of racism in electoral process, 236, 315n13

and merit-based voting rights, 241–42, 317nn28, 31, 318n32

and metropolitan voting blocs, 224

and underlying count problem, 129

and voting instructions, 117, 125, 237–38

Mississippi Freedom Democratic Party, 255

Moore, G. E., 196

Nader, Ralph

and debates, 315n7

as Green Party candidate, 158, 226, 252–53, 307n8

votes to, 60, 158, 222, 252–53, 307n9, 314n4

National Commission on Federal Election Reform, 215

National Democratic Party (NDP) (Canada), 255–56

National Opinion Research Center, 13

New Party, 169, 322n84

New York Times, 13, 15, 70, 231, 263, 288n6, 289n9

New Zealand, 260, 324nn102, 105, 325nn106, 108

Newman, JoNel, 318n33

Nixon, Richard, 220, 221, 278, 288n5

O'Connor, Justice Sandra Day

activism of, 64

and Article II grounds for decision, 210

and conservative alliance on Court, 124

and *Davis v. Bandemer,* 243

and *Roe v. Wade,* 143

and *Rogers v. Tennessee,* 111

on vote-counting standards and voter intent, 238, 316n18

Oregon Democratic central committee, 222

"originalism," 291n44

Overton, Spencer, 243, 250, 321n72

Palm Beach County

Buchanan vote, 4, 58, 59, 107, 288n6

butterfly ballot, 4, 23, 30, 58, 59–60, 107, 129, 266

first sample recount, 188, 190

Florida Supreme Court ruling on recount results, 191

Gore vote, 288n6

Nader vote, 60, 288n6

re-vote in, 61, 288n6

recount deadline, 189

vote-counting standards and equal protection problem, 83–84, 89, 128, 208

party system

computerized polling's impact on, 226

decay of, 225–27

decrease in party identification, 226

and direct elections, 227–28, 271, 274–77, 278

party system (*cont.*)
   and electoral college system, 227–28, 271
   grassroots and locally-based progressive
      parties, 253–56, 260, 321nn78–79,
      322nn84, 86
   minor-party politics and independent
      candidates, 157–59
   primary system, 161–68, 309n49
   proportional representation, 256–60
   regulation and democratizing of, 161–63,
      166, 308n24
   television's impact on, 226
   two-party system, 243, 254–55, 319n42
   See also third parties
Patent Reform Act, 142
Pennzoil v. Texaco, 293n10
Perot, Ross, 158, 226, 270
Philips, Howard, 307n8
Pierce, Neal, 224
Pildes, Richard, 11, 244, 245–46, 319n44
Planned Parenthood of Pennsylvania v.
   Casey, 143–44, 301n135, 302n139
Plessy v. Ferguson, 156, 315n10
The Politics of Electoral College Reform
   (Longley and Braun), 223
popular vote
   and electoral college system, 46, 71, 72,
      218–20, 270, 278–79
   Gore and, 50, 221–22
   and minority presidents, 270, 278–79
   and postelection challenges and contests,
      71–72
Populist Party, 169–70
Porter, Charles O., 222
Posner, Richard
   approval of majority opinion, 93–96, 100,
      113, 183
   and Article II, 93, 95, 183, 285n1, 286n16,
      287n27, 295n29
   on attention to issues of individual rights
      and equality, 156, 305n3
   clear voter intent and "legal votes," 116–17
   clear voter intent and manual recounts,
      122–23, 298n82, 299n95

   Dworkin on, 31–43
   on Gore and popular vote, 50
   on weakness of equal protection
      argument, 94–95, 183, 208–10
   and worst-case scenario, 33–38, 93–94,
      183–84, 192–95
   See also pragmatic adjudication;
      pragmatism
Powell, G. Bingham, 254
pragmatic adjudication, 32–43, 91–96,
   198–213
   and appearance of moral authority,
      209–10
   and Article II, 93, 95, 210–13
   and avoidance of national crisis, 183–84,
      203–5
   and character of Supreme Court's
      constitutional decisions, 206–7, 314n31
   and *Clinton v. Jones,* 205, 291n53
   and consequentialist decisions, 37–42,
      287n30
   Dworkin's rebuttal of, 34–43
   and equal protection, 208–10
   formalism and rule utilitarianism,
      200–201
   and future judicial appointments, 38, 94,
      205–7
   and grounds for stopping recount, 203,
      208–13
   and harm to Court's authority, 94, 205–7
   and *Home Building and Loan Association*
      v. Blaisdell, 204–5
   as improvement over legal positivism, 202
   and judicial honesty, 42–43, 209–10
   and justices' conflicts of interest, 203,
      205–7
   and *Korematsu v. United States,* 184,
      203–4
   as positive explanation for majority
      decision, 32, 91–96, 183–84, 203–13
   Posner and, 32–41, 91, 93–96, 183–84,
      187–213, 291n53
   rule of law and "rule consequentialism,"
      39–40, 200–202

and worst-case scenario, 33–38, 93–94, 183–84, 192–95
See also pragmatism
pragmatism
  everyday meaning, 32–33, 195, 200
  meanings of, 32–33, 195–98, 287n23
  orthodox, 33, 41–42, 195–97, 198–99
  Posner and, 32–41, 91, 93–96, 183–84, 187–213, 291n53
  recusant, 33, 195–99, 313nn13, 17
  See also pragmatic adjudication
proportional representation, 256–60
  and democracy, 252, 256–60, 323nn87, 89
  and elections of women, 257, 259–60, 323n89, 324n102
  and electoral system reform, 45–47, 218, 224, 271–72, 277–79, 327n8
  in Israel, 258–59, 323n94
  mixed-member proportional voting (MMP), 259–60
  in New Zealand, 260, 324nn102, 105, 325nn106, 108
  party-list system, 257–59, 323nn87, 89, 324n99
  in post-war Germany, 259–60, 324n102
  risks and criticisms, 259, 324n100
  single-transferable voting (STV), 323n89, 324n99
  in Weimar Germany, 258, 323nn91–93
  and winner-take-all system, 258, 323n92
protest of election, 5, 113, 122

race. *See* African Americans; Hispanics; minority voters
Raskin, Jamin B., 229
Reagan, Ronald, 274
recount
  alternative remedies to Supreme Court's stopping of, 181–82
  and Article II, 192, 210–13
  and clear voter intent, 5, 89, 115, 120–23, 124–27, 189, 267–68, 299n95, 302n149
  equal protection problems of stopping, 135–39, 209

and errors in vote tabulation, 22–26
  first ruling to stay, 183
  Florida election law and mandated recount, 117, 129, 187–88, 297n74
  Florida Supreme Court ruling to continue, 62, 78, 80–81
  Gore and hand recount, 188, 267
  and "legal votes," 117–18, 189
  and machine recount standards, 124–27
  and manual recount standards, 5, 120–23, 124–27, 302n149
  and partisanship, 121, 299n101
  precedents for, 86–87
  and question of possible harm from continuing, 81
  safe harbor deadline, 63, 66–67, 90–91, 110, 192, 209, 294n21
  scenario if Supreme Court had affirmed recount, 91–93, 94, 103
  Supreme Court final ruling to stop, 64–65, 80–89, 90–91, 135–39, 288n8
  and underlying count issue, 128–30
  and unequal treatments of "overvotes" and "undervotes," 13–15, 65, 84, 133–34, 302n148
  vote-counting standards and equal protection argument, 6, 8, 13–14, 62–63, 65–66, 83–89, 124–27, 133–34, 208–10, 237, 302n149
Rehnquist, Chief Justice William
  activism of, 64
  Bush v. Gore opinions, 110, 111, 116, 122–23, 205, 209, 297n62
  and clear voter intent and defective ballots, 116, 297n62
  and conservative alliance on Court, 124
  on Florida Supreme Court incapable of interpreting its code, 110, 111
  and "legal votes," 116–17, 297n68
  and manual recounts, 122–23
  and pragmatic considerations in majority opinion, 205, 209
  and voting instructions, 117, 297n68
Religious Freedom Restoration Act, 143

remand to Florida Supreme Court
  and Article II, 20–21, 108–9, 190, 211,
    285n4
  better remedy to remand a second time,
    63, 103, 110, 181, 209
  initial remand, 63, 76, 78–80, 114, 190,
    289n12
  possible explanations for, 80–81
Reynolds v. Sims, 236
Rice, Condoleezza, 232
Roberts, Clayton, 188
Roe v. Wade, 64, 143–44, 153
Rogers v. Tennessee, 111, 112, 295nn23, 26–27
Roosevelt, Franklin D., 226
Roosevelt, Theodore, 158, 159, 227
Rorty, Richard, 196, 197, 198, 199, 200
run-off elections, 227–28, 275–76, 279
Rust v. Sullivan, 151

"safe harbor" provision
  Florida election law and statutory
    deadline, 110, 113–15, 136–38, 188,
    294n21
  and Florida Supreme Court, 6–7, 66–67,
    90–91, 110, 113–15, 136–38, 189, 190,
    294n21, 296n42
  and Harris' adherence to statutory
    deadline, 5, 23, 78, 113, 188, 189
  original enactment of, 137, 293n9
  Supreme Court ruling on, 6–7, 63, 66–67,
    90–91, 136–38, 192, 209, 289n9
  and Supreme Court's interpretation of
    Florida Supreme Court rulings, 6–7,
    110, 136–38
Sauls, N. Sanders, 5
Scalia, Justice Antonin
  activism of, 64
  and Article II grounds for decision, 95,
    212
  as Bush's favorite justice, 38, 64, 206
  and conservative alliance on Court, 124
  on Court's function in establishing
    precedent, 9
  on equal protection, 10–11

  on freedom of action in his opinions,
    212
  halting recount to avert harm to Bush,
    64–65, 141–42, 288n8
  on majority opinion as for present
    circumstances only, 212–13
  "originalism" and, 291n44
  and pragmatism in majority opinion, 205,
    209, 212
  Rogers v. Tennessee, 111
  on rule of law, 144
  in support of the first stay, 206
  and two-party system, 319n42
Schmitt, Carl, 200
Section Five of United States Code, 82
Shapiro, Ian, 234, 315n12
Shapley, Lloyd, 326n5
Shelby, Richard, 270
Sherman, John, 177
Slonim, Shlomo, 216
Souter, Justice David
  agreement with equal protection ruling, 8,
    65, 129–30, 146, 180, 289nn9–10
  and *Arkansas Educational Television
    Commission v. Forbes,* 174
  Bush v. Gore dissents, 8, 111
  and *Bush v. Gore* remedies, 135, 192
  and conservative alliance on Court, 124
  and *Roe v. Wade,* 143
  and *Rogers v. Tennessee,* 111
  and *Timmons v. Twin Cities Area New
    Party,* 172, 310n69
  on vote-counting standards, 316n18
stare decisis, 131
statutory deadline. *See* "safe harbor"
  provision
statutory interpretation, 26–29
Stevens, Justice John Paul
  and *Arkansas Educational Television
    Commission v. Forbes,* 174, 175
  Bush v. Gore dissents, 65, 126, 137, 206
  and *California Democratic Party v. Jones,*
    165–66
  on risks of majority opinion, 67, 248–49

and *Rogers v. Tennessee,* 111
and *Timmons v. Twin Cities Area New Party,* 171
Stevenson, Adlai, 195
Summers, Lawrence, 34, 37, 94, 194, 203
Supreme Court. *See Bush v. Gore* majority opinion; remand to Florida Supreme Court; Supreme Court, Rehnquist Court
Supreme Court, Burger Court, 301n134
Supreme Court, Rehnquist Court
    absence of liberals on, 77, 104, 290n7
    concern for appearance of equality only, 126, 300n111
    conservatism of, 64, 75–76, 123–24, 289n1
    and constitutionalization of democracy, 180–85
    on federal intervention in state affairs, 109–10, 294nn18–19
    judicial activism of, 64, 75–76
    merit-based democracy and ambivalence toward democratic institutions, 182–84, 243–45, 318n38, 319nn42–43
    minimalism of, 75–77, 85, 104
    "one person, one vote" rulings and due process, 133
    pretensions of, 142–45

Taft, Robert A., 221
Taft, William Howard, 227
Tashjian v. Republican Party of Connecticut, 309n51
television
    Bush v. Gore images, 124
    network projections, 265, 326n1
    and party system, 226
third parties
    and challenges to traditional forms of democracy, 157–59, 160, 168–72, 310n69
    and direct elections, 227–28
    and electoral college system, 227–28, 270, 278–79, 280

and inclusion in debates, 173–76
and progressive reforms, 252–56, 321nn78–79, 322nn84, 86
and run-off elections, 227–28, 275–76
and *Timmons v. Twin Cities Area New Party,* 43–44, 169–72, 175
See also party system
Thomas, Justice Clarence
    activism of, 64
    and Article II grounds for decision, 95, 212
    Bush's approval of, 38
    and conservative alliance on Court, 124
    "originalism" and, 291n44
    and pragmatism in majority opinion, 205, 209, 212
    and *Rogers v. Tennessee,* 111
Thurmond, Strom, 34, 194, 226, 278
Tilden, Samuel J., 219–20
Timmons v. Twin Cities Area New Party, 43–44, 123, 151, 169–72, 175, 319n44
To Assure Pride and Confidence in the Electoral Process (National Commission on Federal Election Reform), 215
Tocqueville, Alexis de, 225
Trademark Remedy Clarification Act, 143
Tribe, Laurence
    on new election in Palm Beach County, 288n6
    role in *Bush v. Gore,* 108, 293n1
Truman, Harry, 220, 278
Tushnet, Mark, 306n4
Twelfth Amendment, 141, 144, 150, 194, 217, 266
Twentieth Century Fund Task Force on Reform of the Presidential Election Process, 228, 279, 314n1

United States Chamber of Commerce, 221
University of California at Berkeley, 240, 317n26
University of Texas, 240

Ventura, Jesse, 176
Volusia County, 188
voter turnout, 246–48, 250, 251–52
voting instructions
    and Hispanic voters, 117, 125
    "legal votes" and, 117, 237–38, 297n68
    varying or nonexistent, 117, 297n68
    and voter intent, 117, 125, 127, 237–38,
        297n68
voting machinery
    clear voter intent and "legal votes,"
        116–18, 125, 127, 237, 267
    and defective ballots, 116
    and equal protection, 65–66, 88–89,
        124–25, 130, 237, 267, 301n131
    and errors in vote tabulation, 22–24, 30
    establishing uniform standards for, 70,
        289n14
    and Florida election code, 59
    and merit-based democracy, 241–42,
        317nn28, 31
    and voting instructions, 125, 127, 297n68
    See also ballot design
voting rights
    and collective democratic ideals, 48–50
    and disenfranchisement of minority
        voters, 237–38, 241–42, 244–47,
        317nn28, 31; 318nn32–33, 319n46,
        320n59
    equality in, 97–98
    and individual moral and political rights,
        50–53, 59

and merit-based democracy, 240–42, 244,
    245–46, 247, 317n28, 31, 318nn32–34
and potential effects of Bush v. Gore, 76,
    96–99, 103–4
and "substantial compliance," 119–20,
    298n86
Voting Rights Act of 1965, 238, 318n33

Wallace, George, 158, 221, 226, 270, 278, 279
Wallace, Henry, 226, 278
Warren, Earl, 290n7
Warren Court, 64, 301n134, 319n43
Washington, Booker T., 244
W.E.B. Du Bois Institute, 249
Wells, Chief Justice, 116, 140, 296n60,
    302n146
Wiencek, Henry, 236, 263, 315n13
Wilmerding, Lucius, Jr., 217
Wilson, James, 216
Wilson, Woodrow, 220
winner-take-all system
    and electoral college, 217, 218, 271,
        273–74, 275
    and proportional representation, 258,
        323n92
Wittgenstein, Ludwig, 196–97
worst-case scenario of postelection, 33–38,
    93–94, 183–84, 192–95, 201, 203. See
    also pragmatic adjudication

Yale University, 231, 263
Yoo, John, 100